Pheeeew! It's over!
A lot happened along the way, but I'm really glad I kept going until it was complete.
Now it's time for a little break...
But there's no time for that!! I gotta write more manga!

—HIROSHI SHIIBASHI,
2013

HIROSHI SHIIBASHI debuted in BUSINESS JUMP magazine with *Aratama*. NURA: RISE OF THE YOKAI CLAN is his breakout hit. He was an assistant to manga artist Hirohiko Araki, the creator of *Jojo's Bizarre Adventure*. *Steel Ball Run* by Araki is one of his favorite manga.

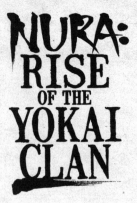

NURA: RISE OF THE YOKAI CLAN

NURA: RISE OF THE YOKAI CLAN
VOLUME 25
SHONEN JUMP Manga Edition

Story and Art by HIROSHI SHIIBASHI

Translation – John Werry
Touch-up Art and Lettering – Annaliese Christman
Graphics and Cover Design – Fawn Lau
Editors – Megan Bates, Joel Enos

Printed in the U.S.A.

Published by VIZ Media, LLC
P.O. Box 77010
San Francisco, CA 94107

10 9 8 7 6 5 4 3 2 1
First printing, February 2015

www.viz.com www.shonenjump.com

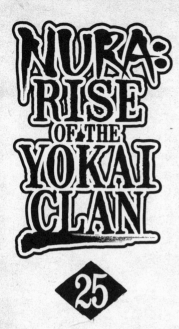

NURA: RISE OF THE YOKAI CLAN

25

HE WHO EQUIPS TRUE FEAR

STORY AND ART BY
HIROSHI SHIIBASHI

CHARACTERS

NURARIHYON

Rikuo's grandfather and the Lord of Pandemonium. He has appointed Rikuo the Third Heir of the Nura clan, a powerful yokai consortium. He's a mischievous sort who enjoys slipping out of diners without paying his bill.

RIKUO NURA

Though he appears to be a human boy, he's actually the grandson of Nurarihyon, a yokai. His grandfather's blood makes him only one-quarter yokai, and he transforms into a yokai at times.

KIYOTSUGU

Rikuo's classmate. He adores yokai, leading him to form the Kiyojuji Paranormal Patrol. He understands Rikuo has yokai blood and encourages him.

YUKI-ONNA

A yokai of the Nura clan who is in charge of looking after Rikuo. She disguises herself as a human and as Tsurara Oikawa attends the same school as Rikuo. Her mother is Setsura.

YURA

Rikuo's classmate and an onmyoji in the Keikain clan. She is able to use Hagun, a feat only possible for those in the clan with the greatest talent.

RYUJI

An onmyoji in the Keikain clan. With his magic, he can use water however he wants. For someone so young, he has a lot of knowledge and experience. He is good at confusing people with his words. Yura is his sister.

ABE NO SEIMEI (NUE)

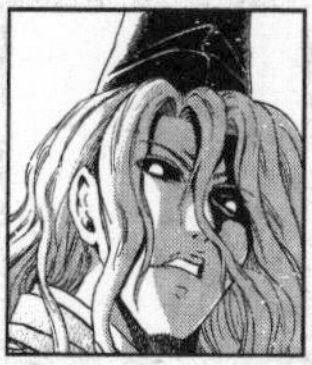

The first leader of the Gokadoin clan. He is an onmyoji, but his mother was an ayakashi (Hagoromo-Gitsune), so he is half yokai. In order to create a world of ayakashi, he has reincarnated and been reborn.

HAGOROMO-GITSUNE

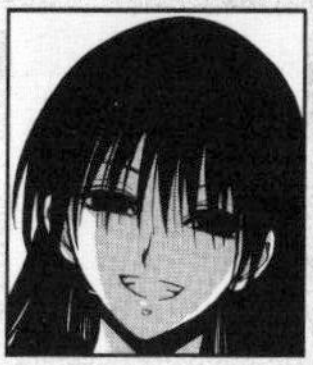

Seimei's mother and an ayakashi. Her vessel is Yamabuki-Otome, the first wife of Rikuo's father Rihan. During the battle in Kyoto, Seimei threw her to Hell.

YUIYUI GOKADOIN

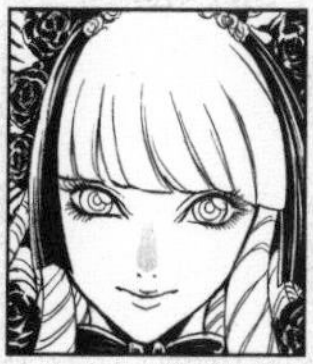

The sixth leader of the Gokadoin. Black-garbed. She attacks the ayakashi of the San'in Region during the Purification. She often uses voodoo-like dolls and has the ability to control opponents.

ABE NO ARIYUKI

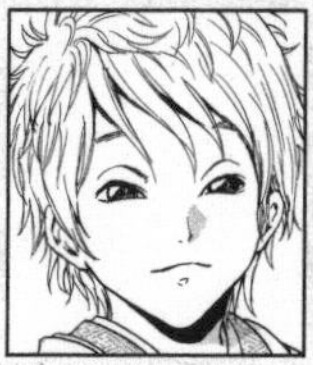

The fourth leader of the Gokadoin clan. White-garbed. During the fight against the Hundred Stories clan, he protected and helped Encho escape. He often accompanies Yosuzume.

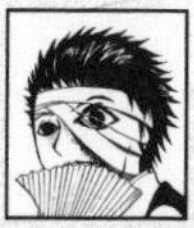

ENCHO

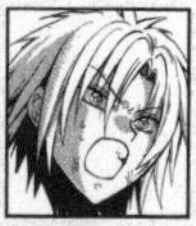

KUBINASHI

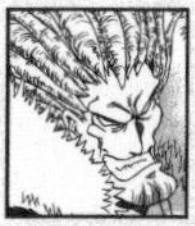

AOTABO

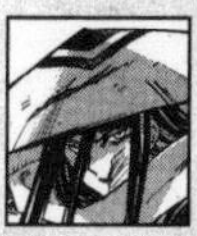

KUROTABO

STORY SO FAR

Rikuo Nura is a seventh-grader at Ukiyoe Middle School. At a glance, he appears to be just another average, normal boy. But he's actually the grandson of the yokai Overlord Nurarihyon. He's also the Third Heir of the powerful Nura clan. He spends his days in hopes that he will someday become a great clan boss who leads a Night Parade of a Hundred Demons.

Through the secret machinations of the Gokadoin clan, Seimei has been reborn from Hell. In order to attack Seimei's base at Aoi Spiral Castle, Ryuji attempts to remove the surrounding barrier, but runs headlong into conflict with its creator, Tenkai! In this battle between onmyoji, Ryuji overcomes his limits and claims victory. At last, the gate to Aoi Spiral Castle is open!!

Aiming for Seimei on the top floor, Rikuo and allies race up the stairs of Aoi Spiral Castle, but leaders of the Gokadoin clan from throughout history stand in their way! Thanks to cooperation from his comrades, Rikuo climbs ever higher... Just before the top, he clashes with Yoshihira—second leader of the enemy clan and Seimei's son! Rikuo and Yoshihira both possess human and ayakashi blood, and now the two opponents with similar backgrounds square off. After a fierce fight, Rikuo defeats Yoshihira and heads for Seimei!

Meanwhile, Seimei has a reunion with his mother, Hagoromo-Gitsune...

TABLE OF CONTENTS

NURA:RISE OF THE YOKAI CLAN

Act 209: Where It Ends

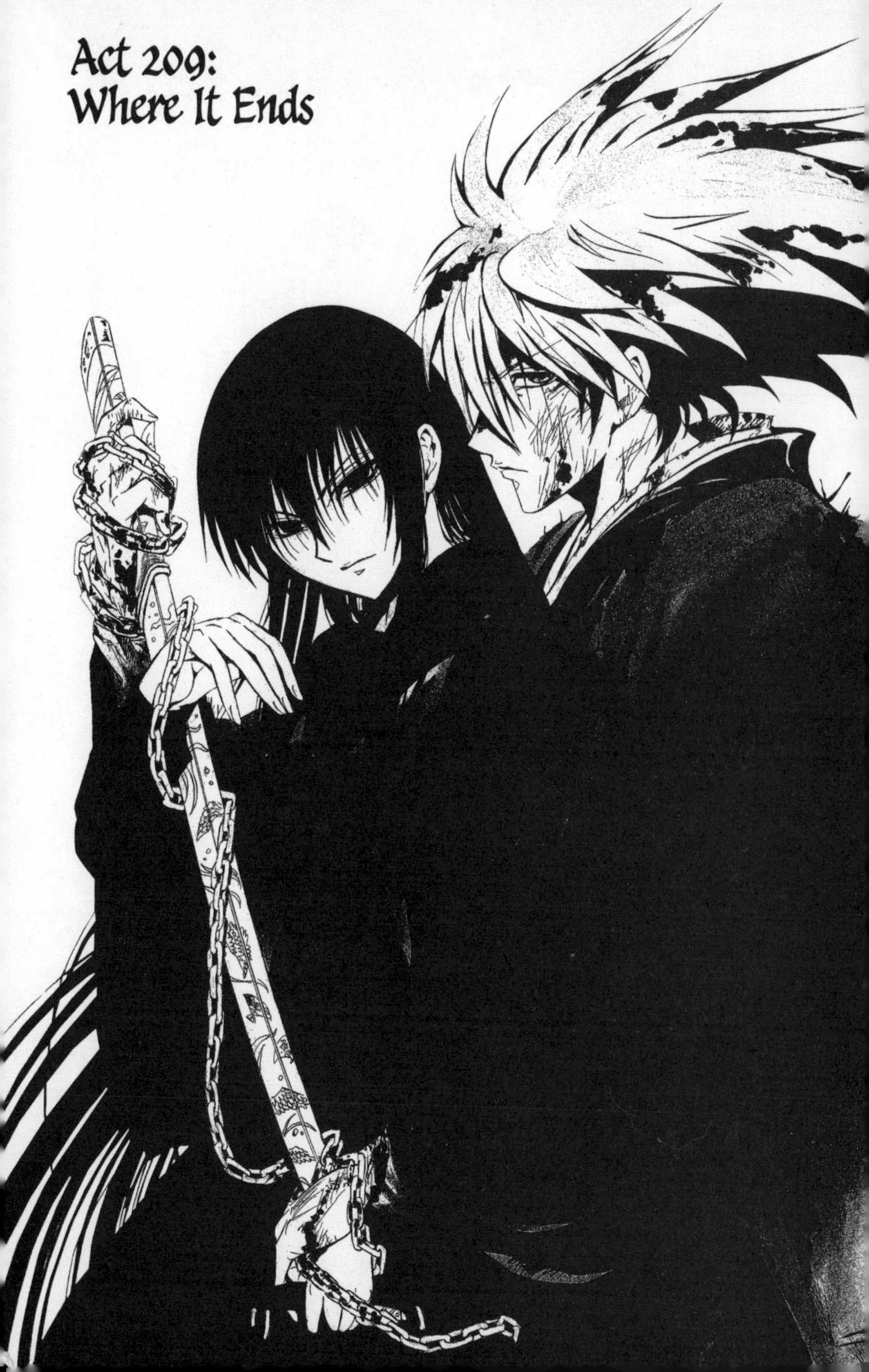

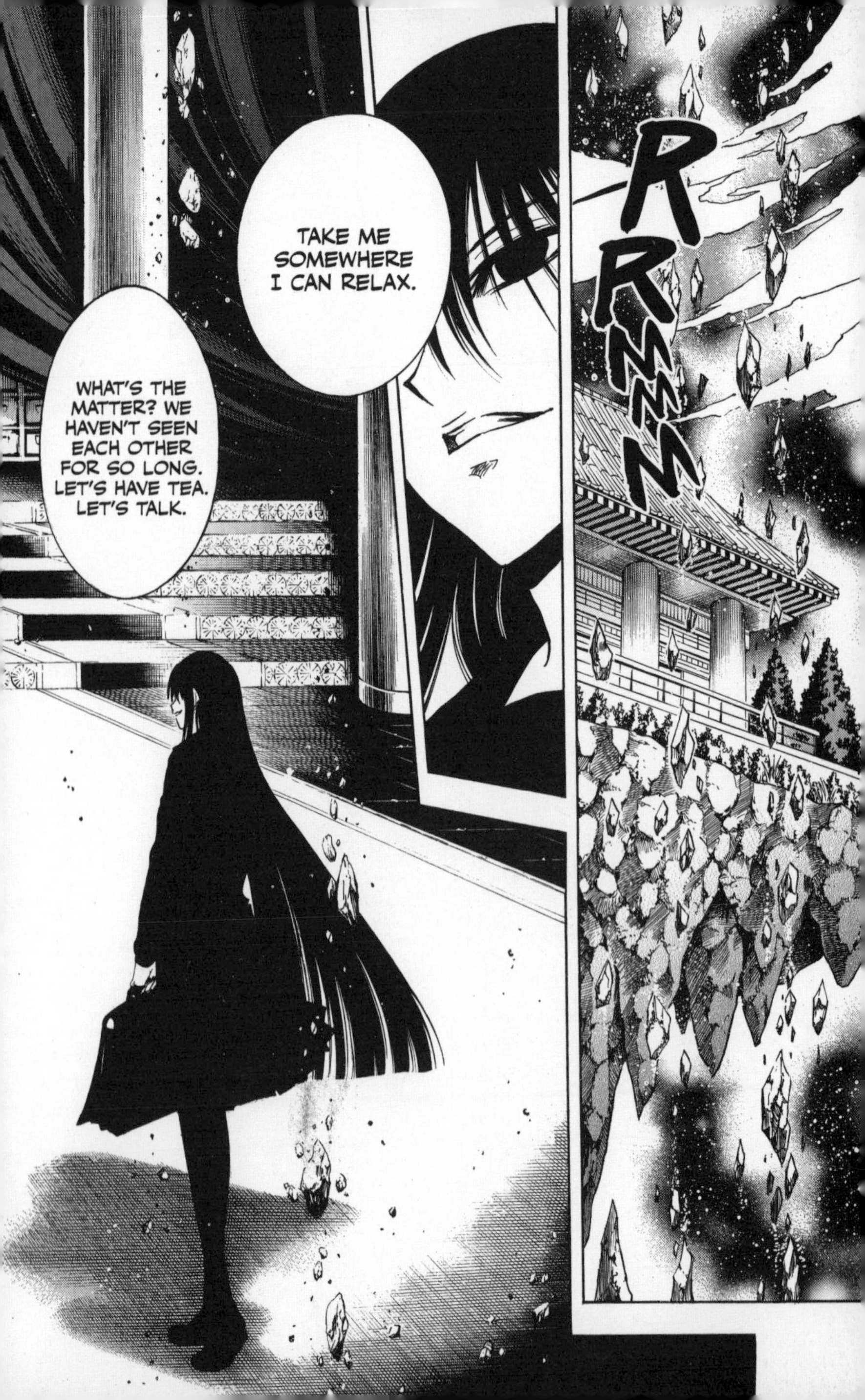
RRMMM
TAKE ME SOMEWHERE I CAN RELAX.
WHAT'S THE MATTER? WE HAVEN'T SEEN EACH OTHER FOR SO LONG. LET'S HAVE TEA. LET'S TALK.

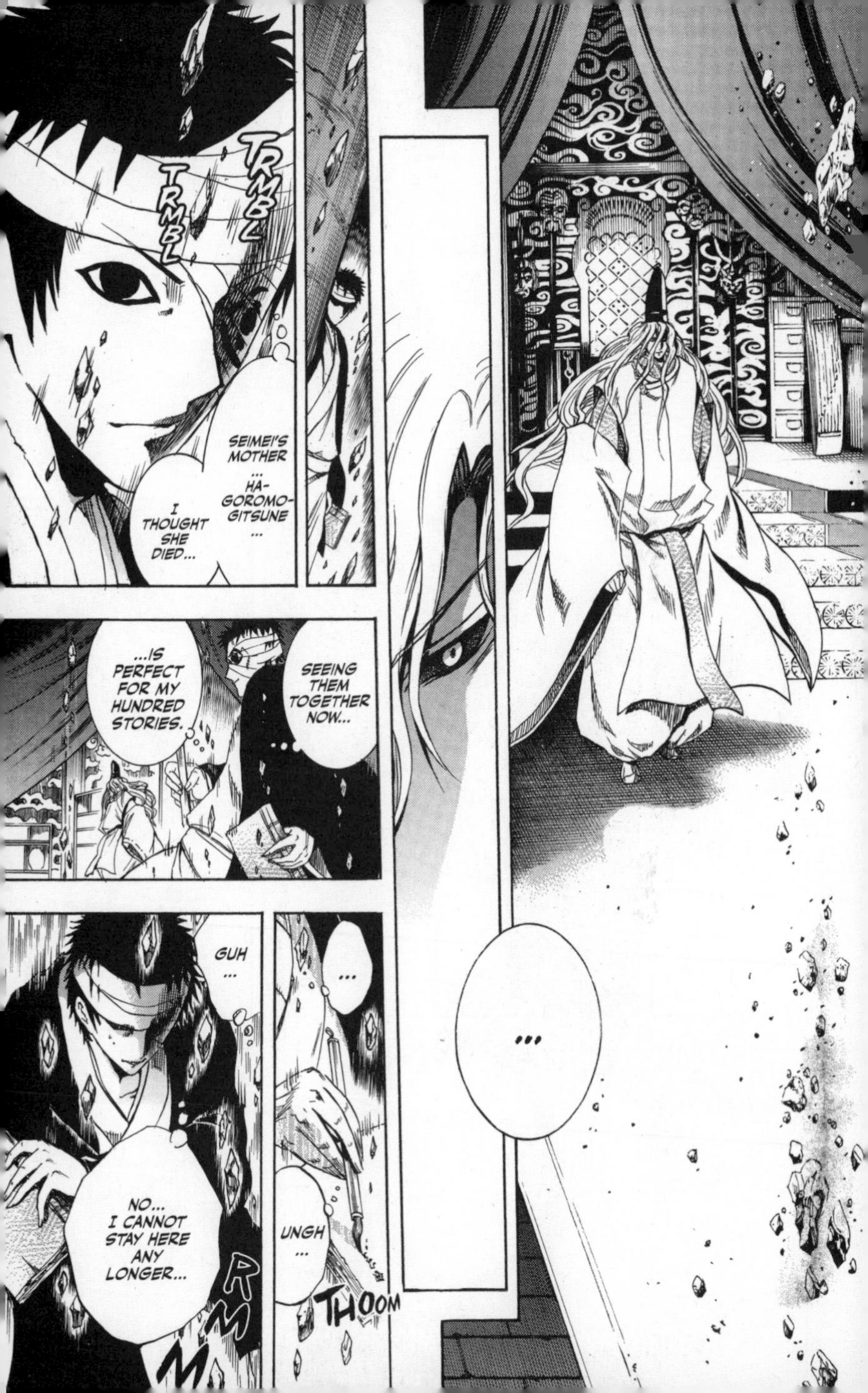

...
TRMBL
TRMBL
SEIMEI'S MOTHER ... HA-GOROMO-GITSUNE ...
I THOUGHT SHE DIED...
SEEING THEM TOGETHER NOW...
...IS PERFECT FOR MY HUNDRED STORIES.
...
UNGH ...
THOOM
GUH ...
NO... I CANNOT STAY HERE ANY LONGER...
RMMM

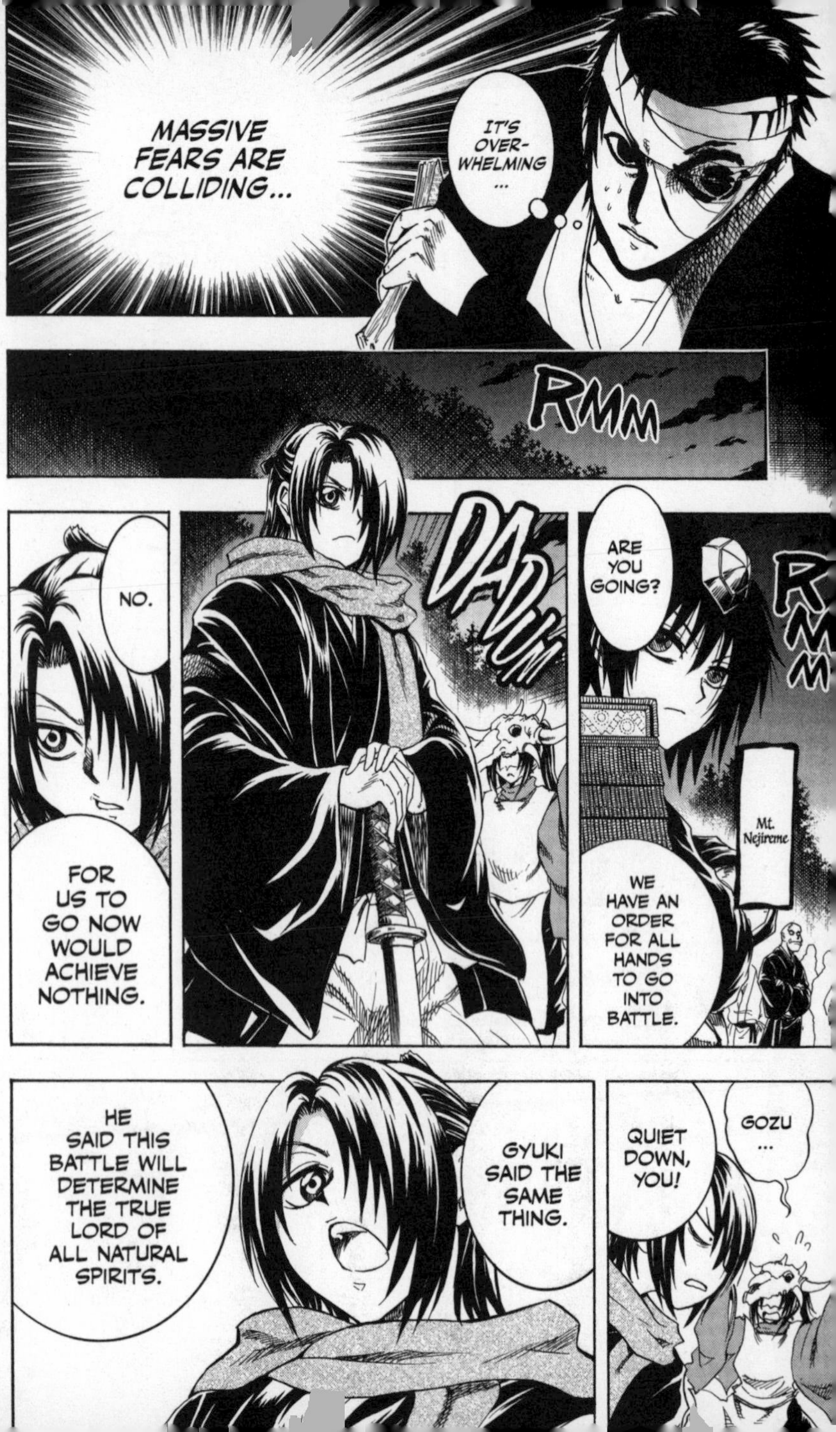
IT'S OVER-WHELMING ...
MASSIVE FEARS ARE COLLIDING...
RMM
RMM
ARE YOU GOING?
Mt. Nejireme
WE HAVE AN ORDER FOR ALL HANDS TO GO INTO BATTLE.
DADUM
NO.
FOR US TO GO NOW WOULD ACHIEVE NOTHING.
GOZU ...
QUIET DOWN, YOU!
GYUKI SAID THE SAME THING.
HE SAID THIS BATTLE WILL DETERMINE THE TRUE LORD OF ALL NATURAL SPIRITS.

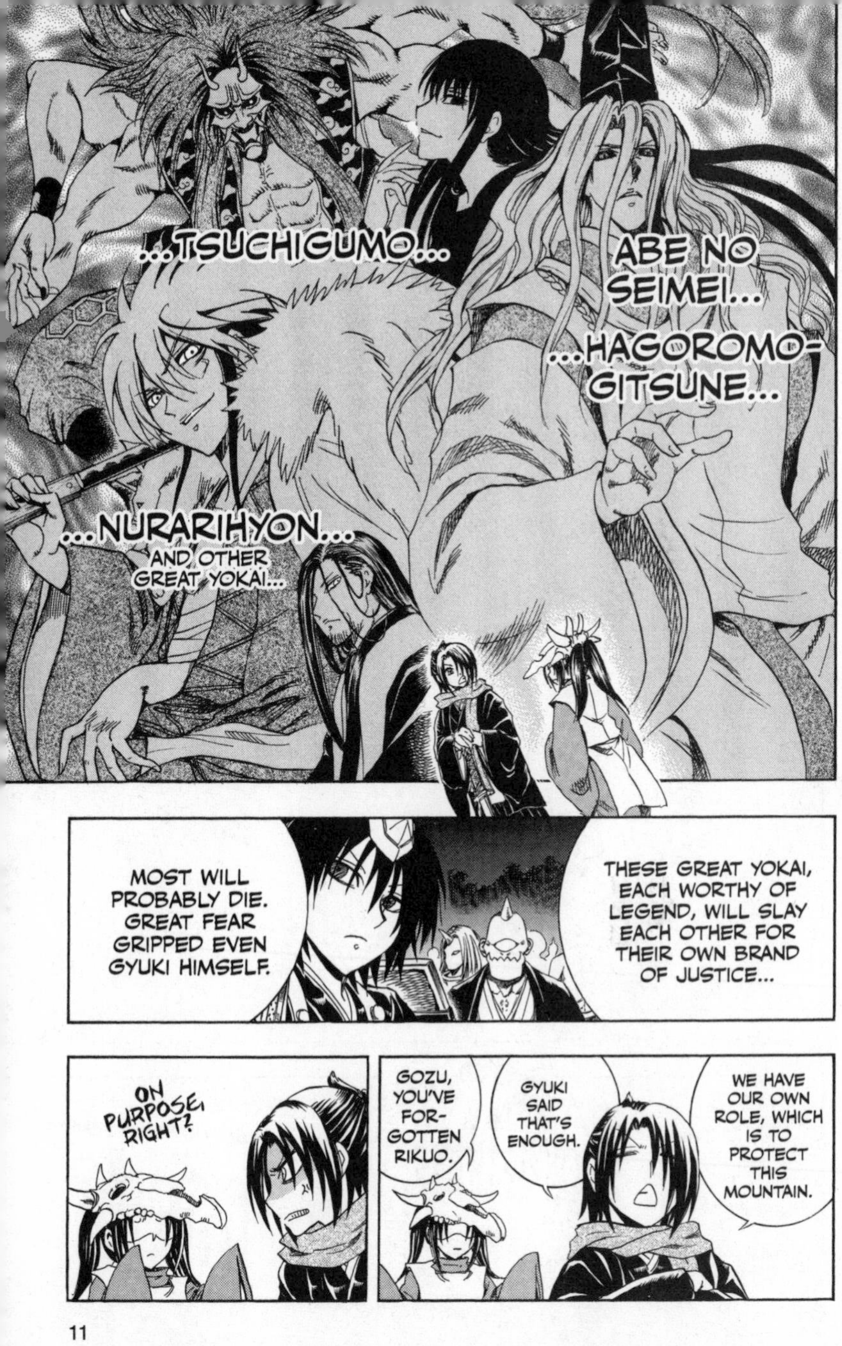
ABE NO SEIMEI...
...HAGOROMO-GITSUNE...
...TSUCHIGUMO...
...NURARIHYON...
AND OTHER GREAT YOKAI...
THESE GREAT YOKAI, EACH WORTHY OF LEGEND, WILL SLAY EACH OTHER FOR THEIR OWN BRAND OF JUSTICE...
MOST WILL PROBABLY DIE. GREAT FEAR GRIPPED EVEN GYUKI HIMSELF.
WE HAVE OUR OWN ROLE, WHICH IS TO PROTECT THIS MOUNTAIN.
GYUKI SAID THAT'S ENOUGH.
GOZU, YOU'VE FOR-GOTTEN RIKUO.
ON PURPOSE, RIGHT?

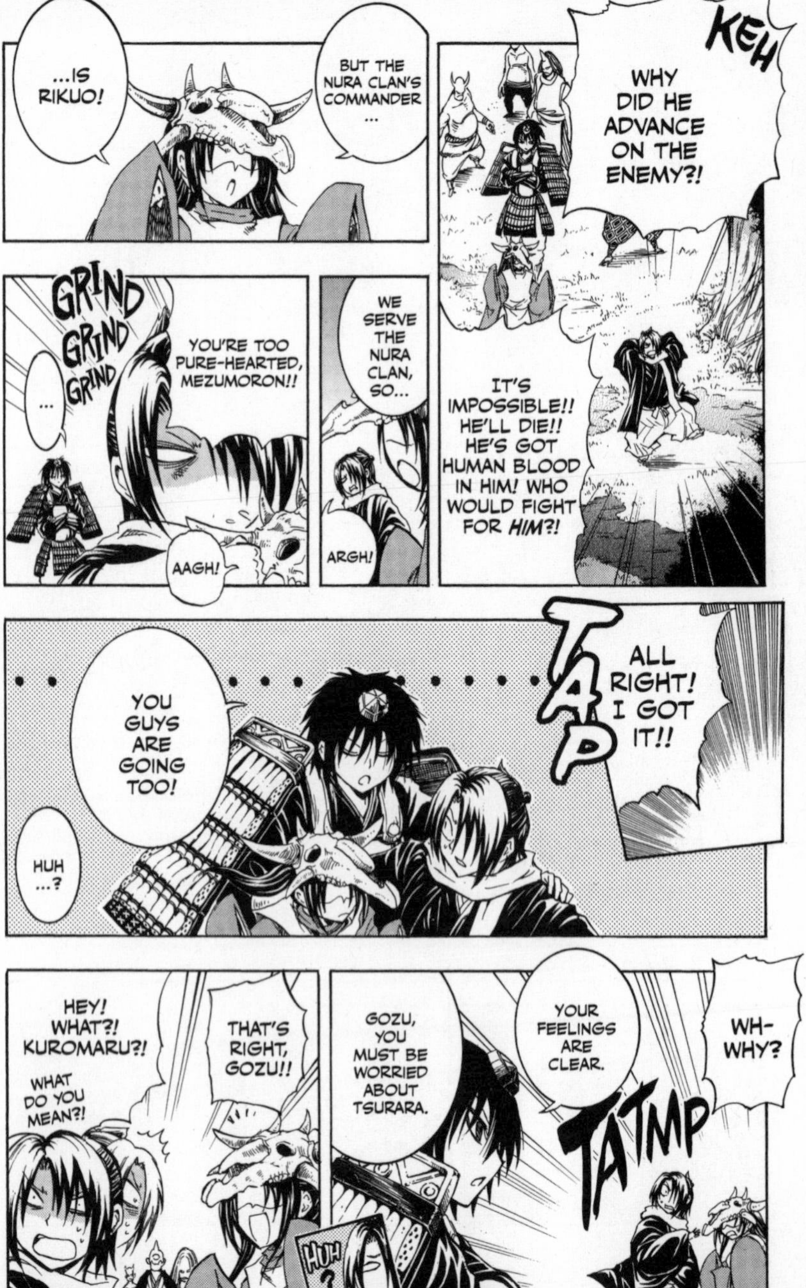
KEH
WHY DID HE ADVANCE ON THE ENEMY?!
IT'S IMPOSSIBLE!! HE'LL DIE!! HE'S GOT HUMAN BLOOD IN HIM! WHO WOULD FIGHT FOR *HIM*?!
BUT THE NURA CLAN'S COMMANDER ...
...IS RIKUO!
WE SERVE THE NURA CLAN, SO...
ARGH!
GRIND GRIND GRIND
YOU'RE TOO PURE-HEARTED, MEZUMORON!!
...
AAGH!
ALL RIGHT! I GOT IT!!
TAP
YOU GUYS ARE GOING TOO!
HUH ...?
WH-WHY?
YOUR FEELINGS ARE CLEAR.
TATMP
GOZU, YOU MUST BE WORRIED ABOUT TSURARA.
HUH ?
THAT'S RIGHT, GOZU!!
HEY! WHAT?! KUROMARU?!
WHAT DO YOU MEAN?!

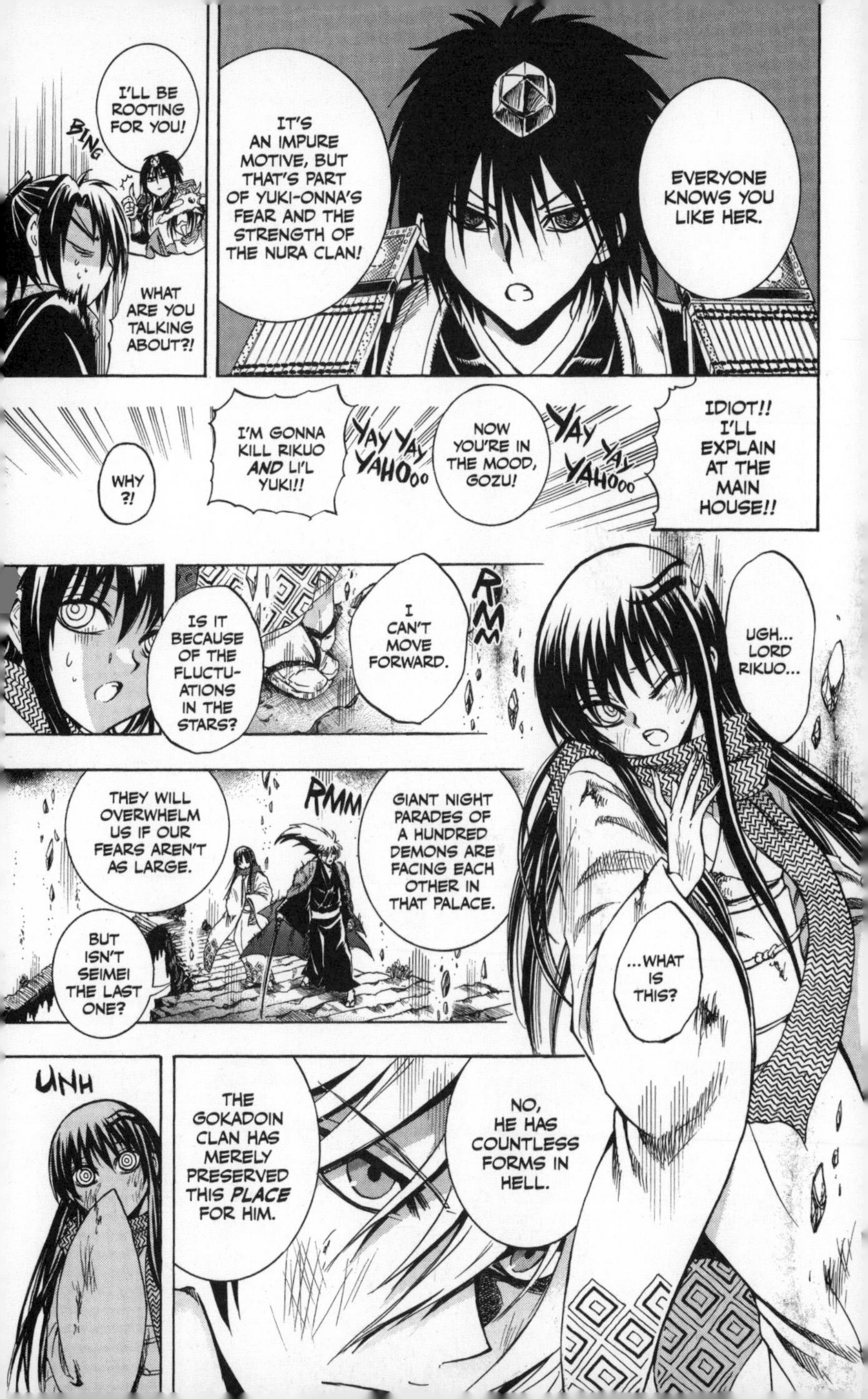
EVERYONE KNOWS YOU LIKE HER.
IT'S AN IMPURE MOTIVE, BUT THAT'S PART OF YUKI-ONNA'S FEAR AND THE STRENGTH OF THE NURA CLAN!
I'LL BE ROOTING FOR YOU!
BING
WHAT ARE YOU TALKING ABOUT?!
IDIOT!! I'LL EXPLAIN AT THE MAIN HOUSE!!
YAY YAY YAHOooo
NOW YOU'RE IN THE MOOD, GOZU!
YAY YAY YAHOoo
I'M GONNA KILL RIKUO *AND* LI'L YUKI!!
WHY?!
UGH... LORD RIKUO...
RMM
I CAN'T MOVE FORWARD.
IS IT BECAUSE OF THE FLUCTU-ATIONS IN THE STARS?
...WHAT IS THIS?
GIANT NIGHT PARADES OF A HUNDRED DEMONS ARE FACING EACH OTHER IN THAT PALACE.
RMM
THEY WILL OVERWHELM US IF OUR FEARS AREN'T AS LARGE.
BUT ISN'T SEIMEI THE LAST ONE?
NO, HE HAS COUNTLESS FORMS IN HELL.
THE GOKADOIN CLAN HAS MERELY PRESERVED THIS *PLACE* FOR HIM.
UNH

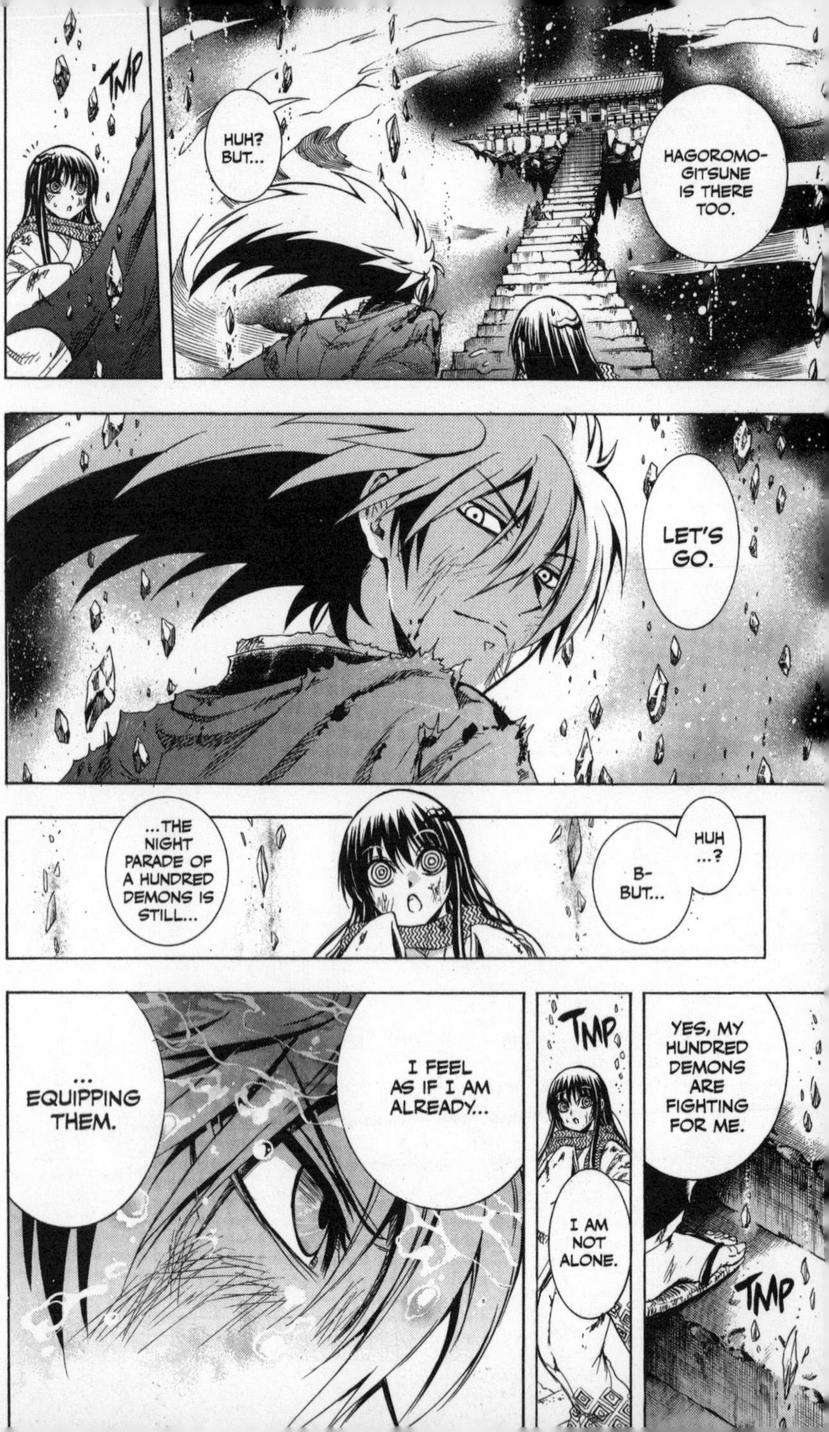
HAGOROMO-GITSUNE IS THERE TOO.
HUH? BUT...
TMP
LET'S GO.
HUH ...?
B-BUT...
...THE NIGHT PARADE OF A HUNDRED DEMONS IS STILL...
YES, MY HUNDRED DEMONS ARE FIGHTING FOR ME.
TMP
TMP
I AM NOT ALONE.
I FEEL AS IF I AM ALREADY...
... EQUIPPING THEM.

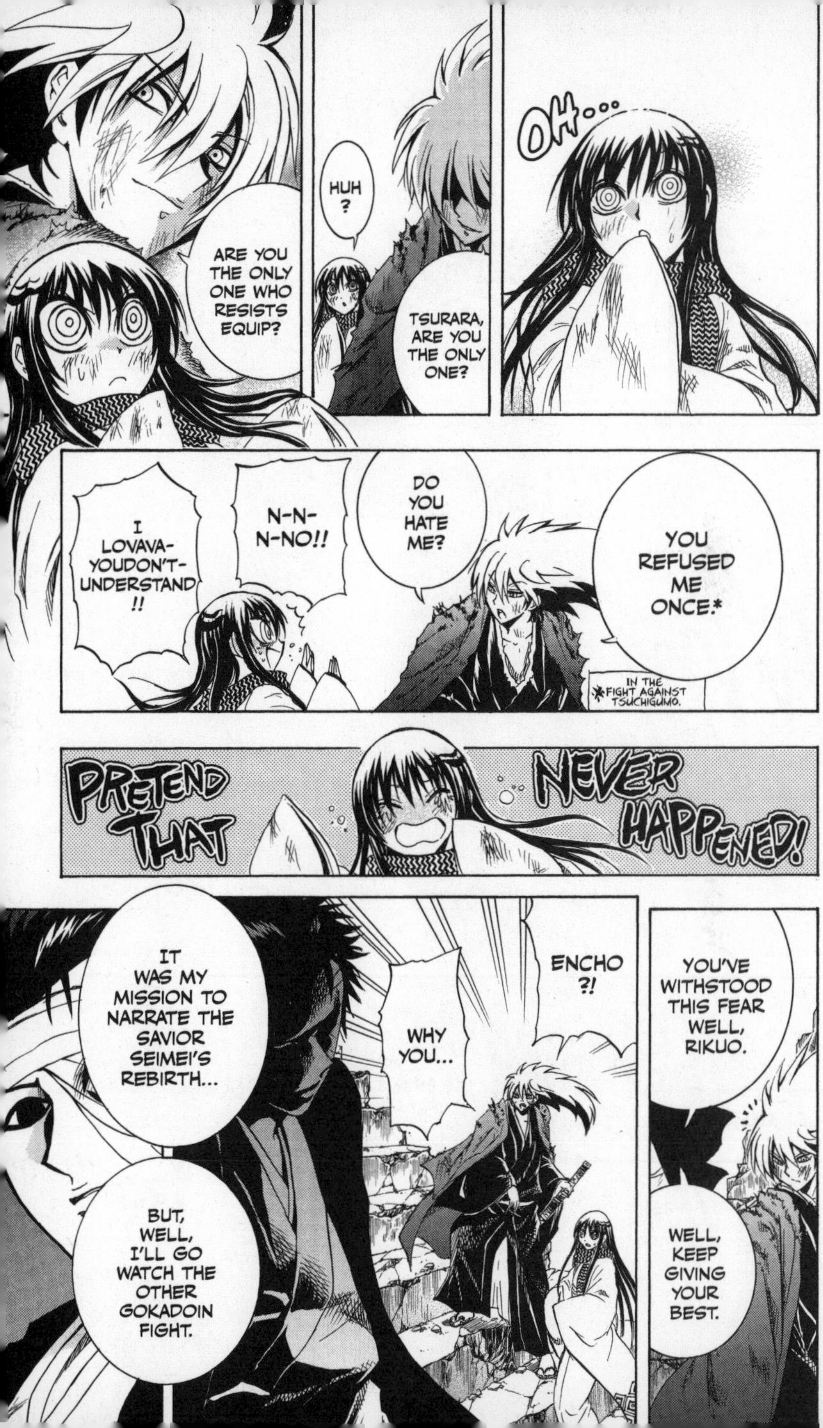
OH...
HUH?
TSURARA, ARE YOU THE ONLY ONE?
ARE YOU THE ONLY ONE WHO RESISTS EQUIP?
YOU REFUSED ME ONCE.*
*IN THE FIGHT AGAINST TSUCHIGUMO.
DO YOU HATE ME?
N-N-N-NO!!
I LOVAVA-YOUDON'T-UNDERSTAND!!
PRETEND THAT NEVER HAPPENED!
YOU'VE WITHSTOOD THIS FEAR WELL, RIKUO.
WELL, KEEP GIVING YOUR BEST.
ENCHO?!
WHY YOU...
IT WAS MY MISSION TO NARRATE THE SAVIOR SEIMEI'S REBIRTH...
BUT, WELL, I'LL GO WATCH THE OTHER GOKADOIN FIGHT.

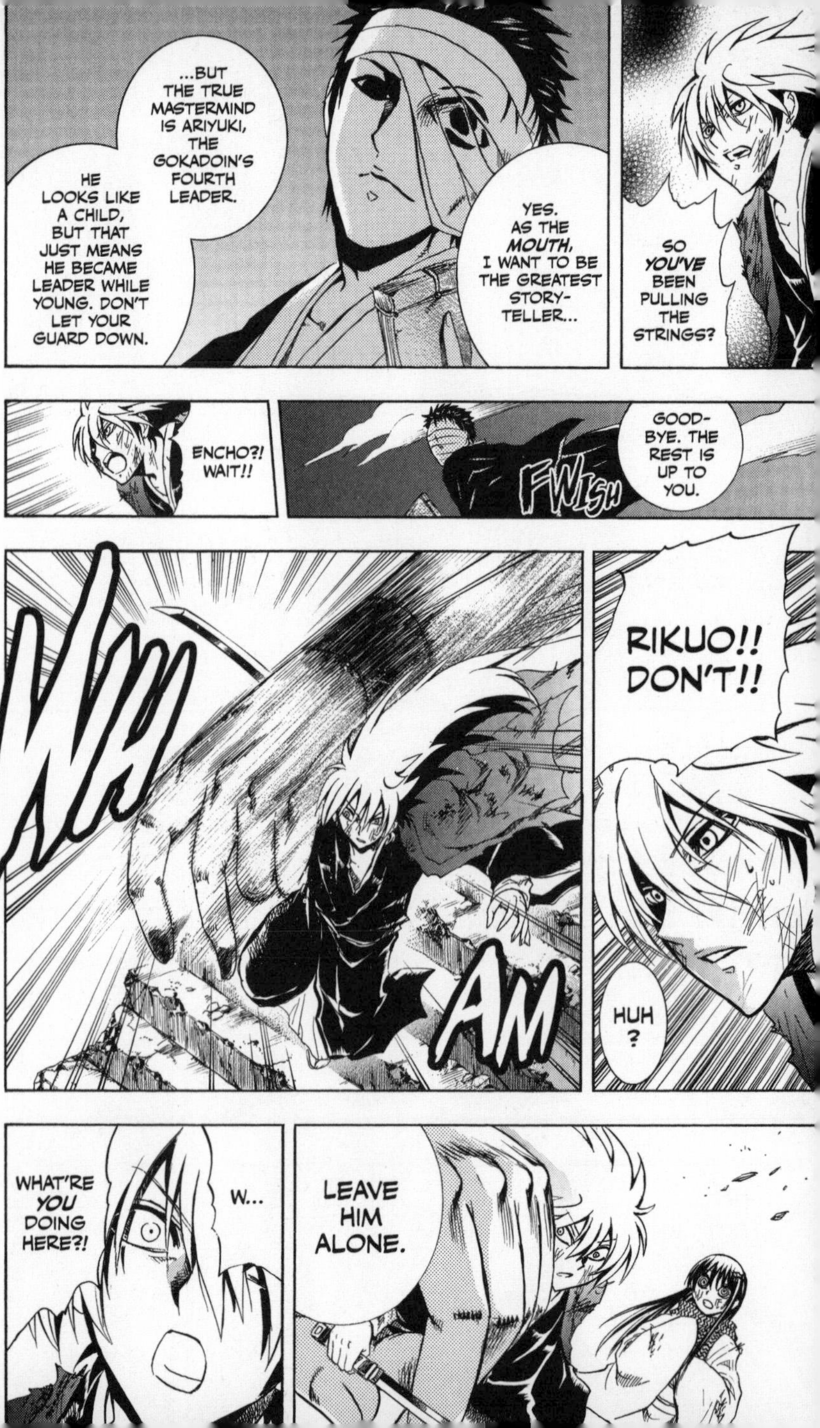
SO *YOU'VE* BEEN PULLING THE STRINGS?
YES. AS THE *MOUTH,* I WANT TO BE THE GREATEST STORY-TELLER...
...BUT THE TRUE MASTERMIND IS ARIYUKI, THE GOKADOIN'S FOURTH LEADER.
HE LOOKS LIKE A CHILD, BUT THAT JUST MEANS HE BECAME LEADER WHILE YOUNG. DON'T LET YOUR GUARD DOWN.
GOOD-BYE. THE REST IS UP TO YOU.
FWISH
ENCHO?! WAIT!!
RIKUO!! DON'T!!
HUH?
WH
AM
LEAVE HIM ALONE.
W...
WHAT'RE *YOU* DOING HERE?!

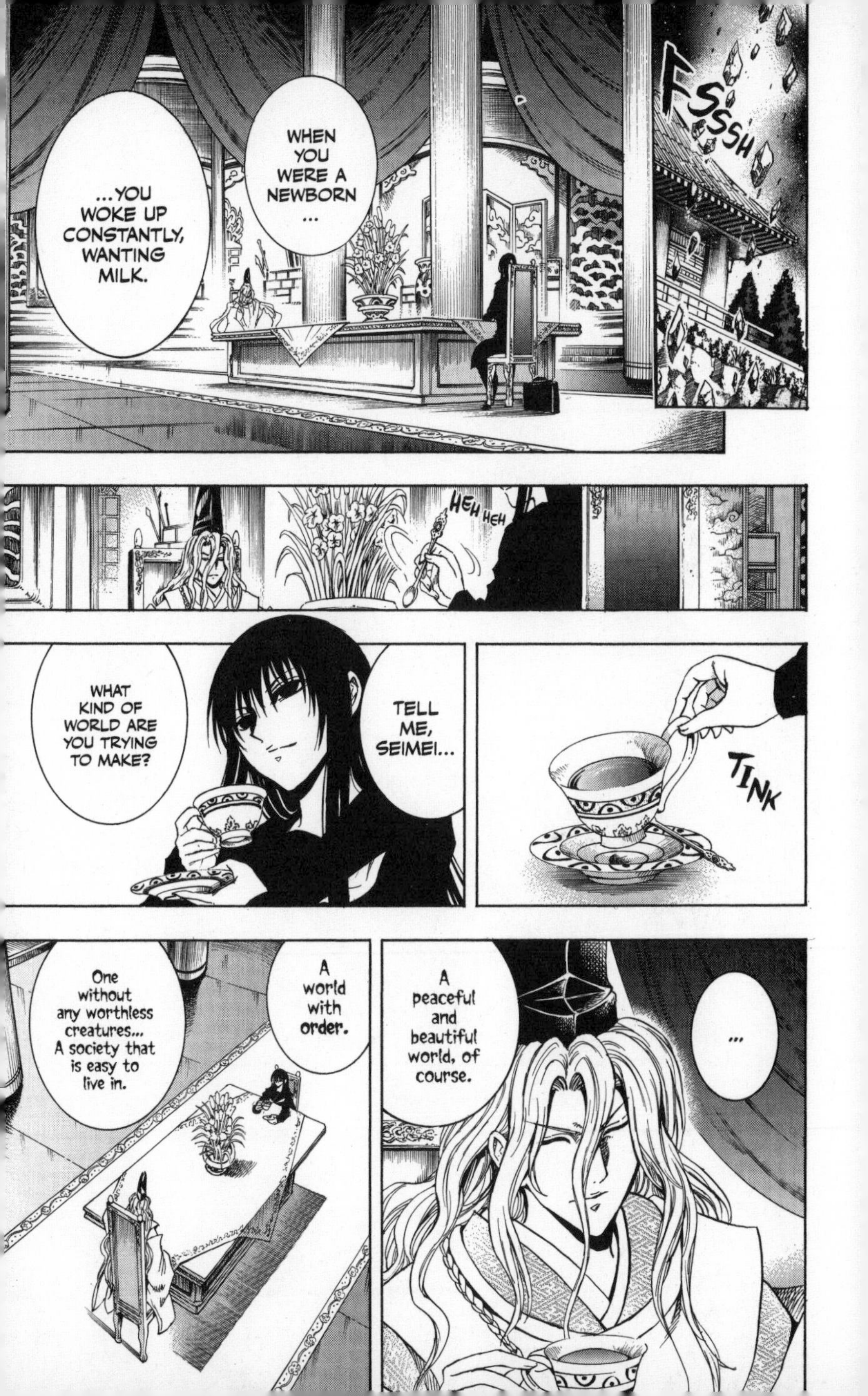
FSSSH
WHEN YOU WERE A NEWBORN ...
...YOU WOKE UP CONSTANTLY, WANTING MILK.
HEH HEH
TINK
TELL ME, SEIMEI...
WHAT KIND OF WORLD ARE YOU TRYING TO MAKE?
...
A peaceful and beautiful world, of course.
A world with **order**.
One without any worthless creatures... A society that is easy to live in.

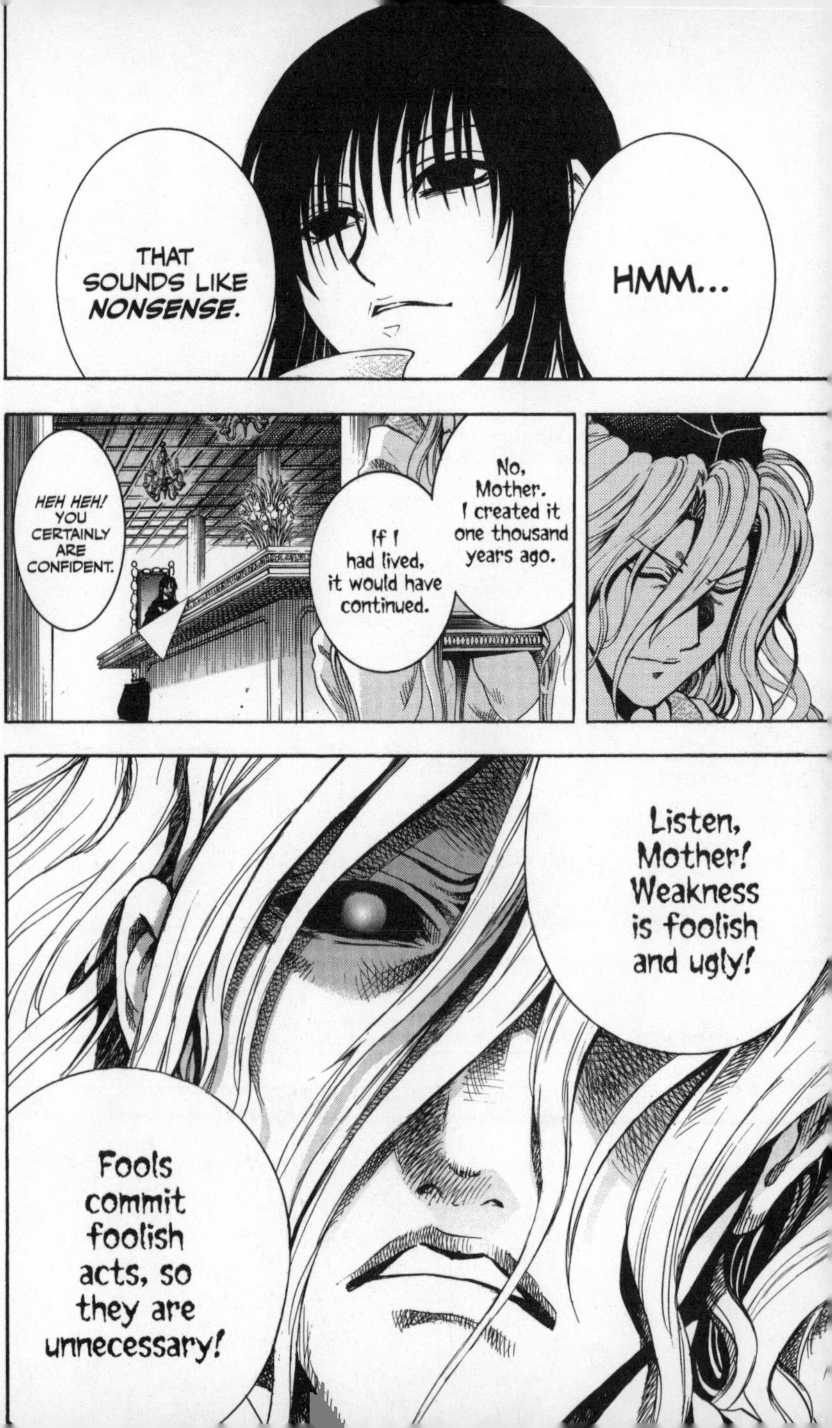
HMM...
THAT SOUNDS LIKE NONSENSE.
No, Mother. I created it one thousand years ago.
If I had lived, it would have continued.
HEH HEH! YOU CERTAINLY ARE CONFIDENT.
Listen, Mother! Weakness is foolish and ugly!
Fools commit foolish acts, so they are unnecessary!

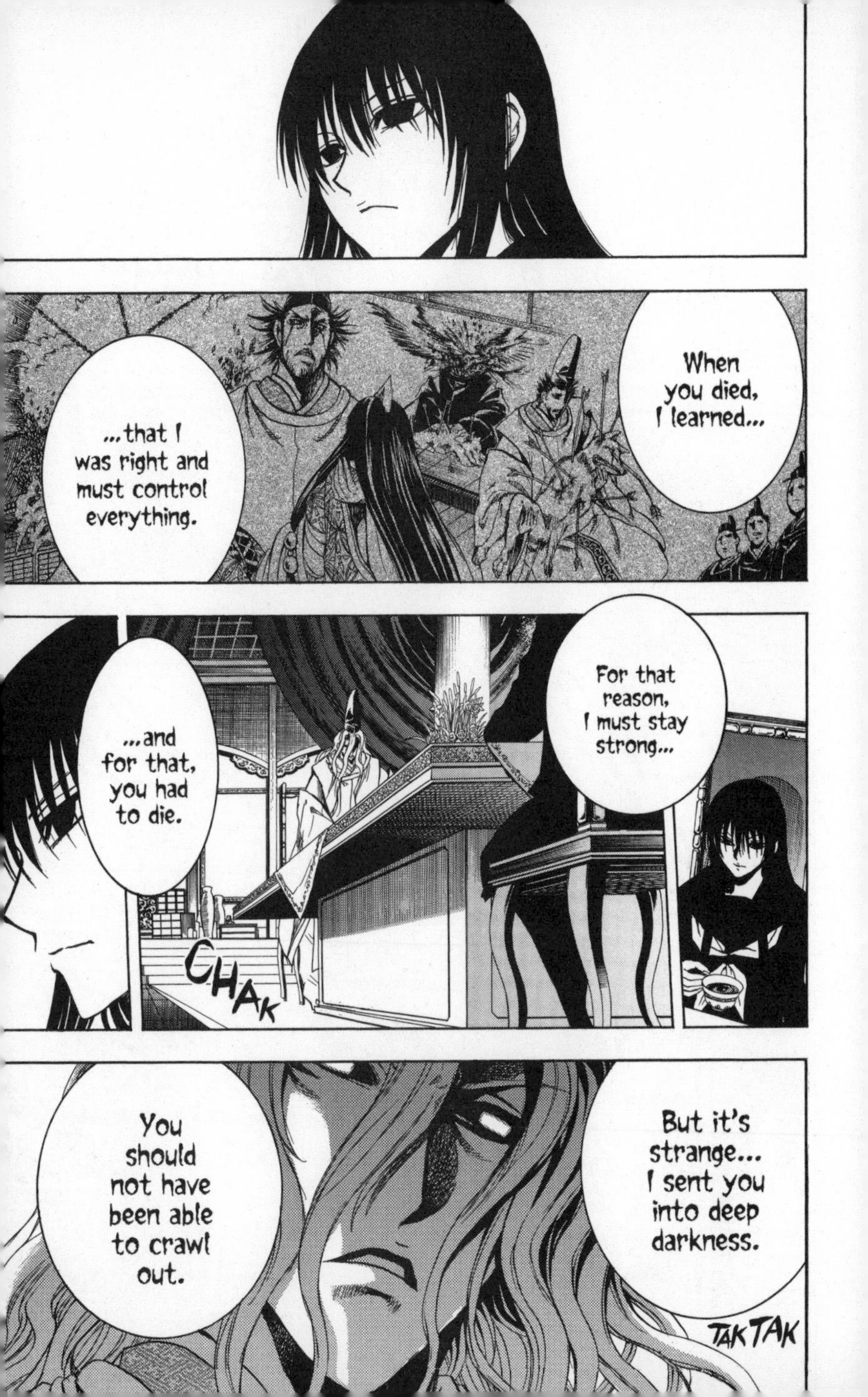
When you died, I learned...
...that I was right and must control everything.
For that reason, I must stay strong...
...and for that, you had to die.
CHAK
But it's strange... I sent you into deep darkness.
TAKTAK
You should not have been able to crawl out.

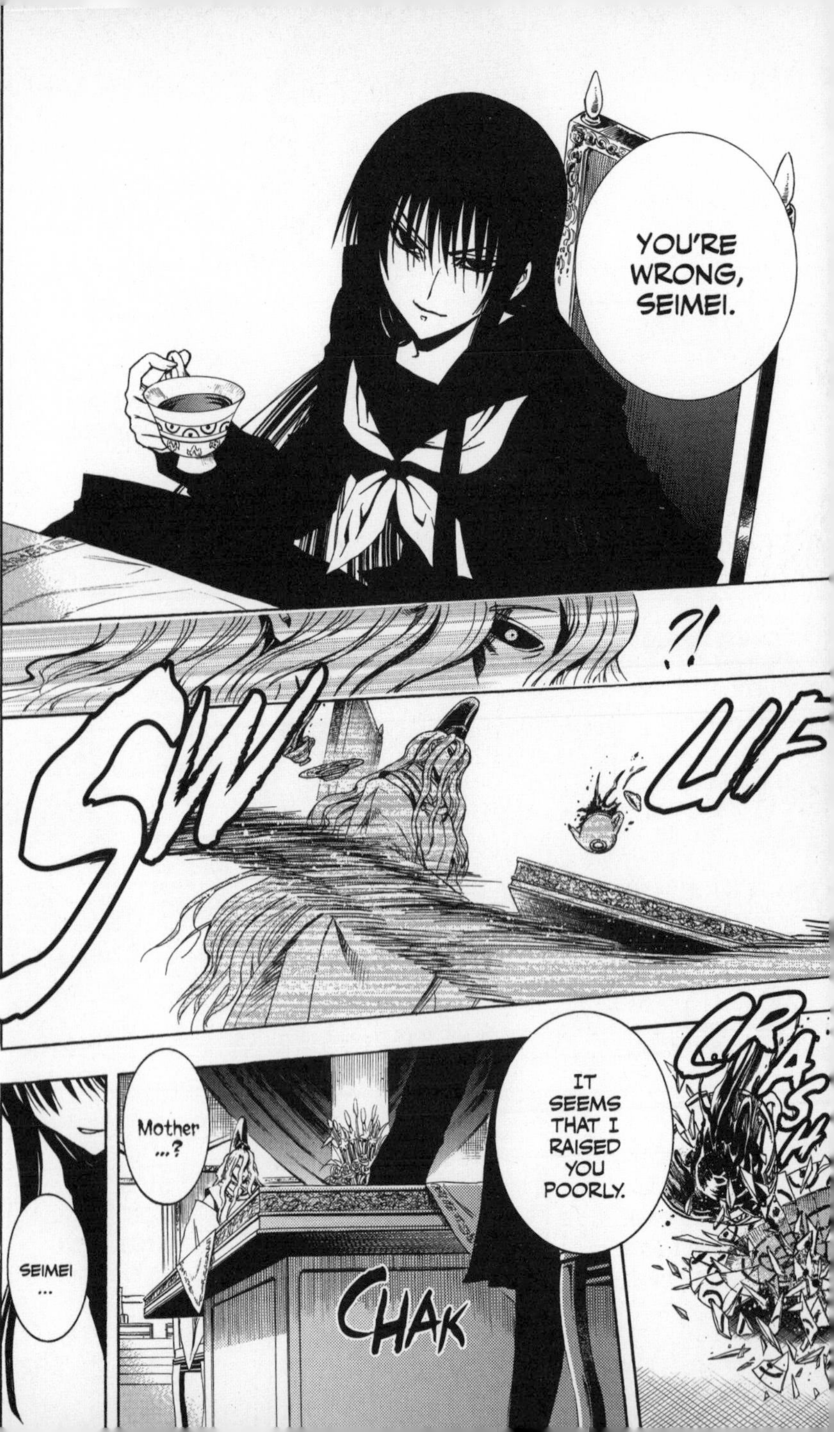
YOU'RE WRONG, SEIMEI.
?!
SWUF
CRASH
IT SEEMS THAT I RAISED YOU POORLY.
CHAK
Mother ...?
SEIMEI ...

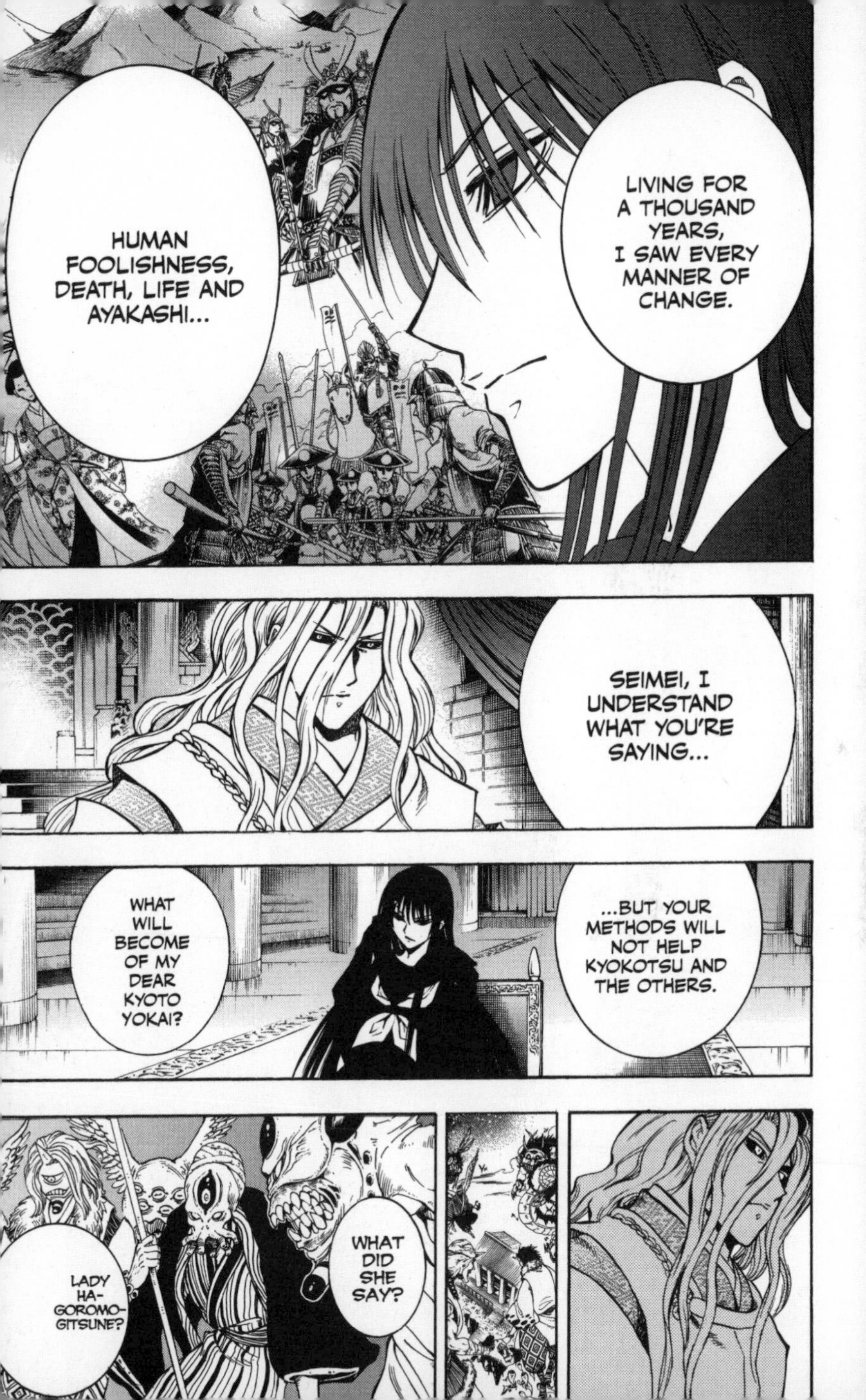

LIVING FOR A THOUSAND YEARS, I SAW EVERY MANNER OF CHANGE.
HUMAN FOOLISHNESS, DEATH, LIFE AND AYAKASHI...
SEIMEI, I UNDERSTAND WHAT YOU'RE SAYING...
...BUT YOUR METHODS WILL NOT HELP KYOKOTSU AND THE OTHERS.
WHAT WILL BECOME OF MY DEAR KYOTO YOKAI?
WHAT DID SHE SAY?
LADY HAGOROMO-GITSUNE?

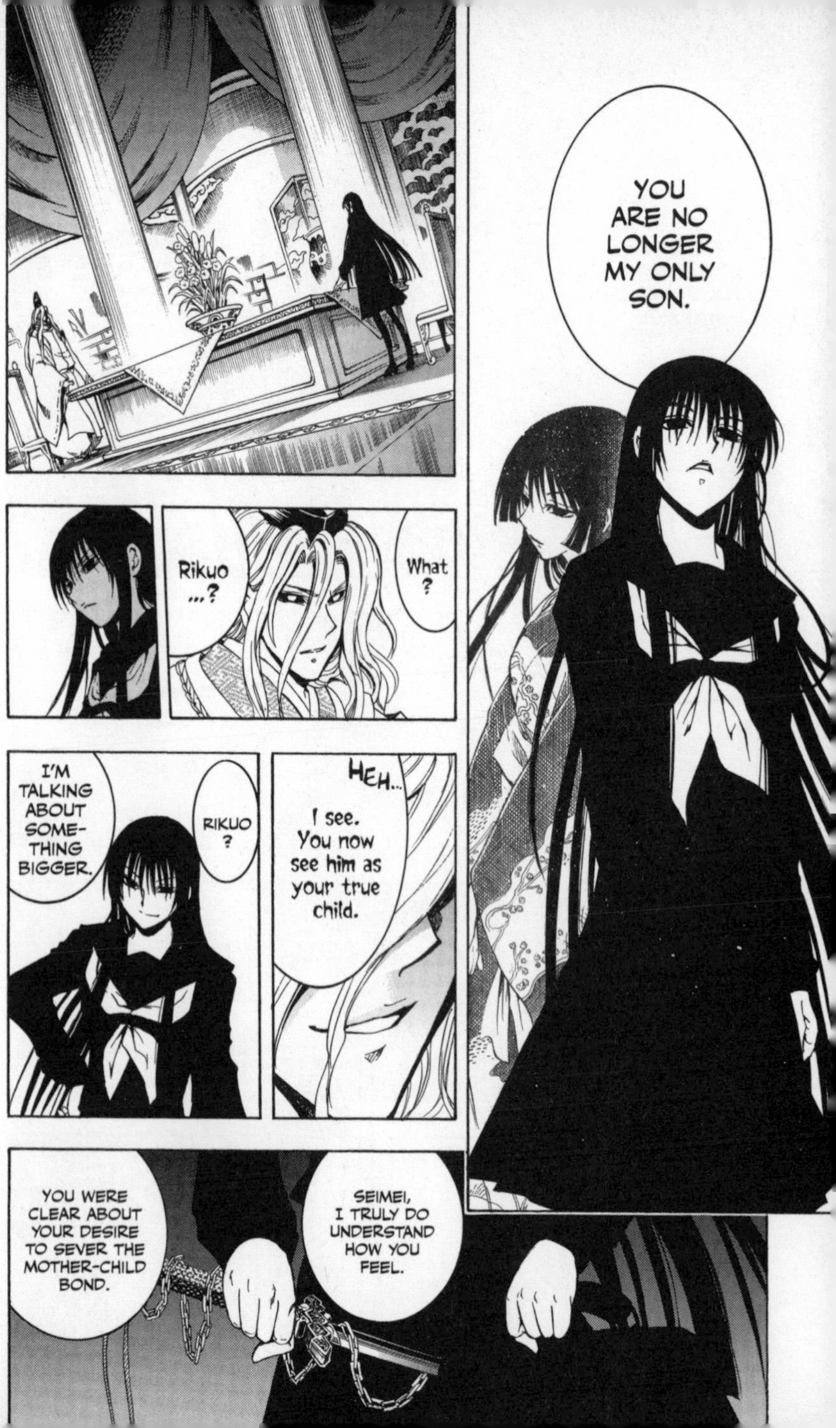
YOU ARE NO LONGER MY ONLY SON.
What?
Rikuo ...?
HEH...
I see. You now see him as your true child.
RIKUO?
I'M TALKING ABOUT SOME-THING BIGGER.
SEIMEI, I TRULY DO UNDERSTAND HOW YOU FEEL.
YOU WERE CLEAR ABOUT YOUR DESIRE TO SEVER THE MOTHER-CHILD BOND.

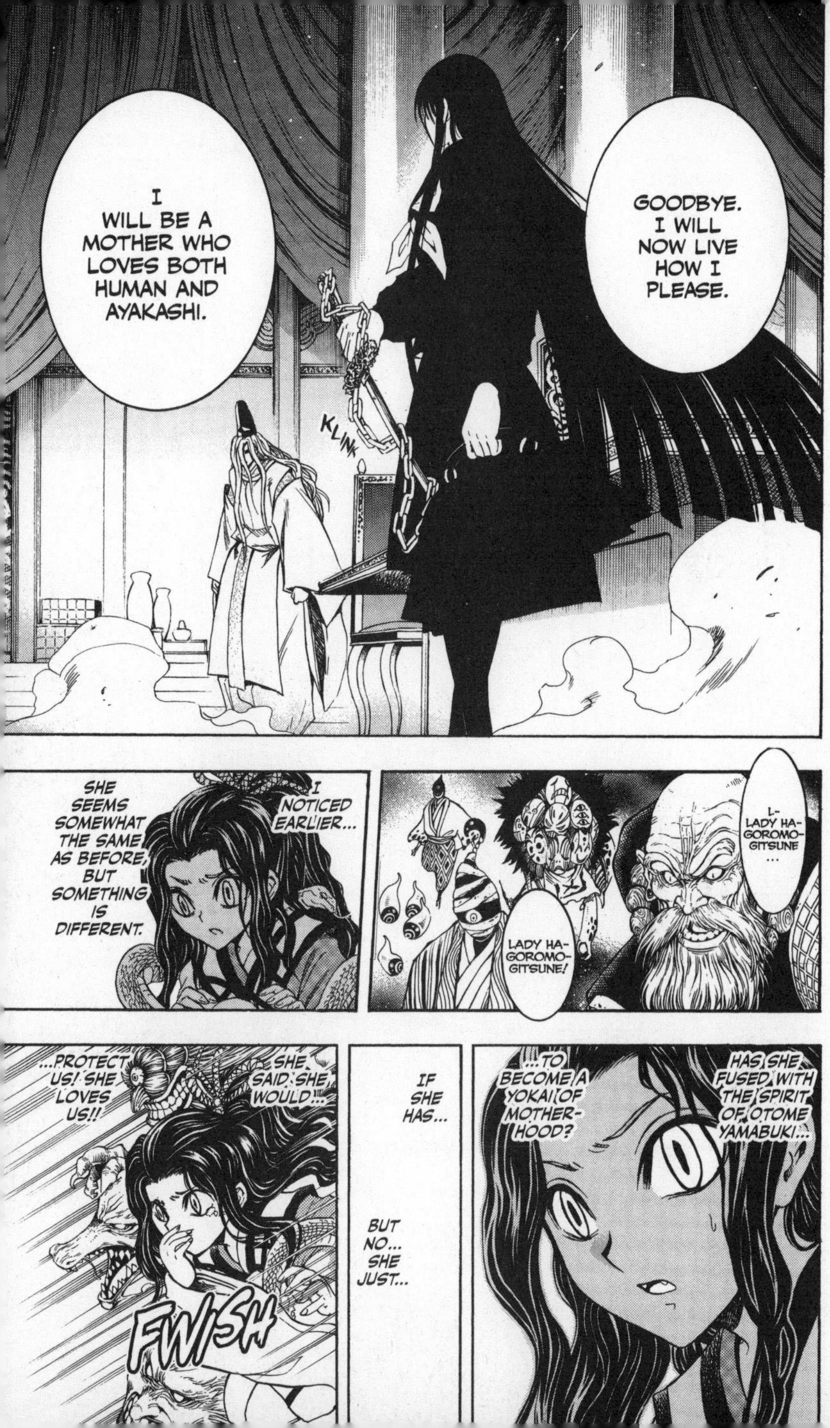
GOODBYE. I WILL NOW LIVE HOW I PLEASE.
I WILL BE A MOTHER WHO LOVES BOTH HUMAN AND AYAKASHI.
KLINK
L-LADY HAGOROMO-GITSUNE...
LADY HAGOROMO-GITSUNE!
I NOTICED EARLIER...
SHE SEEMS SOMEWHAT THE SAME AS BEFORE, BUT SOMETHING IS DIFFERENT.
HAS SHE FUSED WITH THE SPIRIT OF OTOME YAMABUKI...
...TO BECOME A YOKAI OF MOTHER-HOOD?
IF SHE HAS...
BUT NO... SHE JUST...
SHE SAID SHE WOULD...
...PROTECT US! SHE LOVES US!!
FWISH

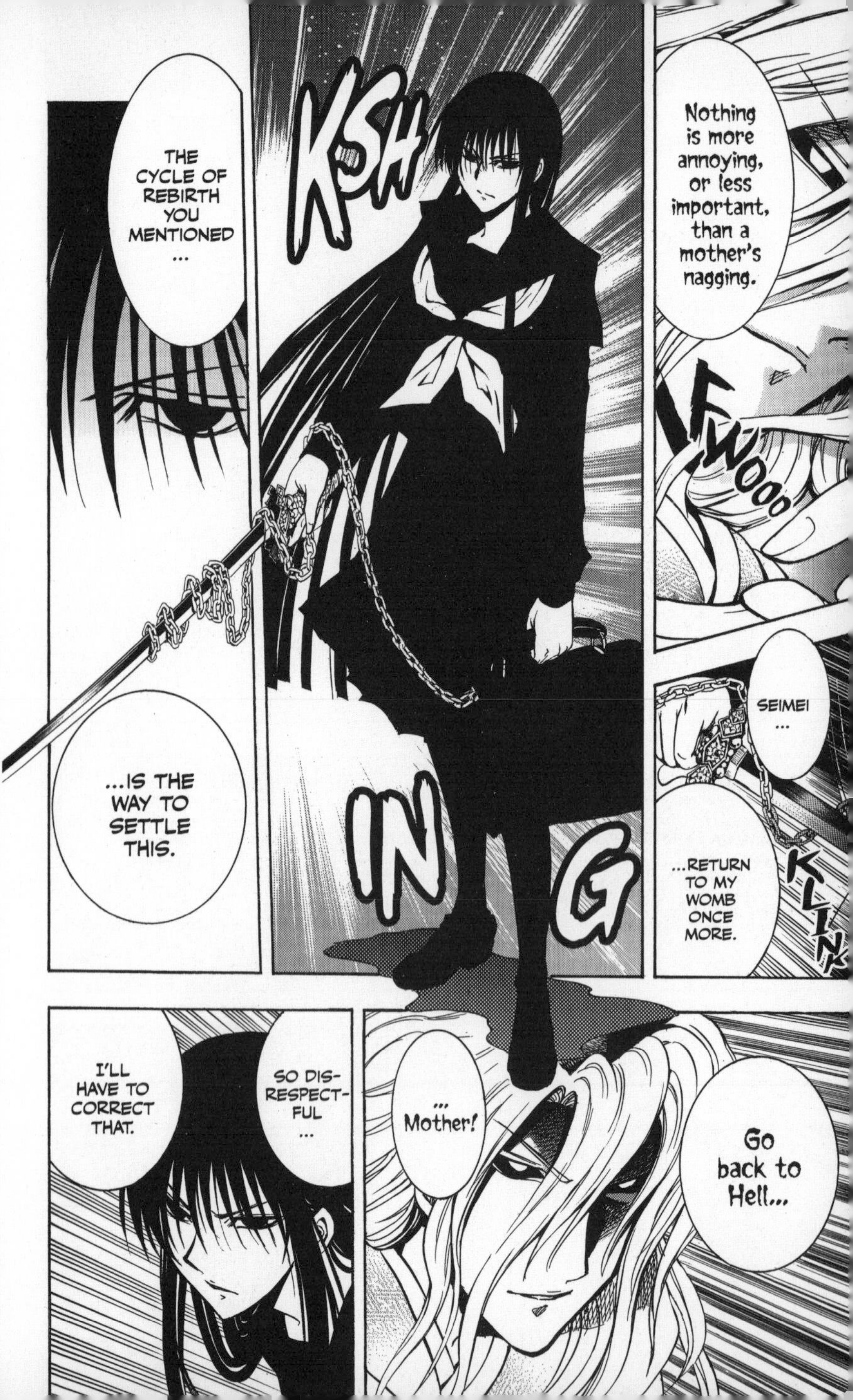
Nothing is more annoying, or less important, than a mother's nagging.
FWOOO
SEIMEI ...
...RETURN TO MY WOMB ONCE MORE.
KLINK
KSH
IN
G
THE CYCLE OF REBIRTH YOU MENTIONED ...
...IS THE WAY TO SETTLE THIS.
Go back to Hell...
... Mother!
SO DIS-RESPECT-FUL ...
I'LL HAVE TO CORRECT THAT.

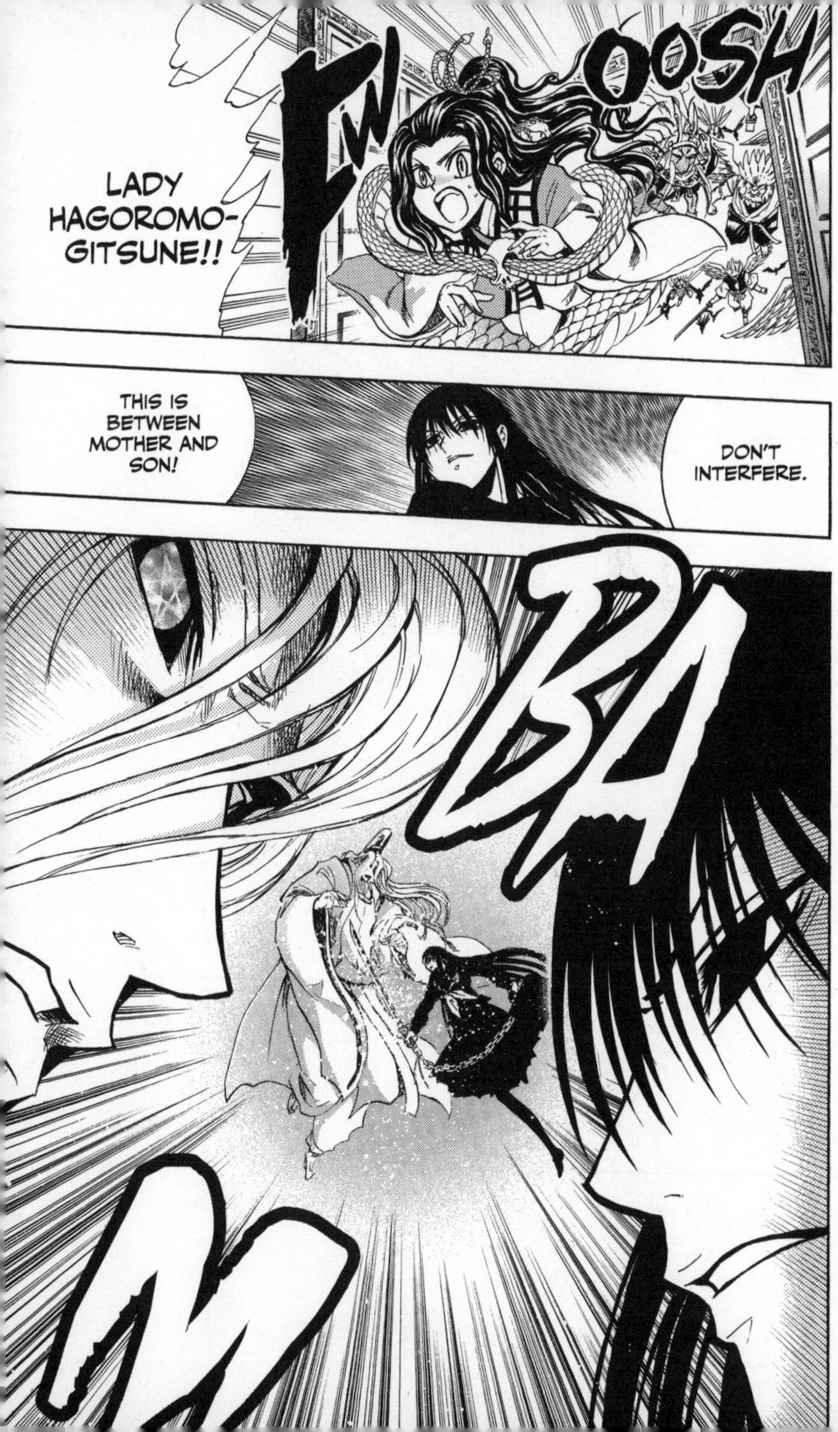
FWOOSH
LADY HAGOROMO-GITSUNE!!
DON'T INTERFERE.
THIS IS BETWEEN MOTHER AND SON!
BA

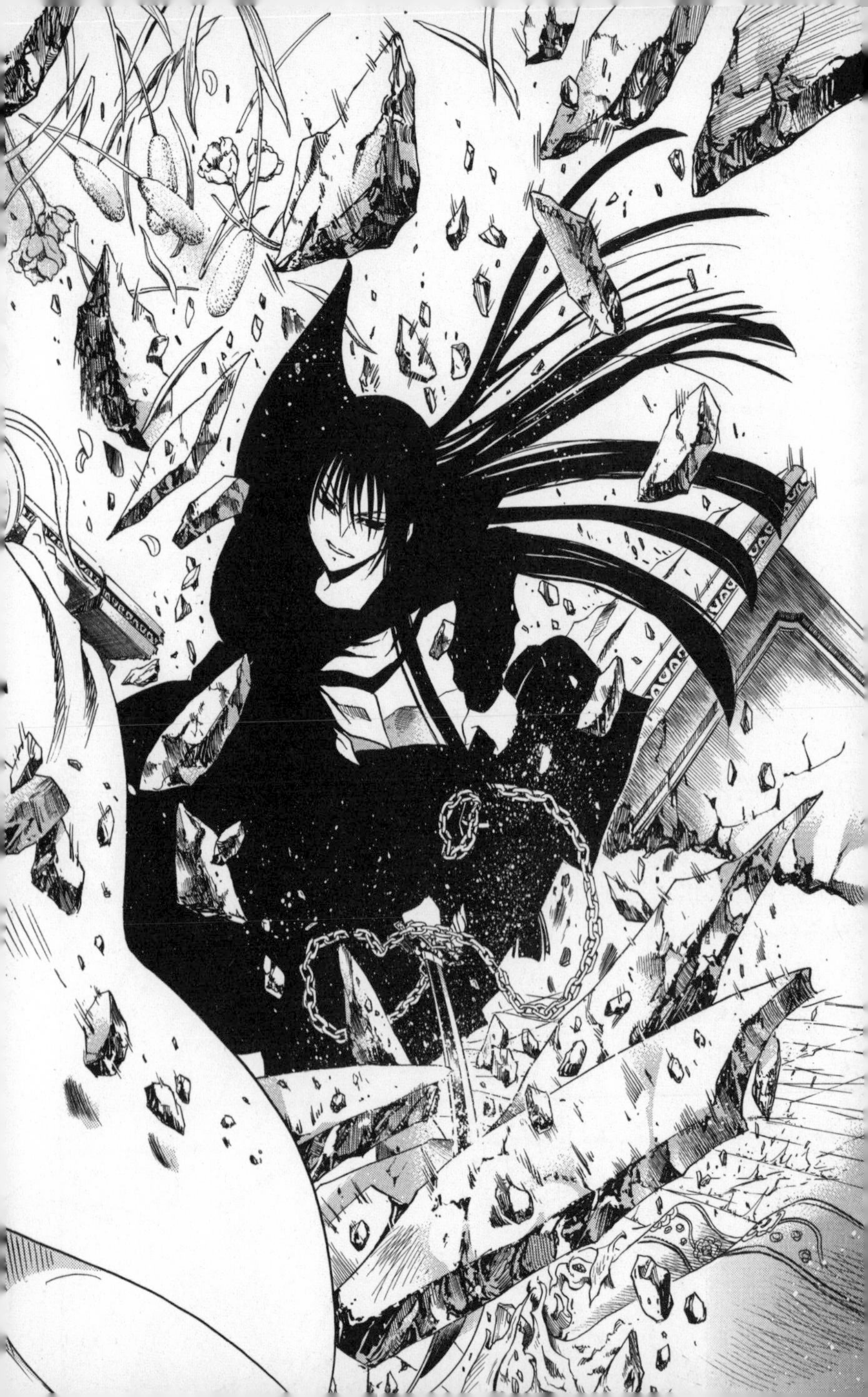

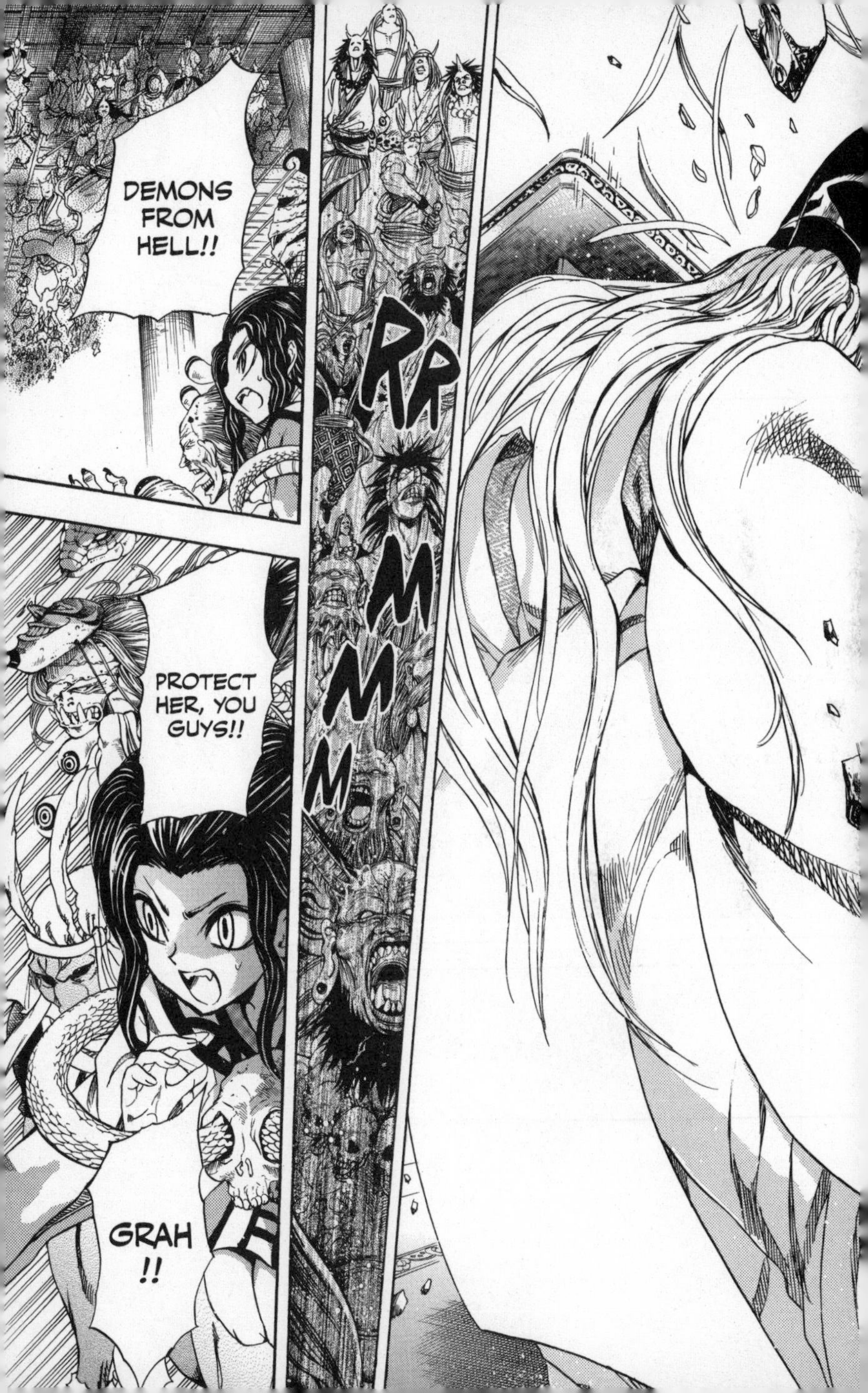
RRMMMM
DEMONS FROM HELL!!
PROTECT HER, YOU GUYS!!
GRAH!!

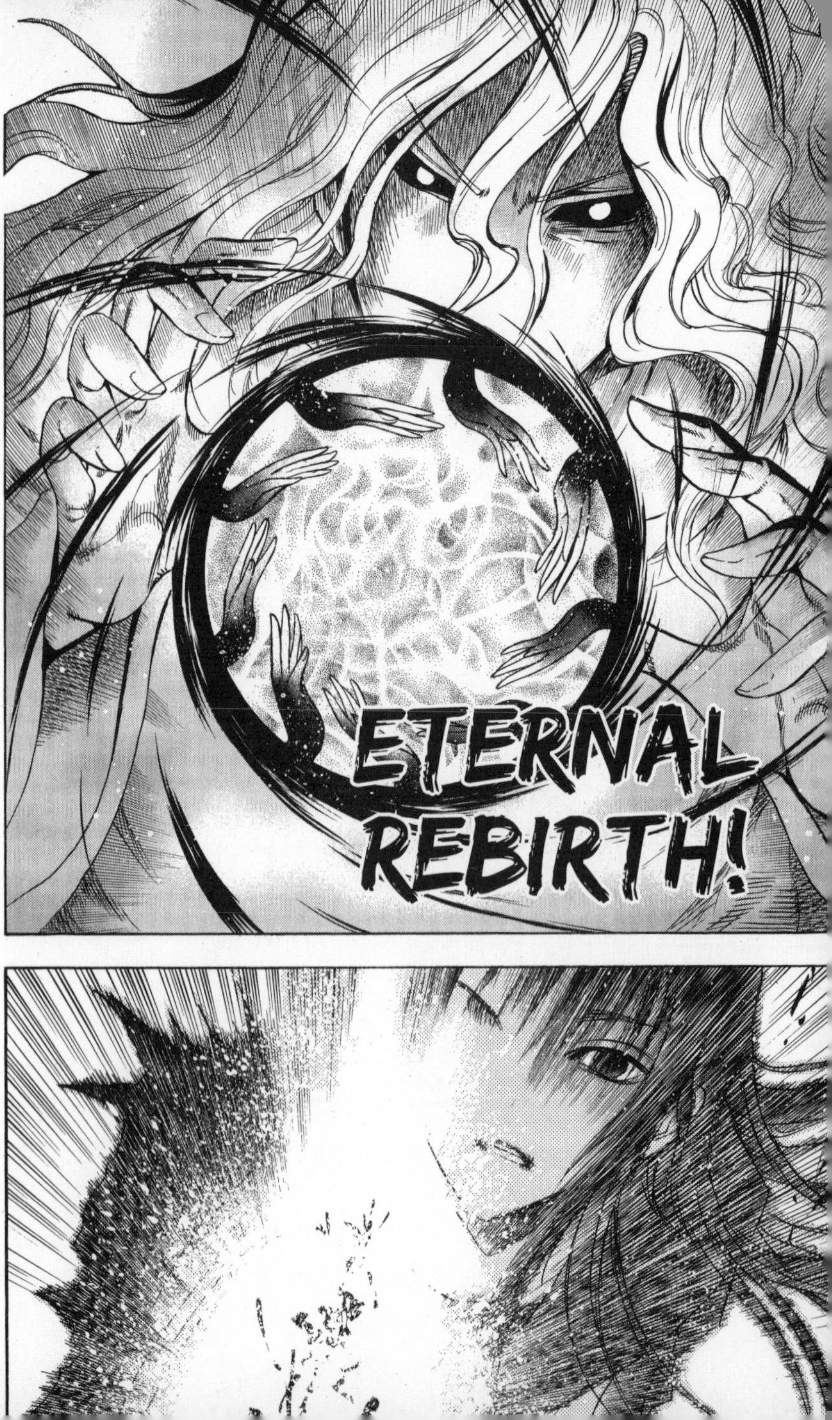
ETERNAL REBIRTH!

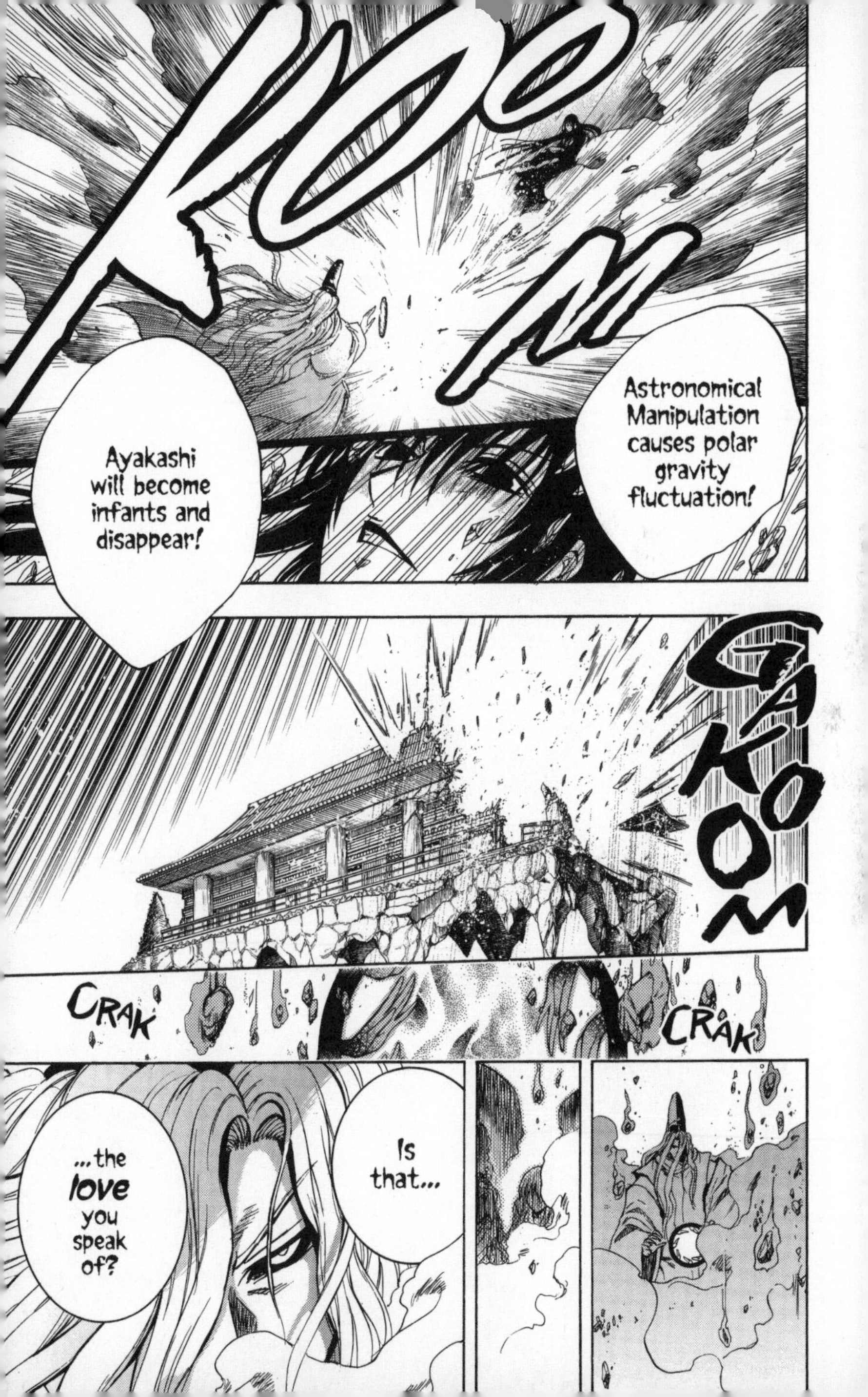
Astronomical Manipulation causes polar gravity fluctuation!
Ayakashi will become infants and disappear!
GAKOOM
CRAK
CRAK
Is that...
...the love you speak of?

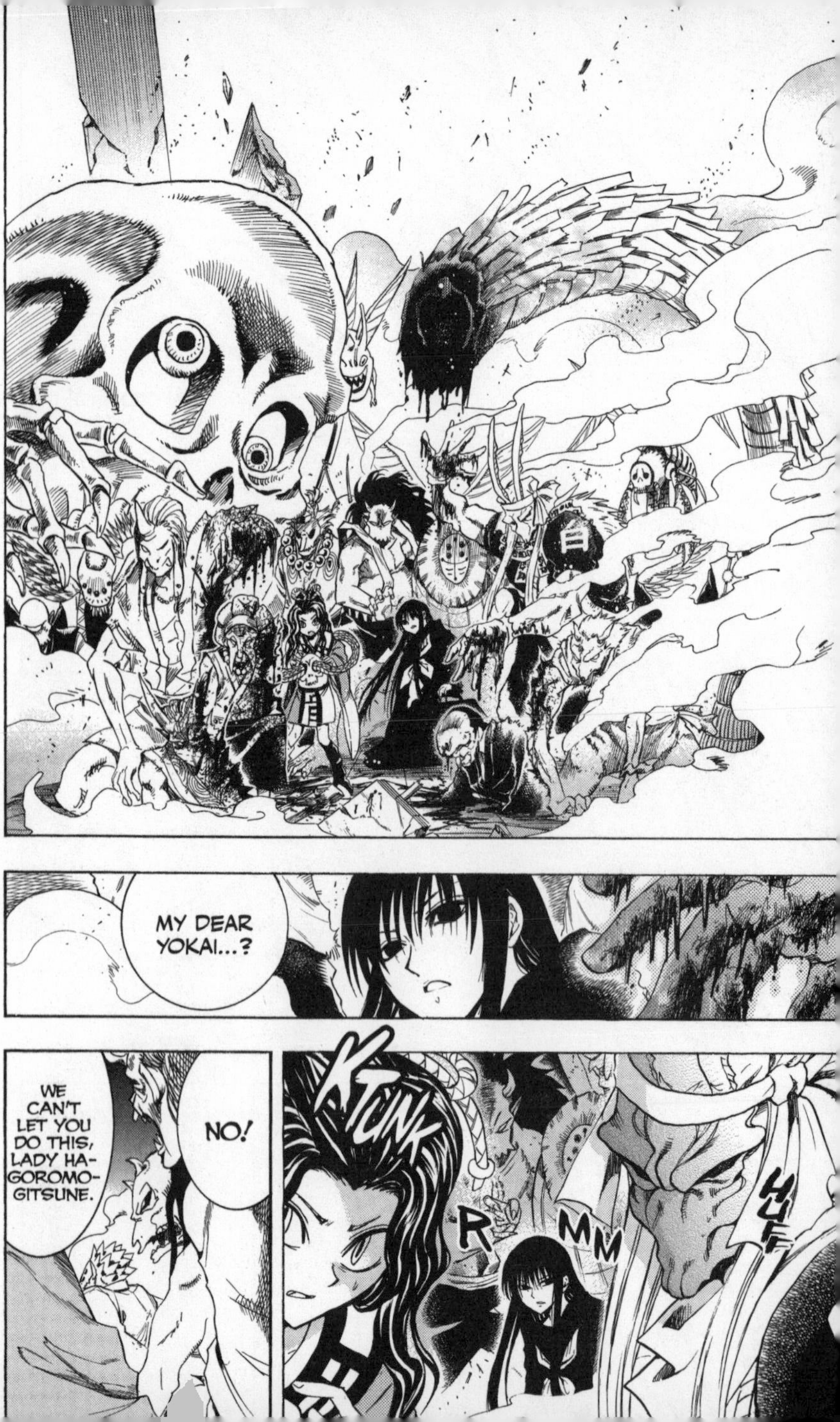
MY DEAR YOKAI...?
K-TUNK
HUF
NO!
WE CAN'T LET YOU DO THIS, LADY HAGOROMO-GITSUNE.
R
MM

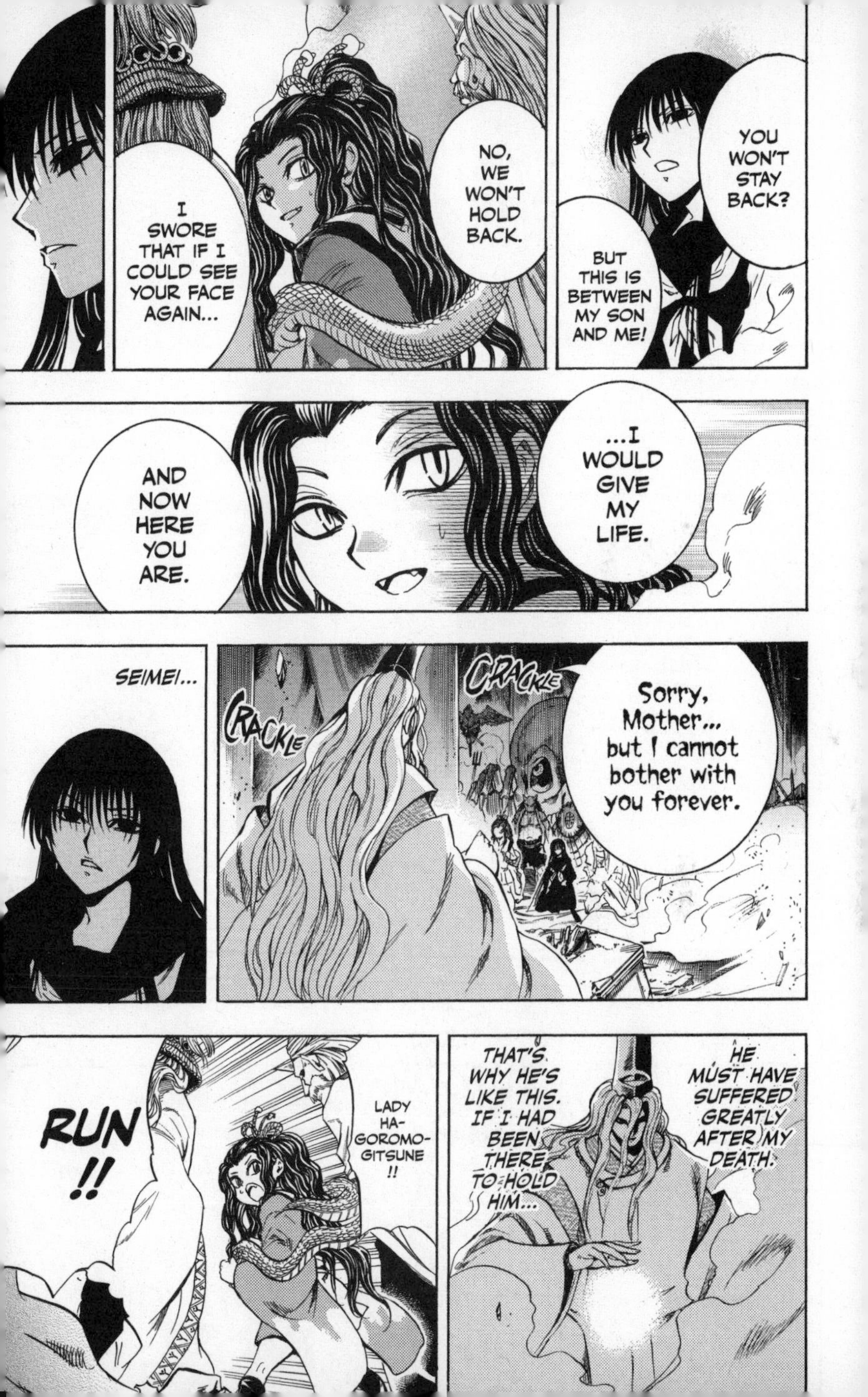
YOU WON'T STAY BACK?
BUT THIS IS BETWEEN MY SON AND ME!
NO, WE WON'T HOLD BACK.
I SWORE THAT IF I COULD SEE YOUR FACE AGAIN...
...I WOULD GIVE MY LIFE.
AND NOW HERE YOU ARE.
CRACKLE
Sorry, Mother... but I cannot bother with you forever.
CRACKLE
SEIMEI...
HE MUST HAVE SUFFERED GREATLY AFTER MY DEATH.
THAT'S WHY HE'S LIKE THIS. IF I HAD BEEN THERE TO HOLD HIM...
LADY HAGOROMO-GITSUNE !!
RUN !!

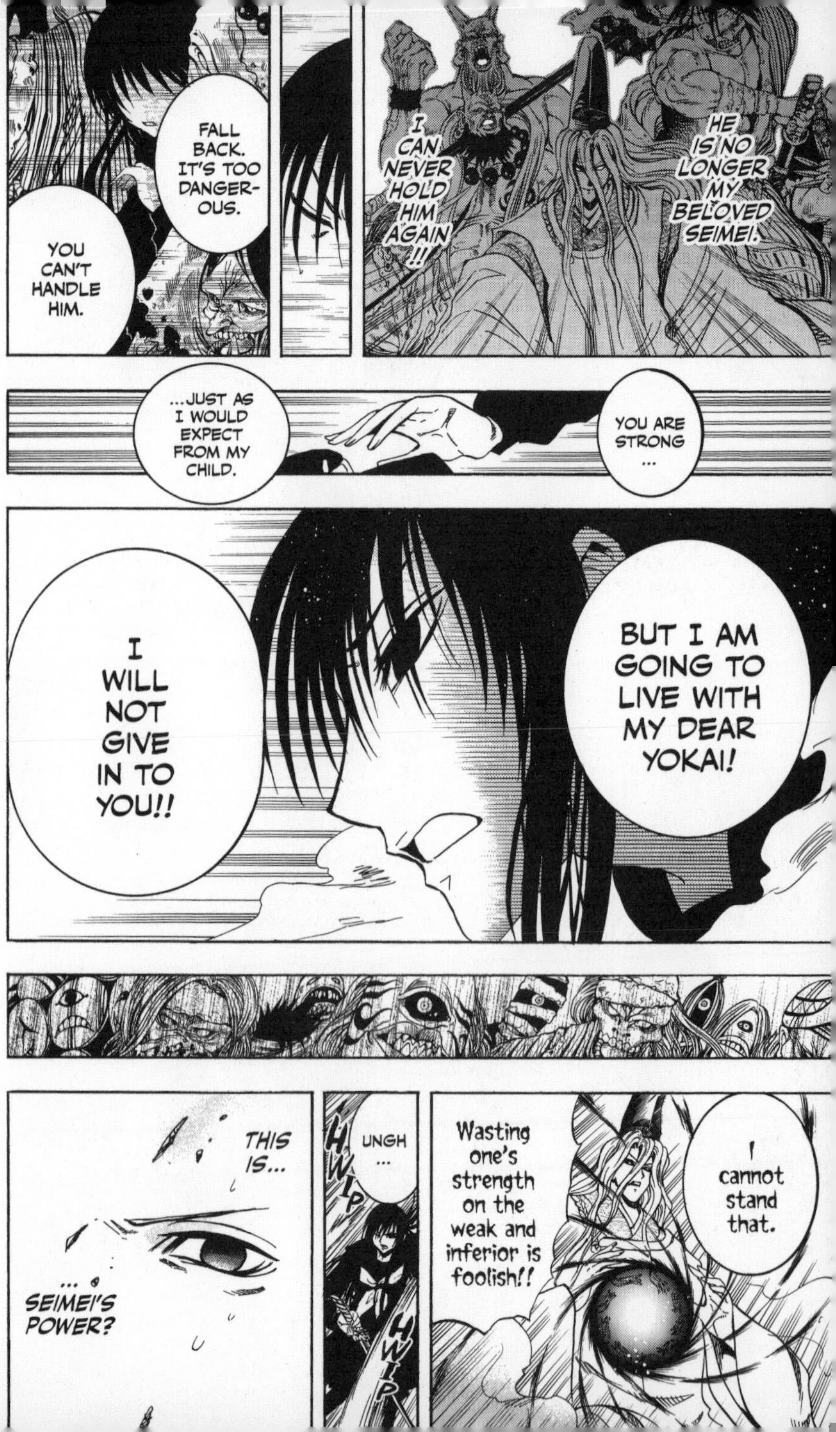
HE IS NO LONGER MY BELOVED SEIMEI.
I CAN NEVER HOLD HIM AGAIN!!
FALL BACK. IT'S TOO DANGER-OUS.
YOU CAN'T HANDLE HIM.
YOU ARE STRONG...
...JUST AS I WOULD EXPECT FROM MY CHILD.
BUT I AM GOING TO LIVE WITH MY DEAR YOKAI!
I WILL NOT GIVE IN TO YOU!!
I cannot stand that.
Wasting one's strength on the weak and inferior is foolish!!
HWIP
UNGH...
HWIP
THIS IS...
...SEIMEI'S POWER?

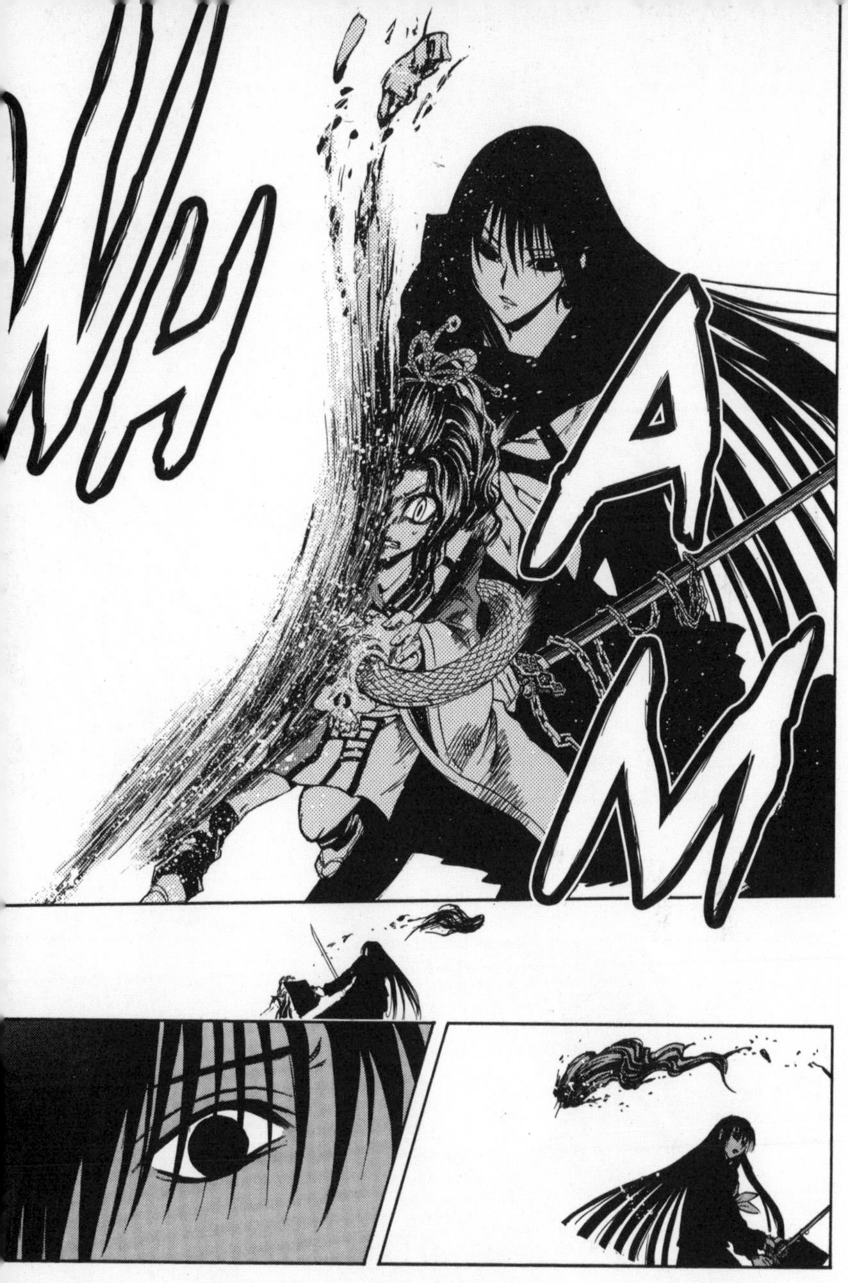

WHAM
KYOKOTSU?

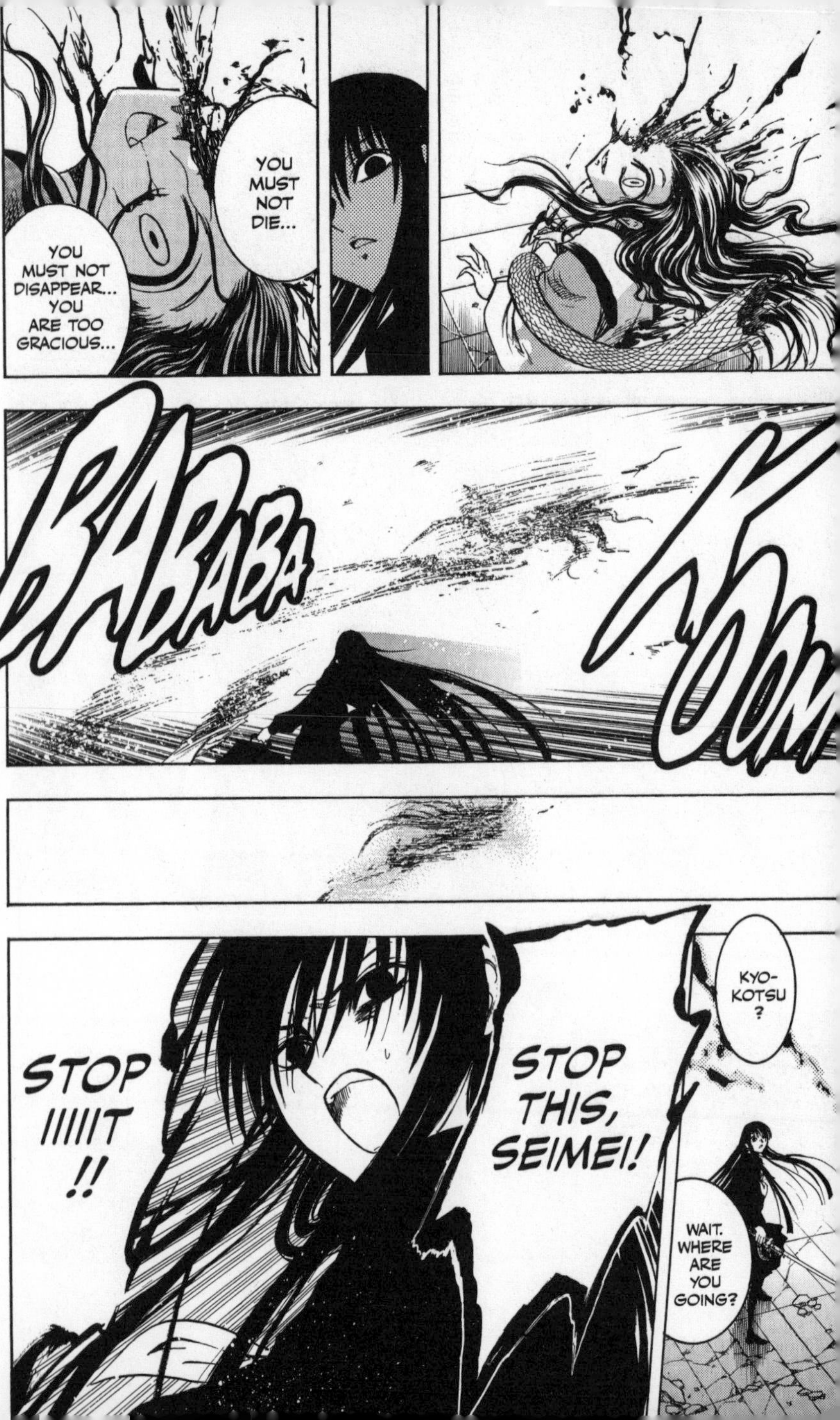
YOU MUST NOT DIE...
YOU MUST NOT DISAPPEAR... YOU ARE TOO GRACIOUS...
BABABA
KYO-KOTSU?
STOP THIS, SEIMEI!
WAIT. WHERE ARE YOU GOING?
STOP IIIIIT!!

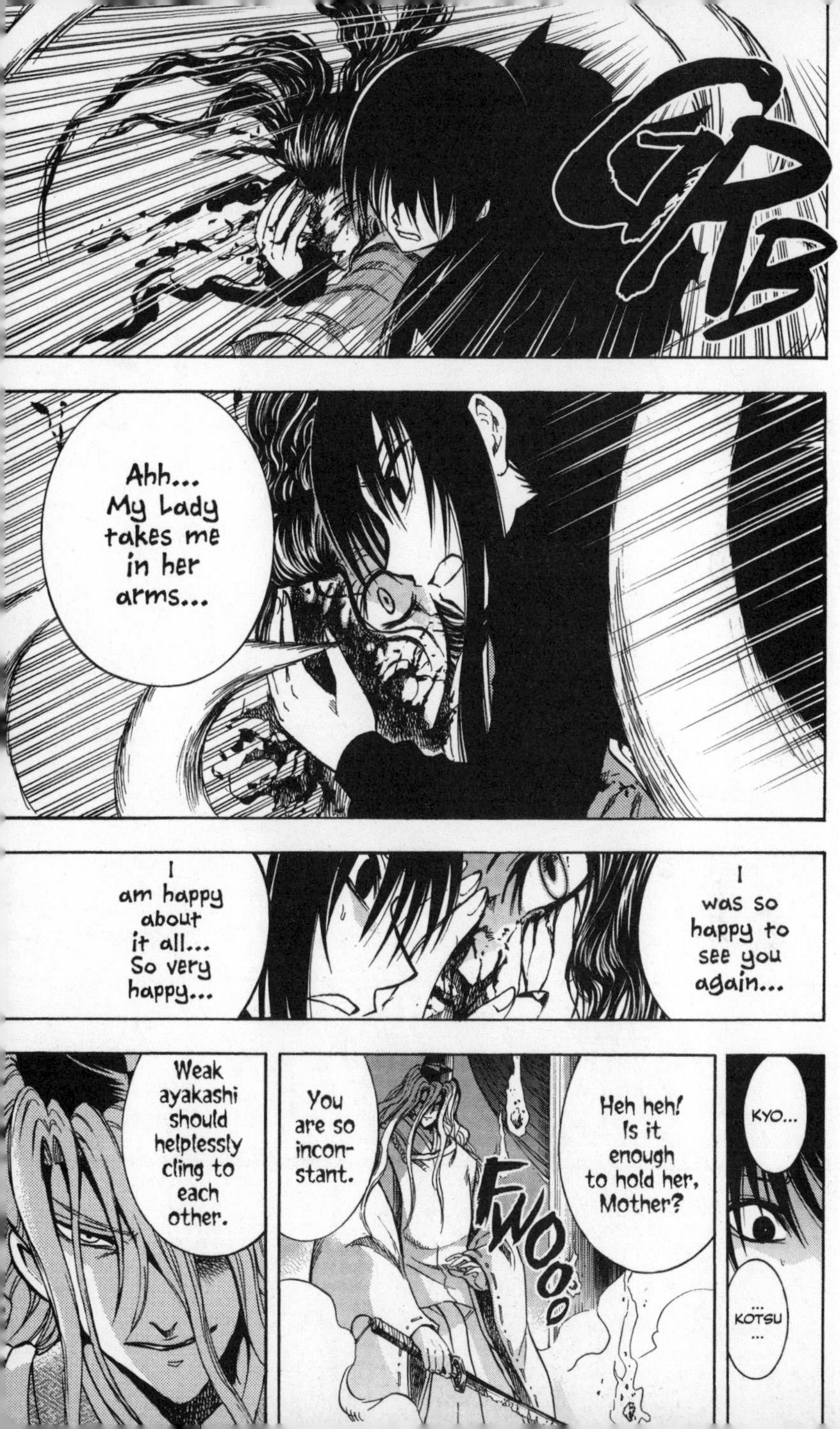
GRB
Ahh... My Lady takes me in her arms...
I was so happy to see you again...
I am happy about it all... So very happy...
KYO...
...KOTSU...
Heh heh! Is it enough to hold her, Mother?
FWOOO
You are so incon-stant.
Weak ayakashi should helplessly cling to each other.

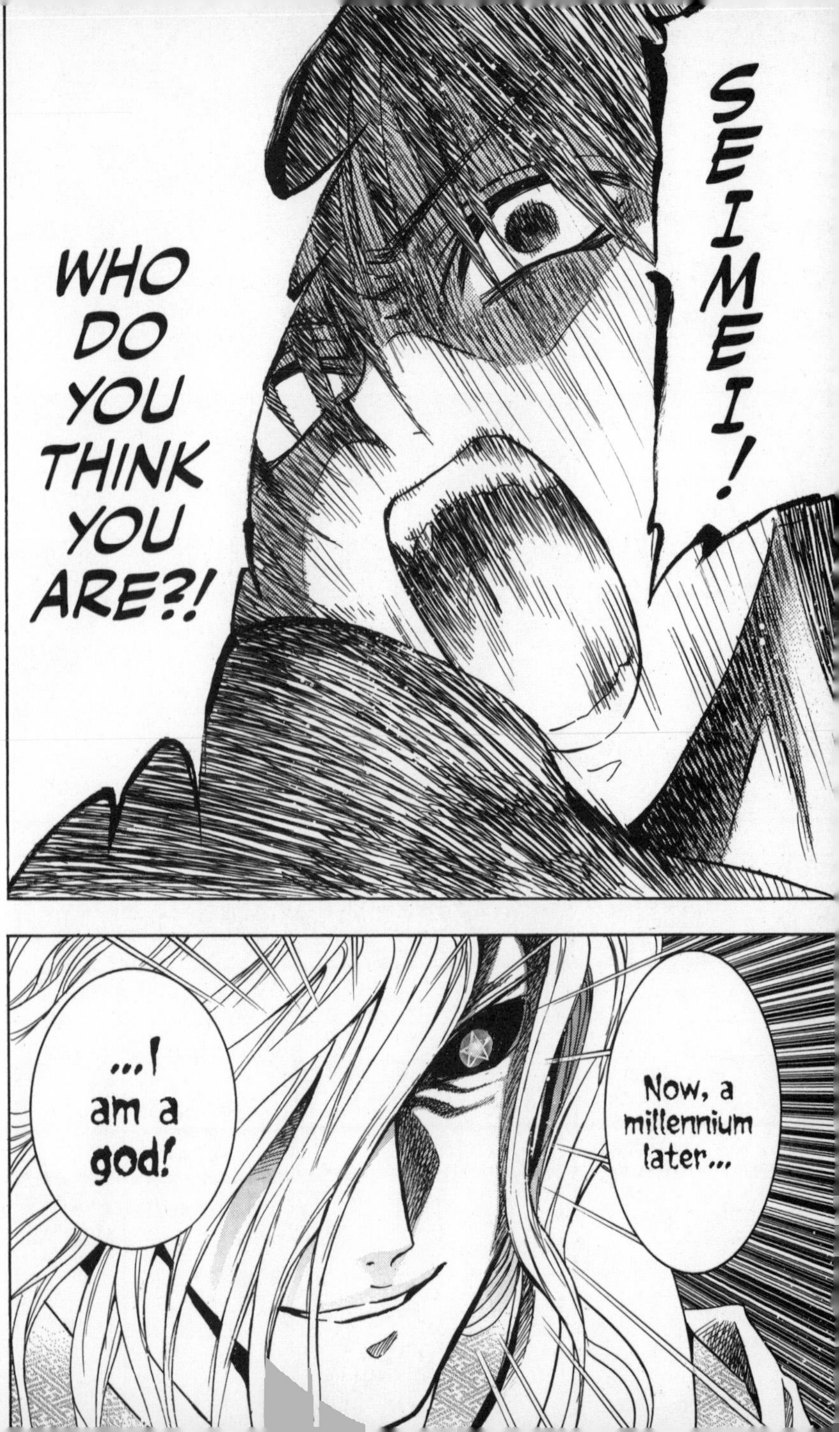
SEIMEI!
WHO DO YOU THINK YOU ARE?!
Now, a millennium later...
...I am a god!

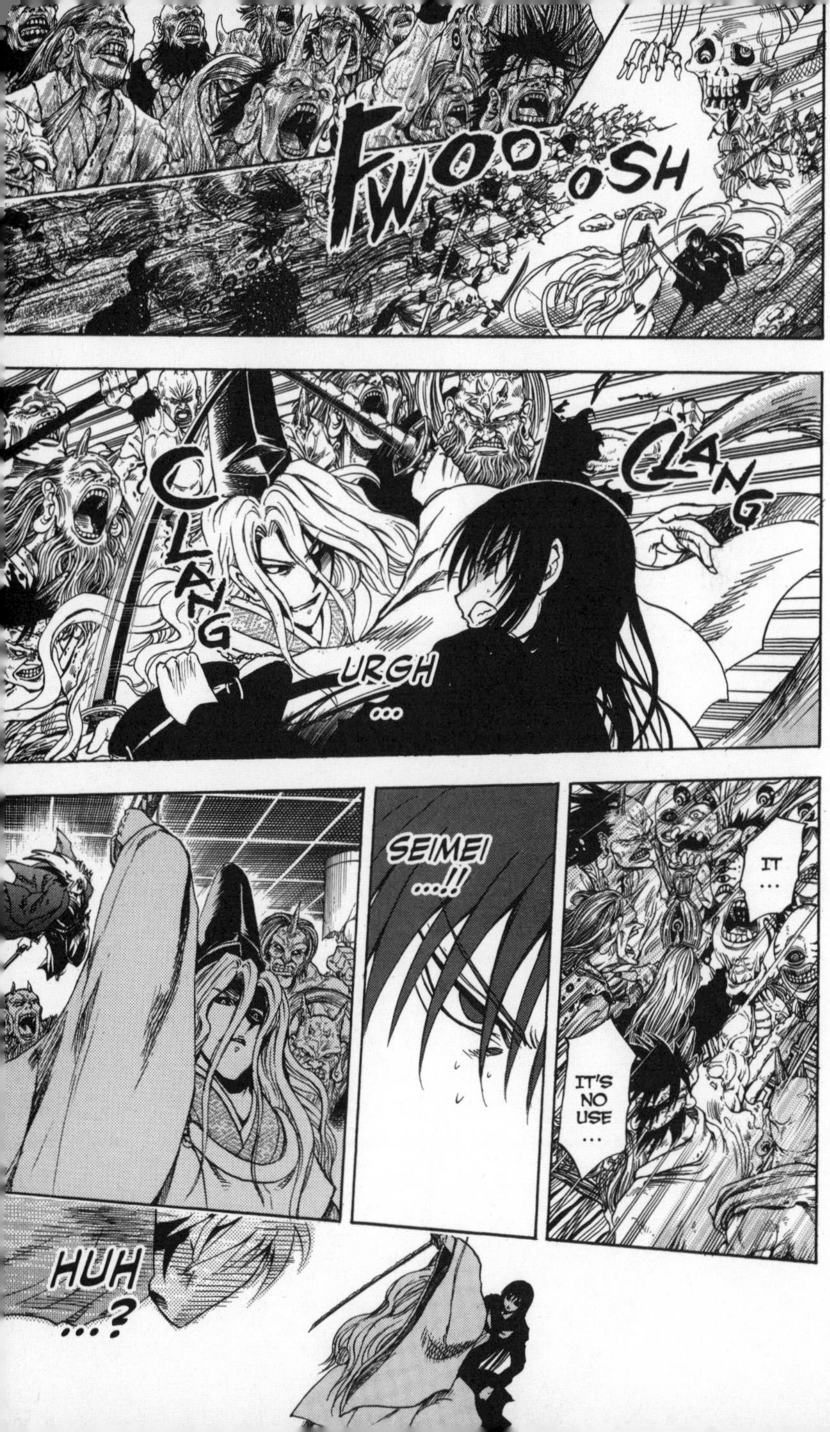
FWOOOSH
CLANG
CLANG
URGH...
IT...
IT'S NO USE...
SEIMEI...!!
HUH...?

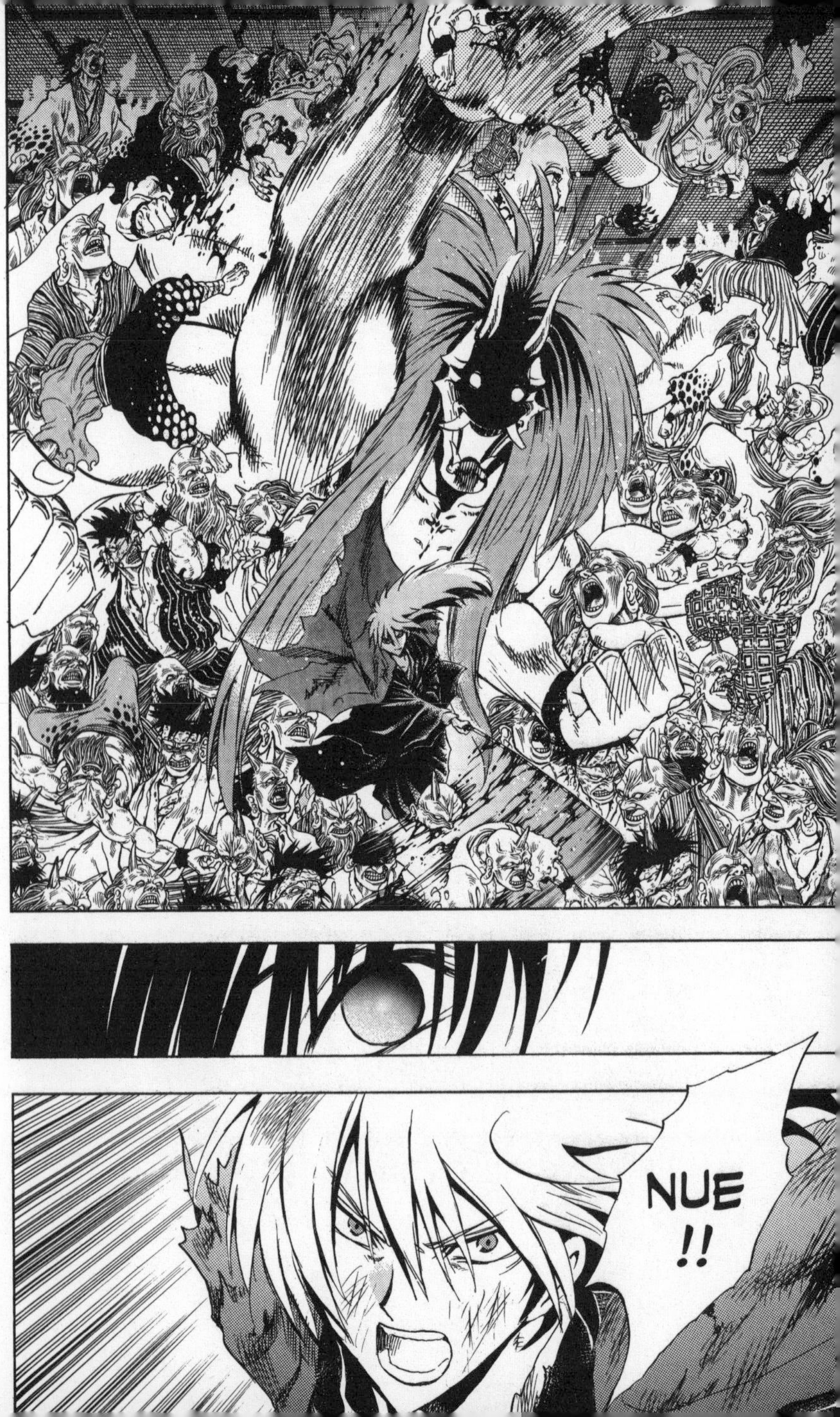
NUE !!

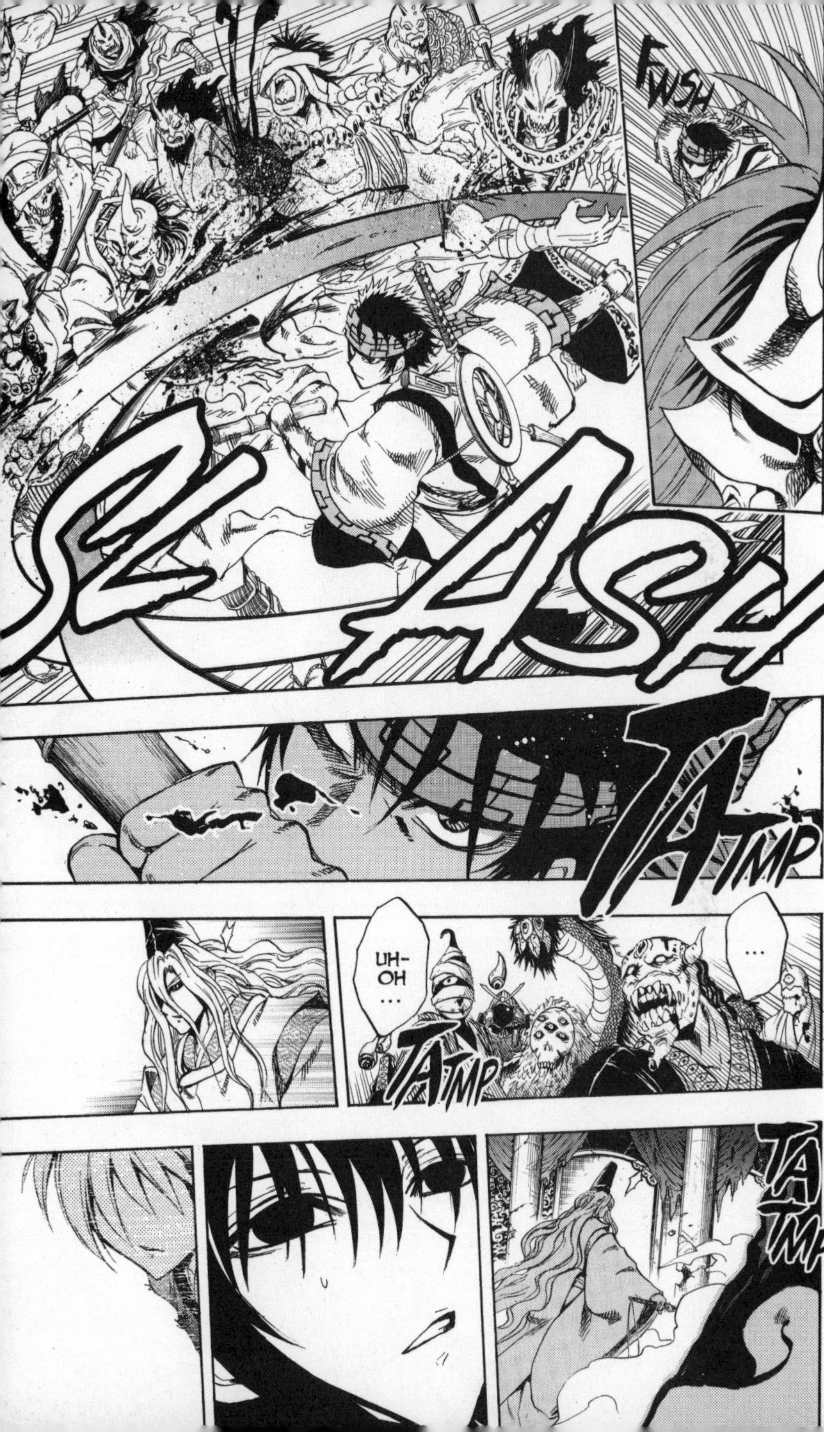
FWSH
SLASH
TATMP
...
UH-OH ...
TATMP
TA TMP

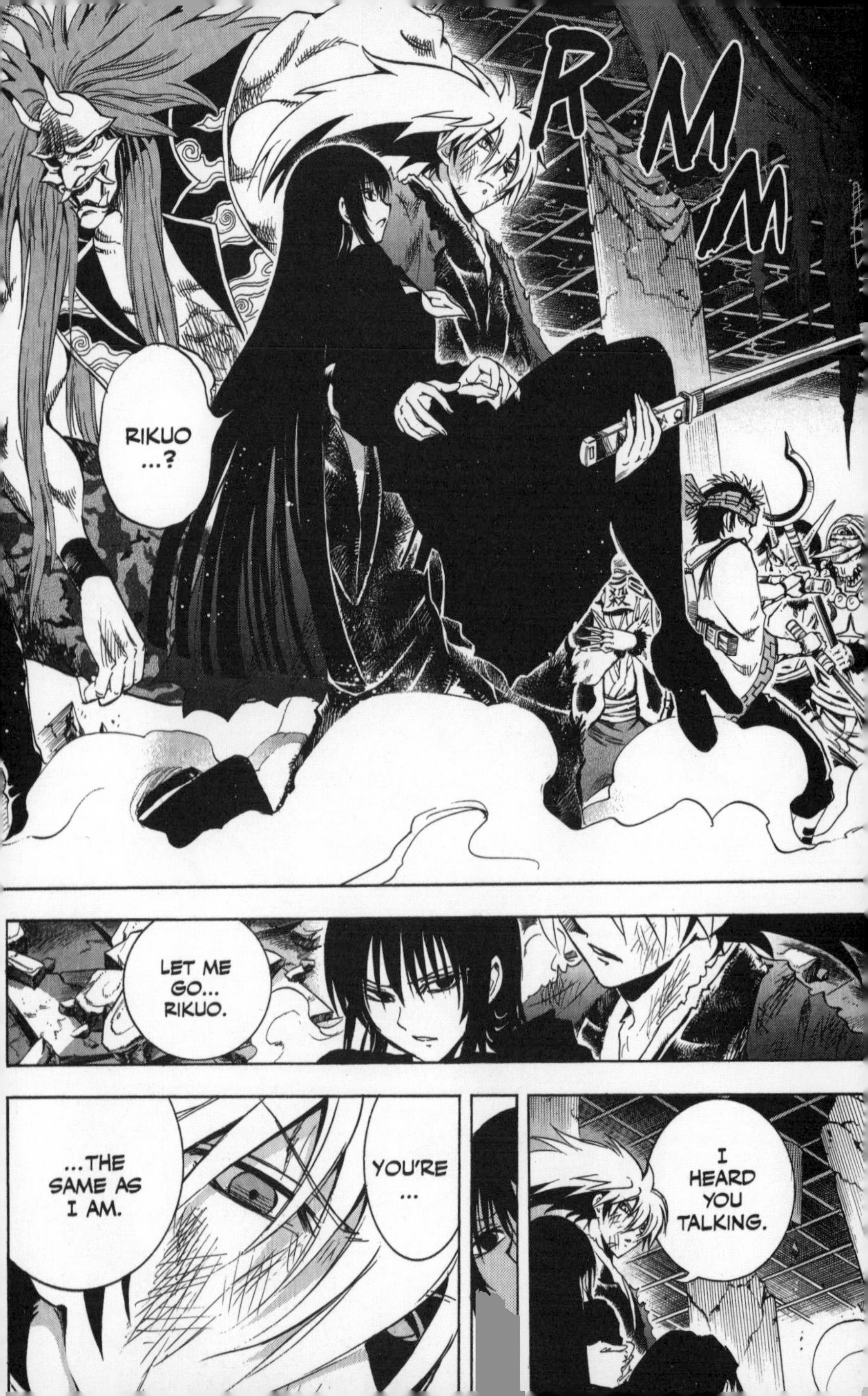
RMM
RIKUO ...?
LET ME GO... RIKUO.
I HEARD YOU TALKING.
YOU'RE ...
...THE SAME AS I AM.

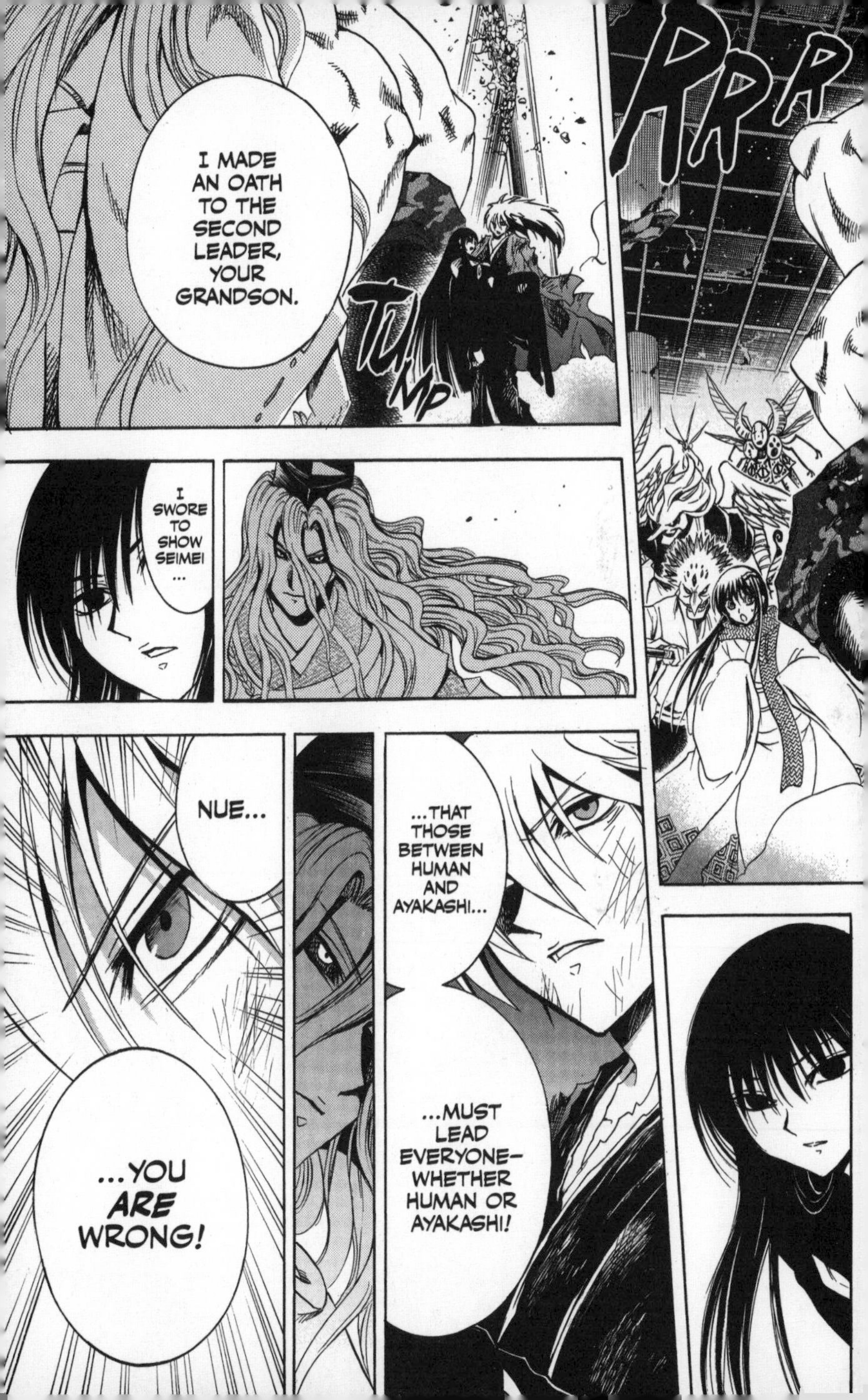
RRR
I MADE AN OATH TO THE SECOND LEADER, YOUR GRANDSON.
TUMP
I SWORE TO SHOW SEIMEI...
...THAT THOSE BETWEEN HUMAN AND AYAKASHI...
...MUST LEAD EVERYONE—WHETHER HUMAN OR AYAKASHI!
NUE...
...YOU **ARE** WRONG!

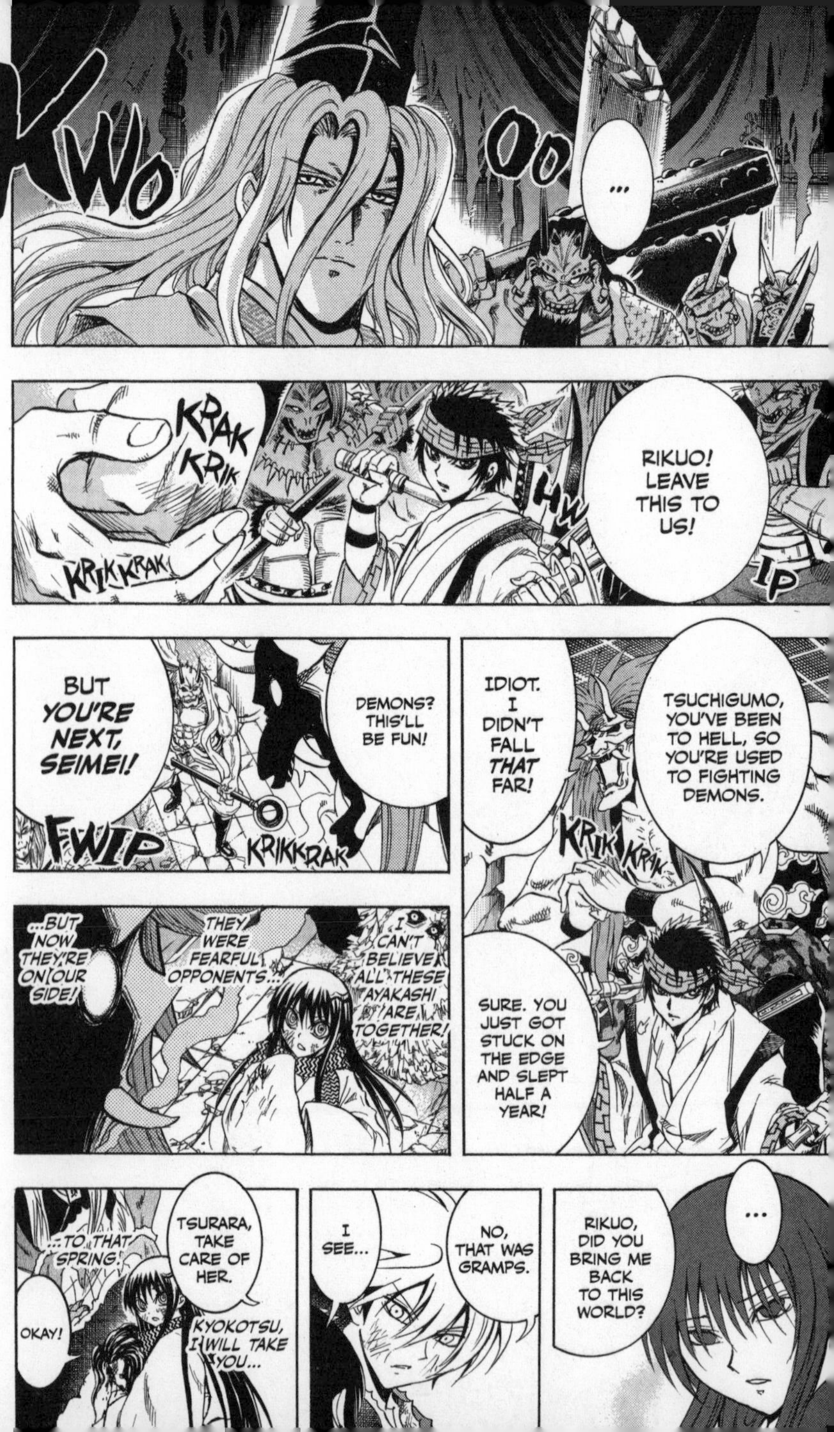
KWOOO
...
RIKUO! LEAVE THIS TO US!
HWIP
KRAK KRIK
KRIKKRAK
TSUCHIGUMO, YOU'VE BEEN TO HELL, SO YOU'RE USED TO FIGHTING DEMONS.
IDIOT. I DIDN'T FALL *THAT* FAR!
KRIKKRAK
SURE. YOU JUST GOT STUCK ON THE EDGE AND SLEPT HALF A YEAR!
DEMONS? THIS'LL BE FUN!
BUT *YOU'RE NEXT, SEIMEI!*
FWIP
KRIKKRAK
I CAN'T BELIEVE ALL THESE AYAKASHI ARE TOGETHER!
THEY WERE FEARFUL OPPONENTS...
...BUT NOW THEY'RE ON OUR SIDE!
...
RIKUO, DID YOU BRING ME BACK TO THIS WORLD?
NO, THAT WAS GRAMPS.
I SEE...
TSURARA, TAKE CARE OF HER.
KYOKOTSU, I WILL TAKE YOU...
...TO THAT SPRING.
OKAY!

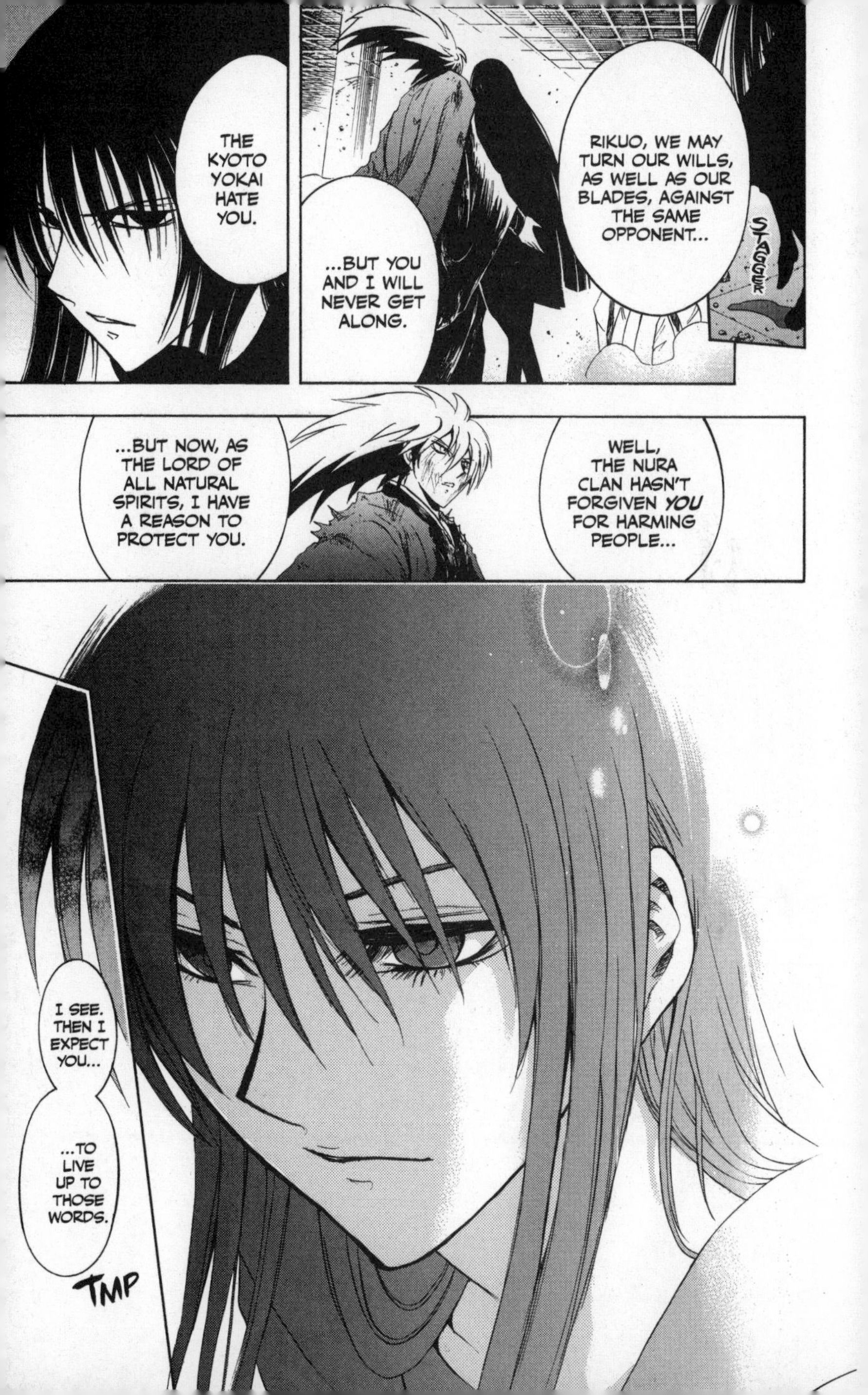
RIKUO, WE MAY TURN OUR WILLS, AS WELL AS OUR BLADES, AGAINST THE SAME OPPONENT...
STAGGER
...BUT YOU AND I WILL NEVER GET ALONG.
THE KYOTO YOKAI HATE YOU.
WELL, THE NURA CLAN HASN'T FORGIVEN *YOU* FOR HARMING PEOPLE...
...BUT NOW, AS THE LORD OF ALL NATURAL SPIRITS, I HAVE A REASON TO PROTECT YOU.
I SEE. THEN I EXPECT YOU...
...TO LIVE UP TO THOSE WORDS.
TMP

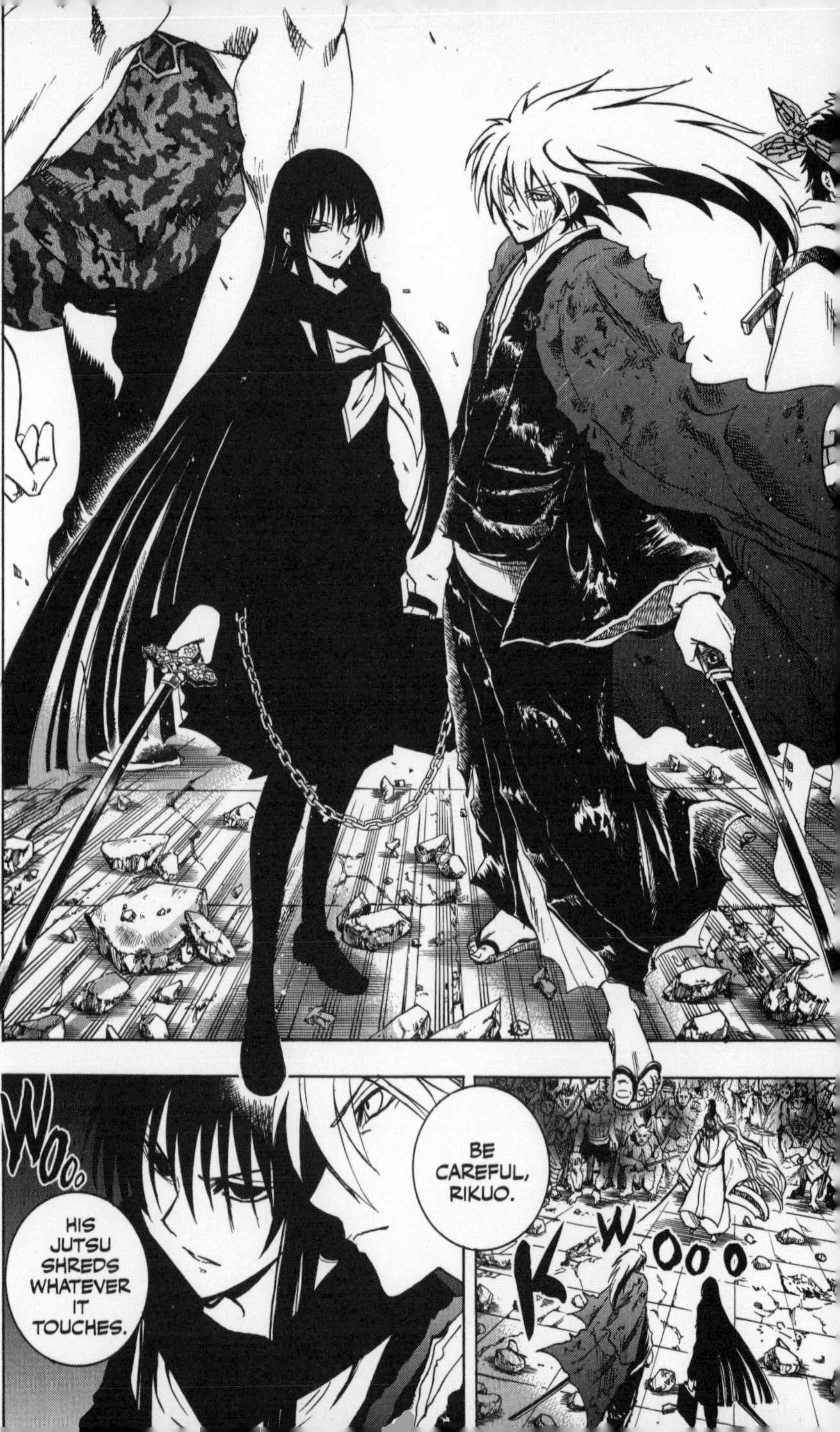
KWOOO
BE CAREFUL, RIKUO.
WOOO
HIS JUTSU SHREDS WHATEVER IT TOUCHES.

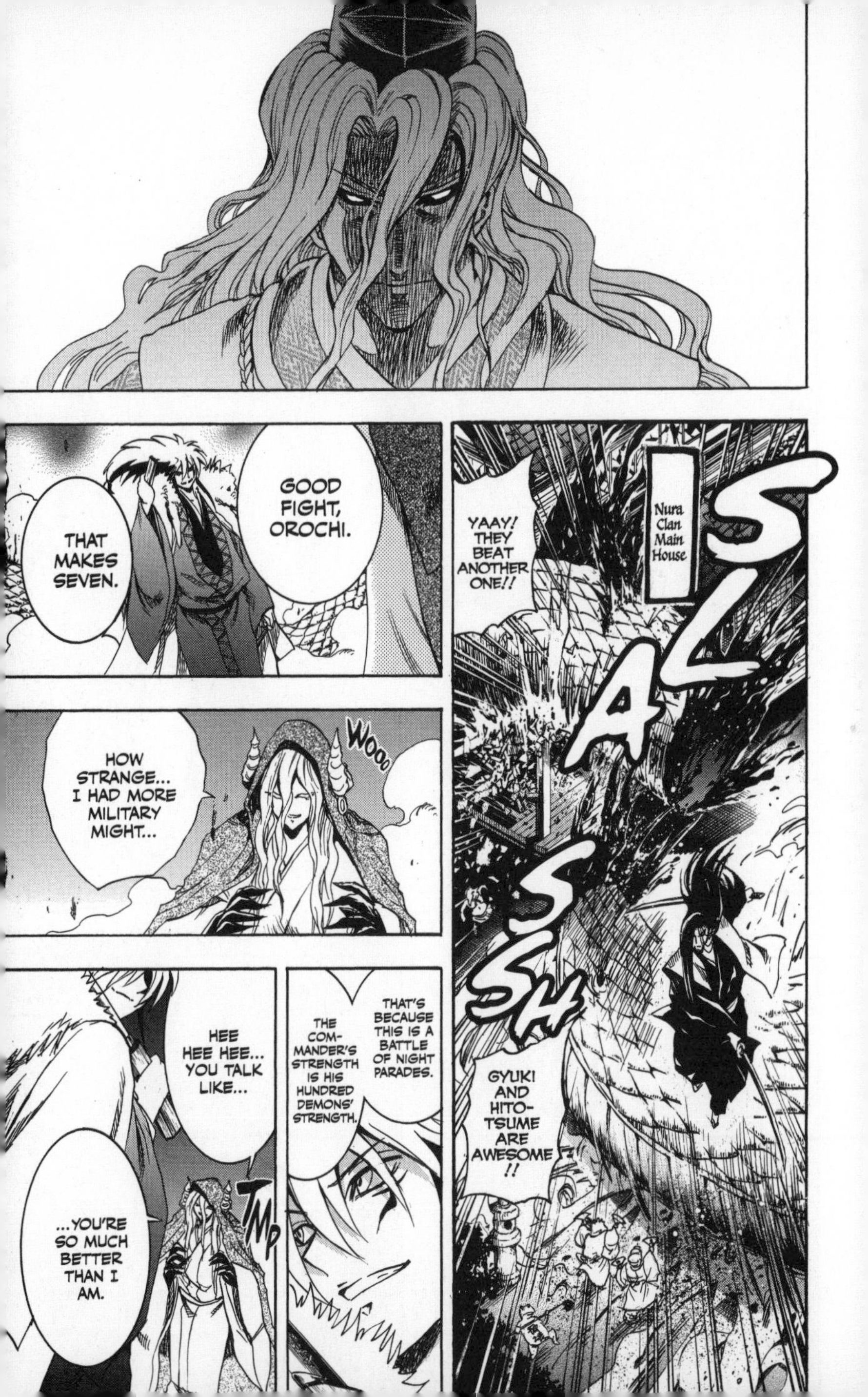
Nura Clan Main House
SLASSH
YAAY! THEY BEAT ANOTHER ONE!!
GYUKI AND HITO-TSUME ARE AWESOME!!
GOOD FIGHT, OROCHI.
THAT MAKES SEVEN.
WOOO
HOW STRANGE... I HAD MORE MILITARY MIGHT...
THAT'S BECAUSE THIS IS A BATTLE OF NIGHT PARADES.
THE COM-MANDER'S STRENGTH IS HIS HUNDRED DEMONS' STRENGTH.
TMP
HEE HEE HEE... YOU TALK LIKE...
...YOU'RE SO MUCH BETTER THAN I AM.

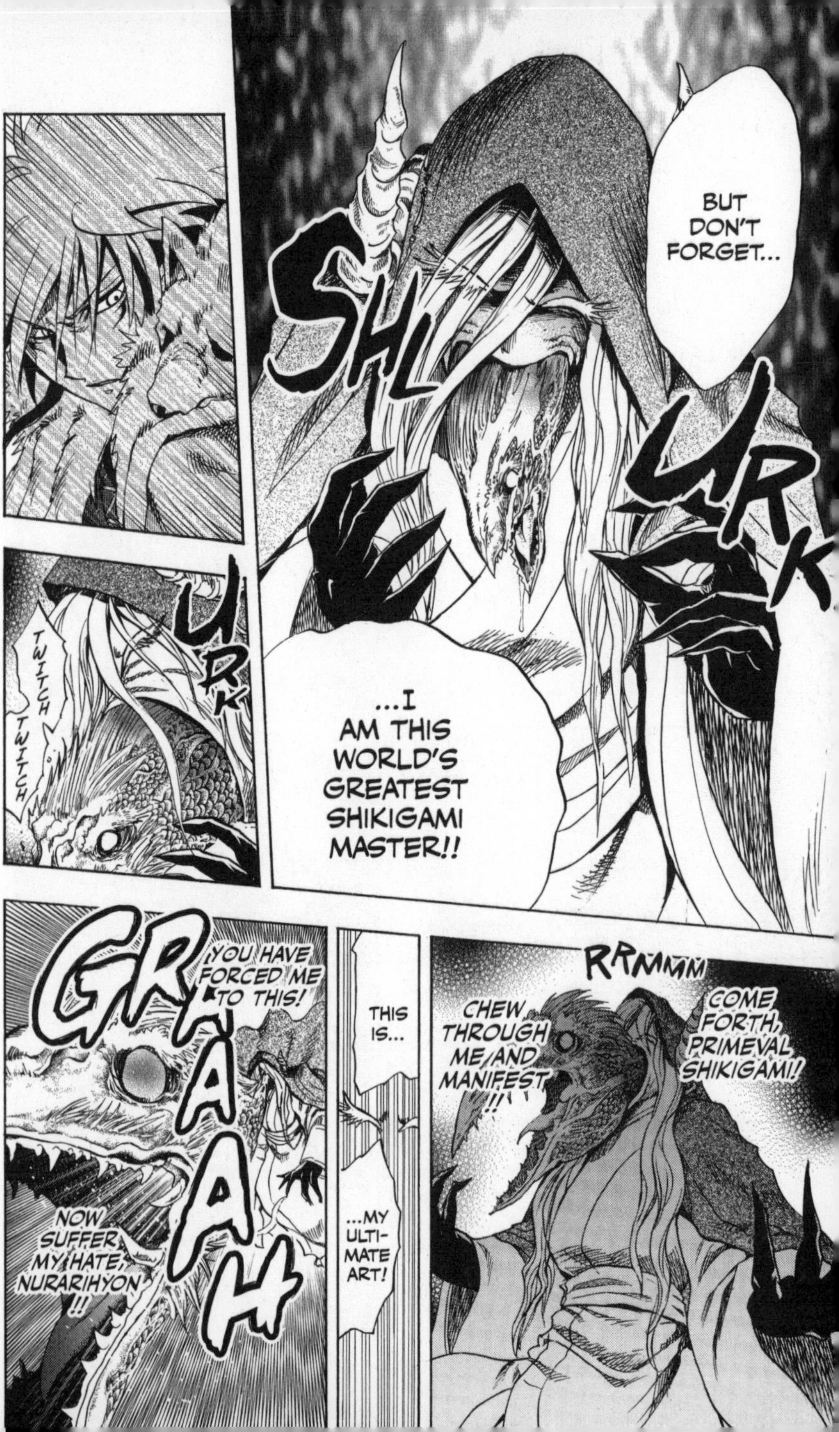
BUT DON'T FORGET...
SHLURK
...I AM THIS WORLD'S GREATEST SHIKIGAMI MASTER!!
URK
TWITCH TWITCH
RRMMM
COME FORTH, PRIMEVAL SHIKIGAMI!
CHEW THROUGH ME AND MANIFEST!!
THIS IS...
...MY ULTIMATE ART!
YOU HAVE FORCED ME TO THIS!
GRAAAH
NOW SUFFER MY HATE, NURARIHYON!!

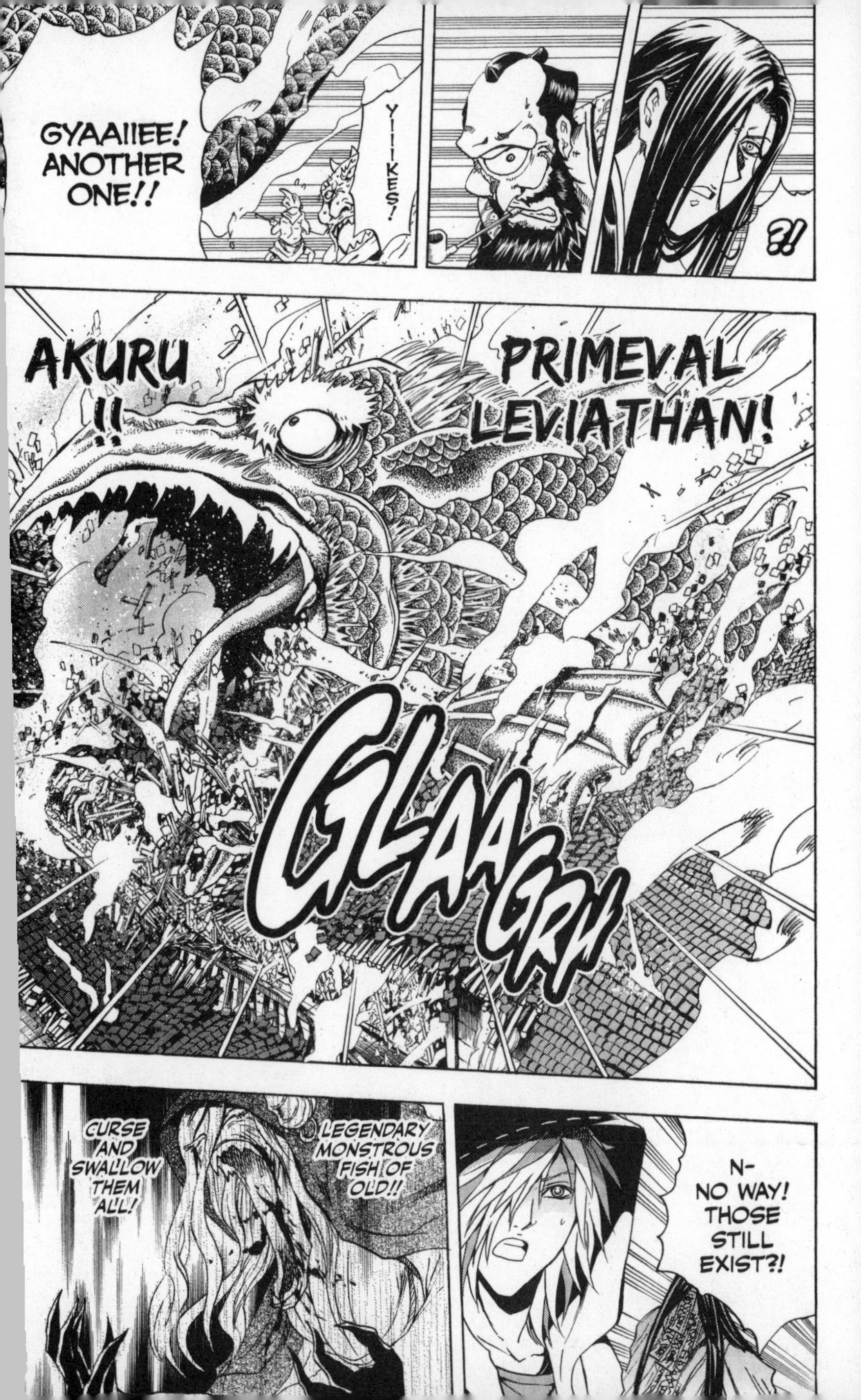
?!
YIIIKES!
GYAAIIEE! ANOTHER ONE!!
PRIMEVAL LEVIATHAN!
AKURU!!
GLAAGRH
N- NO WAY! THOSE STILL EXIST?!
LEGENDARY MONSTROUS FISH OF OLD!!
CURSE AND SWALLOW THEM ALL!

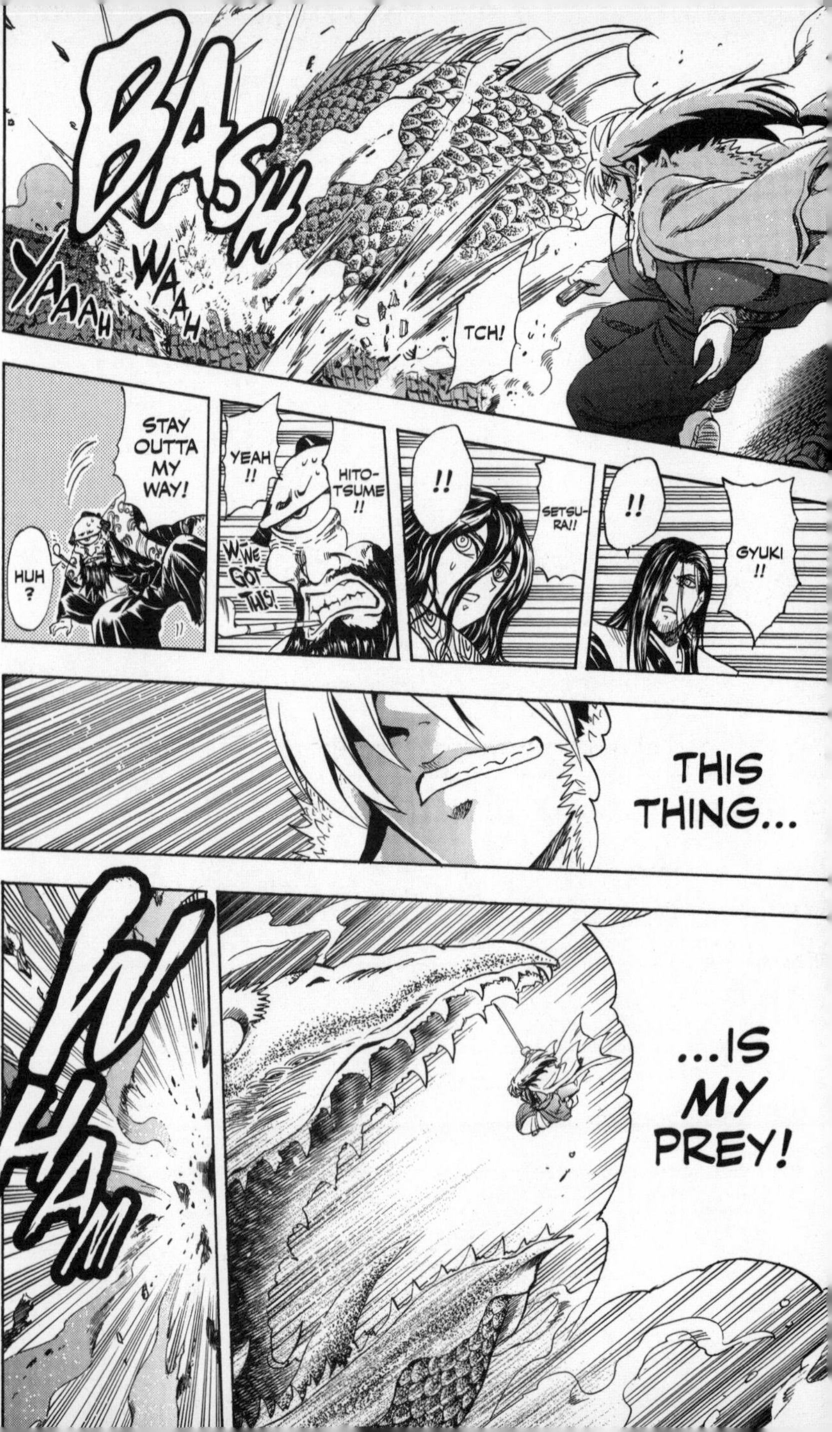
BASH
TCH!
WAAAH
YAAAAH
GYUKI !!
!!
SETSU-RA!!
!!
HITO-TSUME !!
YEAH !!
W-WE GOT THIS!
STAY OUTTA MY WAY!
HUH ?
THIS THING...
...IS MY PREY!
WHAM

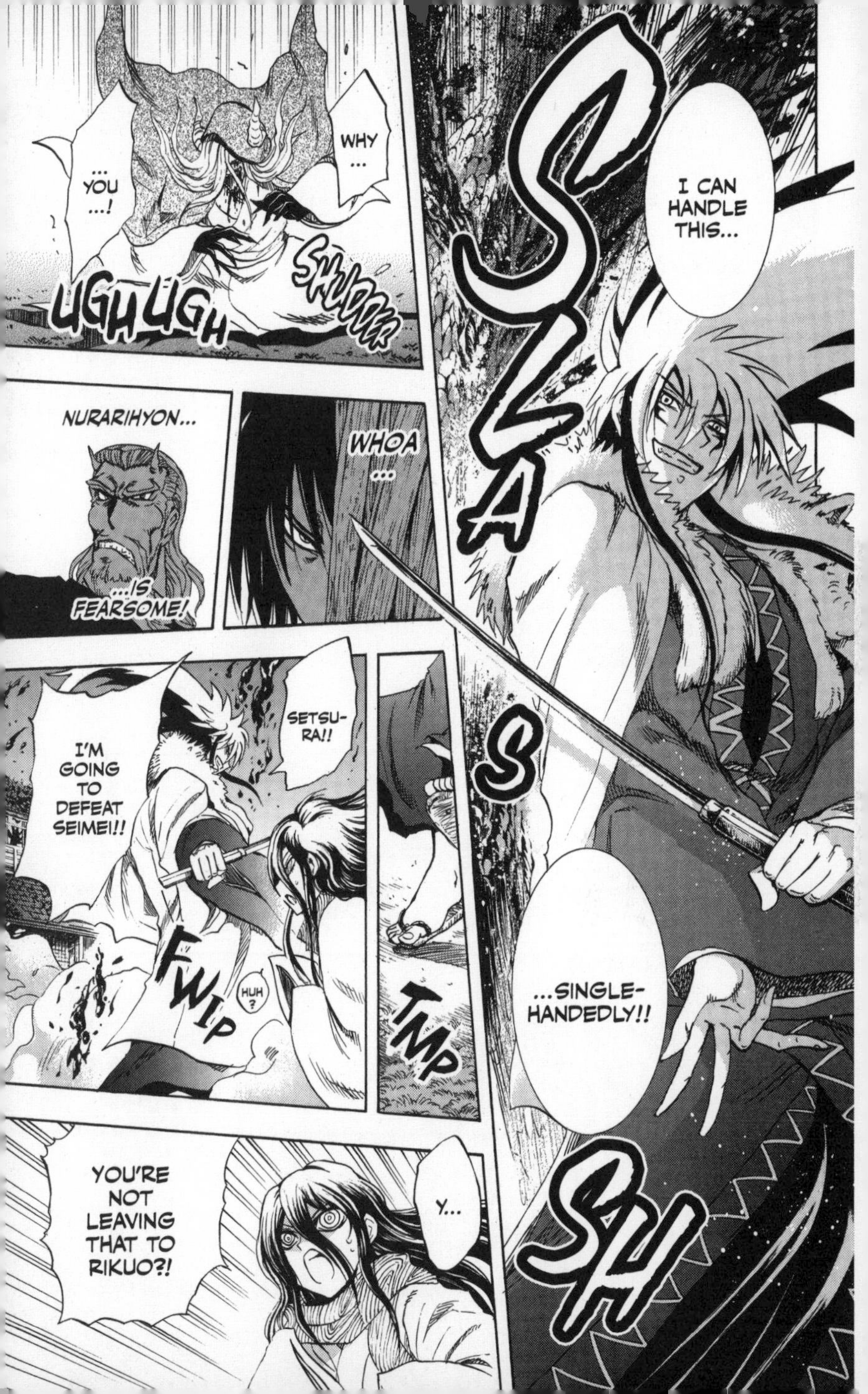
I CAN HANDLE THIS...
SLASSH
...SINGLE-HANDEDLY!!
WHY...
...YOU...!
SHUDDER
UGH UGH
WHOA...
NURARIHYON...
...IS FEARSOME!
TMP
SETSU-RA!!
I'M GOING TO DEFEAT SEIMEI!!
FWIP
HUH?
Y...
YOU'RE NOT LEAVING THAT TO RIKUO?!

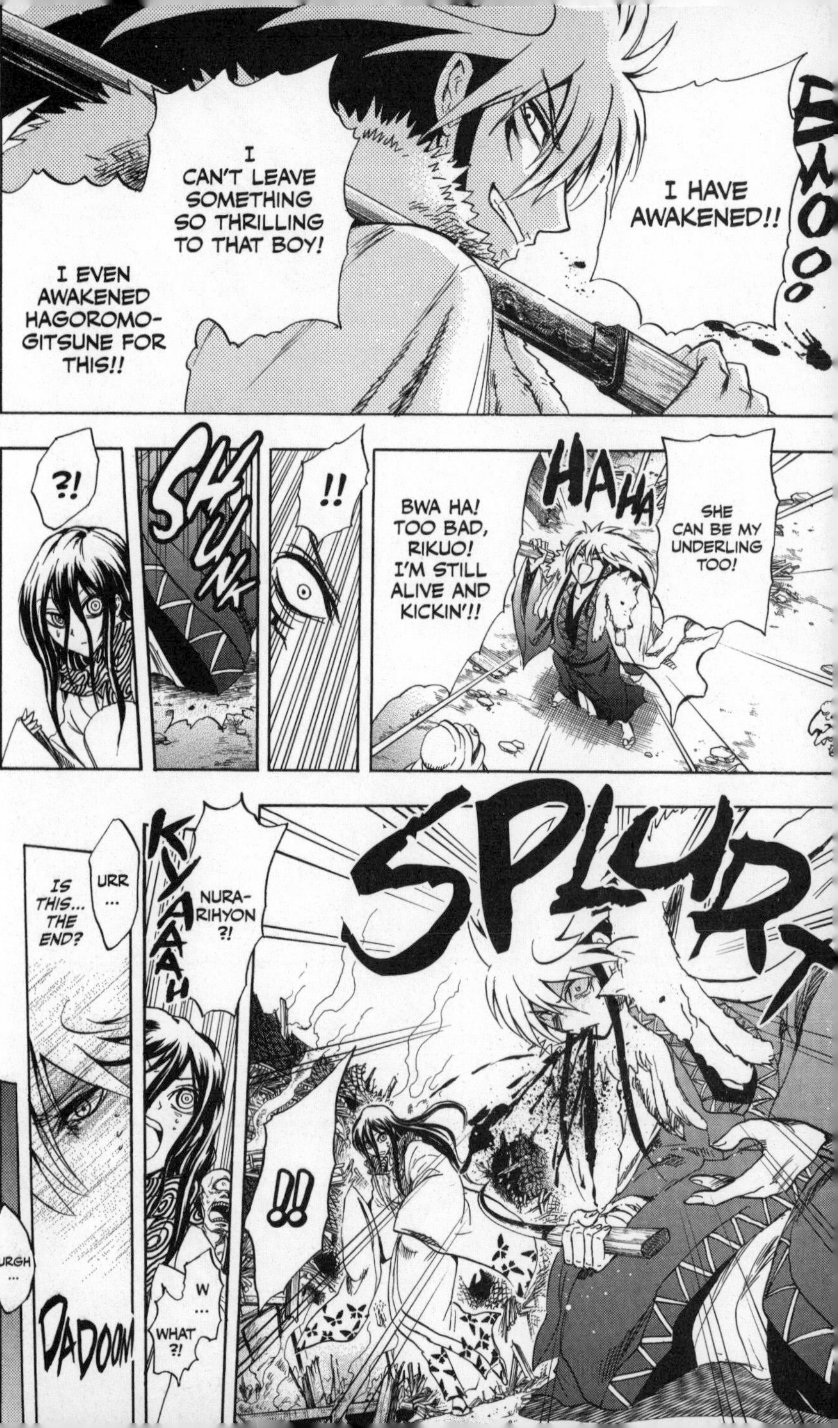
I HAVE AWAKENED!!
I CAN'T LEAVE SOMETHING SO THRILLING TO THAT BOY!
I EVEN AWAKENED HAGOROMO-GITSUNE FOR THIS!!
SHE CAN BE MY UNDERLING TOO!
HAHAHA
BWA HA! TOO BAD, RIKUO! I'M STILL ALIVE AND KICKIN'!!
!!
SHUNK
?!
SPLURT
KYAAAH
NURA-RIHYON ?!
!!
W ... WHAT ?!
URR ...
IS THIS... THE END?
URGH ...
DADOOM

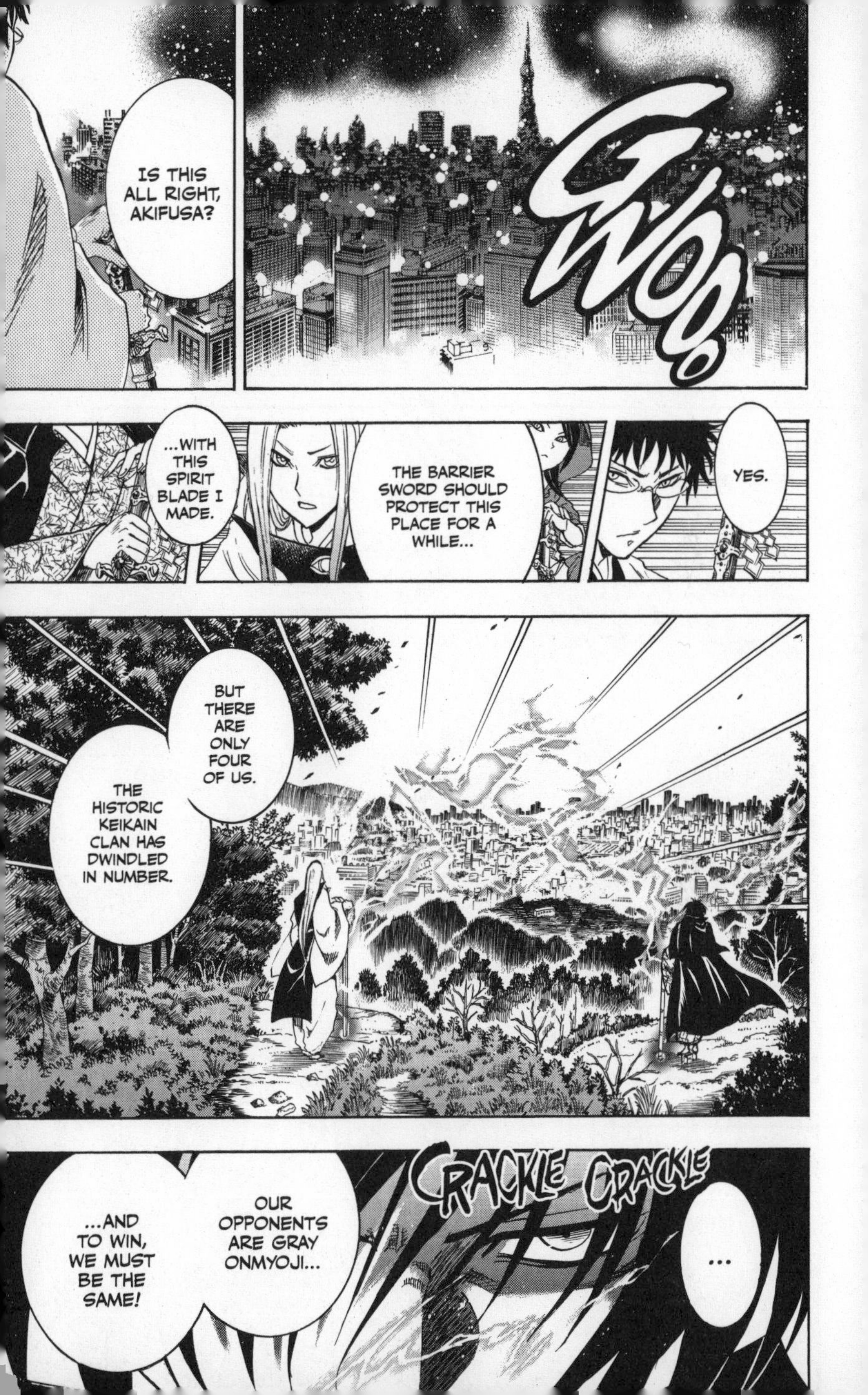
GWOOO
IS THIS ALL RIGHT, AKIFUSA?
YES.
THE BARRIER SWORD SHOULD PROTECT THIS PLACE FOR A WHILE...
...WITH THIS SPIRIT BLADE I MADE.
BUT THERE ARE ONLY FOUR OF US.
THE HISTORIC KEIKAIN CLAN HAS DWINDLED IN NUMBER.
CRACKLE CRACKLE
...
OUR OPPONENTS ARE GRAY ONMYOJI...
...AND TO WIN, WE MUST BE THE SAME!

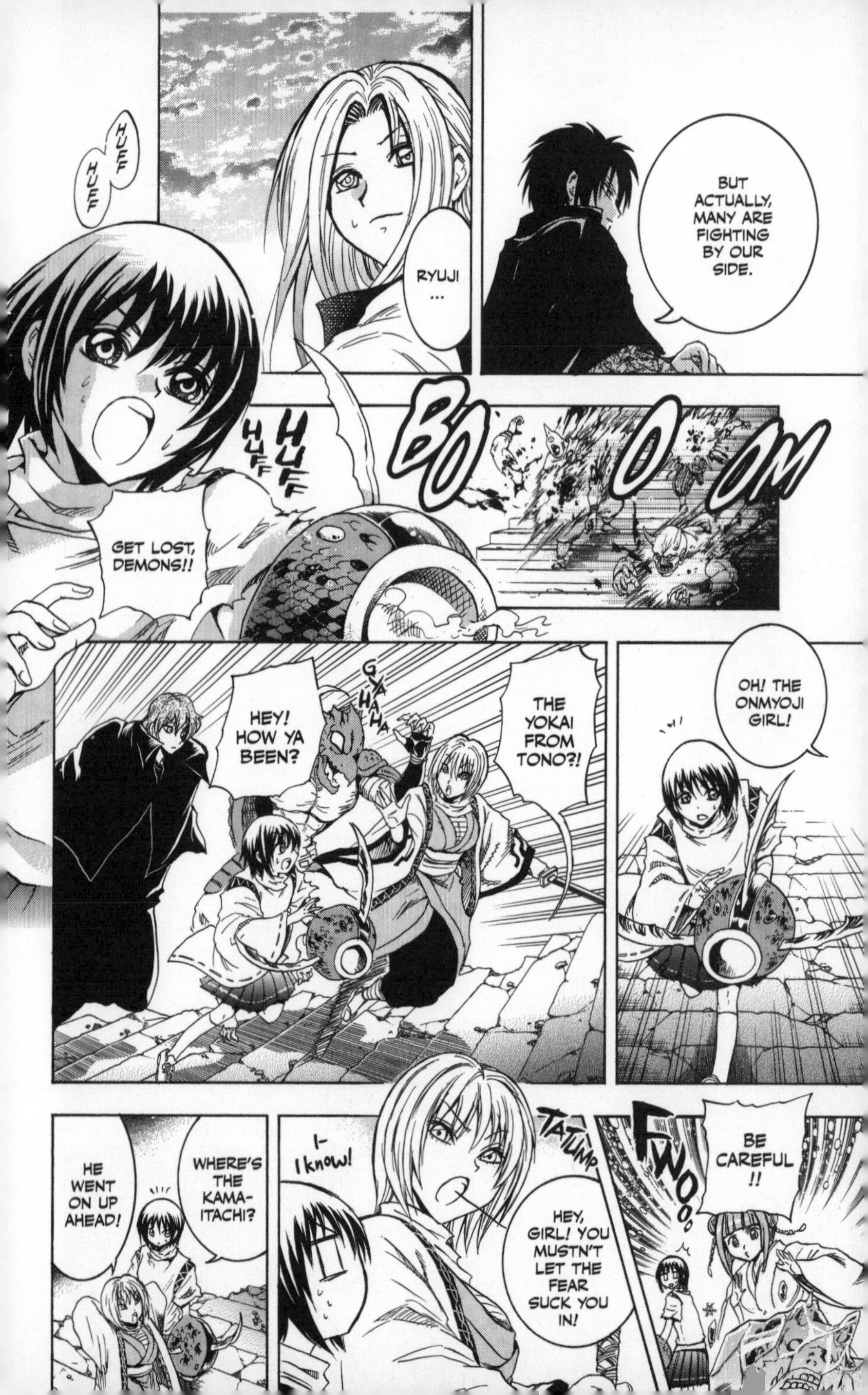
BUT ACTUALLY, MANY ARE FIGHTING BY OUR SIDE.
RYUJI ...
HUFF HUFF
BOOOM
HUFF HUFF
GET LOST, DEMONS!!
OH! THE ONMYOJI GIRL!
THE YOKAI FROM TONO?!
GYAHAHA
HEY! HOW YA BEEN?
BE CAREFUL !!
FWOOO
TATUMP
HEY, GIRL! YOU MUSTN'T LET THE FEAR SUCK YOU IN!
I- I know!
WHERE'S THE KAMA-ITACHI?
HE WENT ON UP AHEAD!

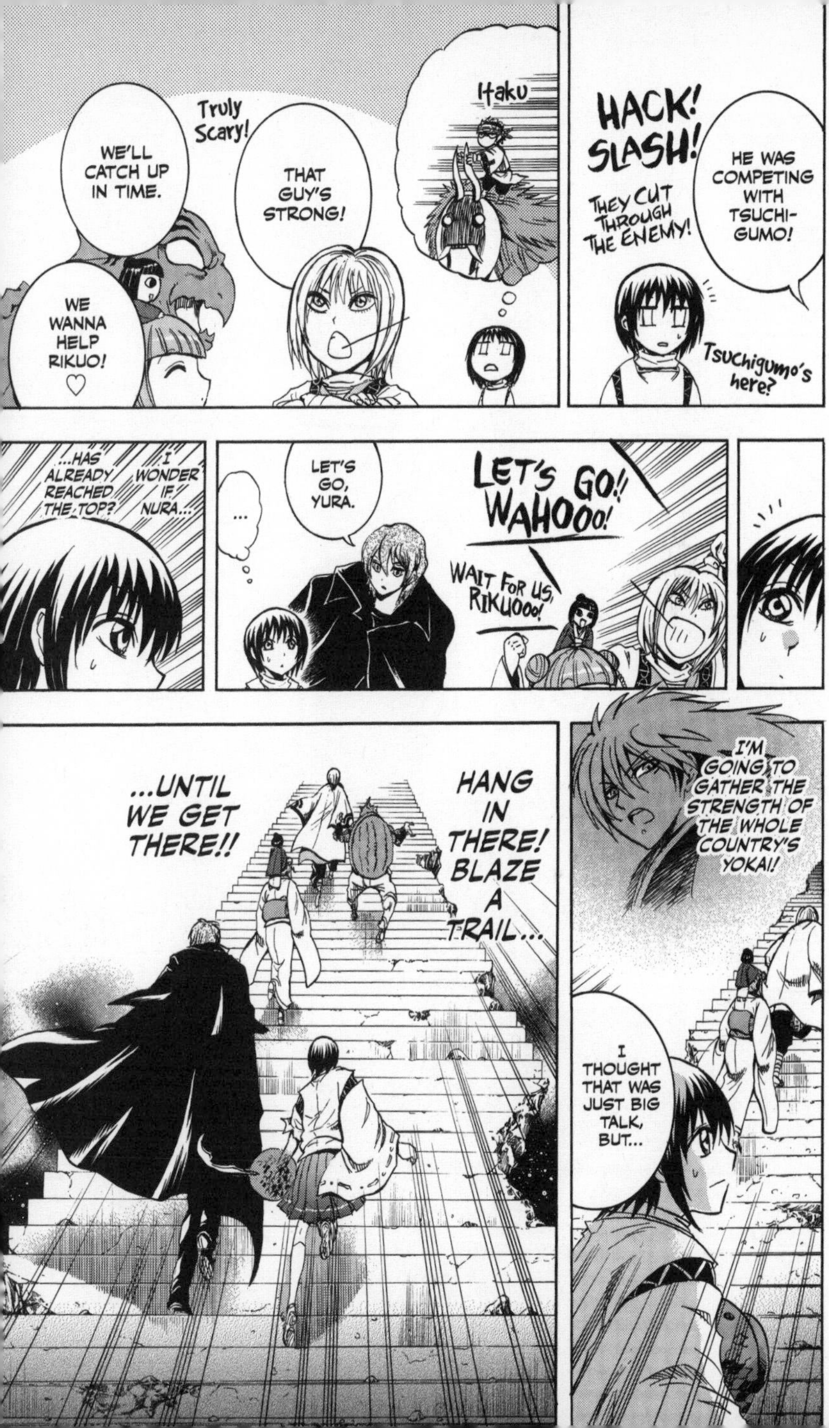
HACK! SLASH!
THEY CUT THROUGH THE ENEMY!
HE WAS COMPETING WITH TSUCHI-GUMO!
Tsuchigumo's here?
Itaku
THAT GUY'S STRONG!
Truly Scary!
WE'LL CATCH UP IN TIME.
WE WANNA HELP RIKUO! ♡
LET'S GO!! WAHOOO!
WAIT FOR US, RIKUOOO!
LET'S GO, YURA.
...
I WONDER IF NURA...
...HAS ALREADY REACHED THE TOP?
I'M GOING TO GATHER THE STRENGTH OF THE WHOLE COUNTRY'S YOKAI!
I THOUGHT THAT WAS JUST BIG TALK, BUT...
HANG IN THERE! BLAZE A TRAIL...
...UNTIL WE GET THERE!!

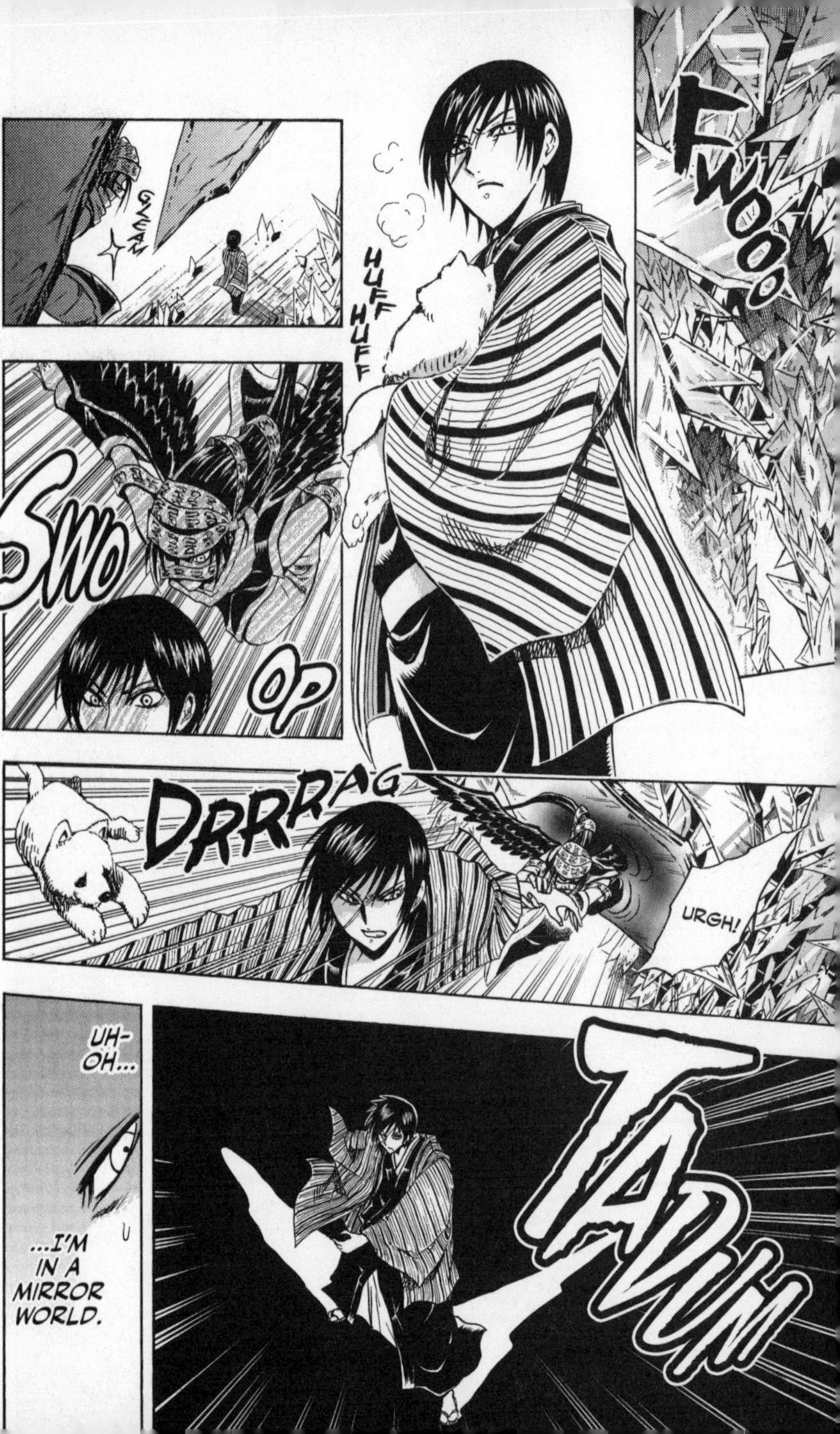
FWOOOO
HUFF HUFF
GLEAM
SWOOP
URGH!
DRRRAG
TADUM
UH-OH...
...I'M IN A MIRROR WORLD.

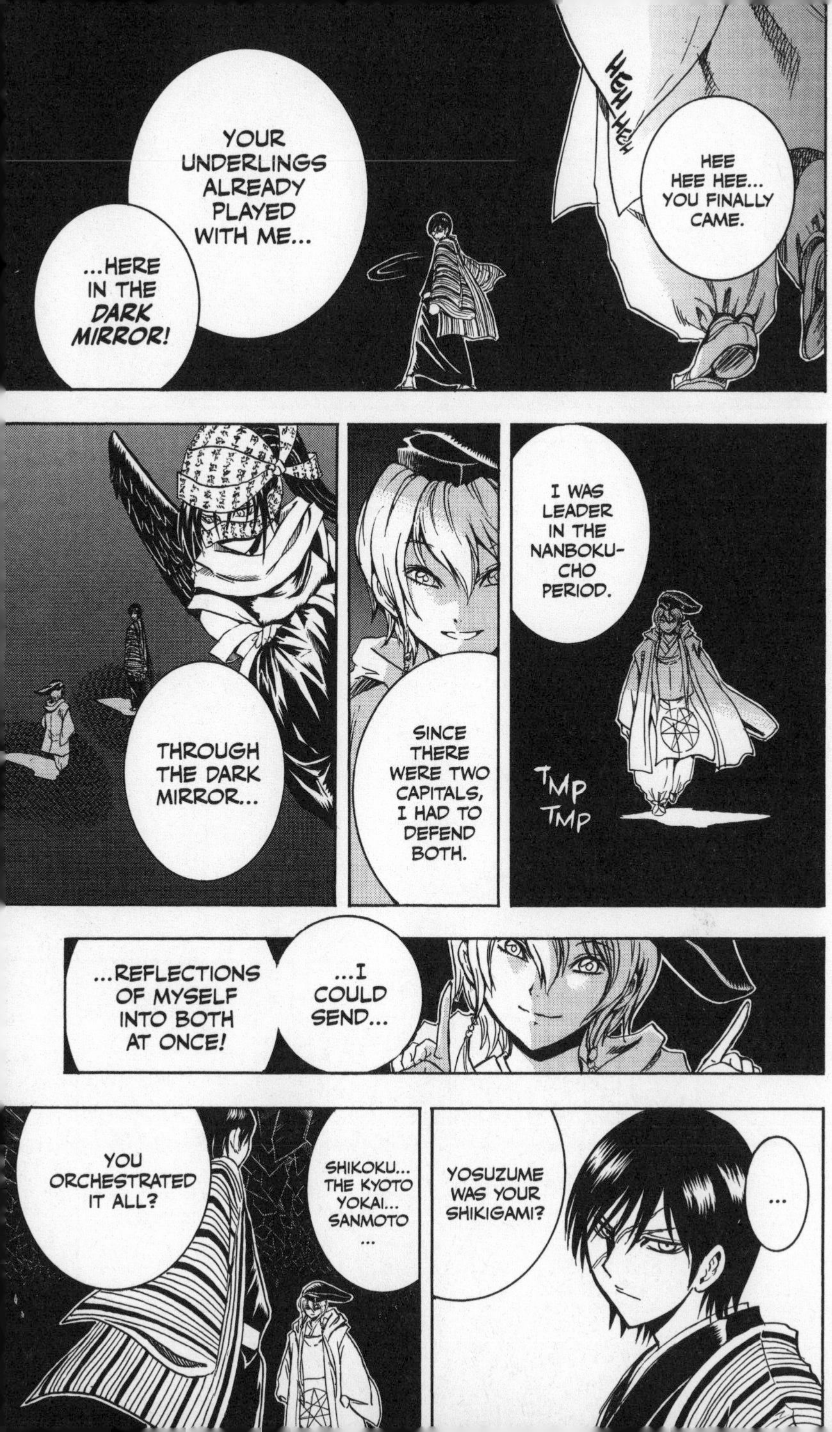
HEH HEH
HEE HEE HEE... YOU FINALLY CAME.
YOUR UNDERLINGS ALREADY PLAYED WITH ME...
...HERE IN THE *DARK MIRROR!*
I WAS LEADER IN THE NANBOKU-CHO PERIOD.
TMP TMP
SINCE THERE WERE TWO CAPITALS, I HAD TO DEFEND BOTH.
THROUGH THE DARK MIRROR...
...I COULD SEND...
...REFLECTIONS OF MYSELF INTO BOTH AT ONCE!
...
YOSUZUME WAS YOUR SHIKIGAMI?
SHIKOKU... THE KYOTO YOKAI... SANMOTO ...
YOU ORCHESTRATED IT ALL?

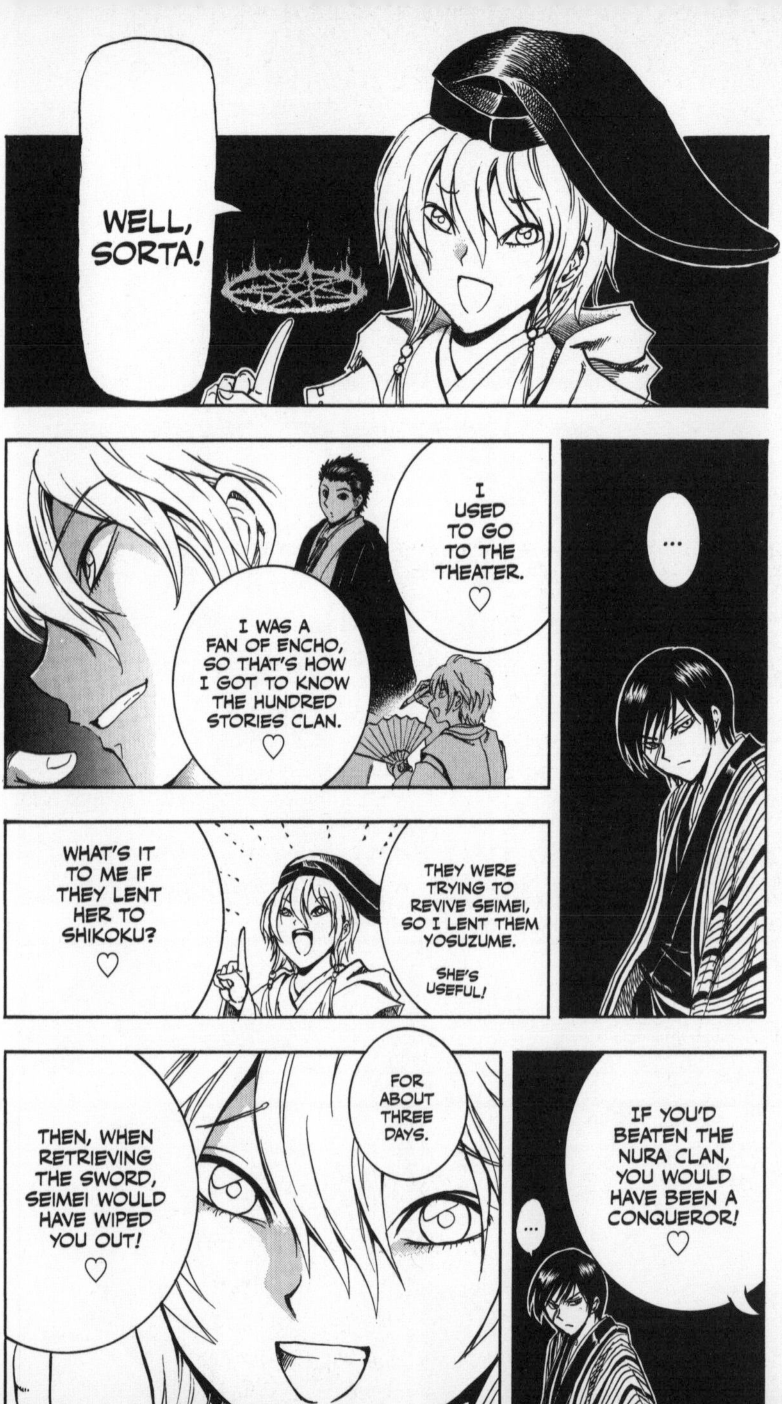
WELL, SORTA!
...
I USED TO GO TO THE THEATER. ♡
I WAS A FAN OF ENCHO, SO THAT'S HOW I GOT TO KNOW THE HUNDRED STORIES CLAN. ♡
THEY WERE TRYING TO REVIVE SEIMEI, SO I LENT THEM YOSUZUME.
SHE'S USEFUL!
WHAT'S IT TO ME IF THEY LENT HER TO SHIKOKU? ♡
IF YOU'D BEATEN THE NURA CLAN, YOU WOULD HAVE BEEN A CONQUEROR! ♡
...
FOR ABOUT THREE DAYS.
THEN, WHEN RETRIEVING THE SWORD, SEIMEI WOULD HAVE WIPED YOU OUT! ♡

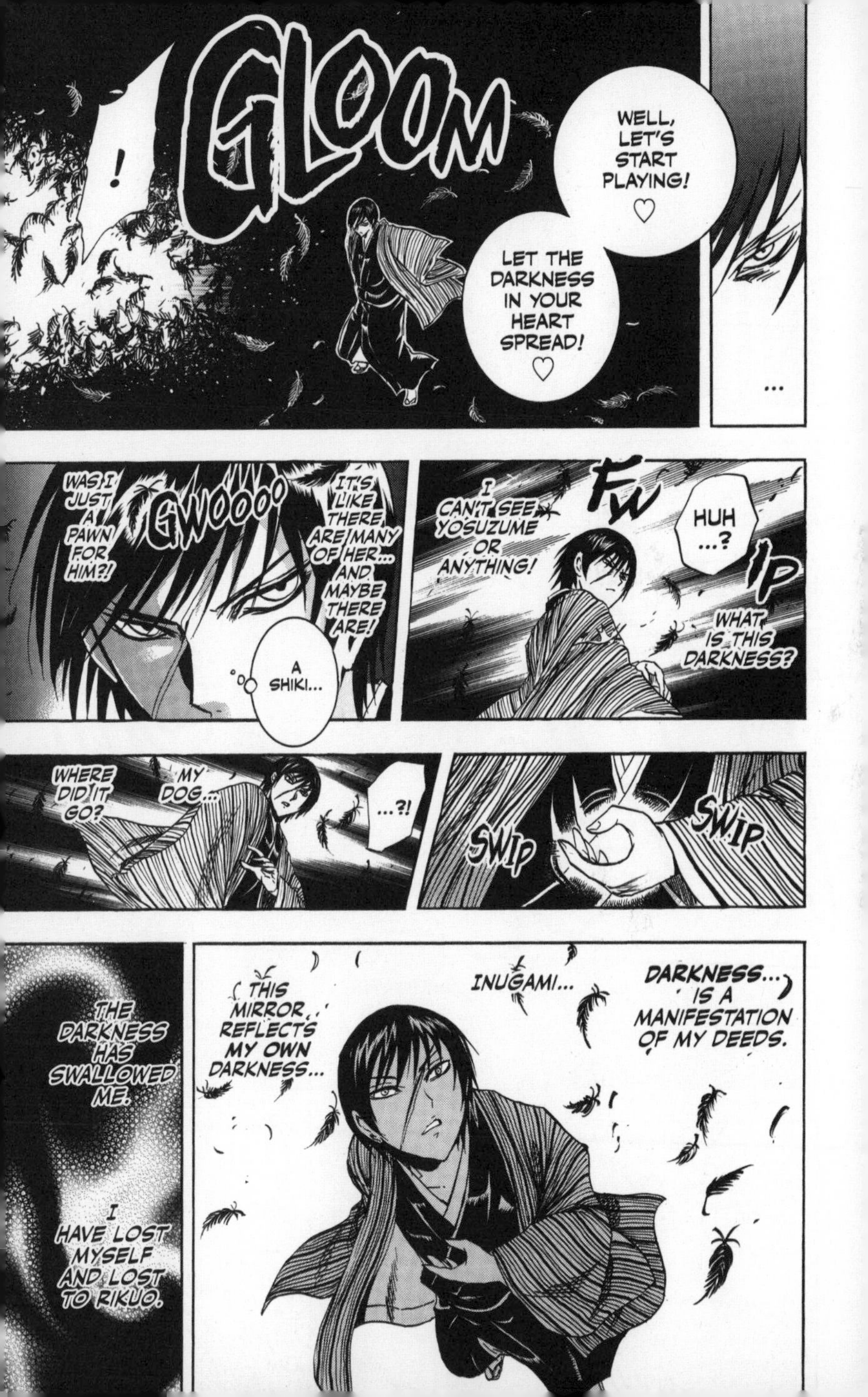
...
WELL, LET'S START PLAYING! ♡
LET THE DARKNESS IN YOUR HEART SPREAD! ♡
GLOOM
!
HUH ...?
FWIP
I CAN'T SEE YOSUZUME OR ANYTHING!
WHAT IS THIS DARKNESS?
IT'S LIKE THERE ARE MANY OF HER... AND MAYBE THERE ARE!
GWOOO
WAS I JUST A PAWN FOR HIM?!
A SHIKI...
SWIP
SWIP
...?!
MY DOG...
WHERE DID IT GO?
DARKNESS... IS A MANIFESTATION OF MY DEEDS.
INUGAMI...
THIS MIRROR REFLECTS MY OWN DARKNESS...
THE DARKNESS HAS SWALLOWED ME.
I HAVE LOST MYSELF AND LOST TO RIKUO.

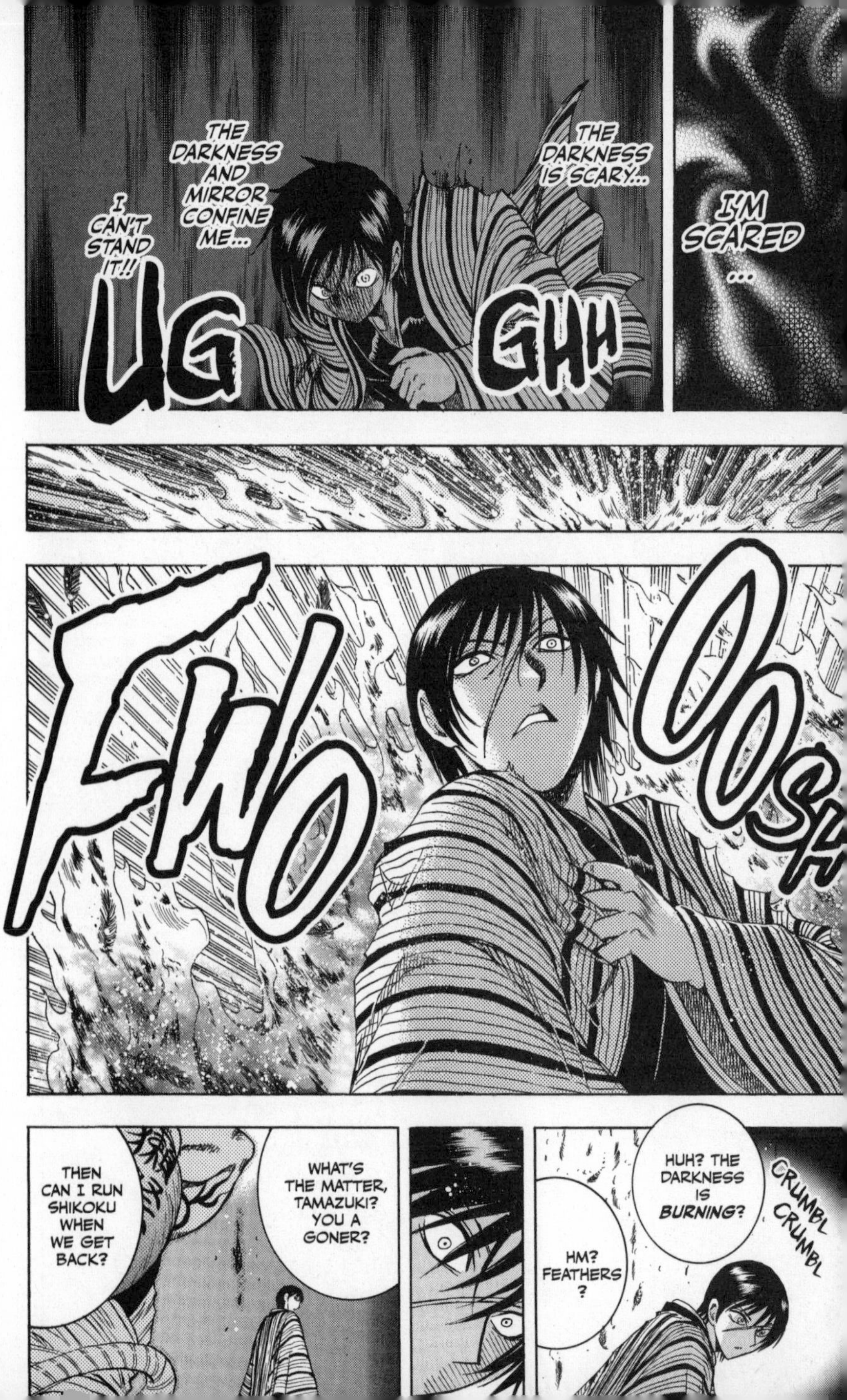
I'M SCARED...
THE DARKNESS IS SCARY...
THE DARKNESS AND MIRROR CONFINE ME...
I CAN'T STAND IT!!
UGGHH
FWOOOSH
CRUMBL CRUMBL
HUH? THE DARKNESS IS *BURNING*?
HM? FEATHERS?
WHAT'S THE MATTER, TAMAZUKI? YOU A GONER?
THEN CAN I RUN SHIKOKU WHEN WE GET BACK?

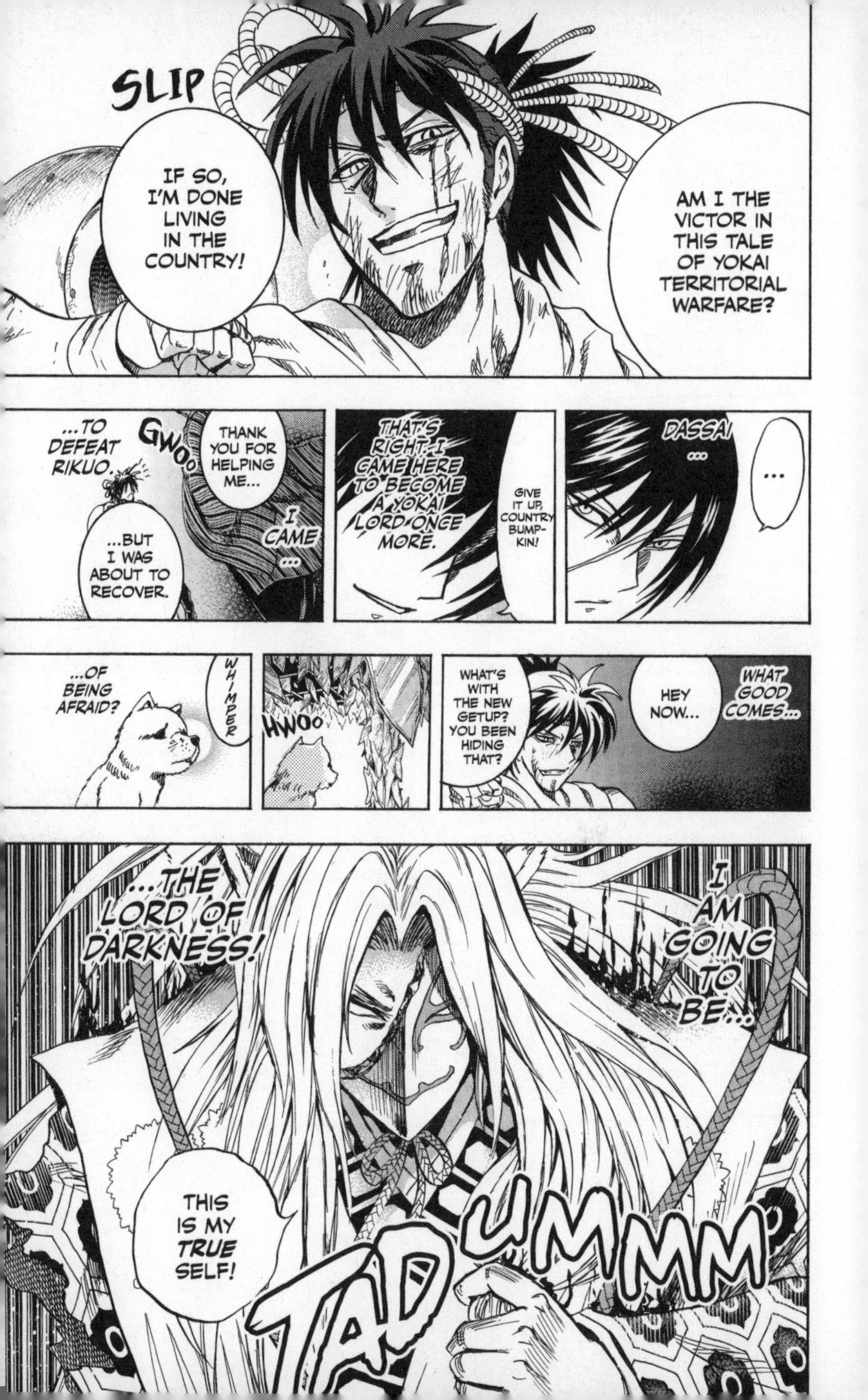
AM I THE VICTOR IN THIS TALE OF YOKAI TERRITORIAL WARFARE?
SLIP
IF SO, I'M DONE LIVING IN THE COUNTRY!
...
DASSAI ...
GIVE IT UP, COUNTRY BUMPKIN!
THAT'S RIGHT. I CAME HERE TO BECOME A YOKAI LORD ONCE MORE.
THANK YOU FOR HELPING ME...
GWOO
...BUT I WAS ABOUT TO RECOVER.
I CAME ...
...TO DEFEAT RIKUO.
WHAT GOOD COMES...
HEY NOW...
WHAT'S WITH THE NEW GETUP? YOU BEEN HIDING THAT?
HWOO
WHIMPER
...OF BEING AFRAID?
I AM GOING TO BE...
...THE LORD OF DARKNESS!
THIS IS MY TRUE SELF!
TADUMMMM

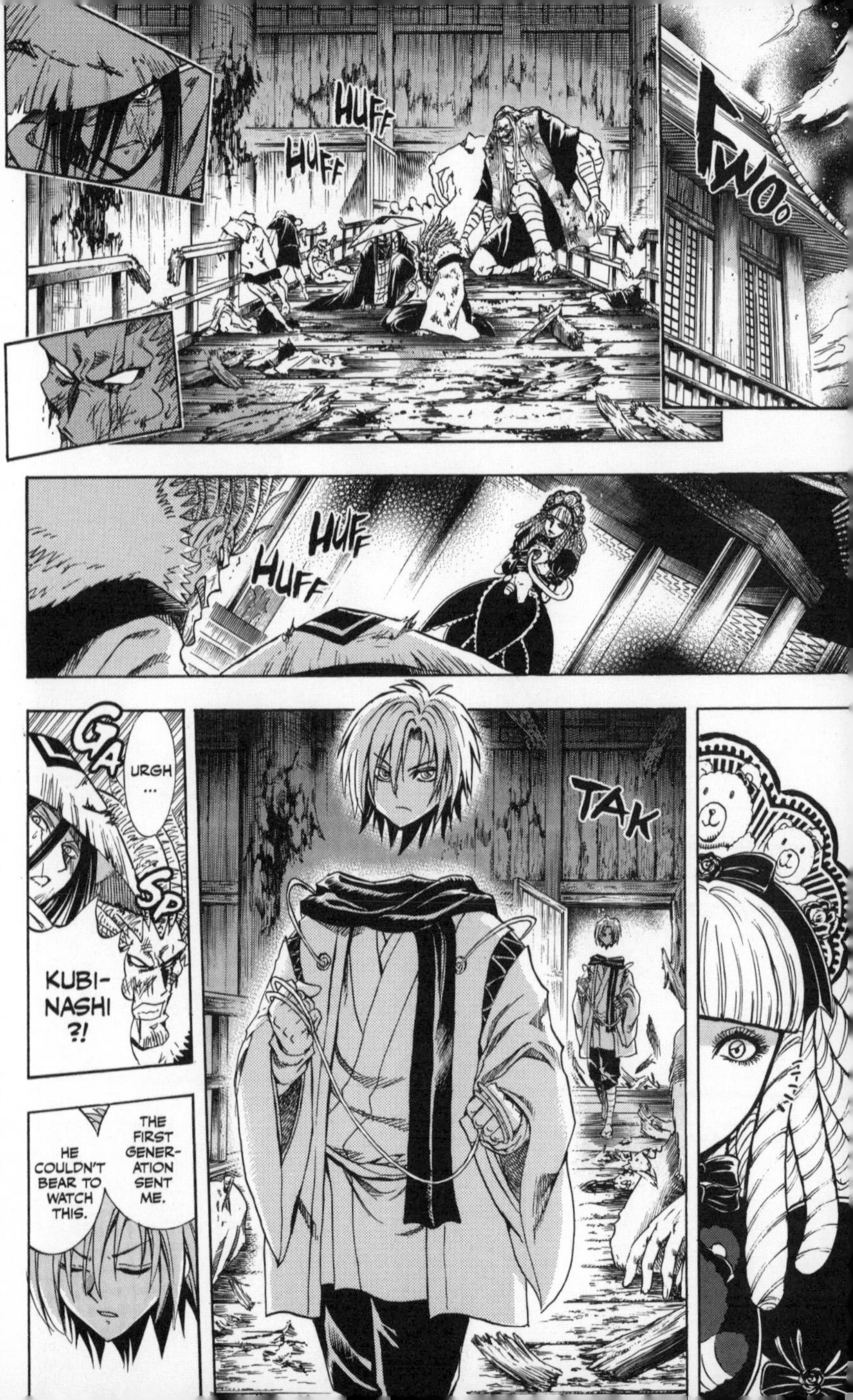
FWOO
HUFF
HUFF
HUFF
HUFF
TAK
GA
URGH...
SP
KUBI-NASHI?!
THE FIRST GENERATION SENT ME.
HE COULDN'T BEAR TO WATCH THIS.

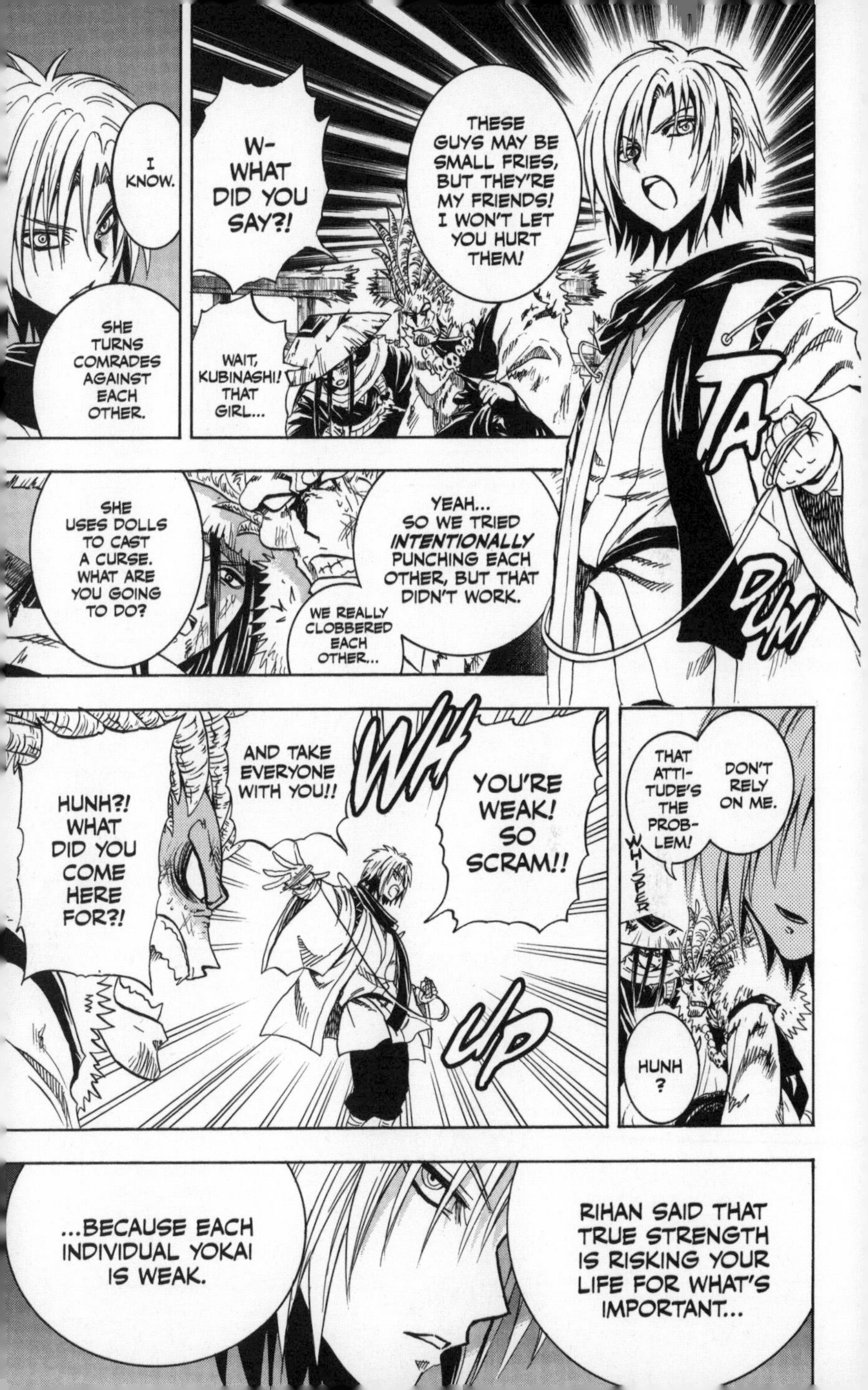
THESE GUYS MAY BE SMALL FRIES, BUT THEY'RE MY FRIENDS! I WON'T LET YOU HURT THEM!
TA
DUM
W- WHAT DID YOU SAY?!
WAIT, KUBINASHI! THAT GIRL...
I KNOW.
SHE TURNS COMRADES AGAINST EACH OTHER.
YEAH... SO WE TRIED *INTENTIONALLY* PUNCHING EACH OTHER, BUT THAT DIDN'T WORK.
WE REALLY CLOBBERED EACH OTHER...
SHE USES DOLLS TO CAST A CURSE. WHAT ARE YOU GOING TO DO?
DON'T RELY ON ME.
THAT ATTI-TUDE'S THE PROB-LEM!
WHISPER
HUNH ?
YOU'RE WEAK! SO SCRAM!!
AND TAKE EVERYONE WITH YOU!!
WH
UP
HUNH?! WHAT DID YOU COME HERE FOR?!
RIHAN SAID THAT TRUE STRENGTH IS RISKING YOUR LIFE FOR WHAT'S IMPORTANT...
...BECAUSE EACH INDIVIDUAL YOKAI IS WEAK.

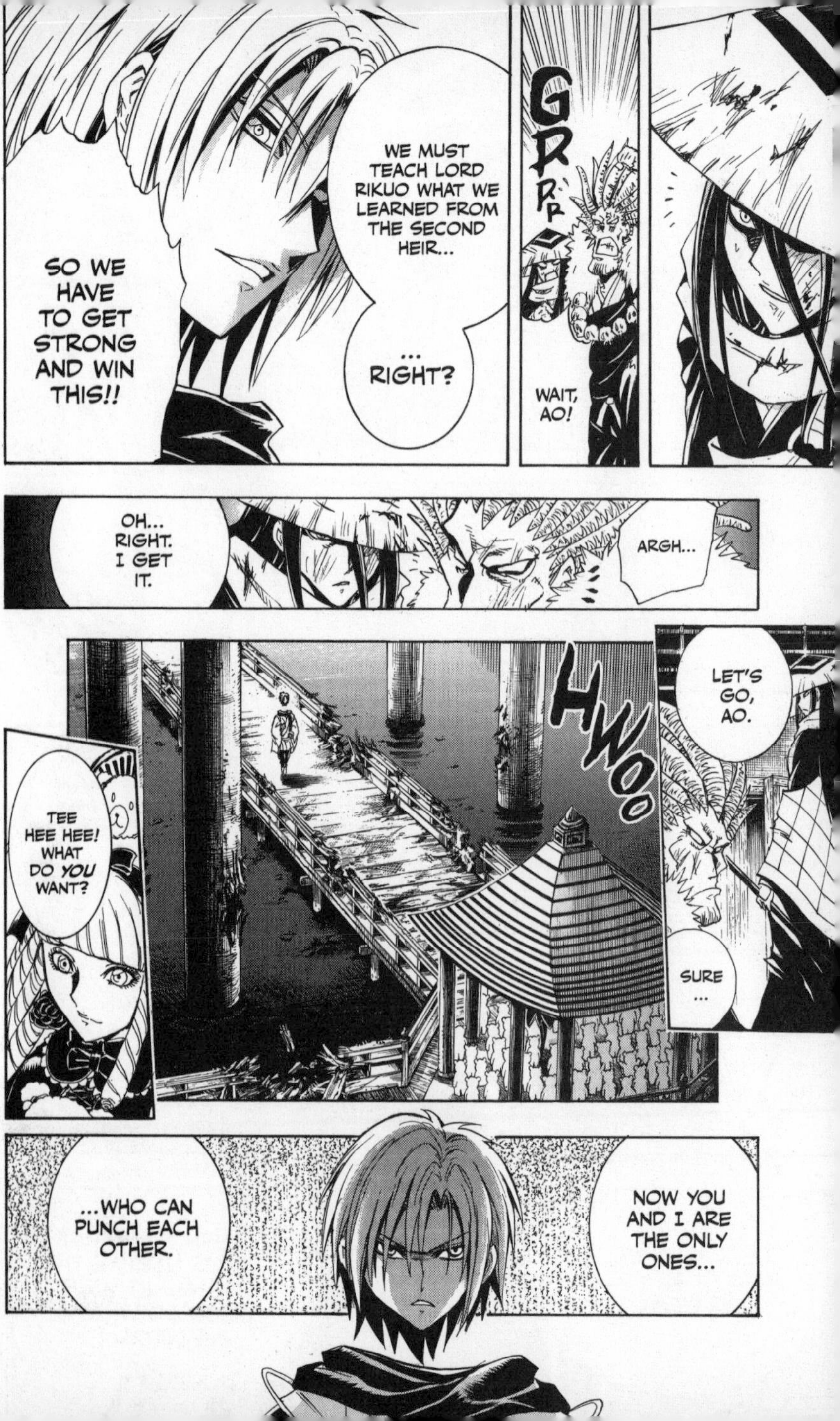
GRRR
WAIT, AO!
WE MUST TEACH LORD RIKUO WHAT WE LEARNED FROM THE SECOND HEIR...
...RIGHT?
SO WE HAVE TO GET STRONG AND WIN THIS!!
ARGH...
OH... RIGHT. I GET IT.
LET'S GO, AO.
SURE...
HWOO
TEE HEE HEE! WHAT DO *YOU* WANT?
NOW YOU AND I ARE THE ONLY ONES...
...WHO CAN PUNCH EACH OTHER.

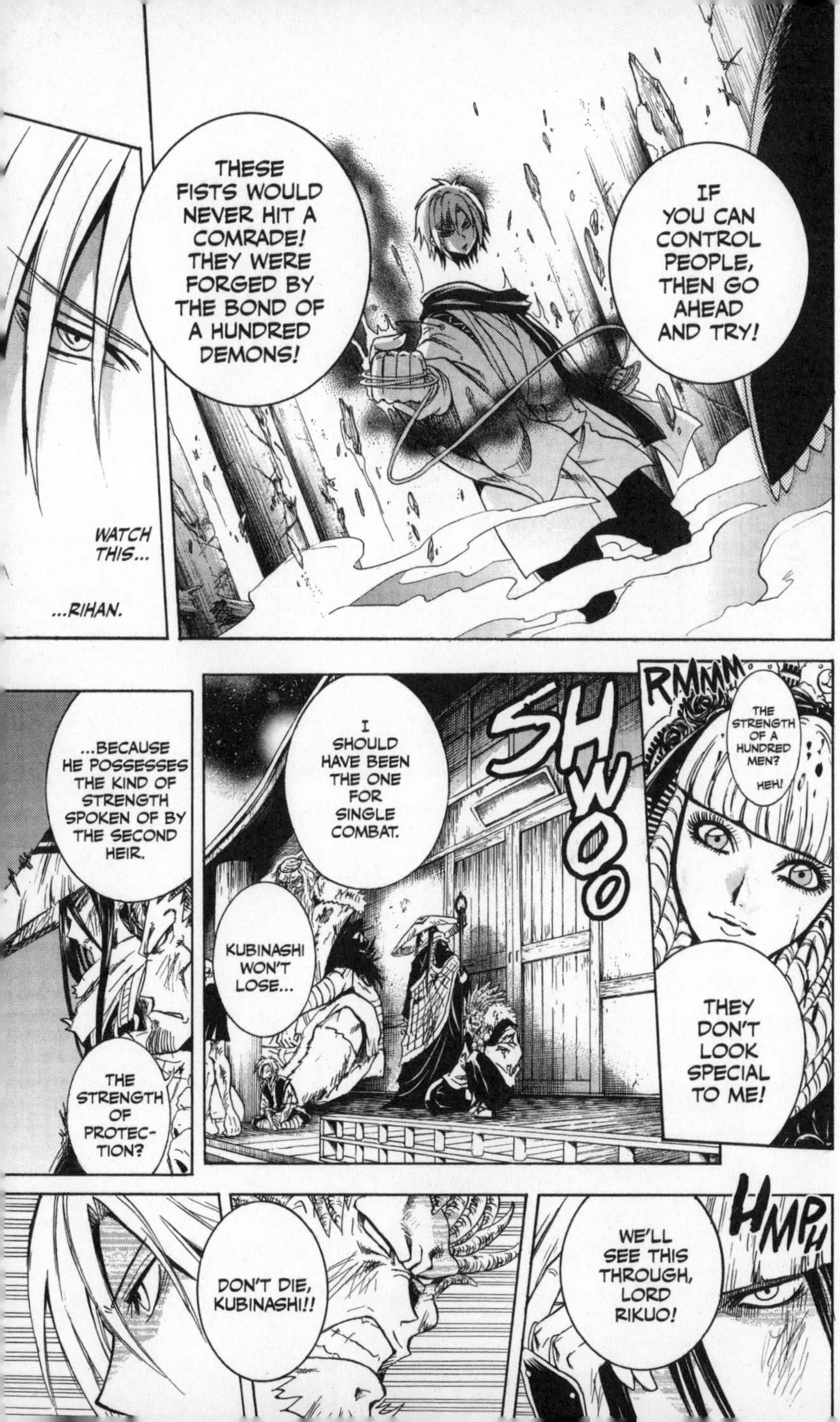
IF YOU CAN CONTROL PEOPLE, THEN GO AHEAD AND TRY!
THESE FISTS WOULD NEVER HIT A COMRADE! THEY WERE FORGED BY THE BOND OF A HUNDRED DEMONS!
WATCH THIS...
...RIHAN.
RMMM
THE STRENGTH OF A HUNDRED MEN? HEH!
THEY DON'T LOOK SPECIAL TO ME!
SHWOO
I SHOULD HAVE BEEN THE ONE FOR SINGLE COMBAT.
KUBINASHI WON'T LOSE...
...BECAUSE HE POSSESSES THE KIND OF STRENGTH SPOKEN OF BY THE SECOND HEIR.
THE STRENGTH OF PROTECTION?
HMPH
WE'LL SEE THIS THROUGH, LORD RIKUO!
DON'T DIE, KUBINASHI!!

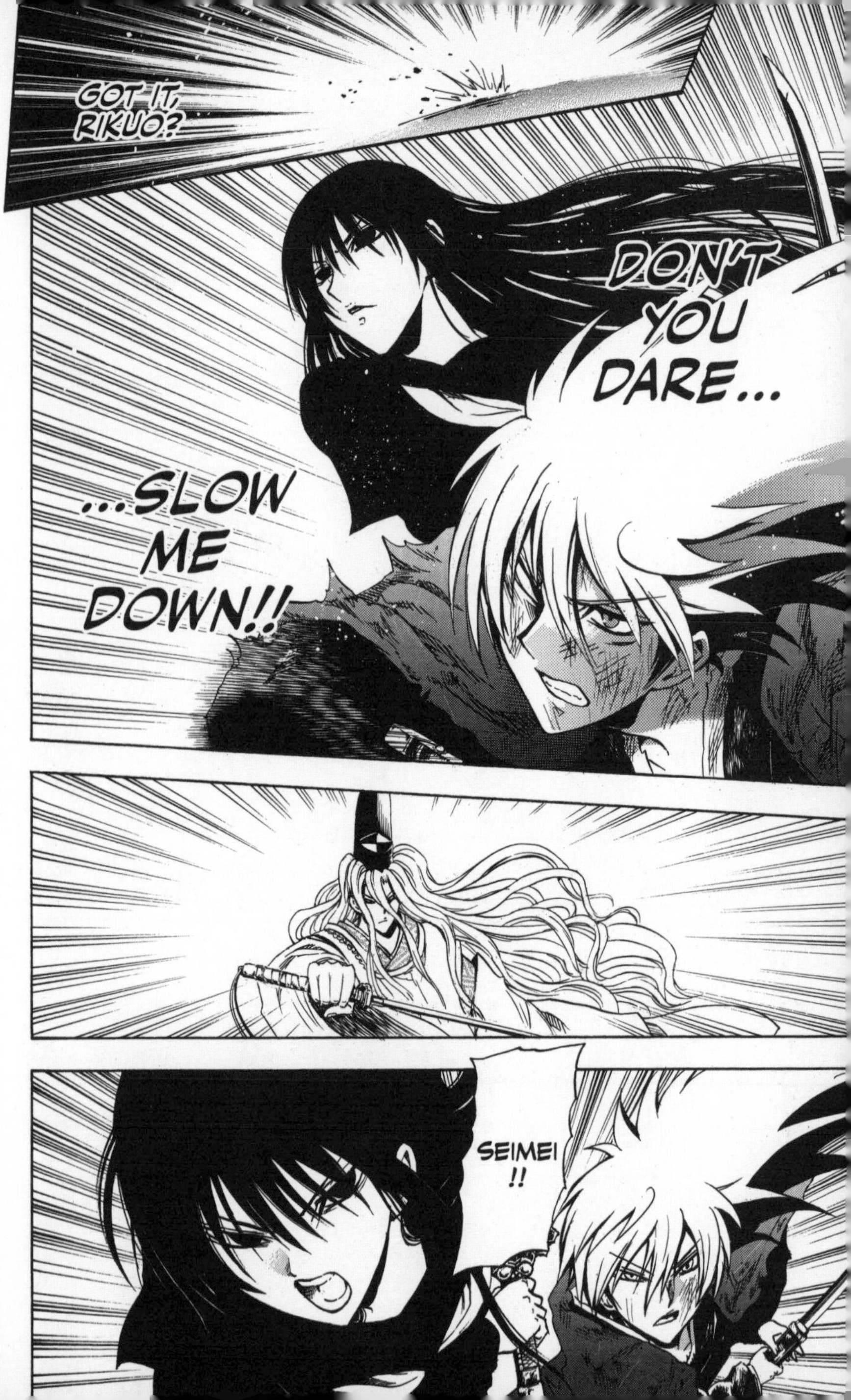
GOT IT, RIKUO?
DON'T YOU DARE...
...SLOW ME DOWN!!
SEIMEI !!

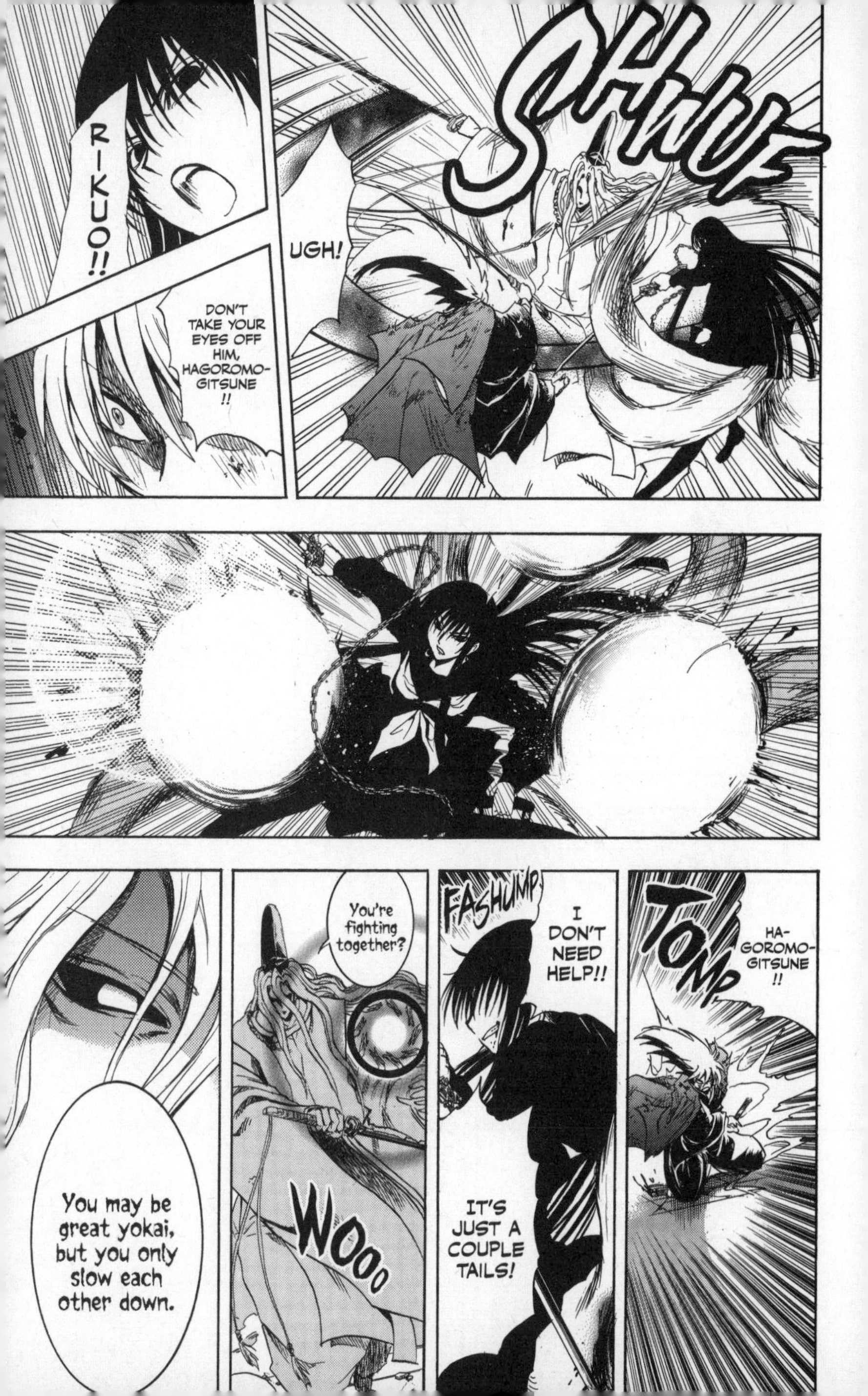
UGH!
RIKUO!!
DON'T TAKE YOUR EYES OFF HIM, HAGOROMO-GITSUNE!!
HA-GOROMO-GITSUNE!!
TOMP
FASHUMP
I DON'T NEED HELP!!
IT'S JUST A COUPLE TAILS!
You're fighting together?
WOOO
You may be great yokai, but you only slow each other down.

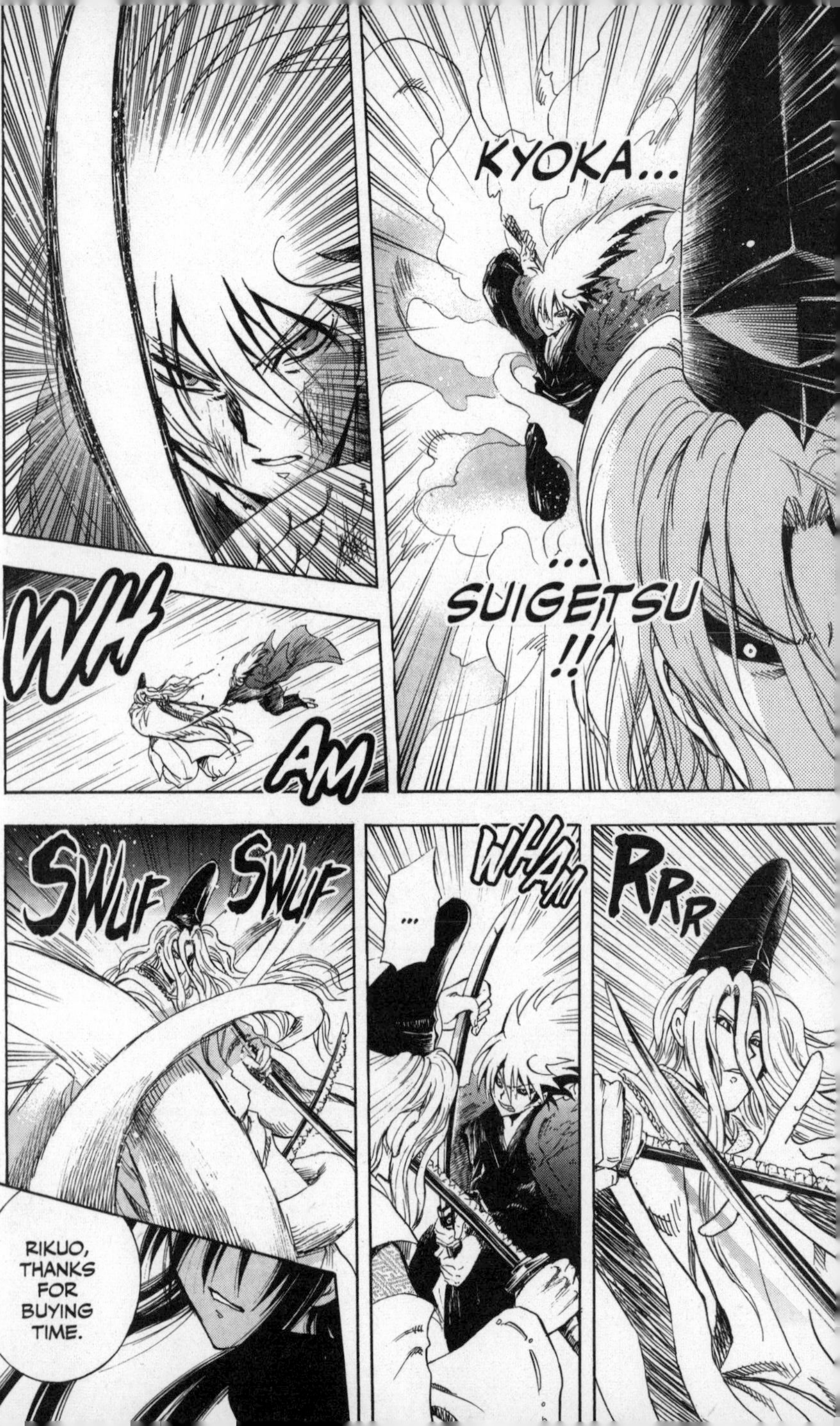
KYOKA...
...SUIGETSU !!
WH AM
RRR
WHAM
...
SWUF SWUF
RIKUO, THANKS FOR BUYING TIME.

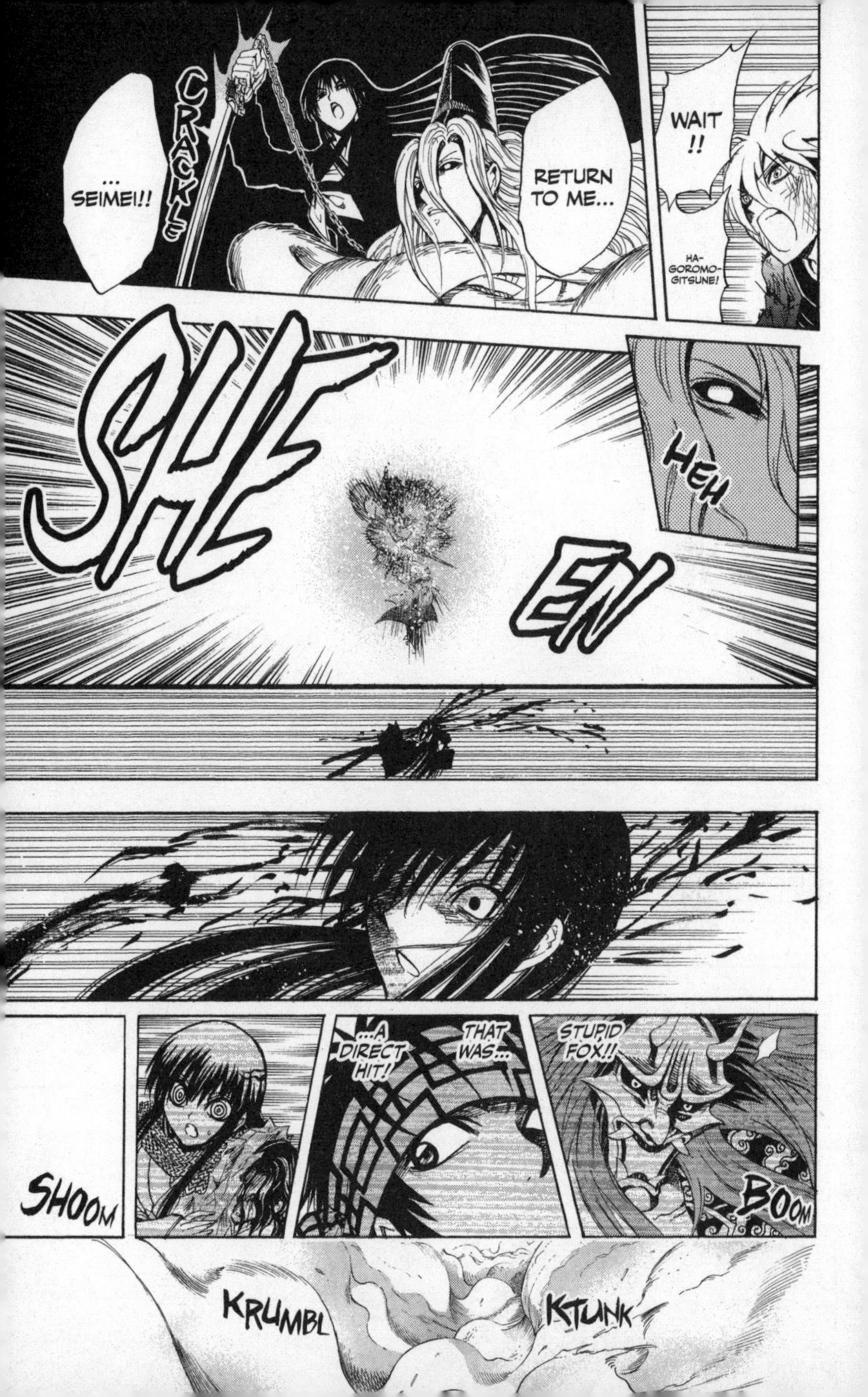
WAIT !!
HA-GOROMO-GITSUNE!
RETURN TO ME...
CRACKLE
... SEIMEI!!
HEH
SHE
EN
STUPID FOX!!
BOOM
THAT WAS...
...A DIRECT HIT!
SHOOM
KTUNK
KRUMBL

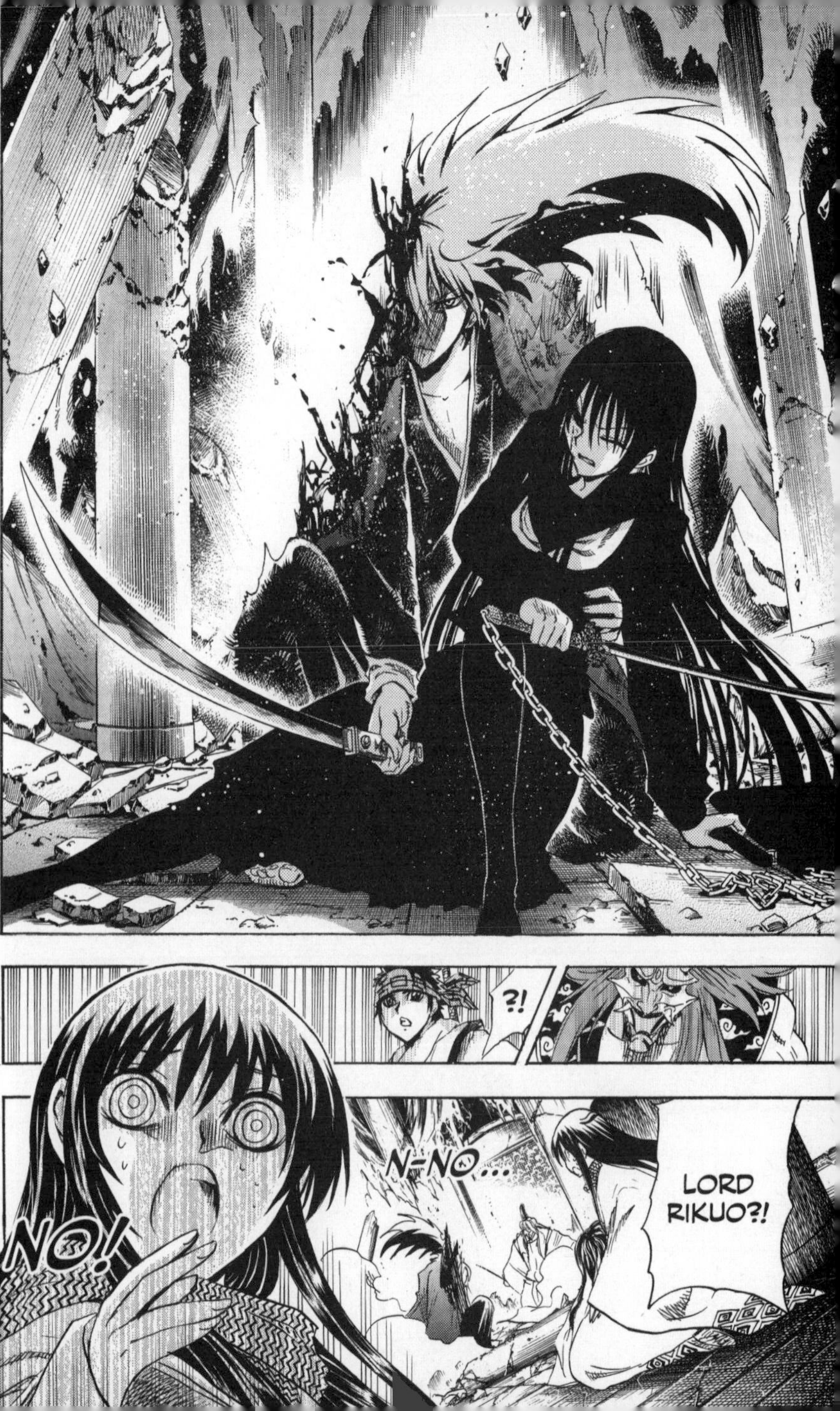
?!
LORD RIKUO?!
N-NO...
NO!

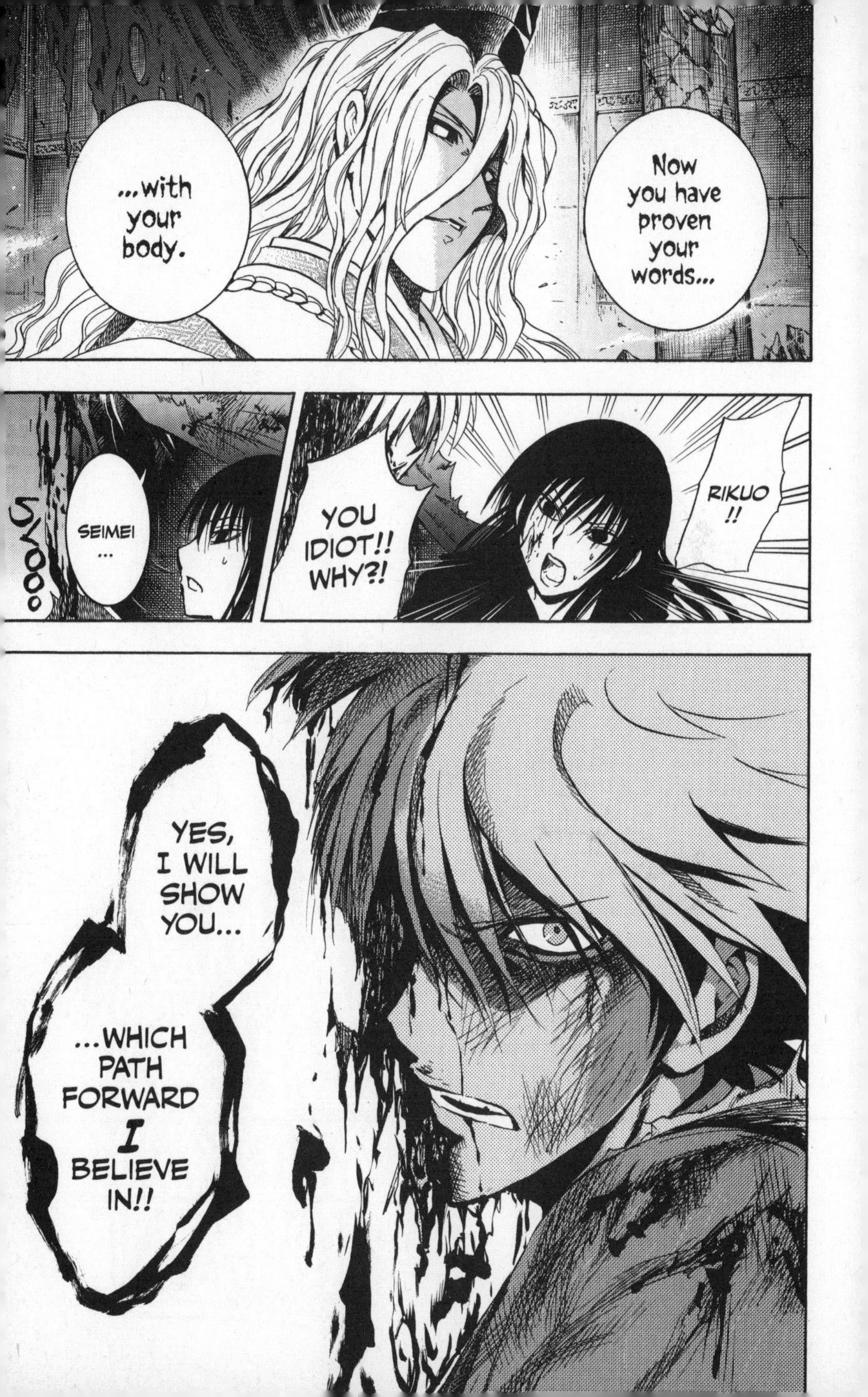
Now you have proven your words...
...with your body.
RIKUO!!
YOU IDIOT!! WHY?!
SEIMEI...
YES, I WILL SHOW YOU...
...WHICH PATH FORWARD I BELIEVE IN!!

NURA: RISE OF THE YOKAI CLAN

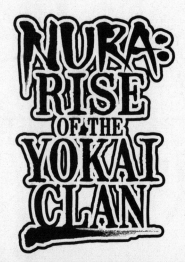

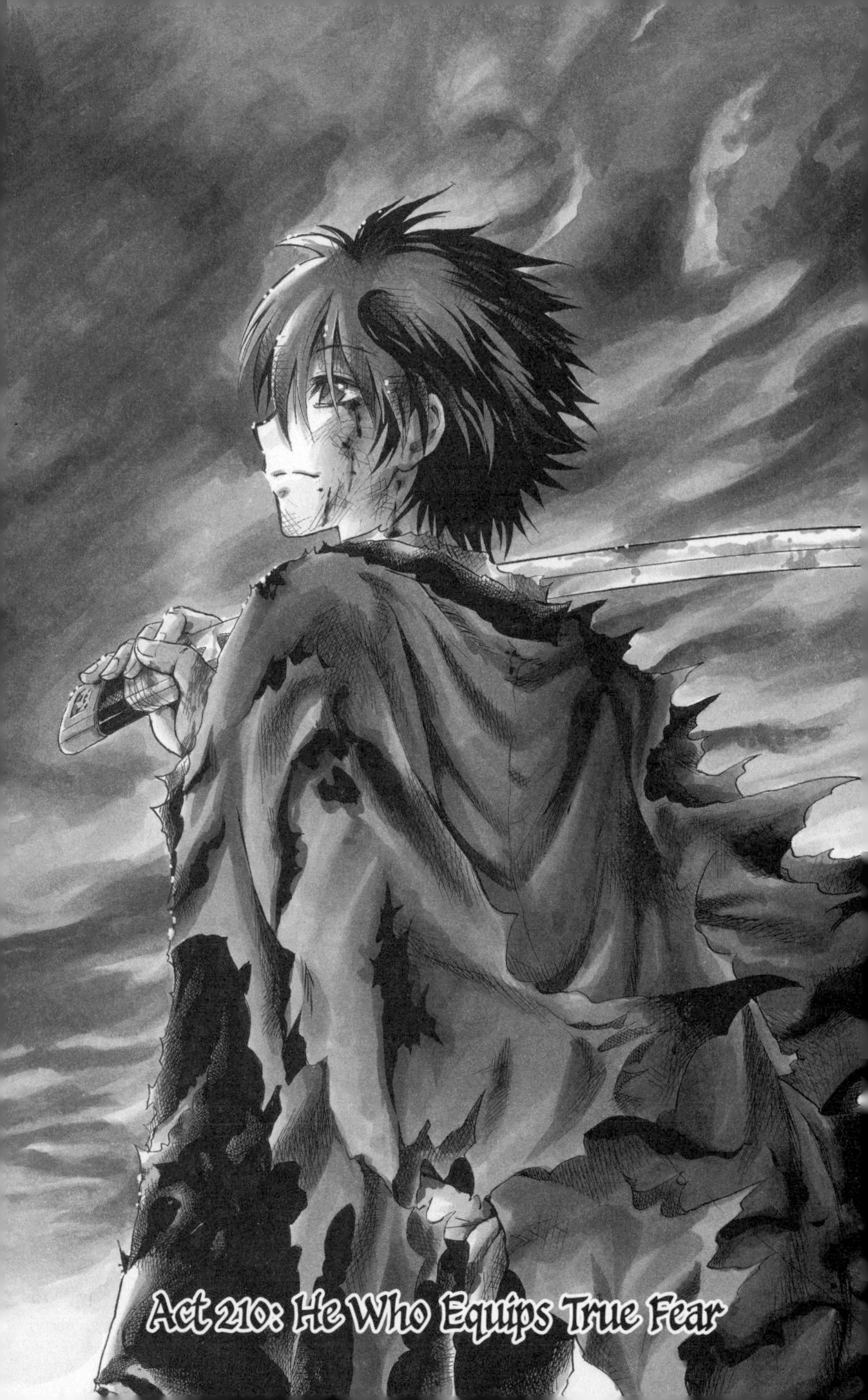
Act 210: He Who Equips True Fear

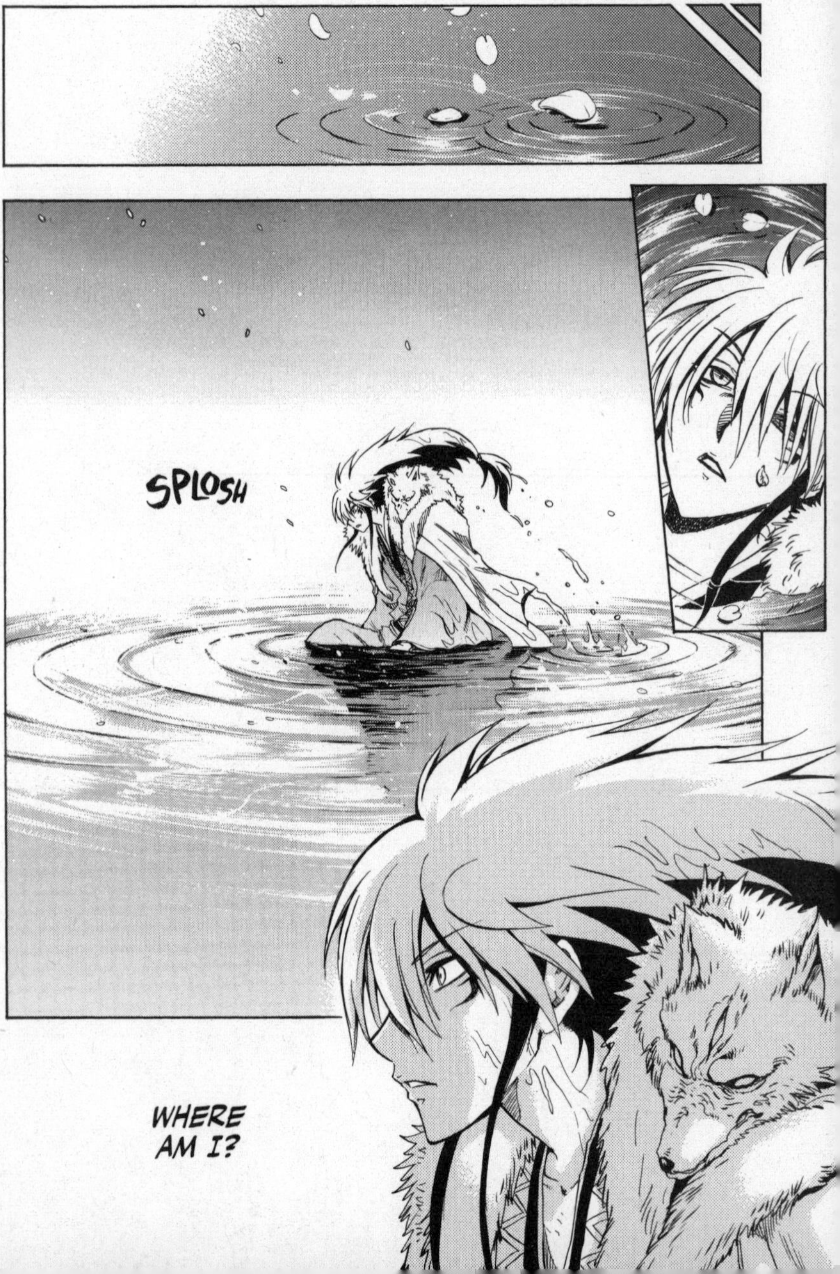
SPLOSH
WHERE AM I?

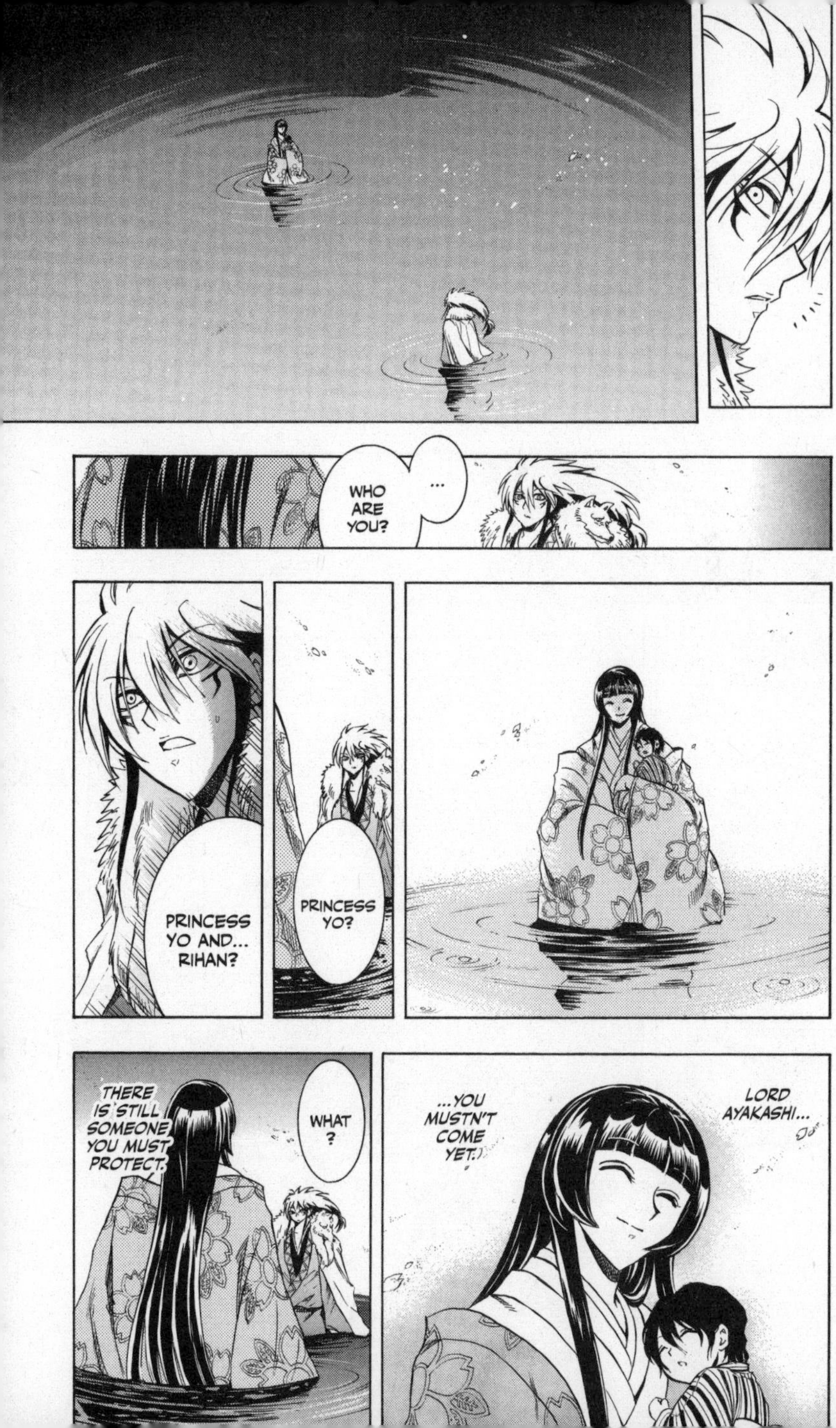
...
WHO ARE YOU?
PRINCESS YO?
PRINCESS YO AND... RIHAN?
LORD AYAKASHI...
...YOU MUSTN'T COME YET.
WHAT?
THERE IS STILL SOMEONE YOU MUST PROTECT.

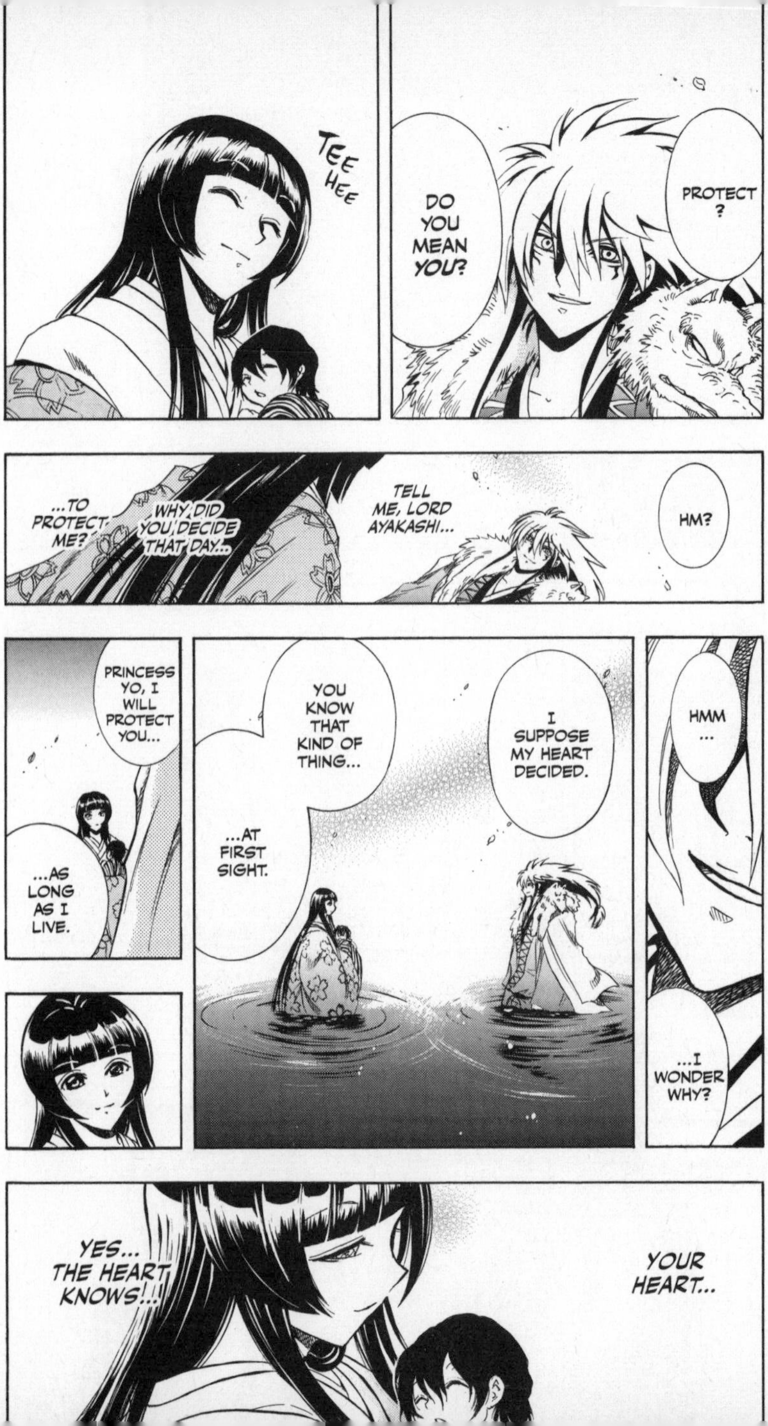
PROTECT ?
DO YOU MEAN YOU?
TEE HEE
HM?
TELL ME, LORD AYAKASHI...
WHY DID YOU DECIDE THAT DAY...
...TO PROTECT ME?
HMM ...
...I WONDER WHY?
I SUPPOSE MY HEART DECIDED.
YOU KNOW THAT KIND OF THING...
...AT FIRST SIGHT.
PRINCESS YO, I WILL PROTECT YOU...
...AS LONG AS I LIVE.
YOUR HEART...
YES... THE HEART KNOWS!...

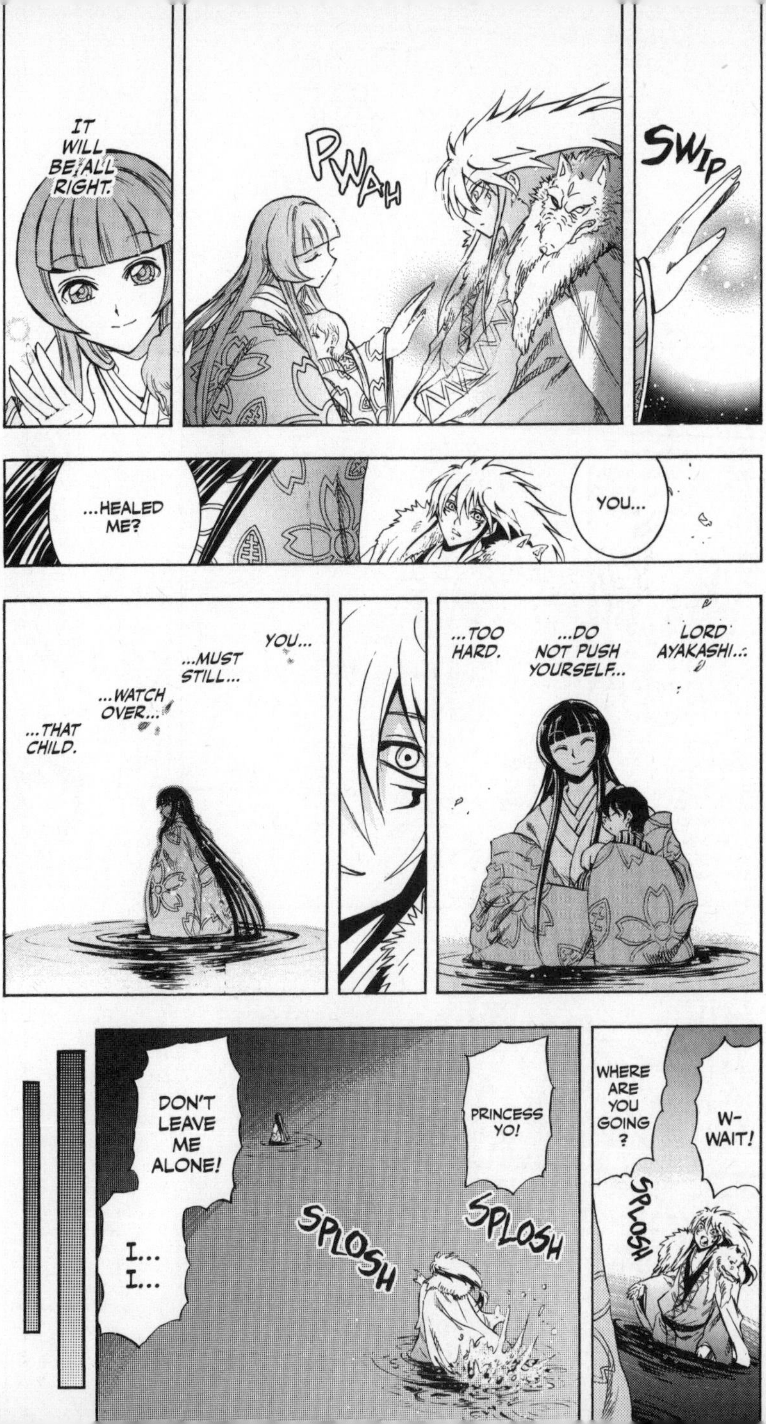
SWIP
PWAH
IT WILL BE ALL RIGHT.
YOU...
...HEALED ME?
LORD AYAKASHI...
...DO NOT PUSH YOURSELF...
...TOO HARD.
YOU...
...MUST STILL...
...WATCH OVER...
...THAT CHILD.
W-WAIT!
WHERE ARE YOU GOING?
SPLOSH
PRINCESS YO!
SPLOSH
SPLOSH
DON'T LEAVE ME ALONE!
I... I...

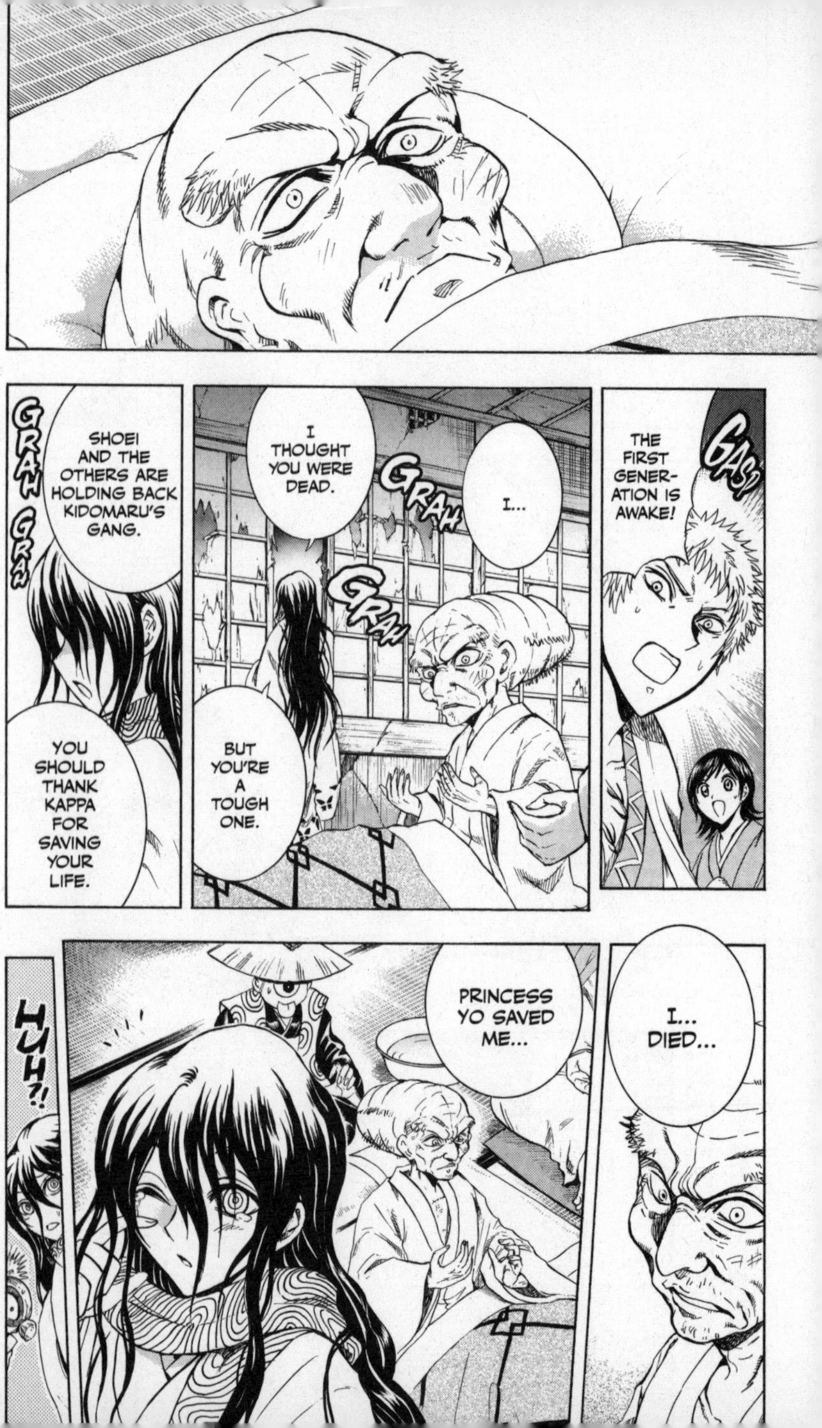
GASP
THE FIRST GENERATION IS AWAKE!
I...
GRAH
I THOUGHT YOU WERE DEAD.
GRAH
BUT YOU'RE A TOUGH ONE.
GRAH GRAH GRAH
SHOEI AND THE OTHERS ARE HOLDING BACK KIDOMARU'S GANG.
YOU SHOULD THANK KAPPA FOR SAVING YOUR LIFE.
I... DIED...
PRINCESS YO SAVED ME...
HUH?!

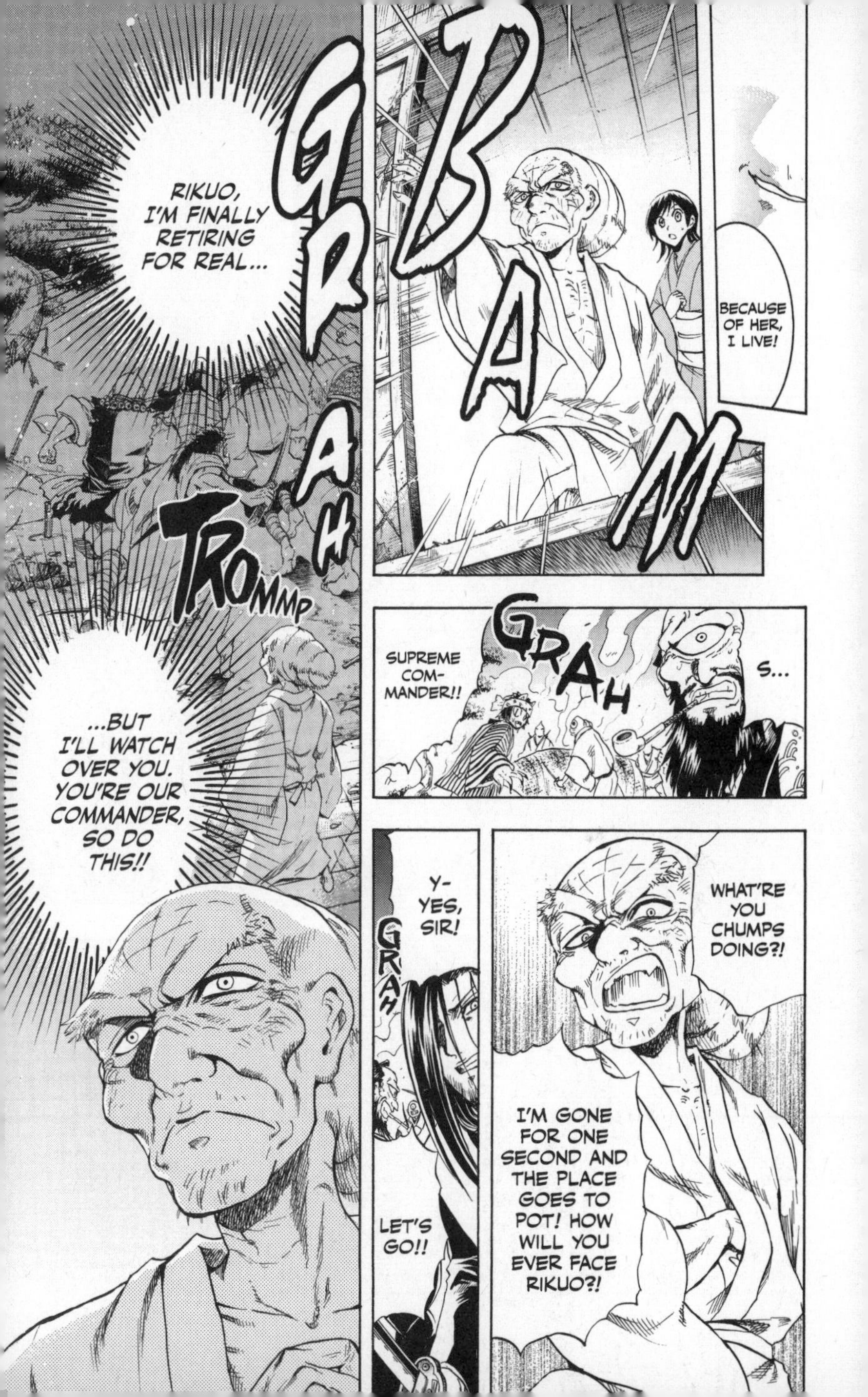
BECAUSE OF HER, I LIVE!
BAM
S...
GRAH
SUPREME COM-MANDER!!
WHAT'RE YOU CHUMPS DOING?!
I'M GONE FOR ONE SECOND AND THE PLACE GOES TO POT! HOW WILL YOU EVER FACE RIKUO?!
Y-YES, SIR!
GRAH
LET'S GO!!
RIKUO, I'M FINALLY RETIRING FOR REAL...
GDAH
TROMMP
...BUT I'LL WATCH OVER YOU. YOU'RE OUR COMMANDER, SO DO THIS!!

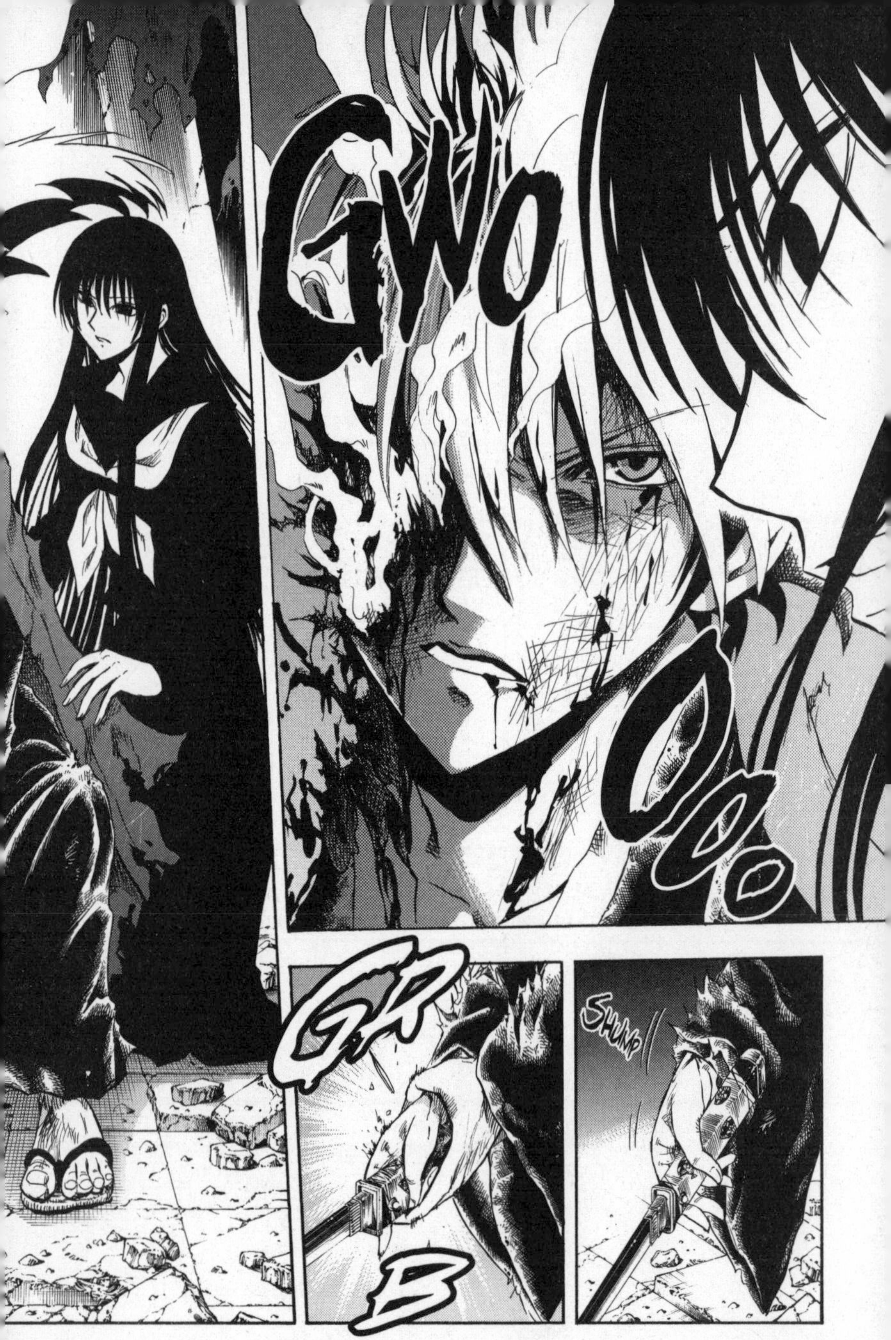
GWOOOOO
SHUMP
GR
B

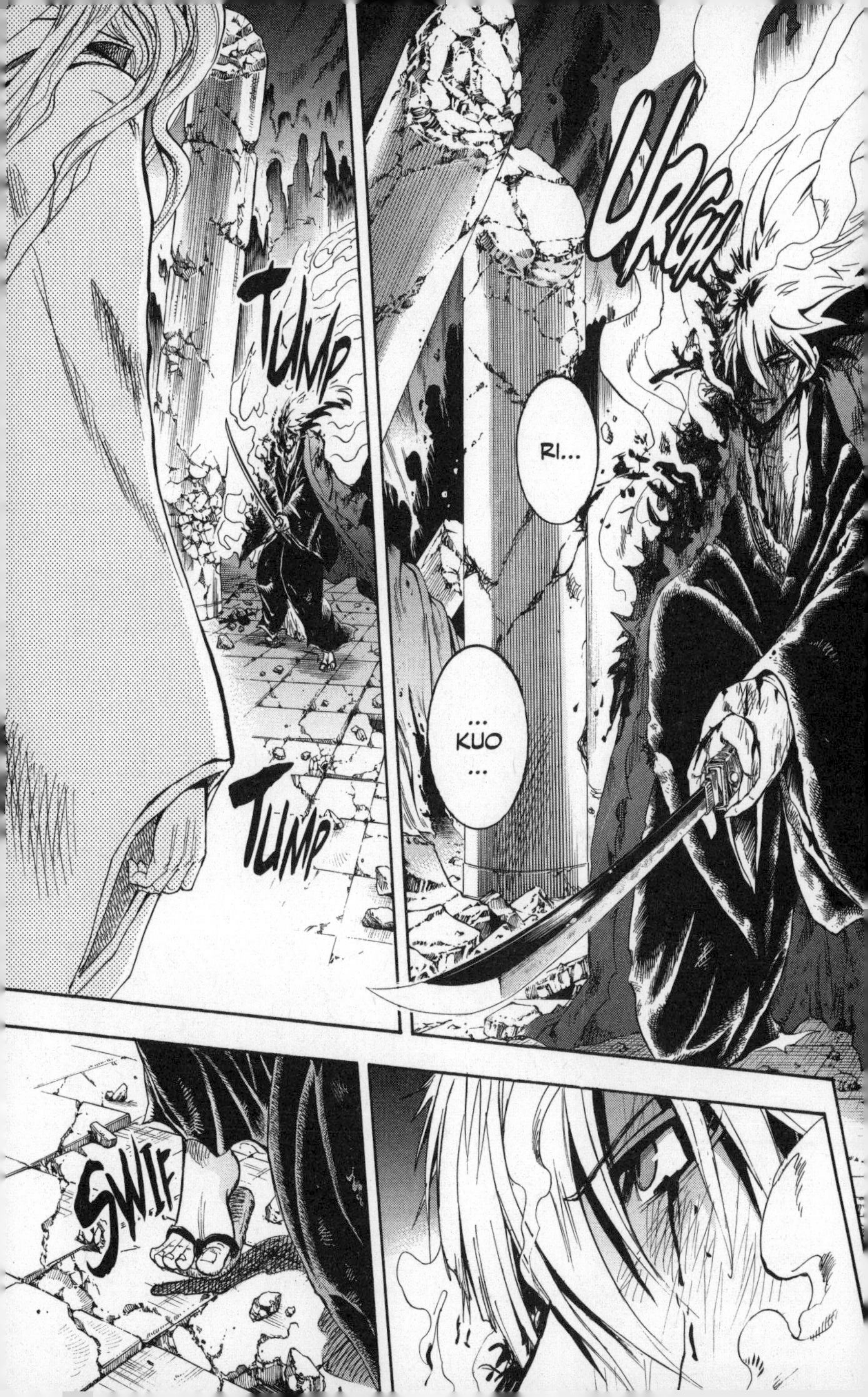
UHGH
RI...
...KUO...
TUMP
TUMP
SWIF

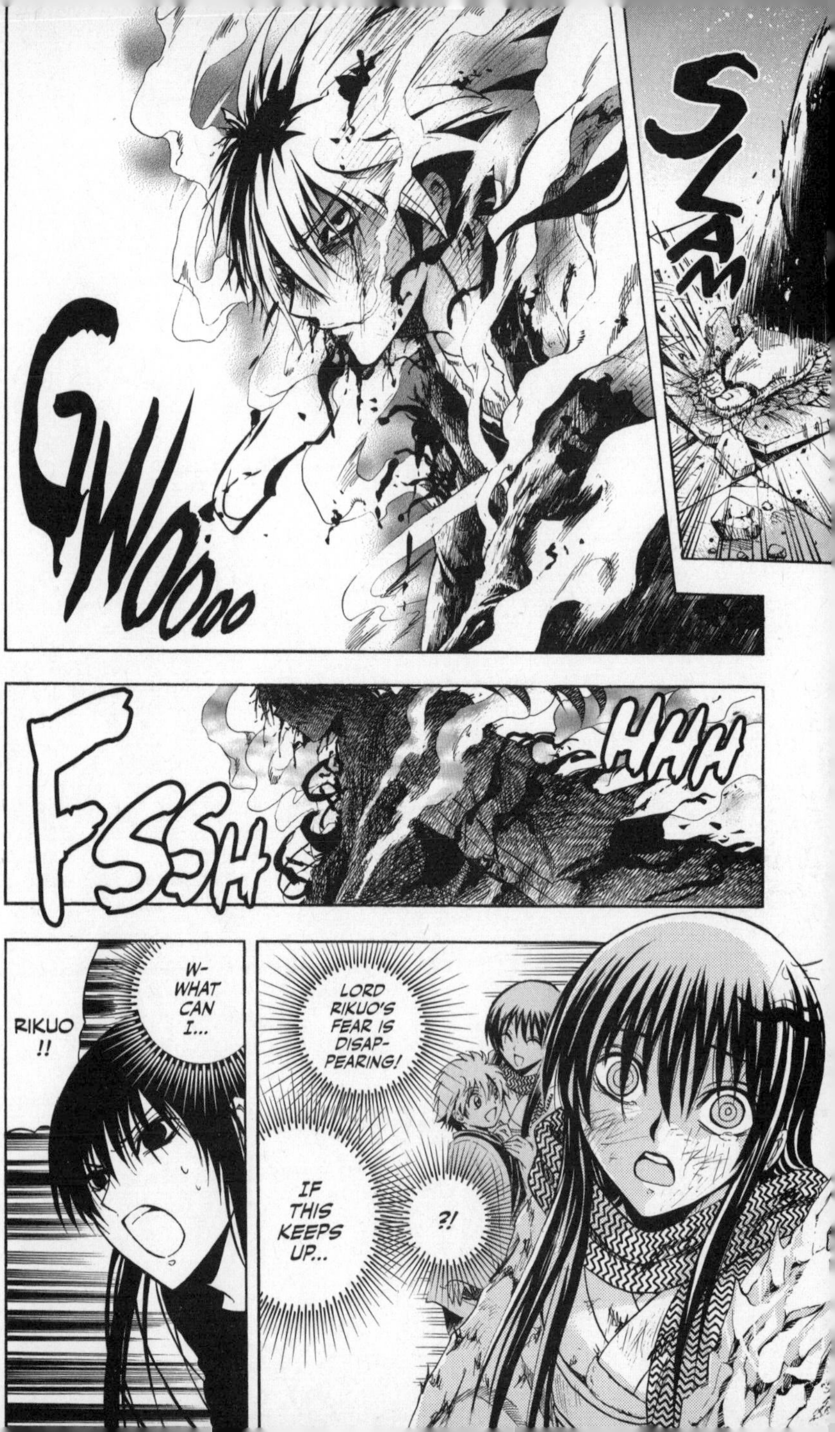
SLAM
GWOOOO
FSSH HHH
LORD RIKUO'S FEAR IS DISAPPEARING!
?!
IF THIS KEEPS UP...
W-WHAT CAN I...
RIKUO!!

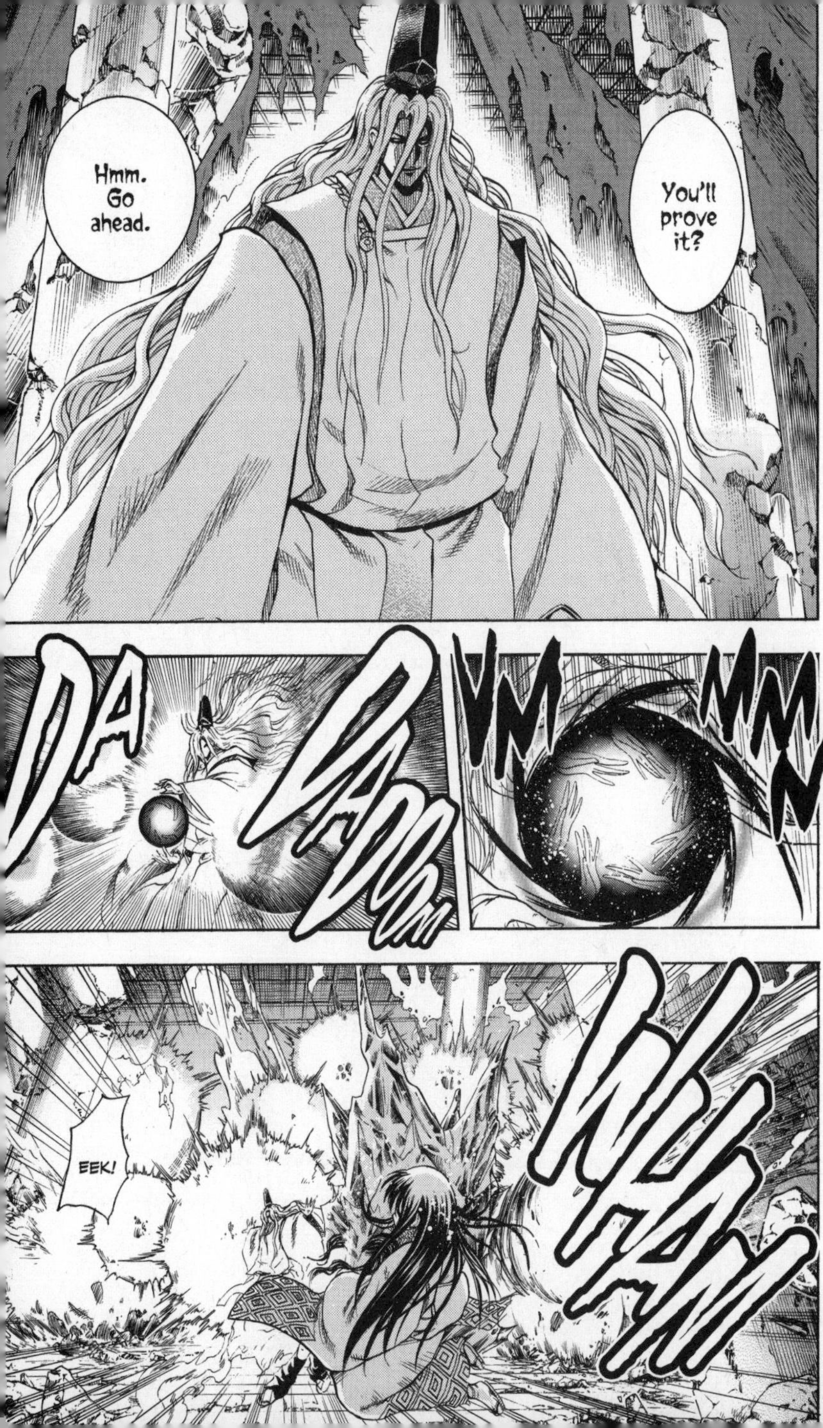
You'll prove it?
Hmm. Go ahead.
VMMMMM
DA
EEK!

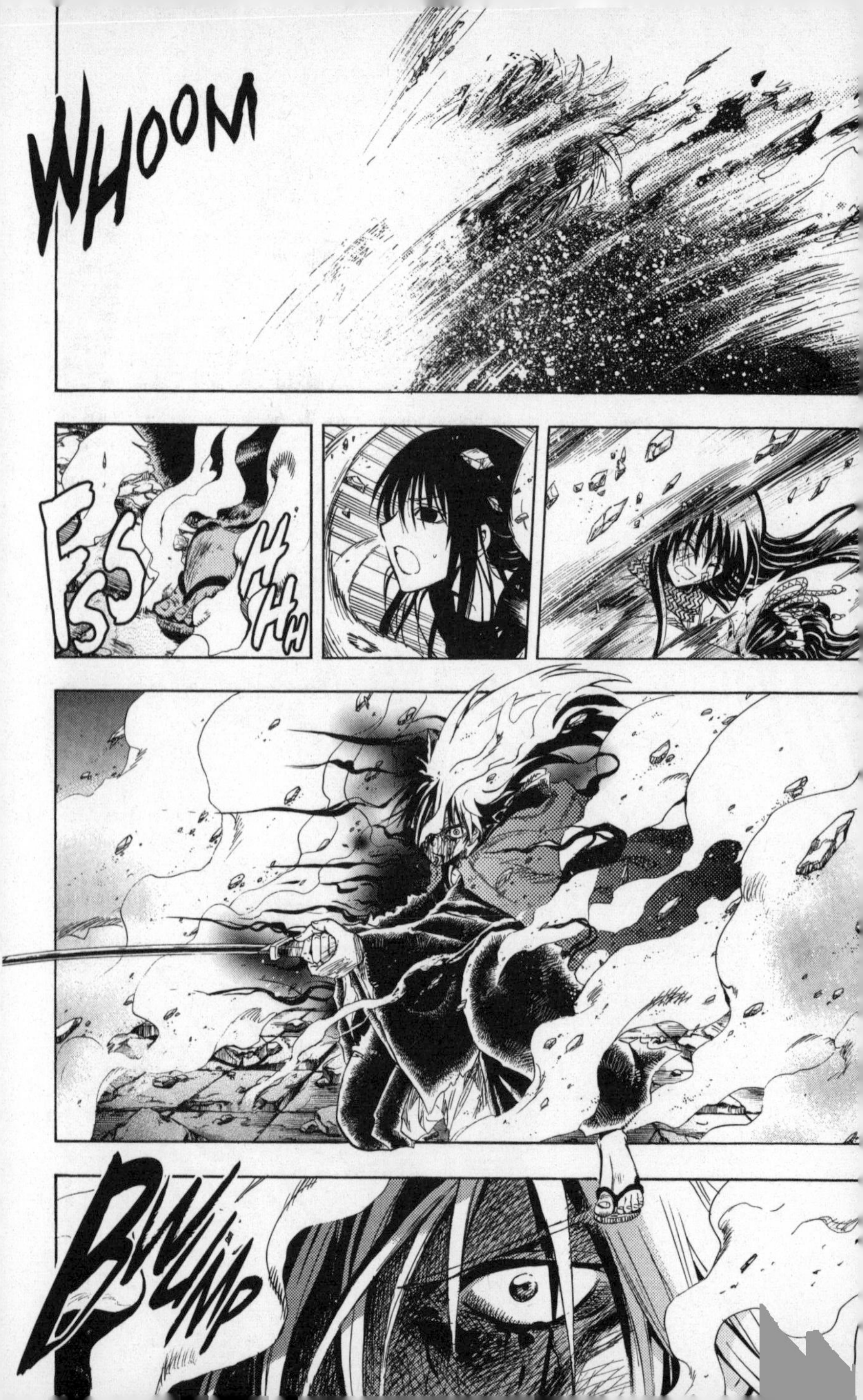
WHOOM
FSSHHH
BUMP

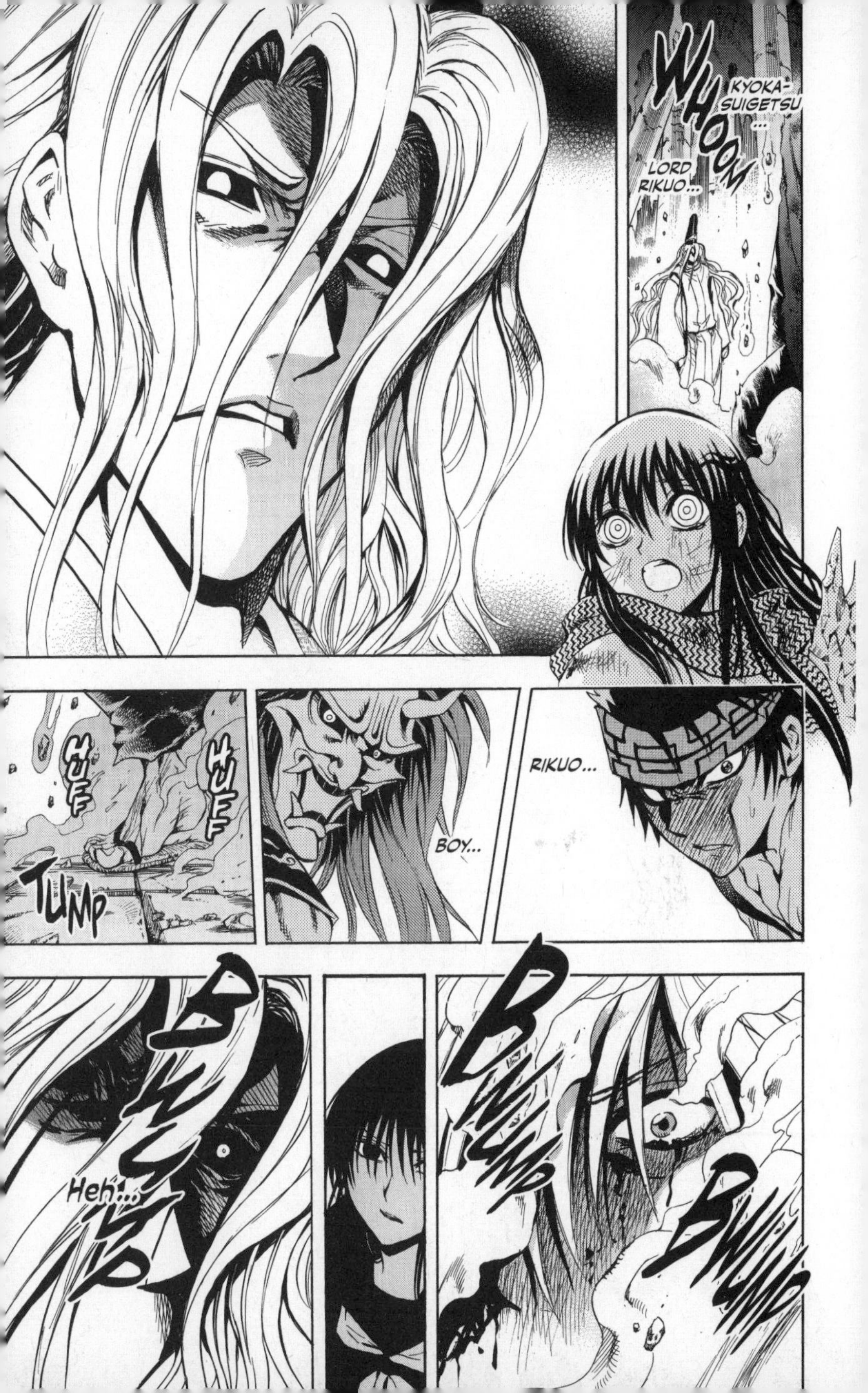
WHOOOM
KYOKA-SUIGETSU...
LORD RIKUO...
RIKUO...
BOY...
HUFF
HUFF
TUMP
BMMMP
BMMMP
BMMMP
Heh...

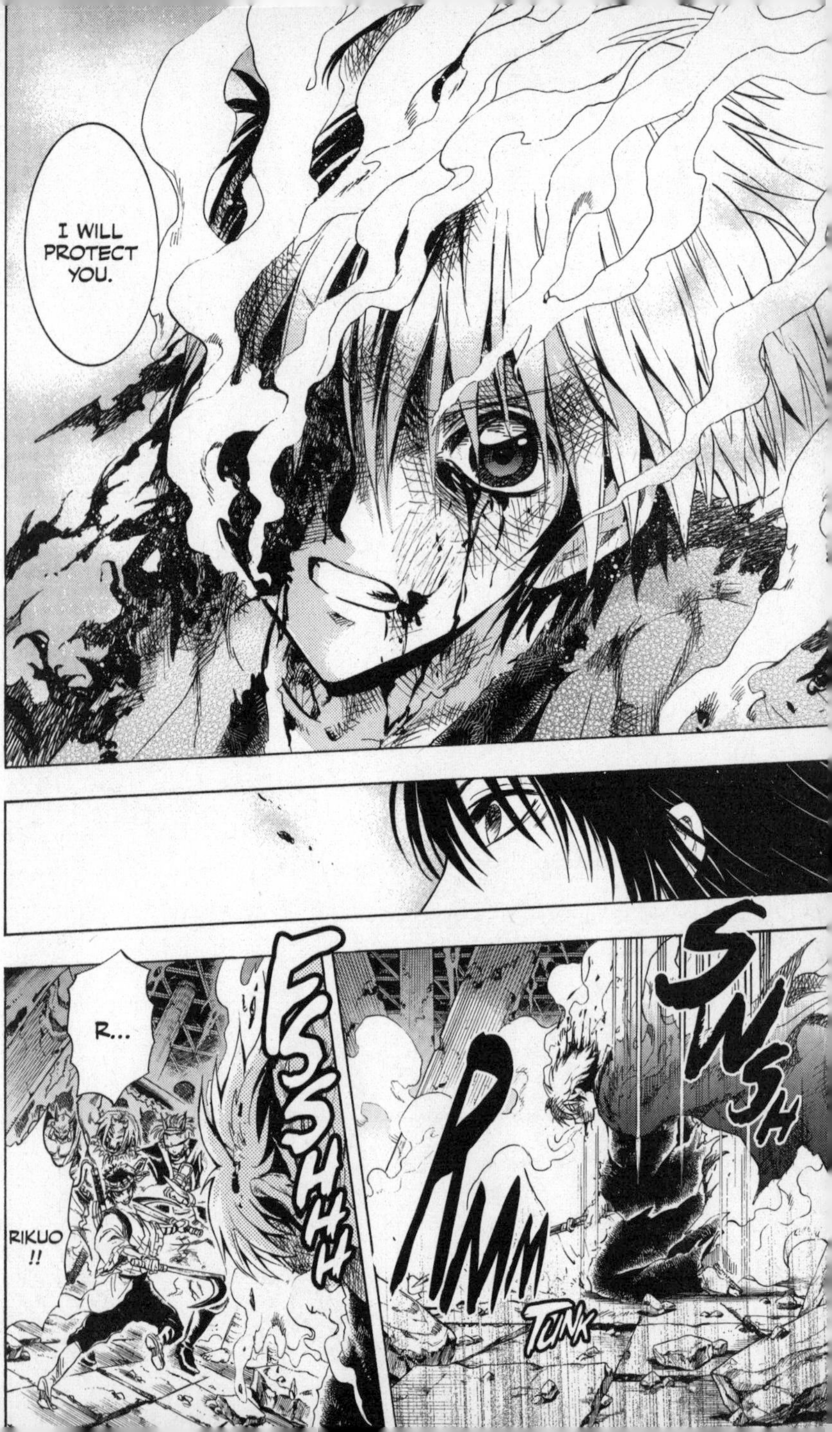
I WILL PROTECT YOU.
SWSH
FSSHHH
R...
RIKUO !!
TCNK

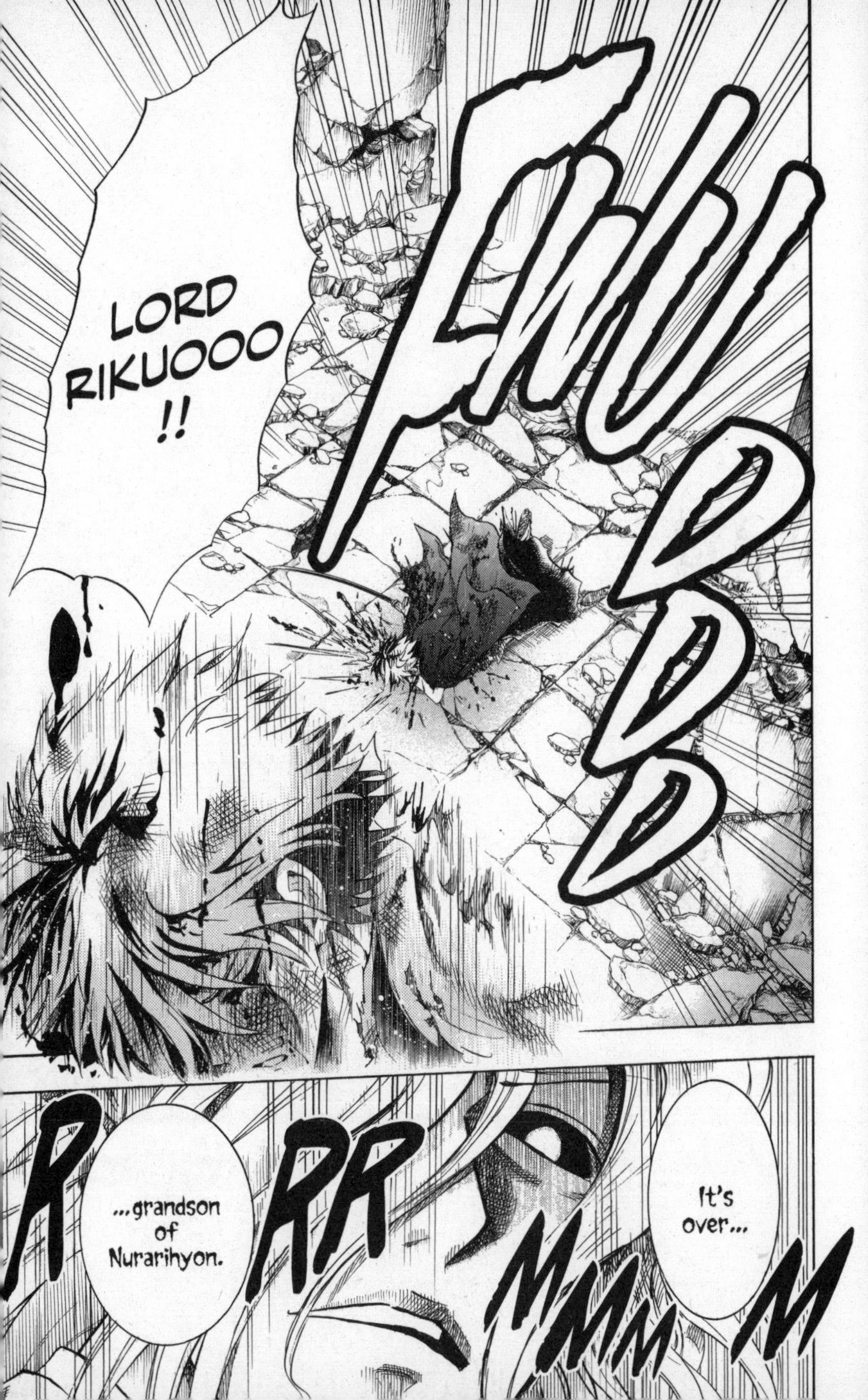
LORD RIKUOOO !!
It's over...
...grandson of Nurarihyon.

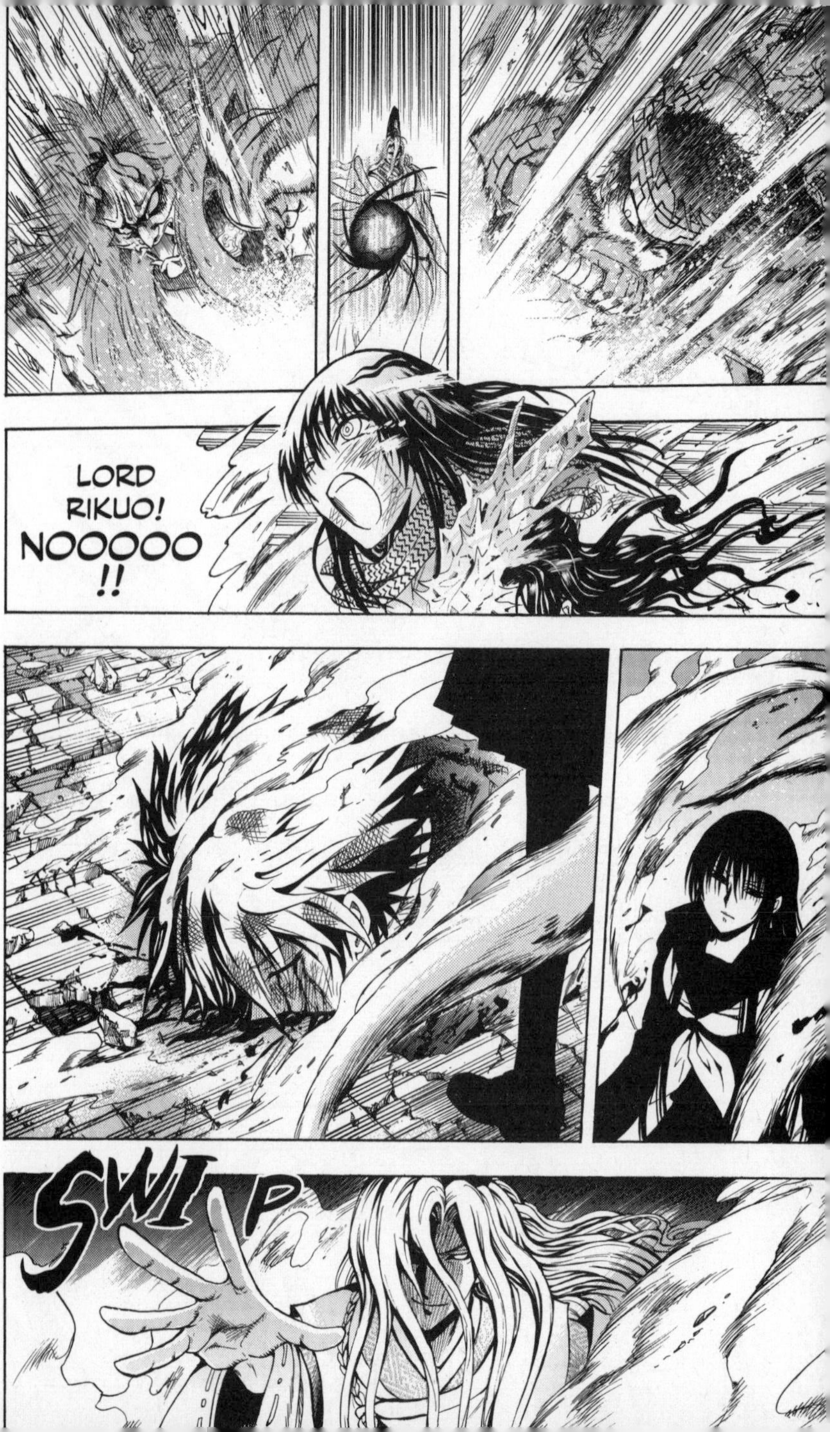
LORD RIKUO! NOOOOO !!
SWIP

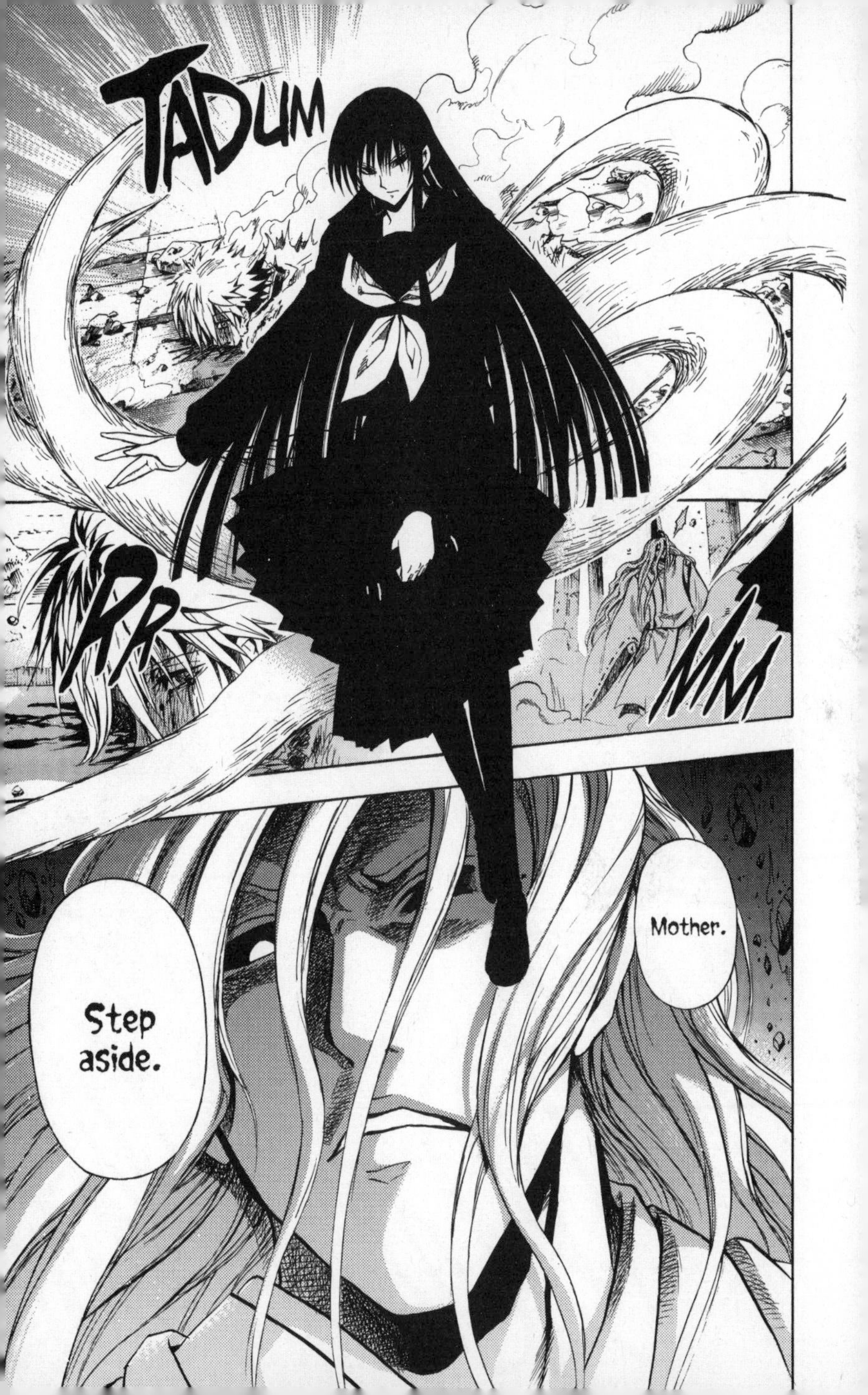
TADUM
MM
RR
Mother.
Step aside.

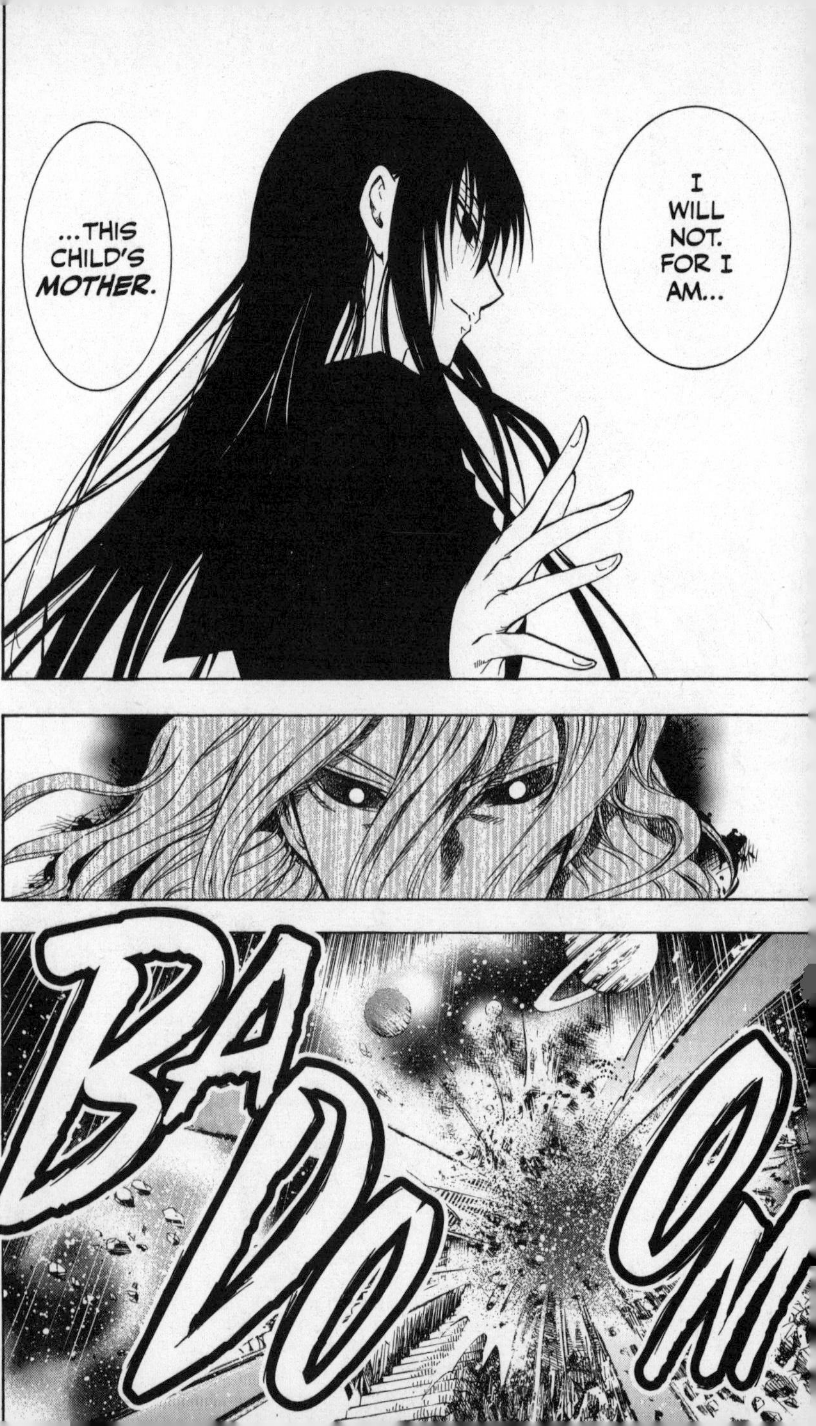
I WILL NOT. FOR I AM...
...THIS CHILD'S *MOTHER*.
BADOGU

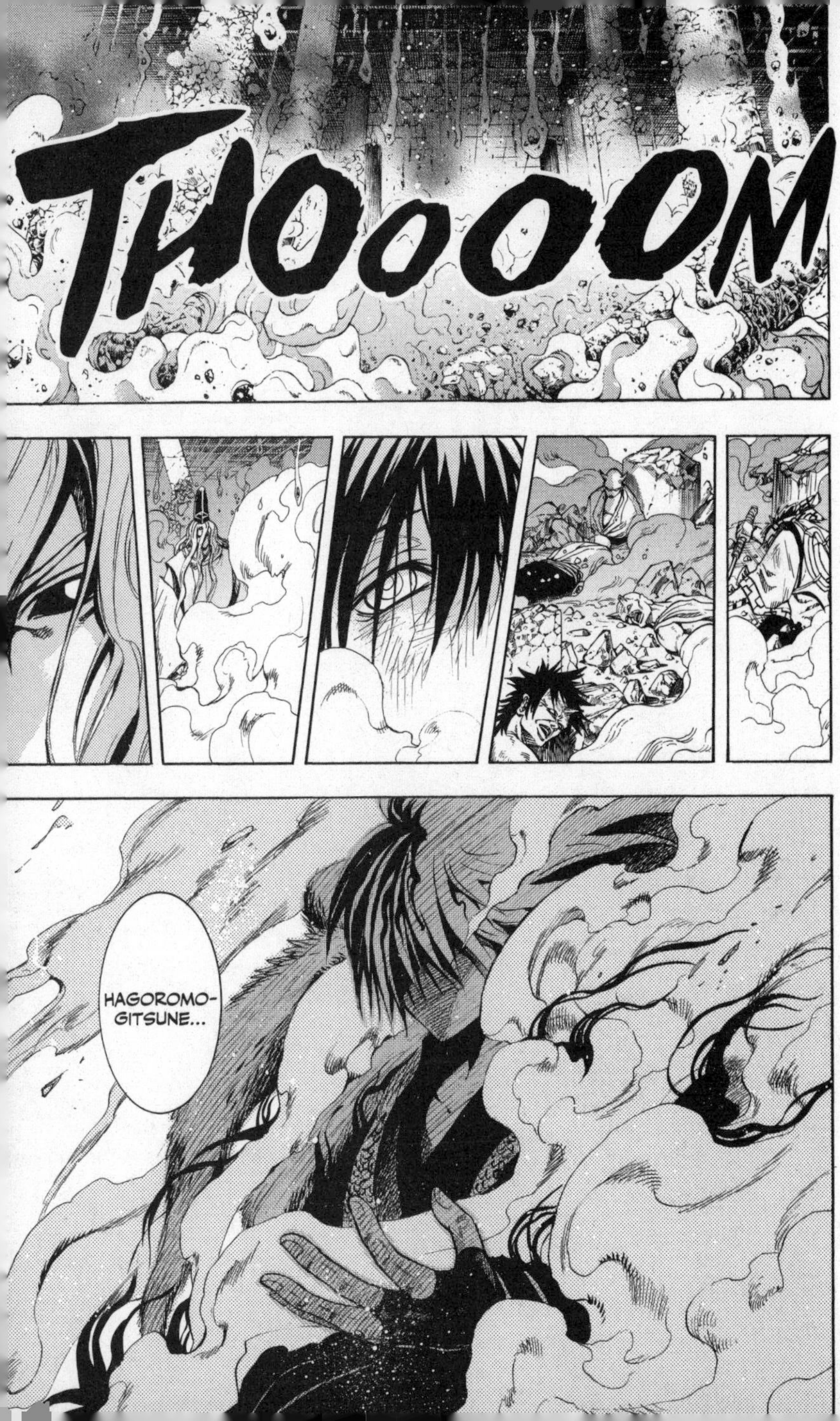
THOOOOM
HAGOROMO-GITSUNE...

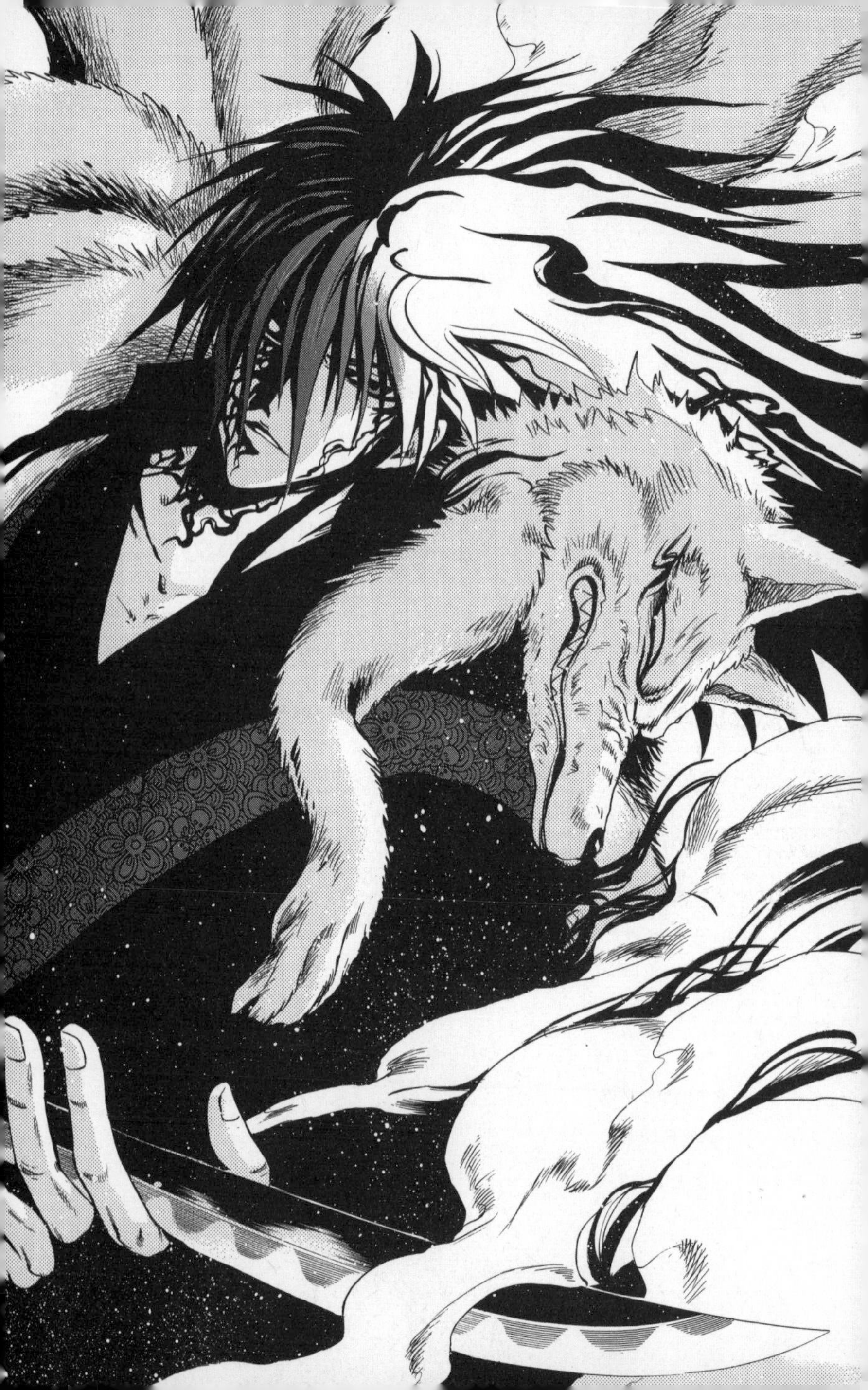

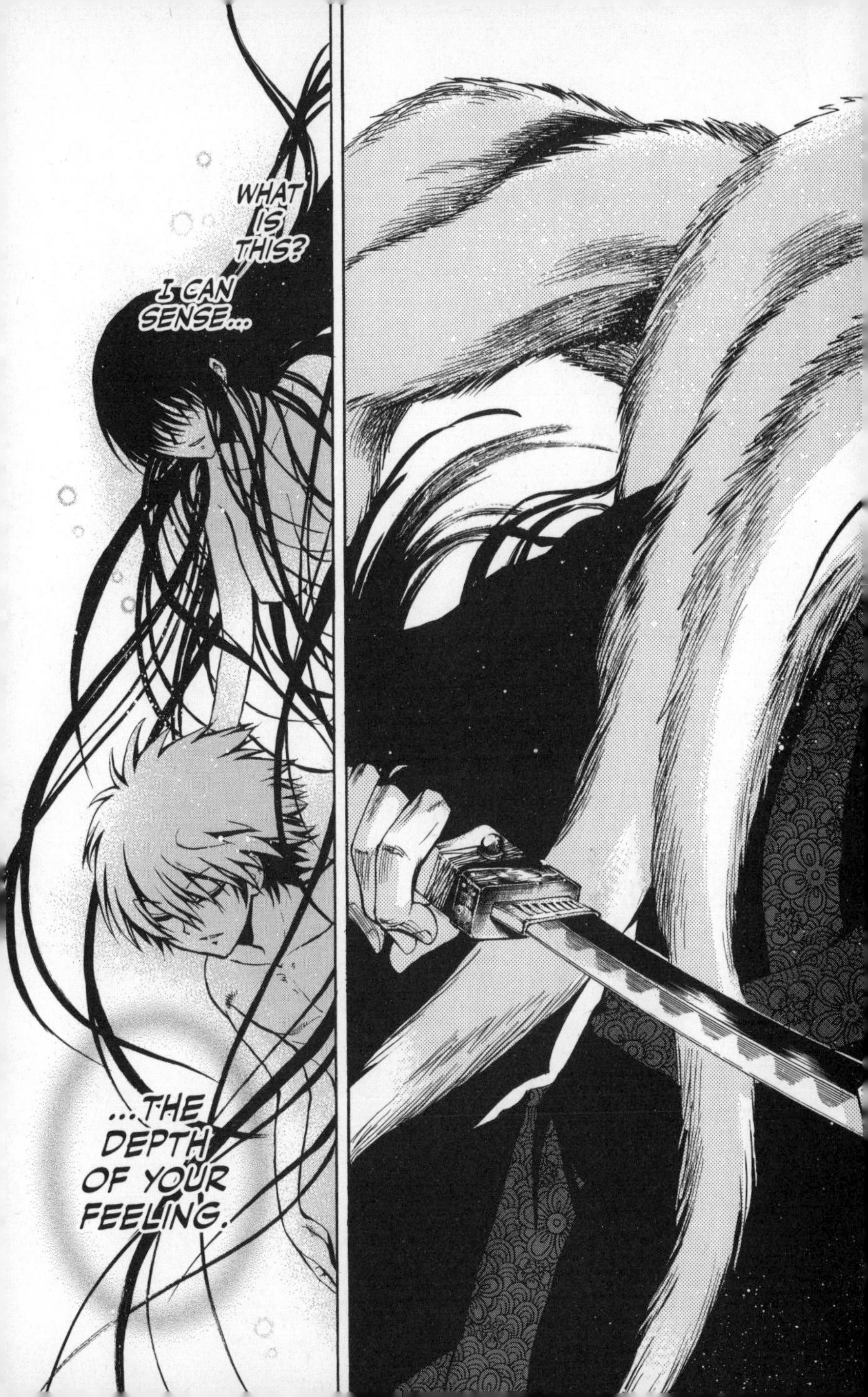
WHAT IS THIS?
I CAN SENSE...
...THE DEPTH OF YOUR FEELING.

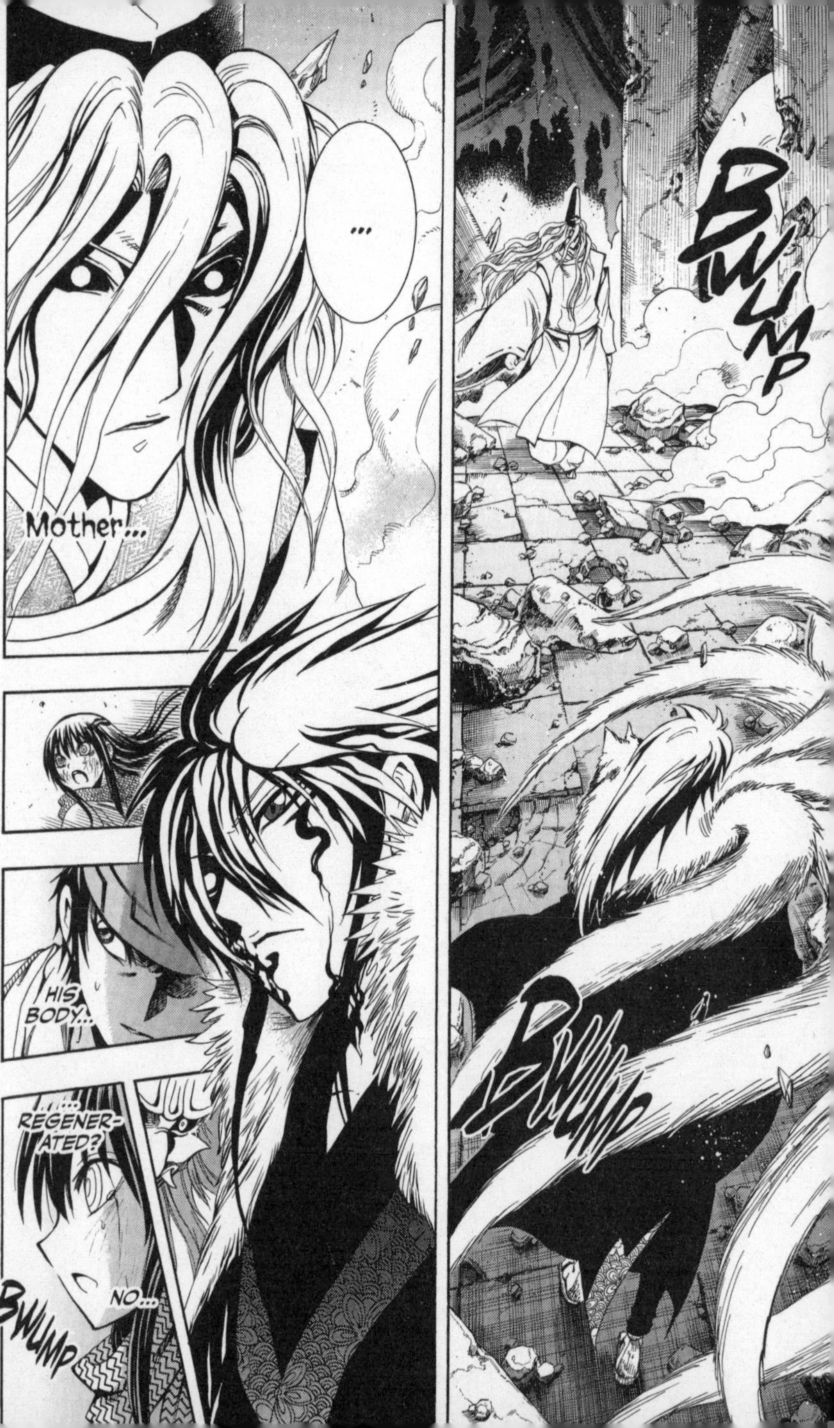
BWUMP
BWUMP
...
Mother...
HIS BODY...
...REGENER-ATED?
NO...
BWUMP

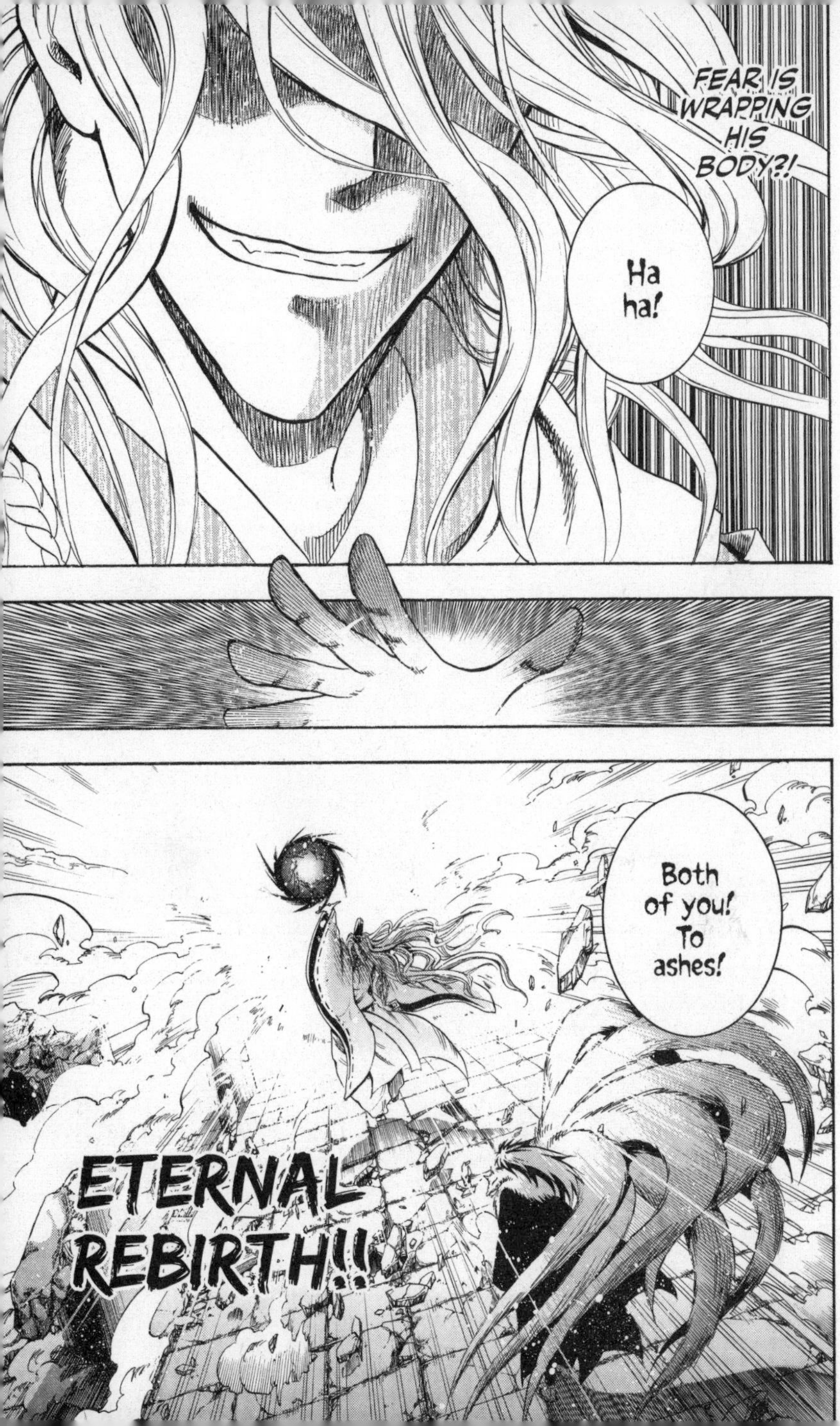
FEAR IS WRAPPING HIS BODY?!
Ha ha!
Both of you! To ashes!
ETERNAL REBIRTH!!

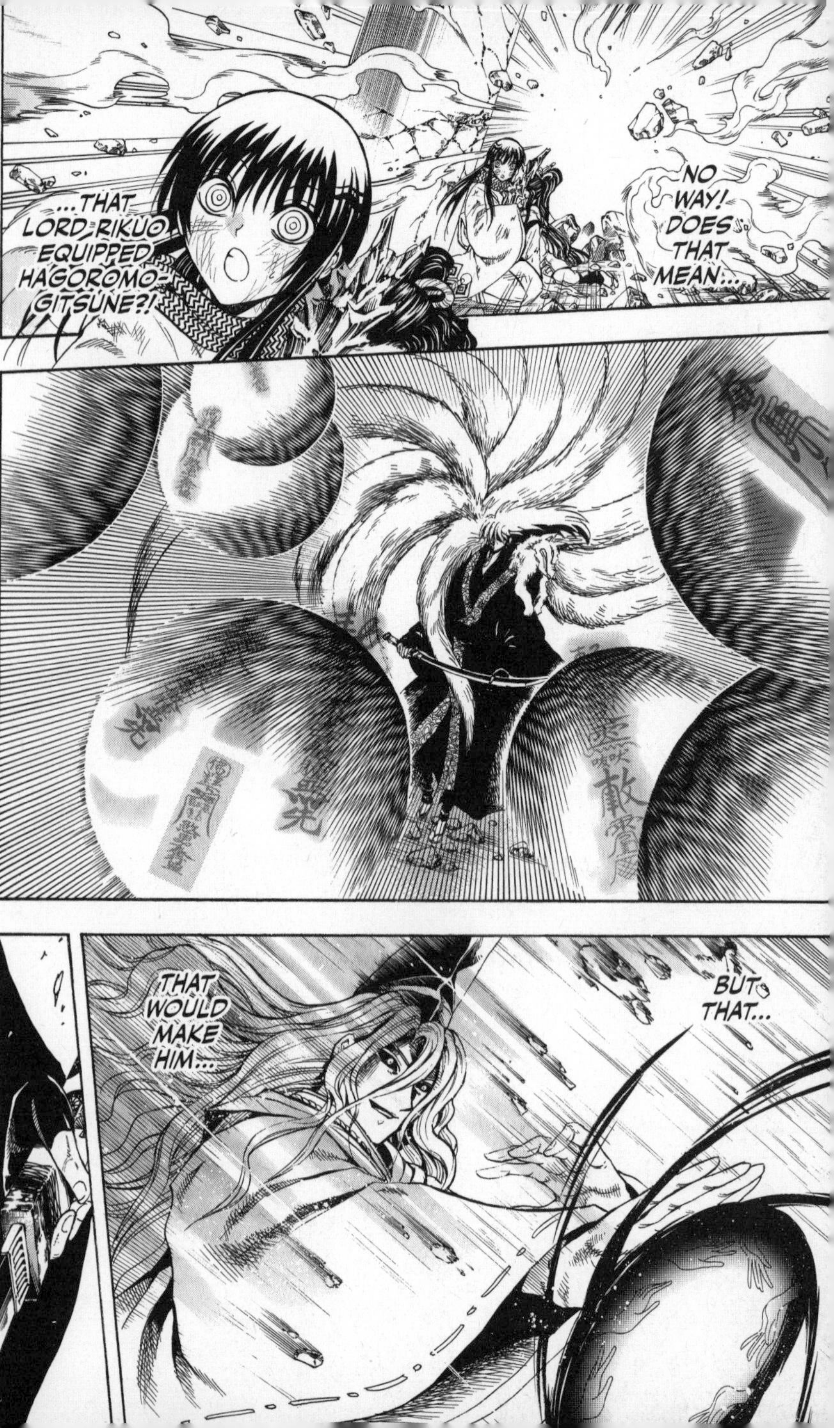
NO WAY! DOES THAT MEAN...
...THAT LORD RIKUO EQUIPPED HAGOROMO-GITSUNE?!
BUT THAT...
THAT WOULD MAKE HIM...

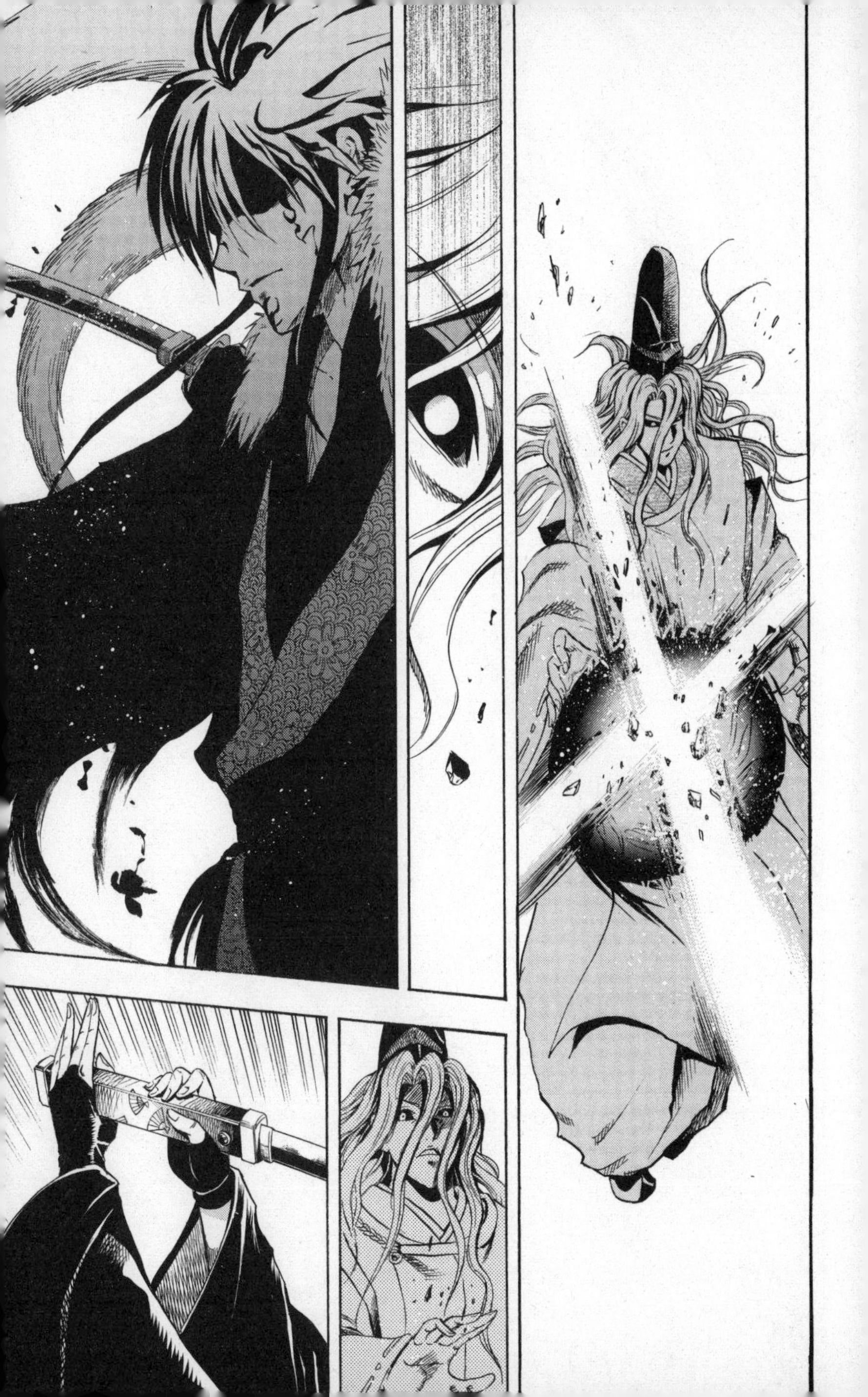

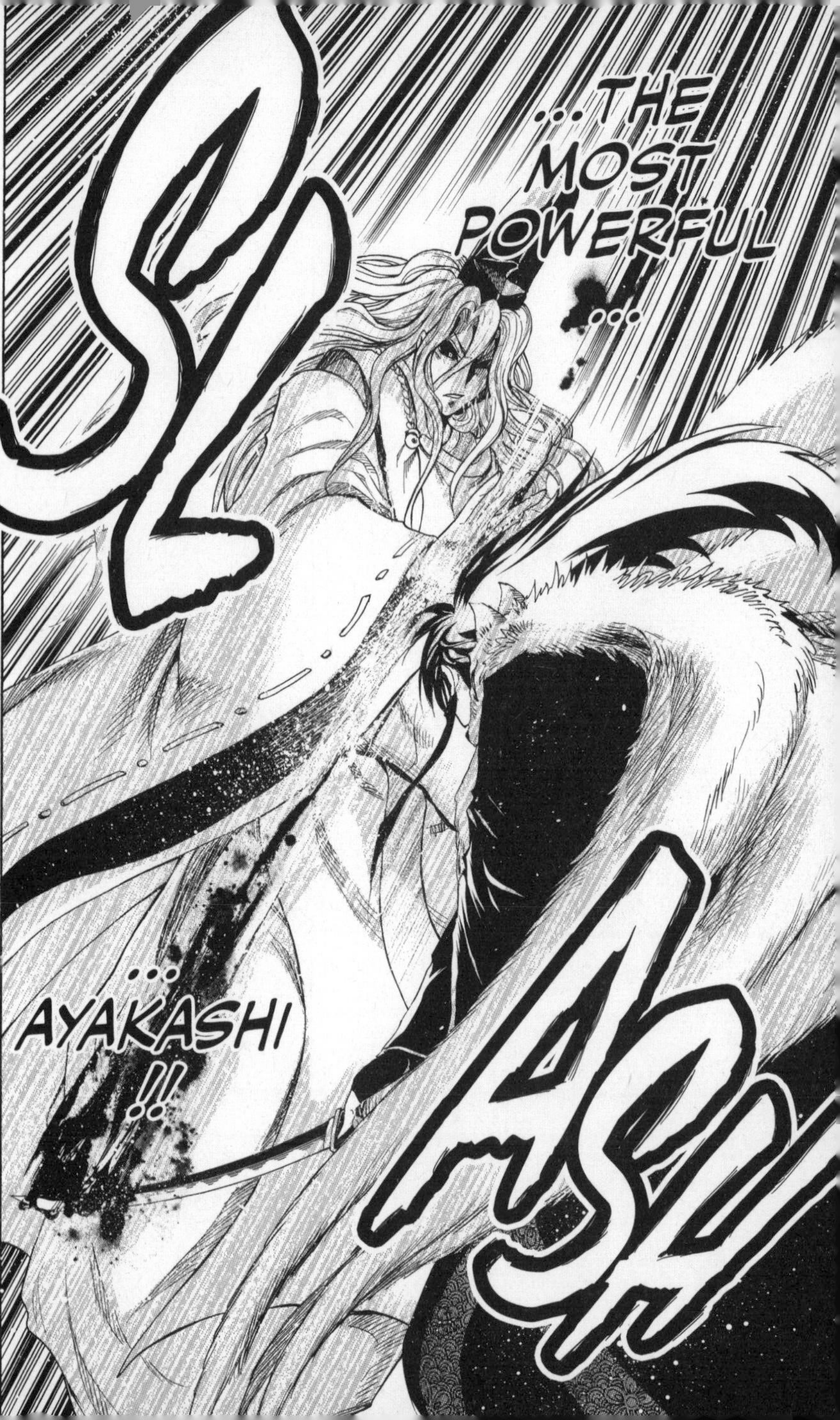
...THE MOST POWERFUL...
...AYAKASHI!!

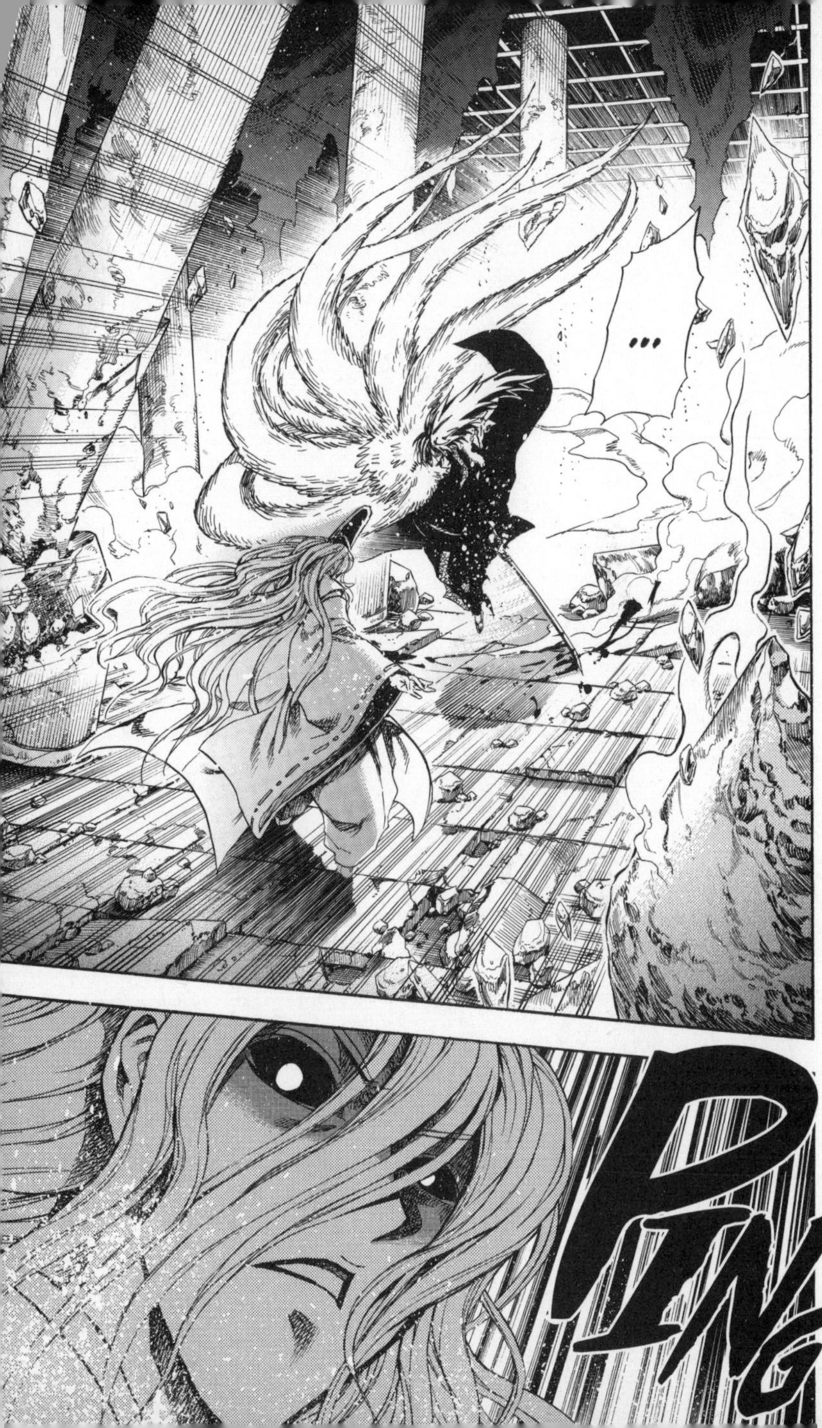
...
DING

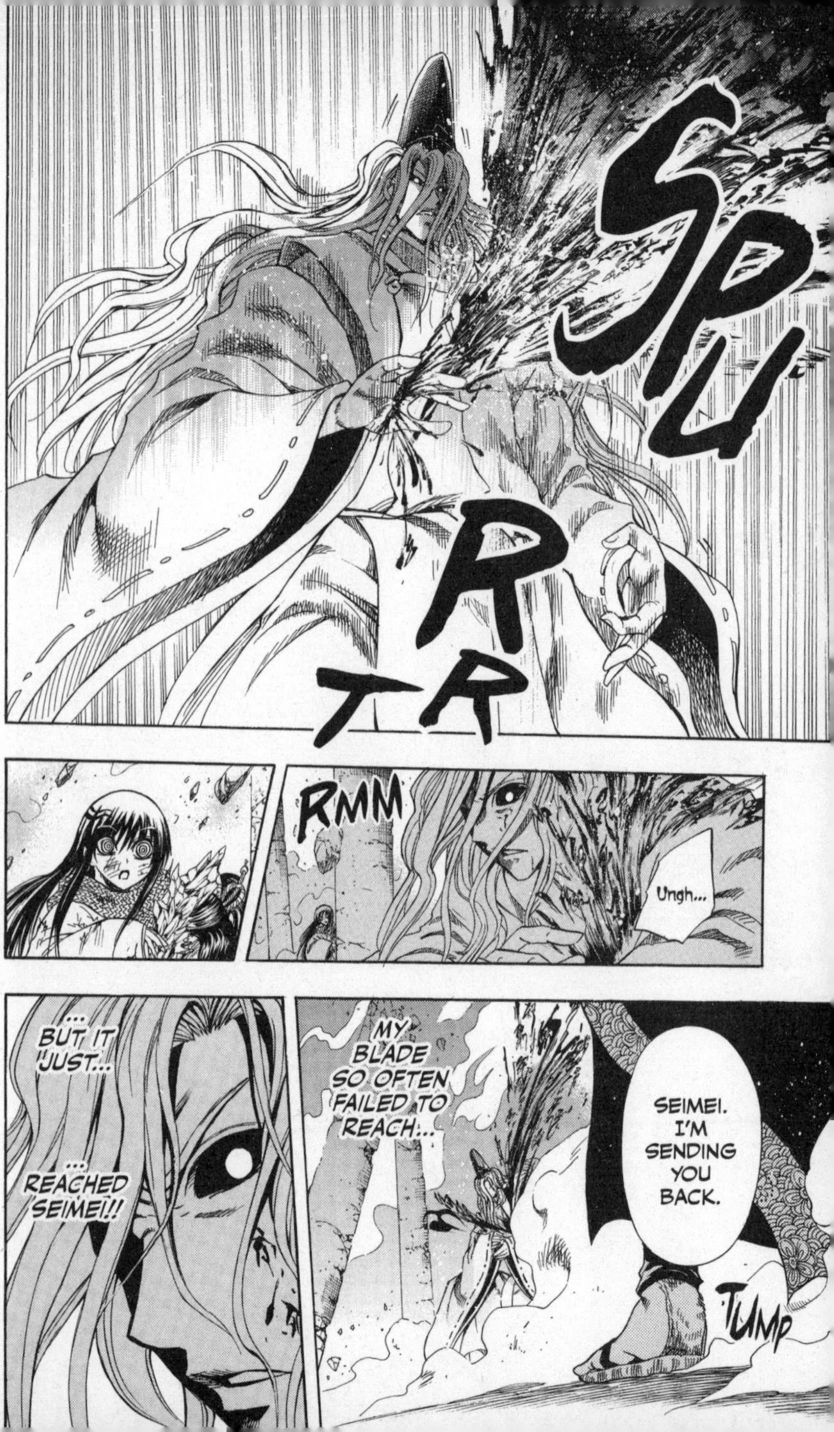
SPU
R
TR
RMM
Ungh...
SEIMEI. I'M SENDING YOU BACK.
MY BLADE SO OFTEN FAILED TO REACH...
TUMP
... BUT IT JUST...
... REACHED SEIMEI!!

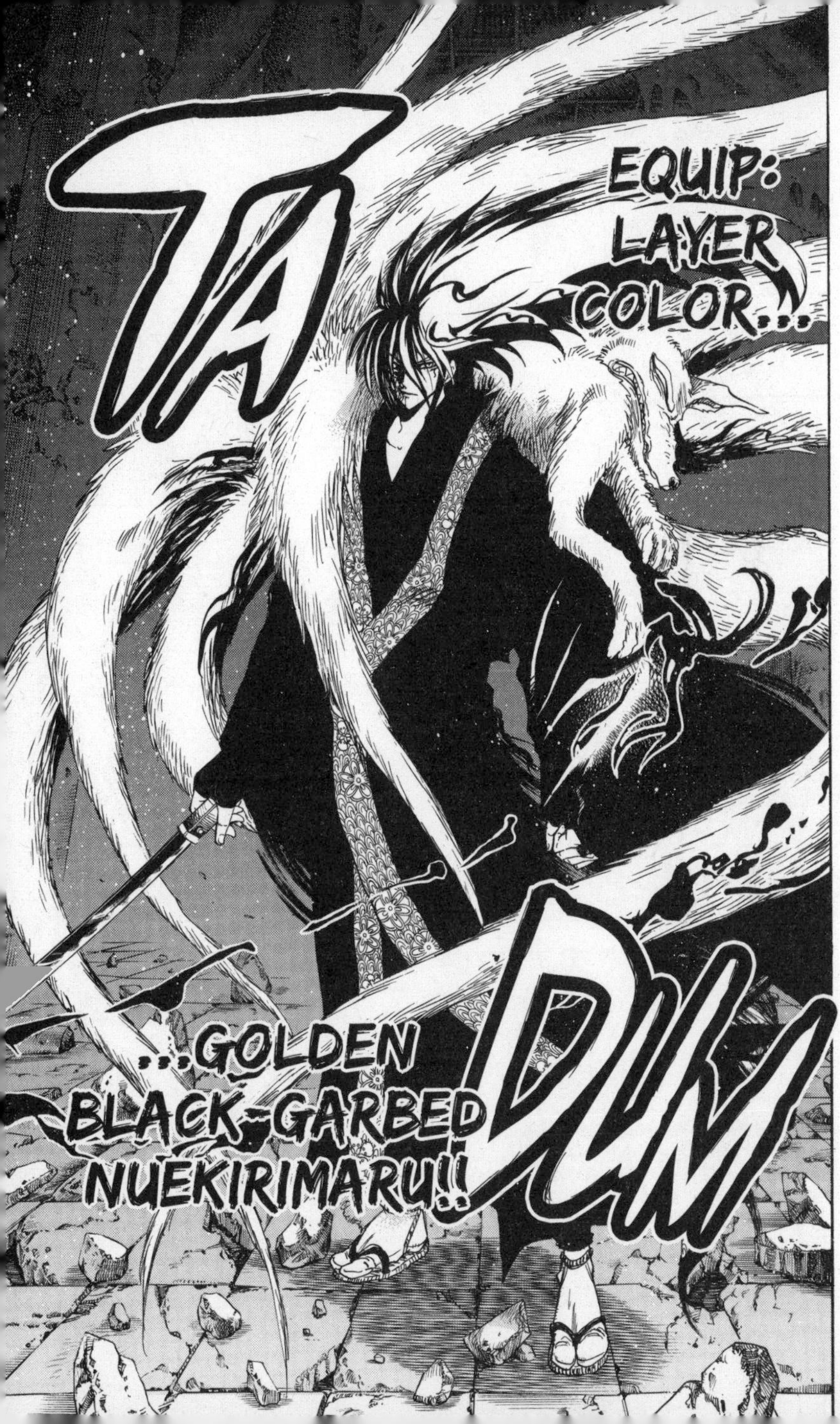
TA
EQUIP: LAYER COLOR...
...GOLDEN BLACK-GARBED NUEKIRIMARU!!
DUN

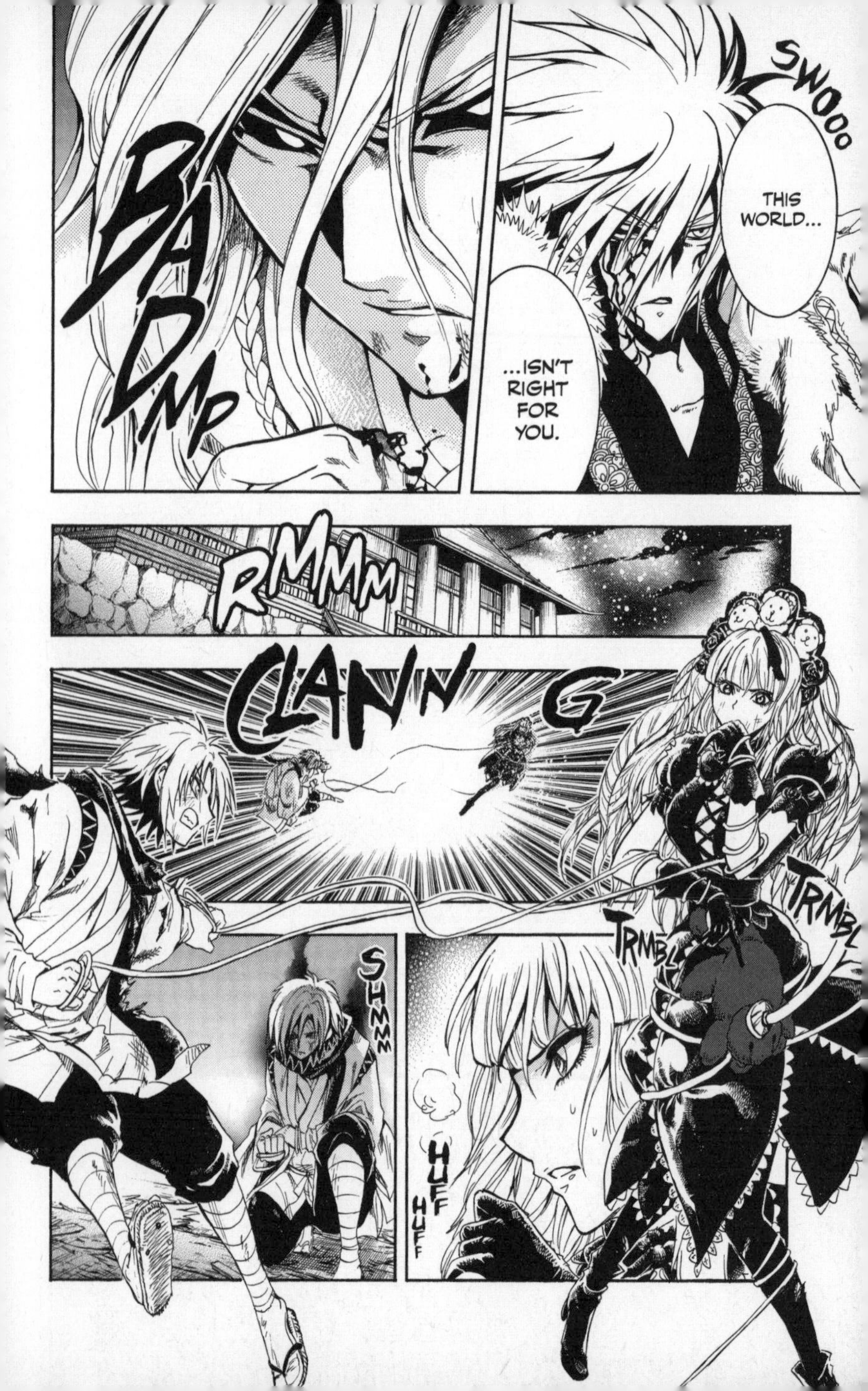
SWOOO
THIS WORLD...
...ISN'T RIGHT FOR YOU.
BADMP
RMMMM
CLANNG
TRMBL
TRMBL
SHMMM
HUFF
HUFF

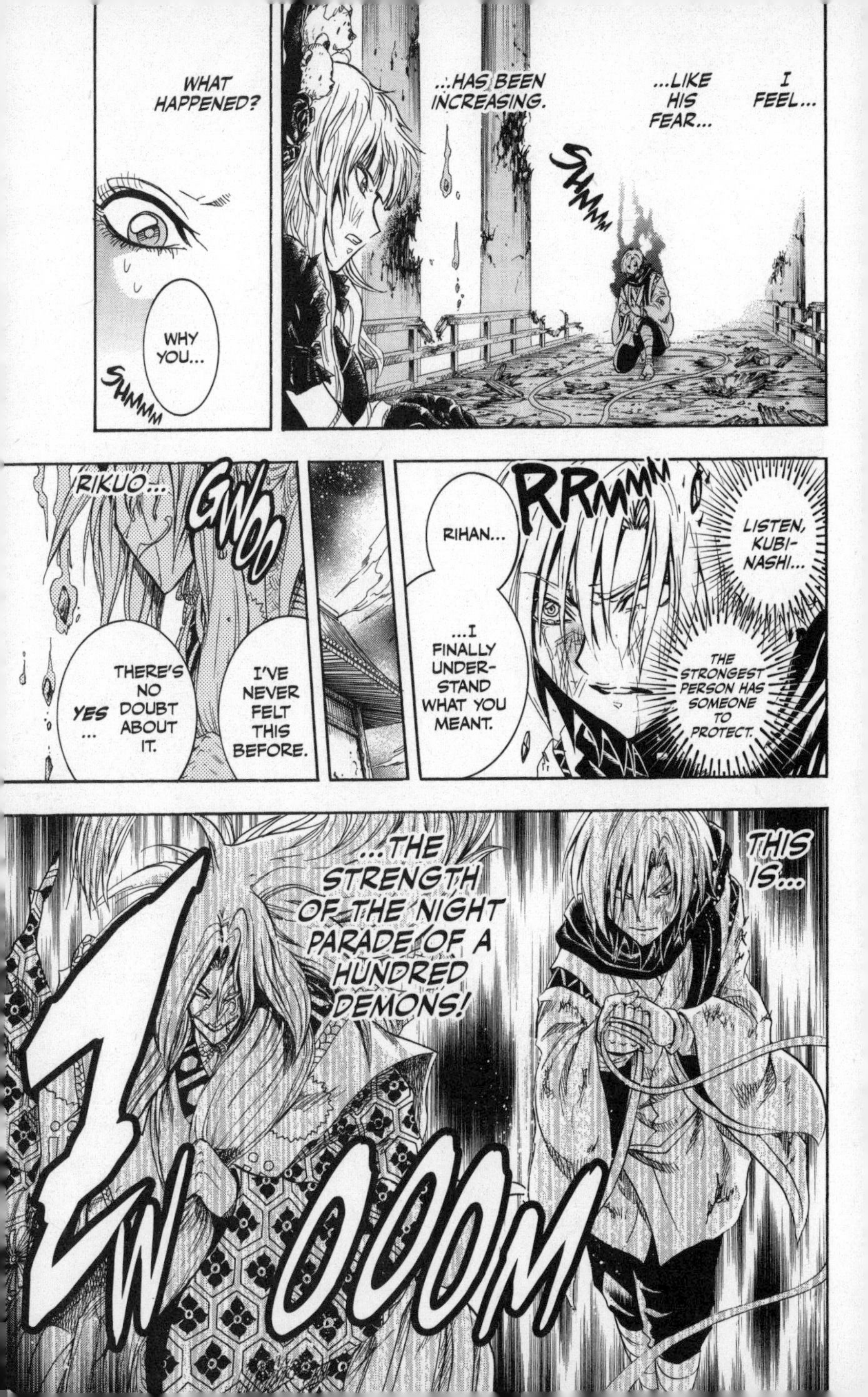
I FEEL...
...LIKE HIS FEAR...
...HAS BEEN INCREASING.
SHMMM
WHAT HAPPENED?
WHY YOU...
SHMMM
LISTEN, KUBINASHI...
THE STRONGEST PERSON HAS SOMEONE TO PROTECT.
RRMMM
RIHAN...
...I FINALLY UNDERSTAND WHAT YOU MEANT.
RIKUO...
GWOOO
I'VE NEVER FELT THIS BEFORE.
THERE'S NO DOUBT ABOUT IT.
YES...
THIS IS...
...THE STRENGTH OF THE NIGHT PARADE OF A HUNDRED DEMONS!
ZWOOOM

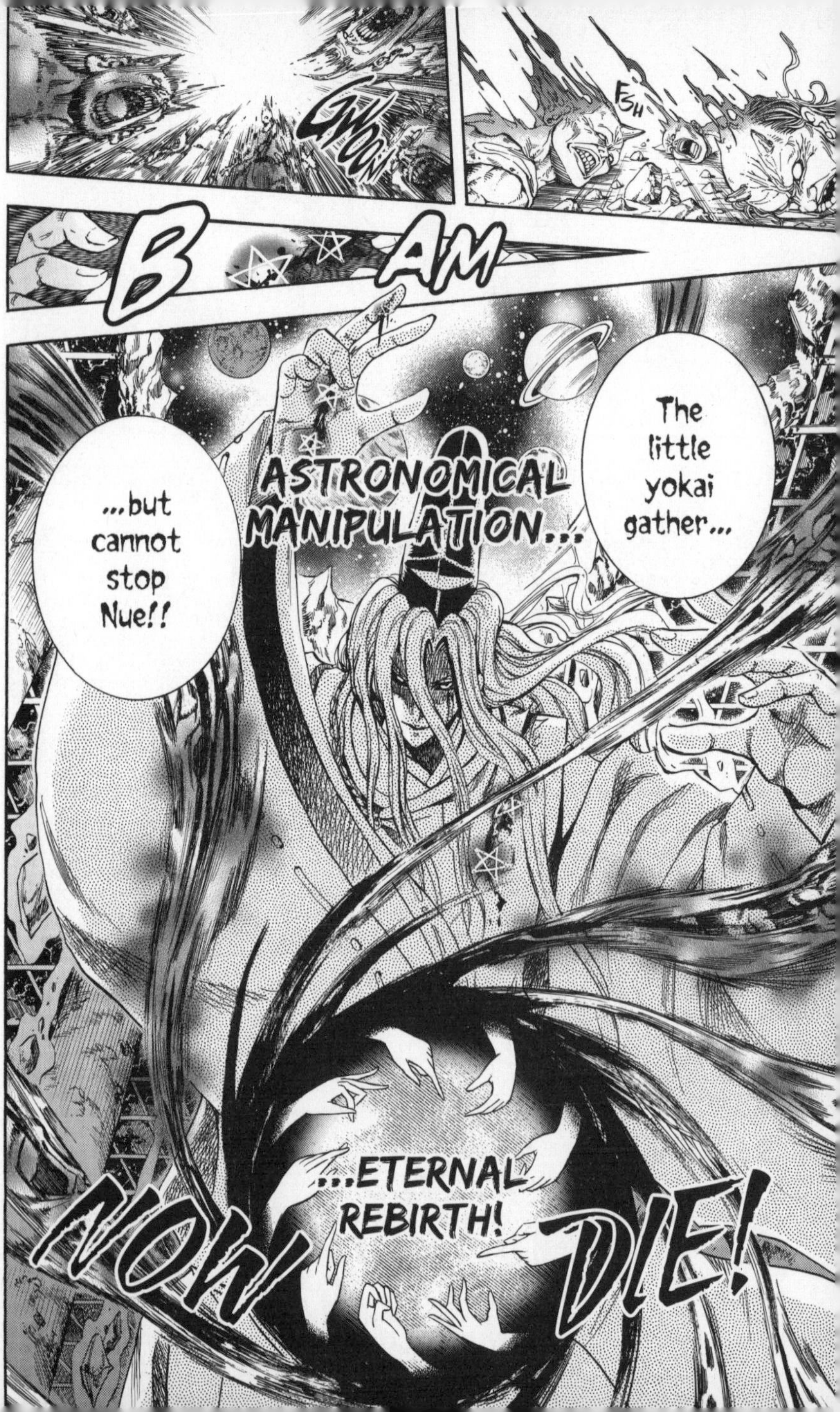
FSH
GWOOON
BAM
The little yokai gather...
...but cannot stop Nue!!
ASTRONOMICAL MANIPULATION...
...ETERNAL REBIRTH!
NOW DIE!

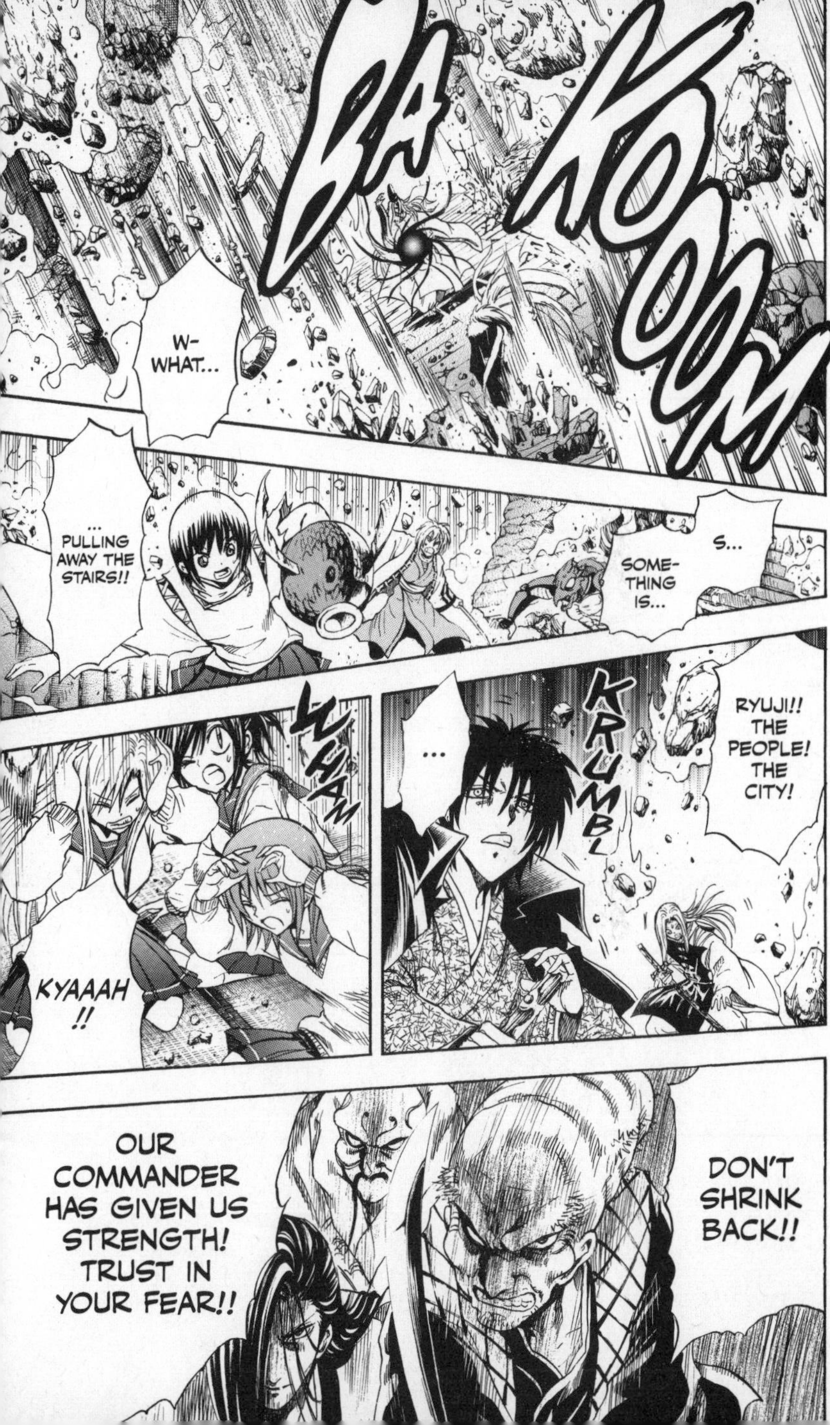
BA KOOOM
W-WHAT...
S...
SOME-THING IS...
... PULLING AWAY THE STAIRS!!
RYUJI!! THE PEOPLE! THE CITY!
KRUMBL
...
WHAM
KYAAAH!!
DON'T SHRINK BACK!!
OUR COMMANDER HAS GIVEN US STRENGTH! TRUST IN YOUR FEAR!!

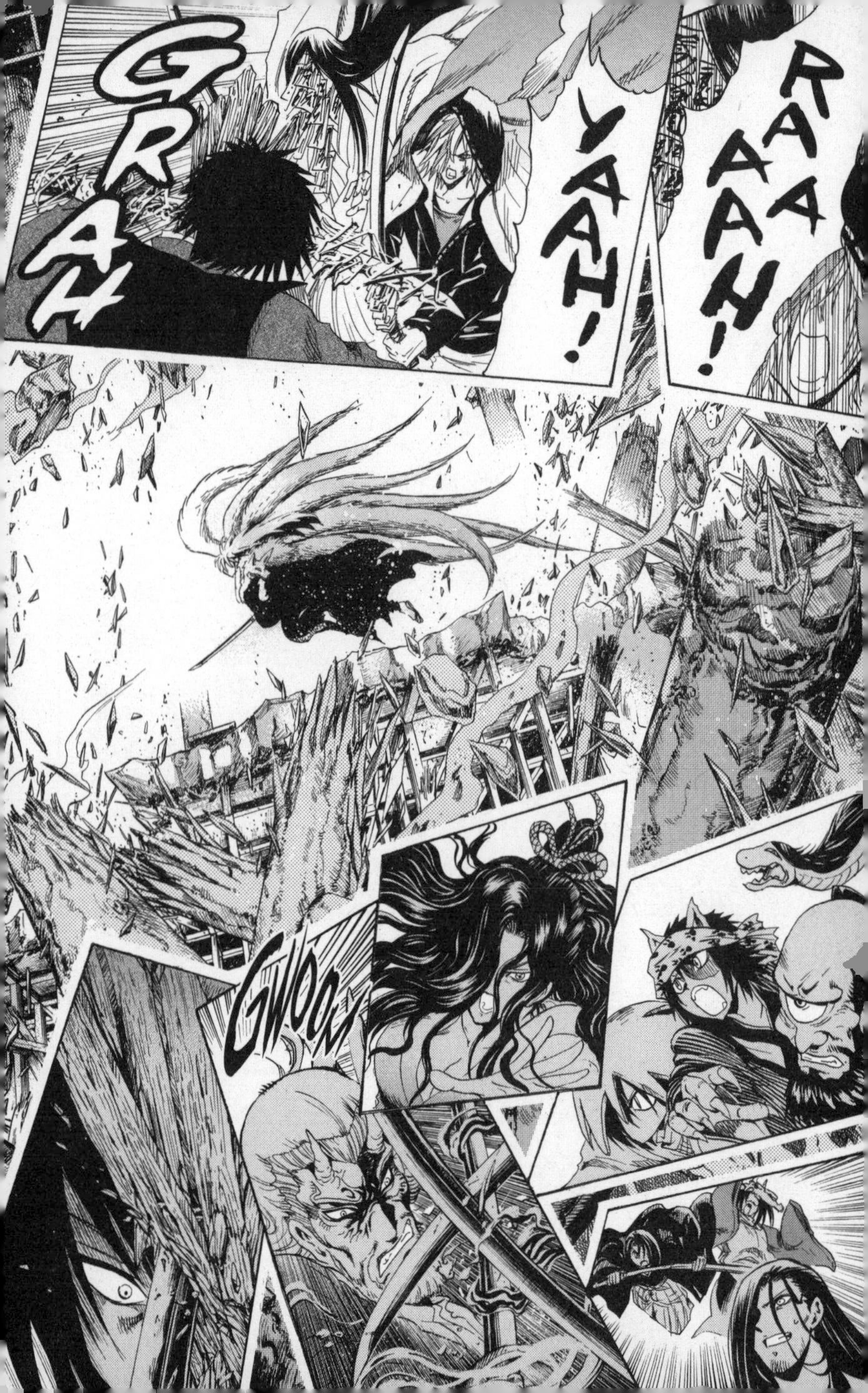
RAAAAH!
YAAH!
GRAH
GWOOM

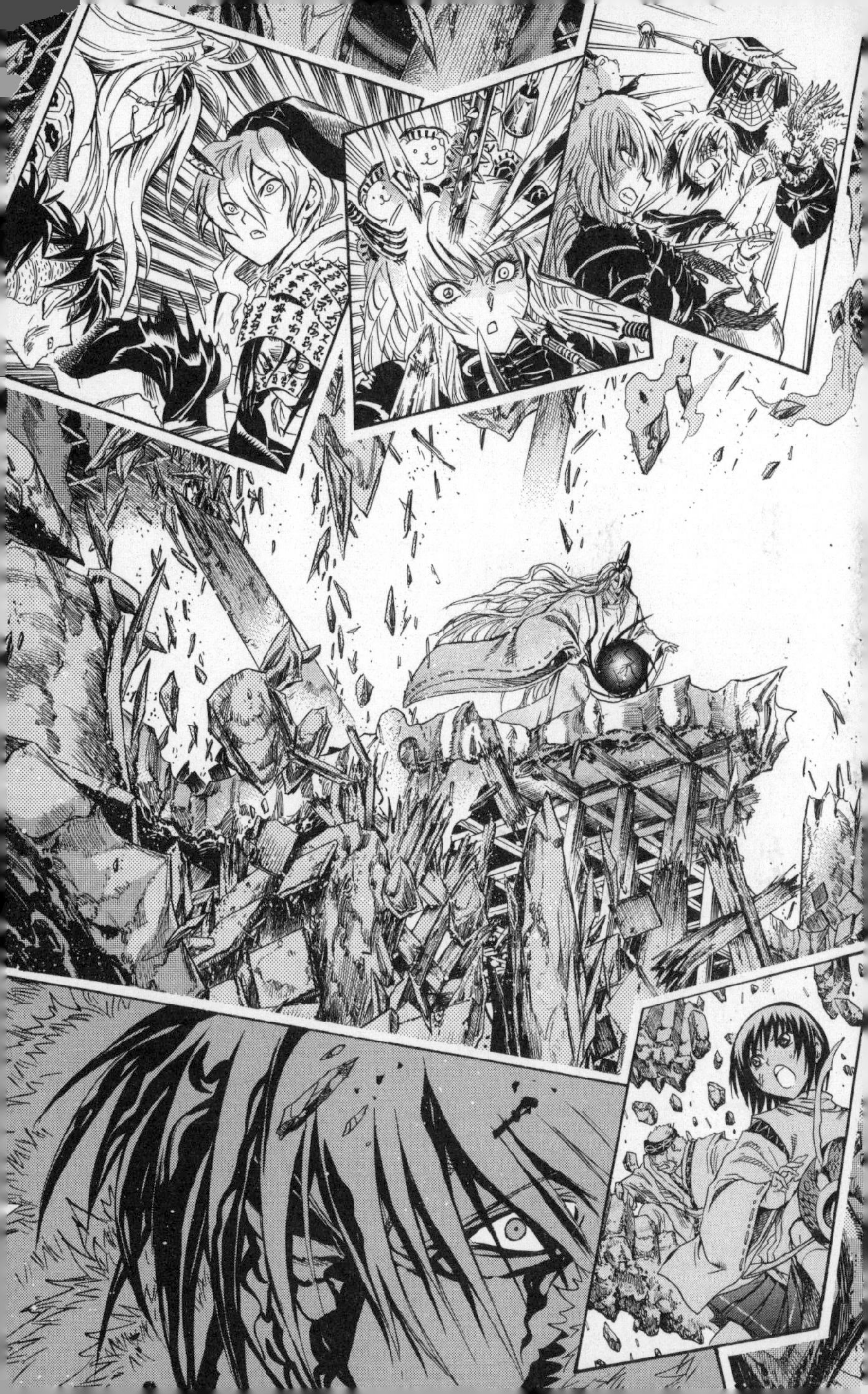

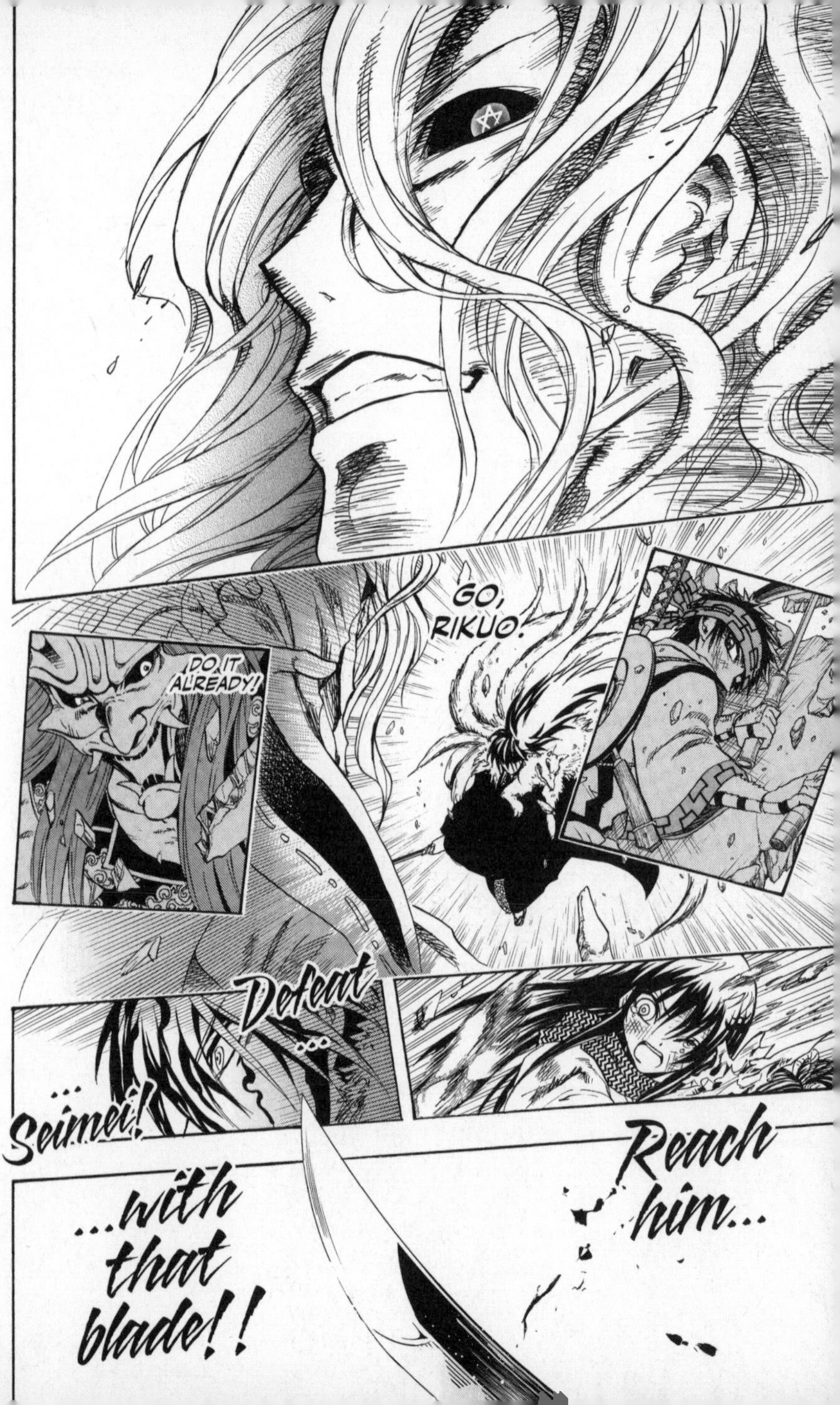
GO, RIKUO!
DO IT ALREADY!
Defeat...
...Seimei!
Reach him...
...with that blade!!

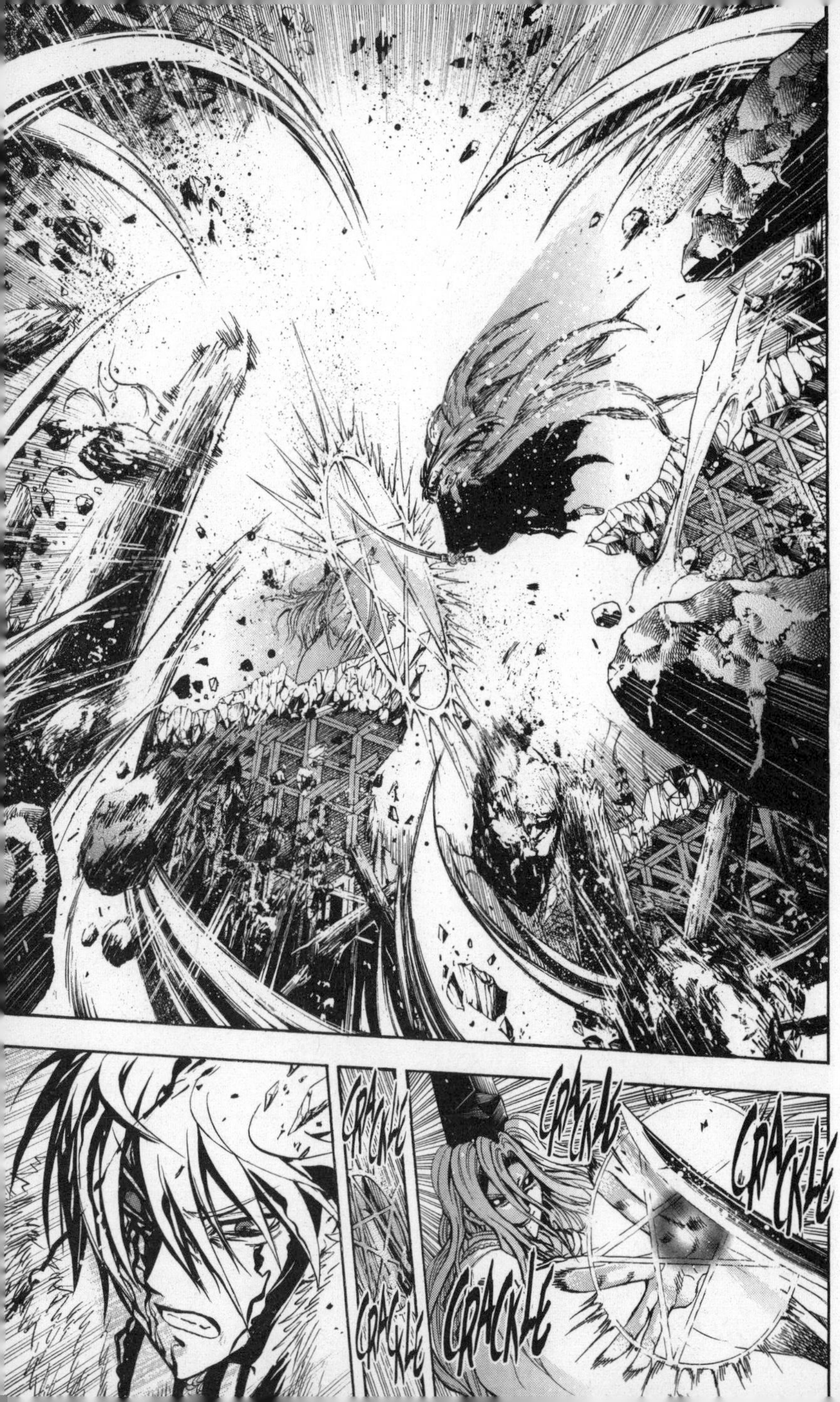
CRACKLE
CRACKLE
CRACKLE
CRACKLE
CRACKLE

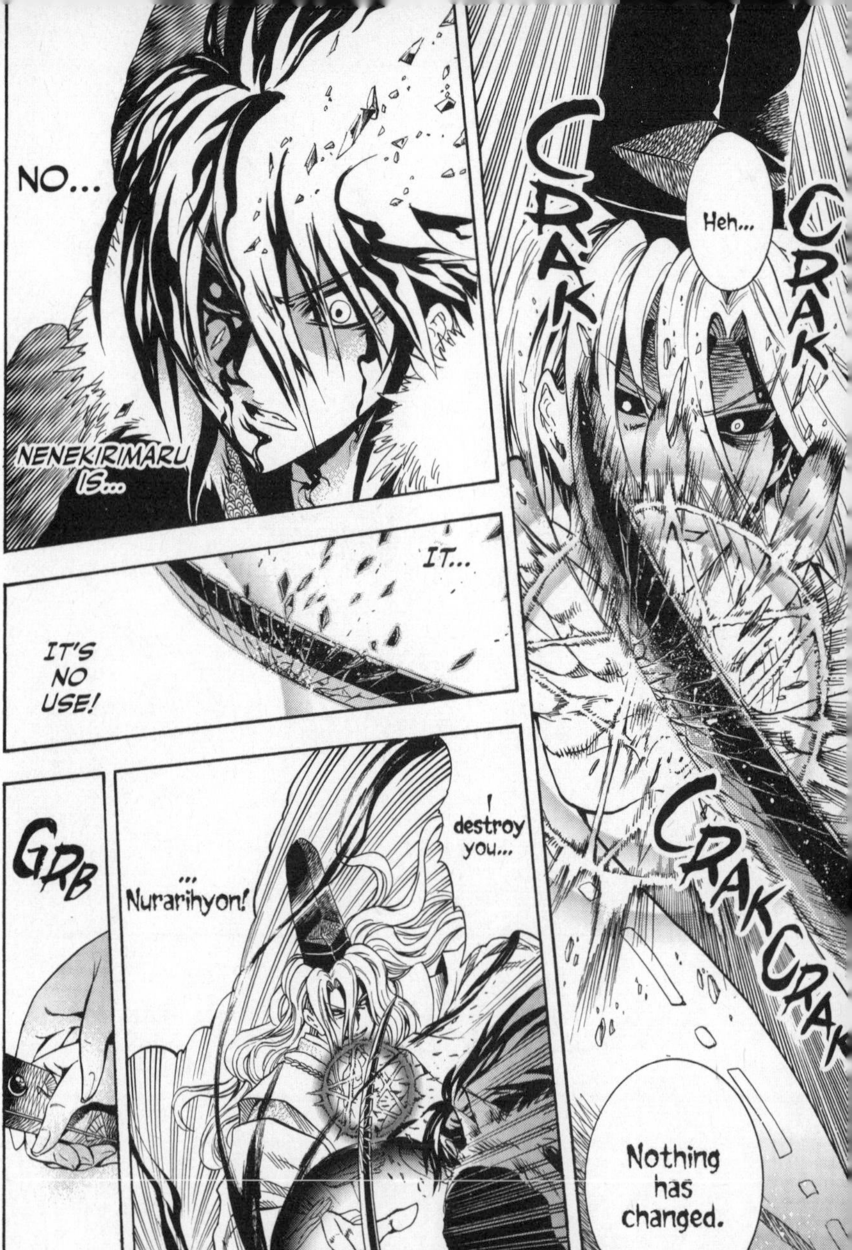
CRAK
Heh...
CRAK
CRAKCRAKCRAK
Nothing has changed.
NO...
NENEKIRIMARU IS...
IT...
IT'S NO USE!
I destroy you...
... Nurarihyon!
GDRB

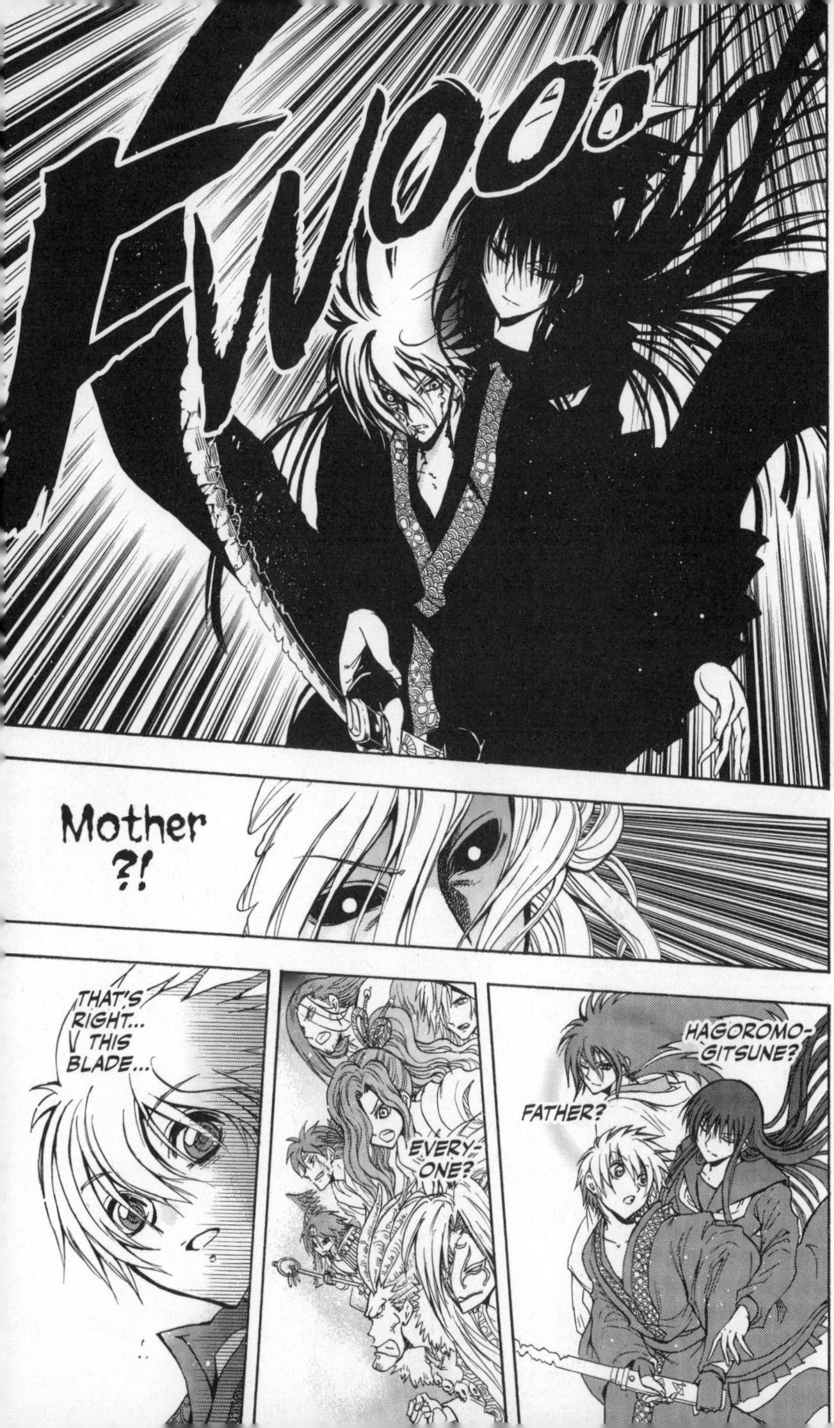
FWOOSH
Mother ?!
HAGOROMO-GITSUNE?
FATHER?
EVERY-ONE?
THAT'S RIGHT... THIS BLADE...

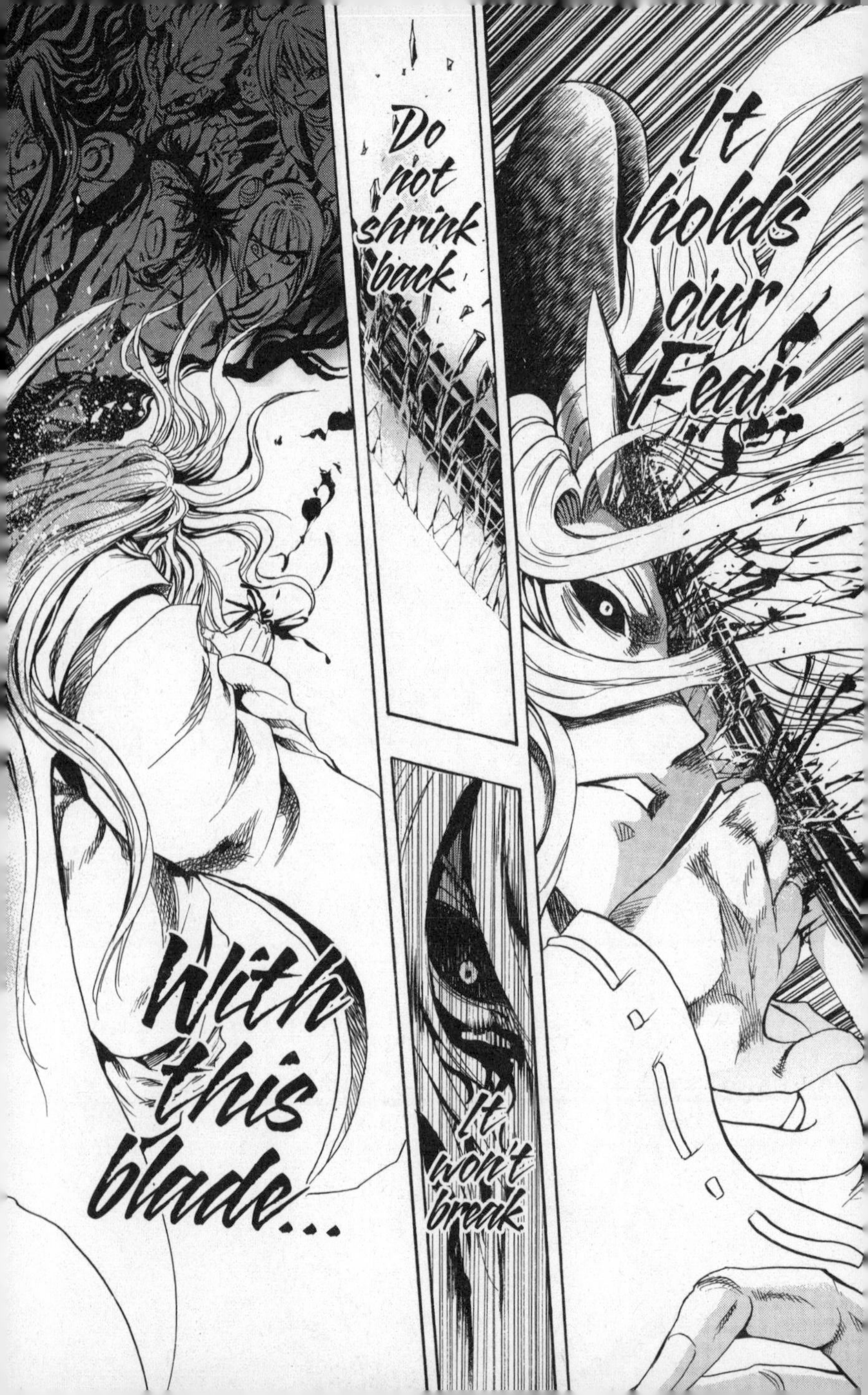
It holds our Fear
Do not shrink back
It won't break
With this blade...

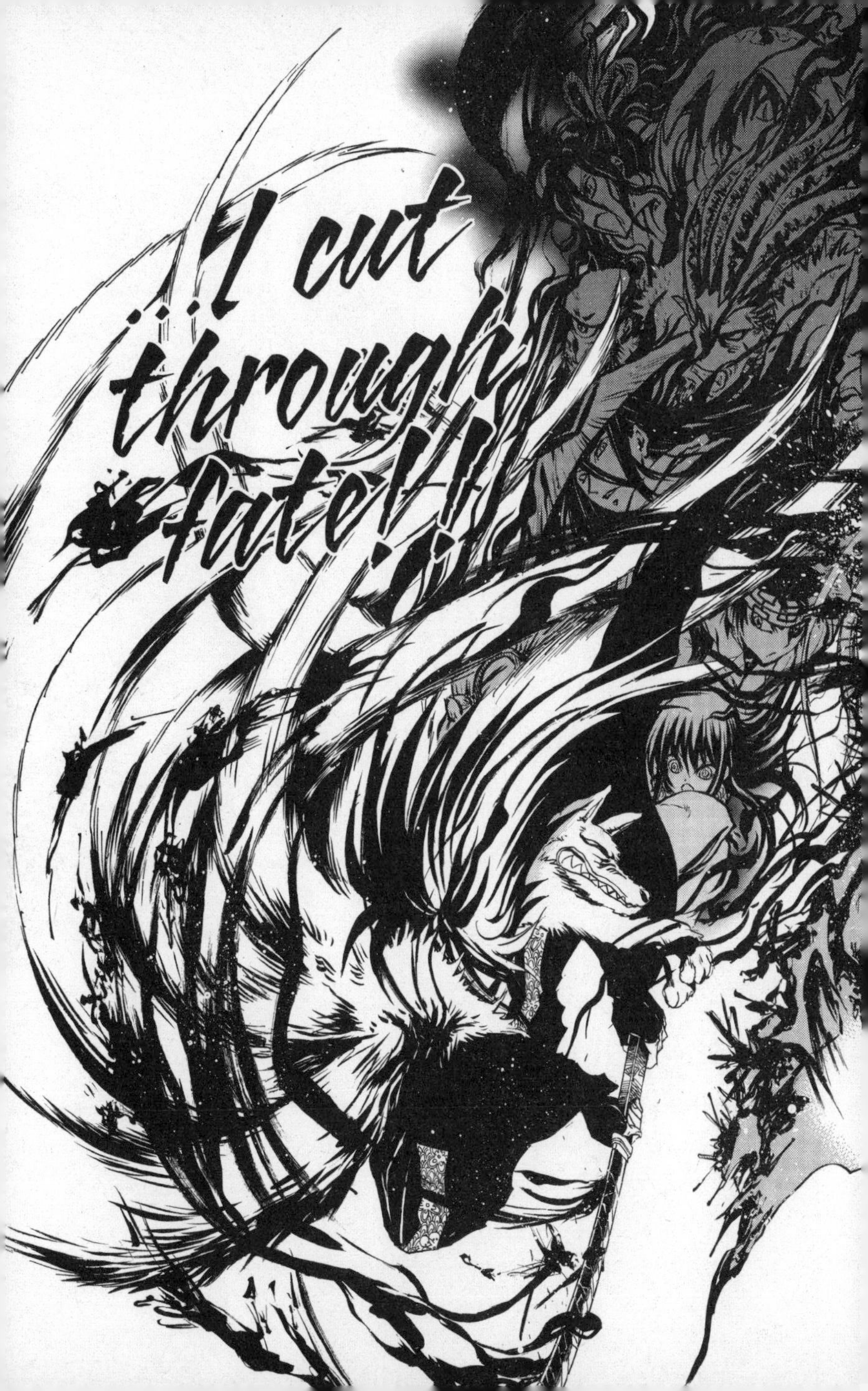
...I cut through fate!!

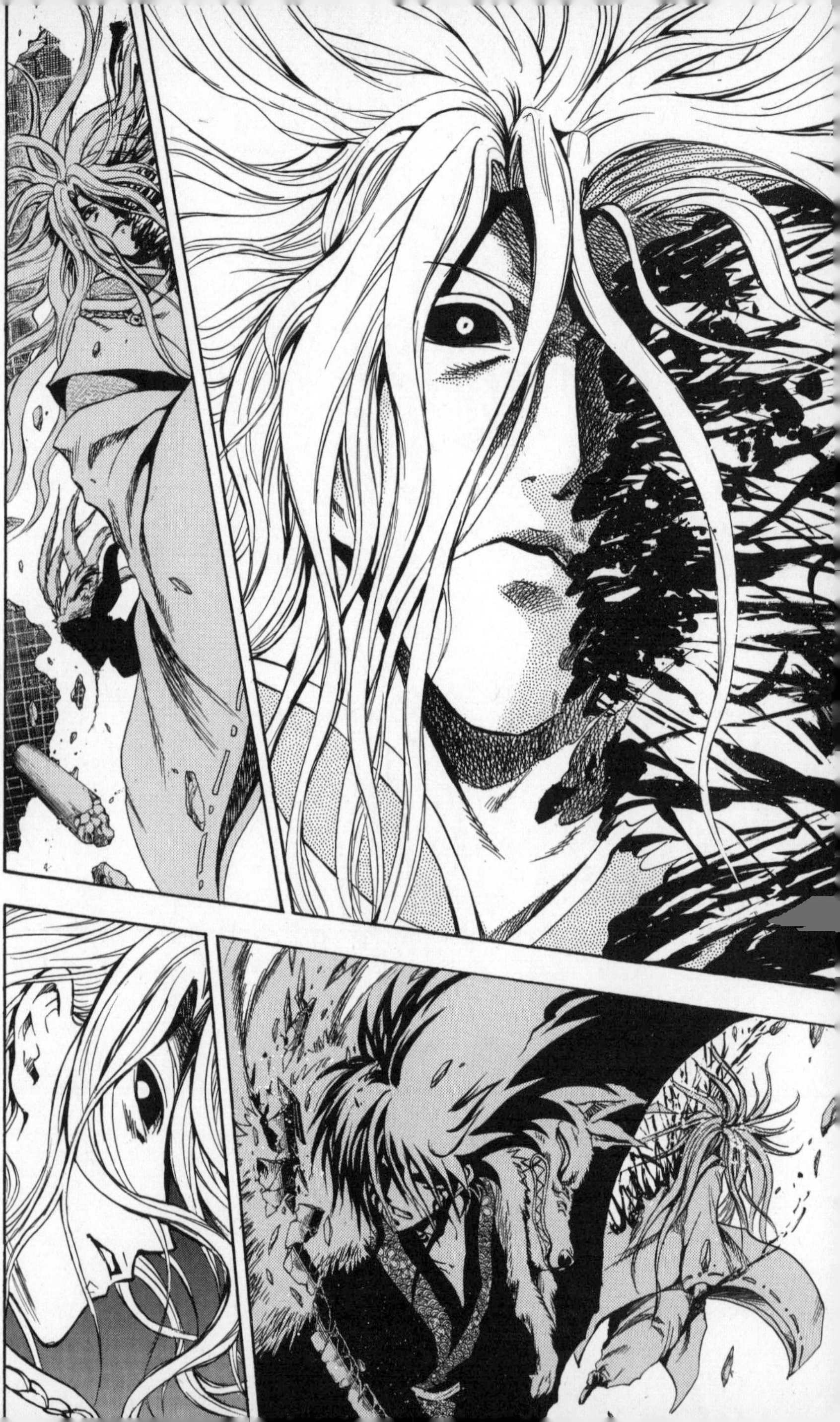

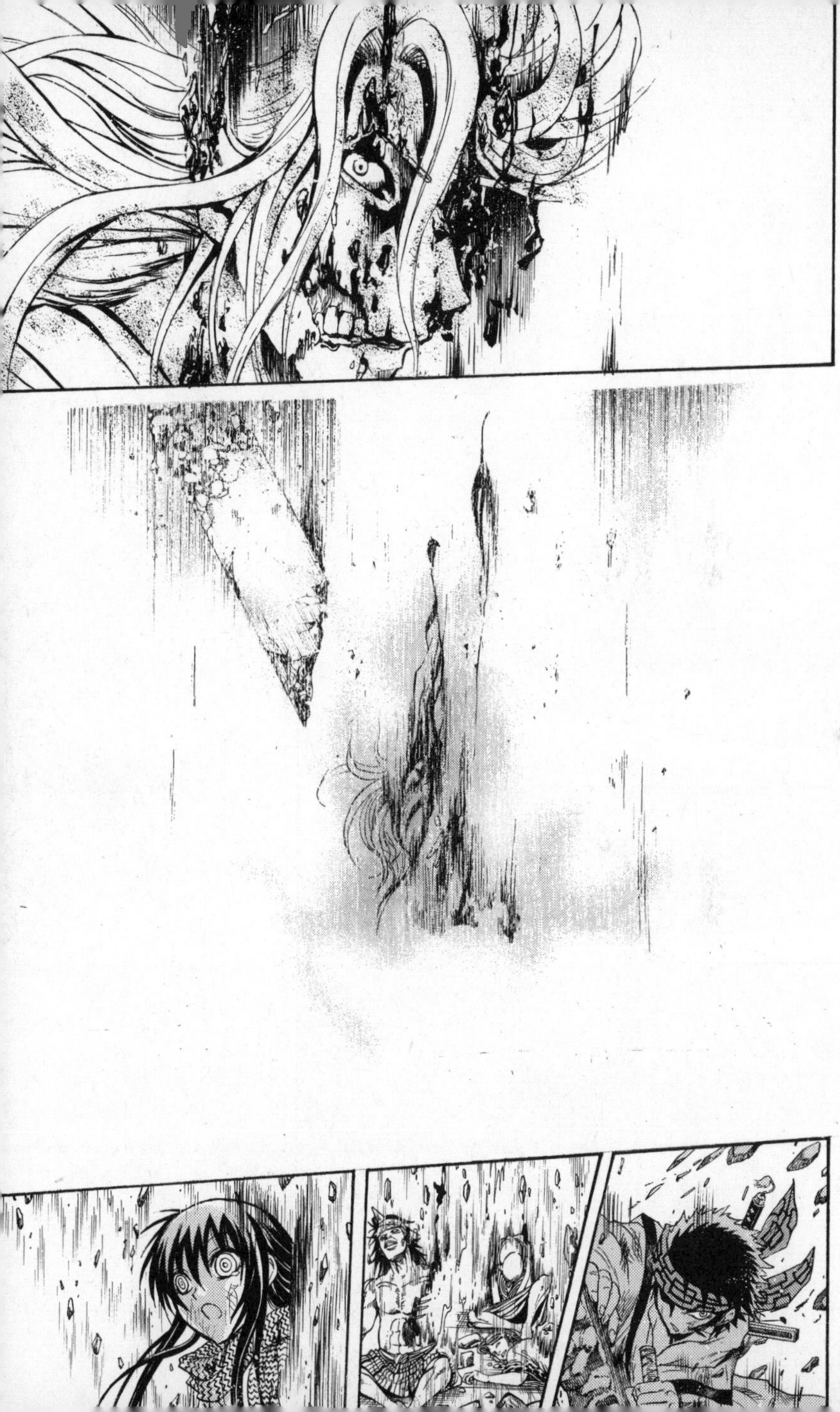

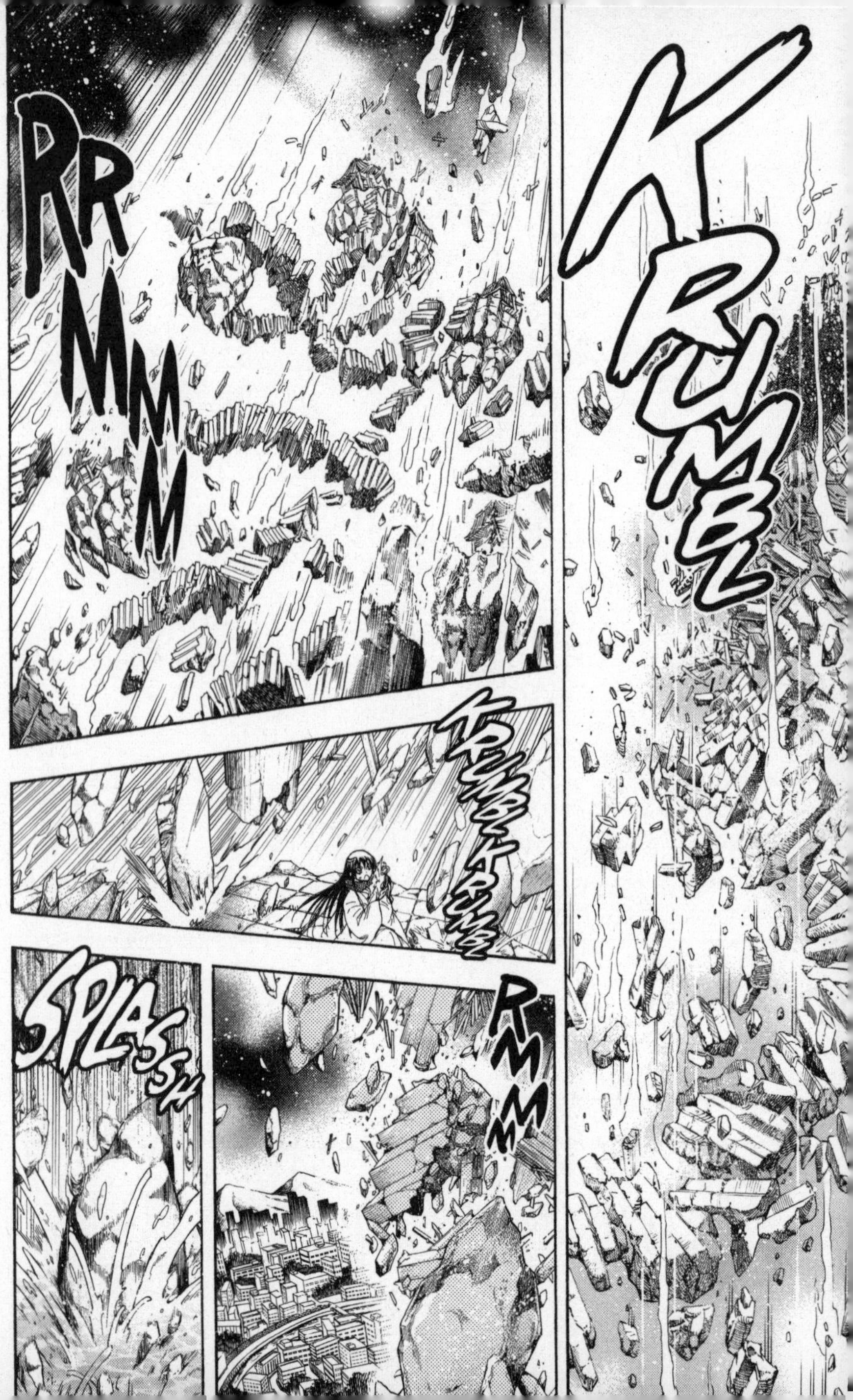
KRUMBL
RRMMMM
KRUMBLKRUMBL
RMMM
SPLASSH

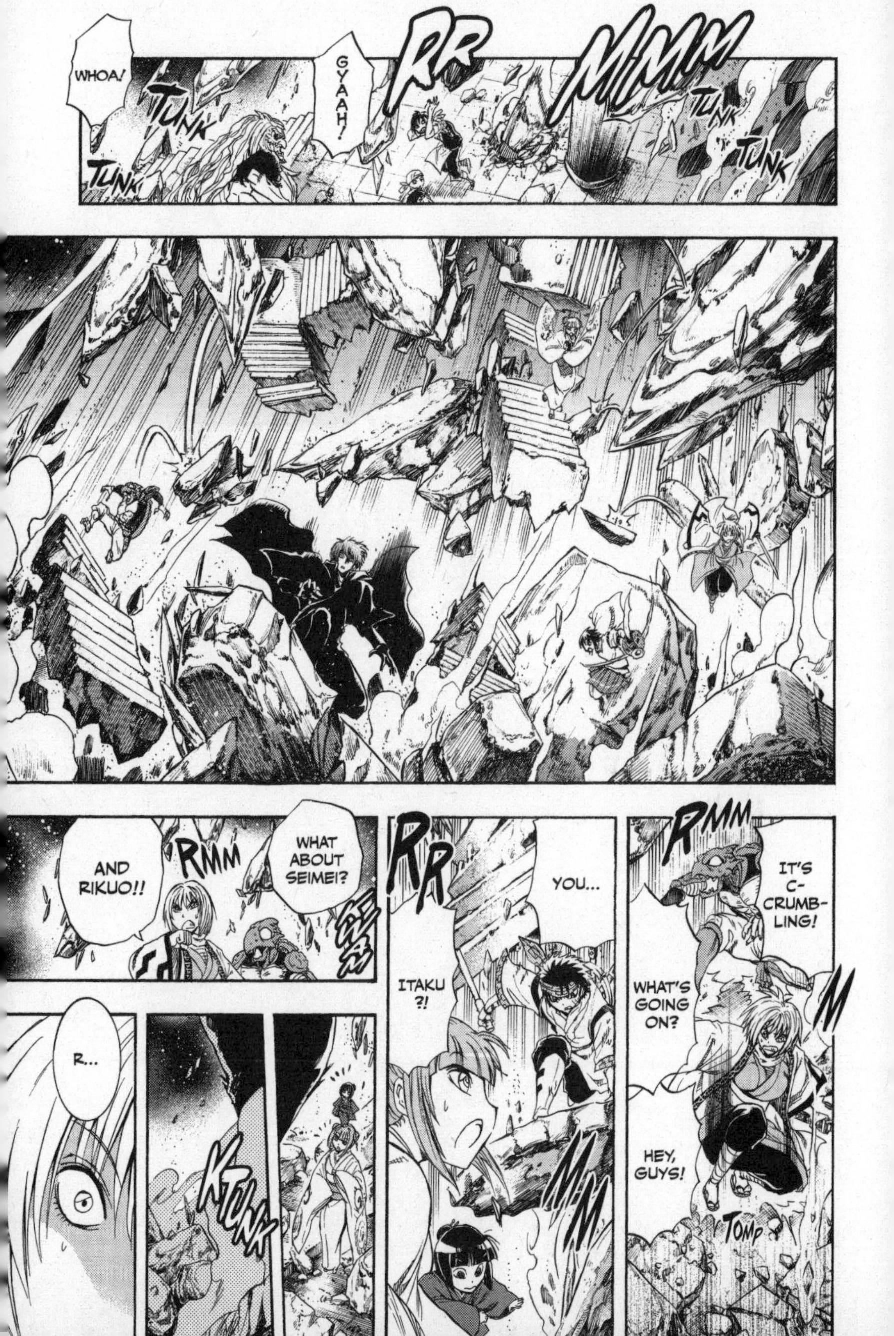
RR MMM
TUNK
TUNK
GYAAH!
WHOA!
TUNK
TUNK
RMM
IT'S C-CRUMBLING!
WHAT'S GOING ON?
HEY, GUYS!
M
TOMP
RR
YOU...
ITAKU?!
MM
RMM
WHAT ABOUT SEIMEI?
AND RIKUO!!
KTUNK
R...

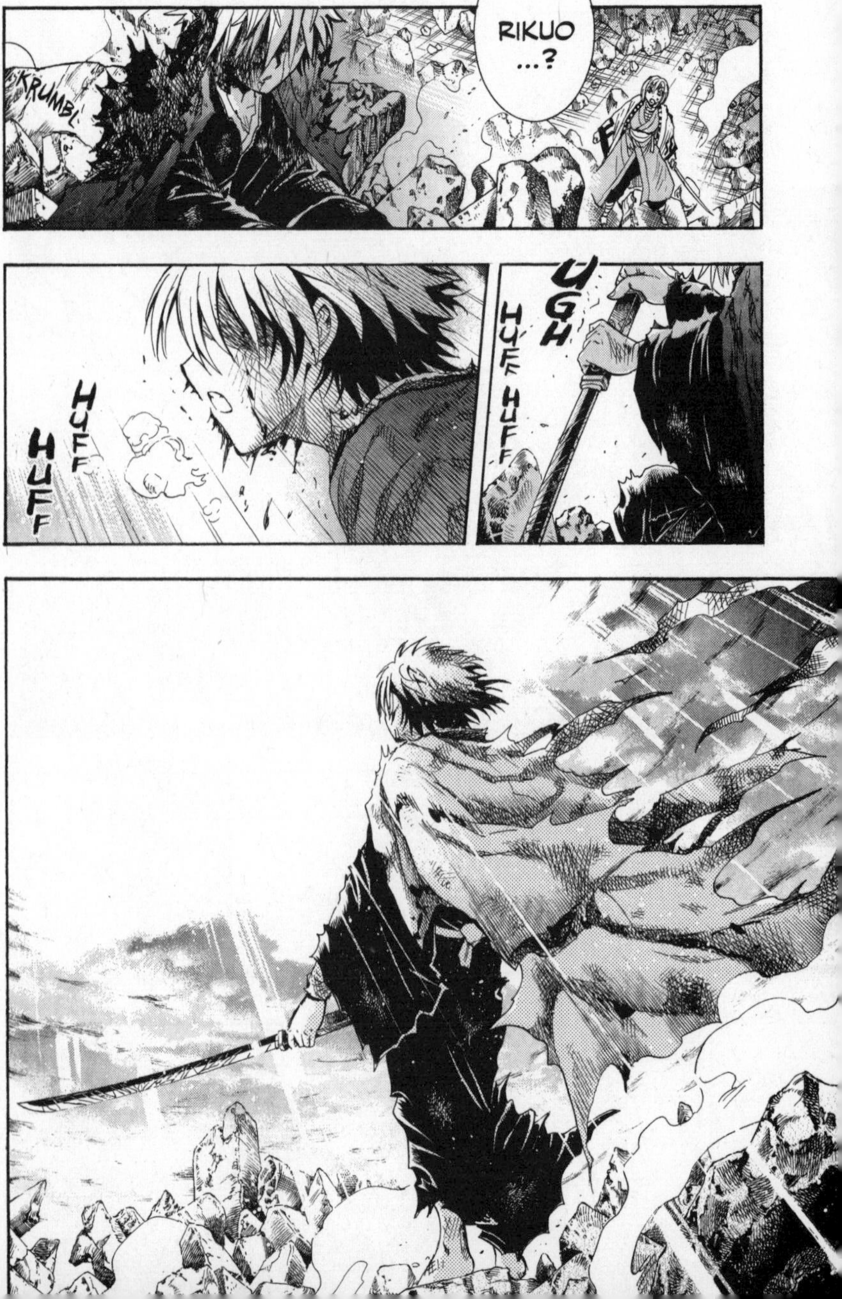
RIKUO ...?
KRUMBL
UGH
HUFF HUFF
HUFF HUFF

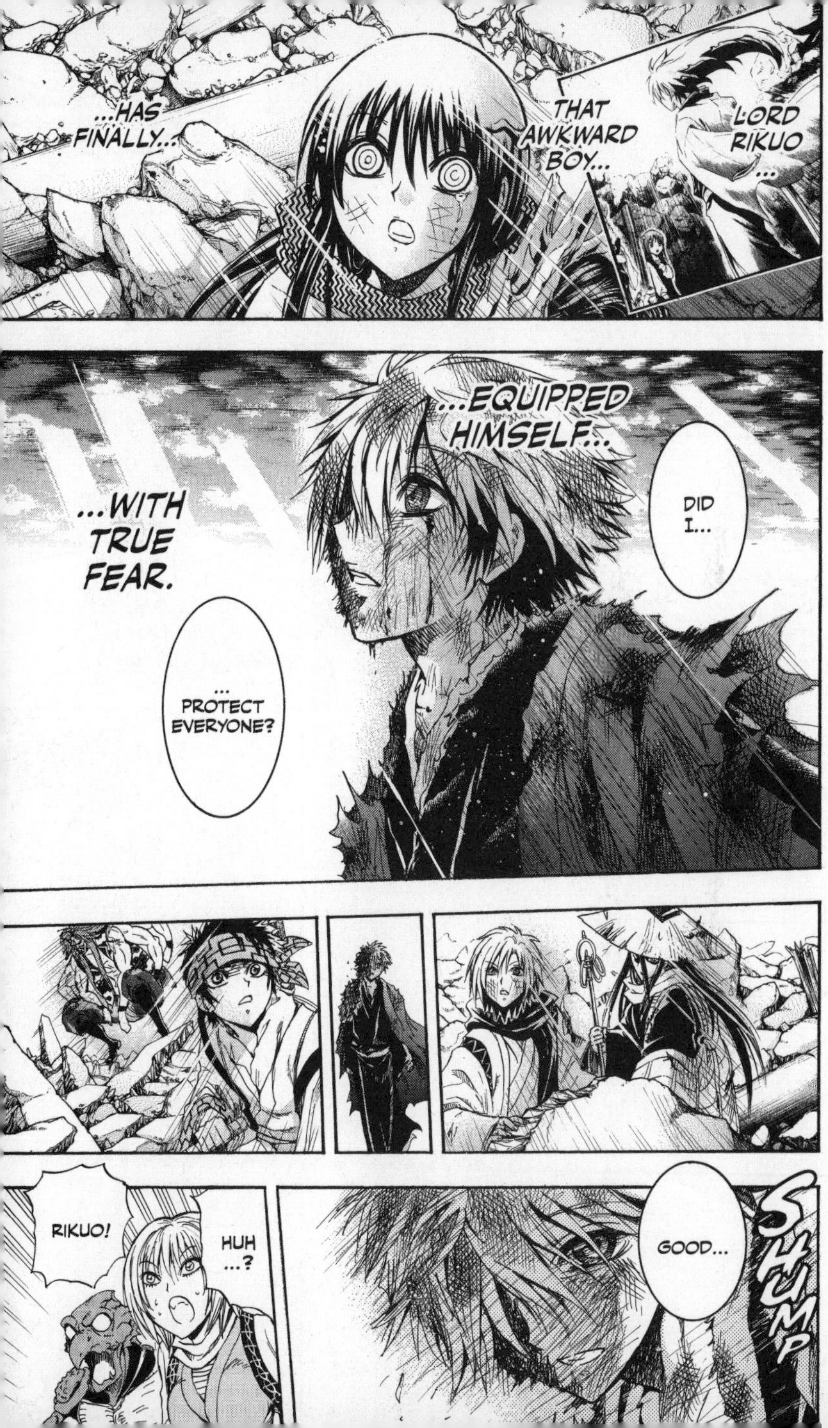
LORD RIKUO ...
THAT AWKWARD BOY...
...HAS FINALLY...
...EQUIPPED HIMSELF...
...WITH TRUE FEAR.
DID I...
... PROTECT EVERYONE?
SHUMP
GOOD...
HUH ...?
RIKUO!

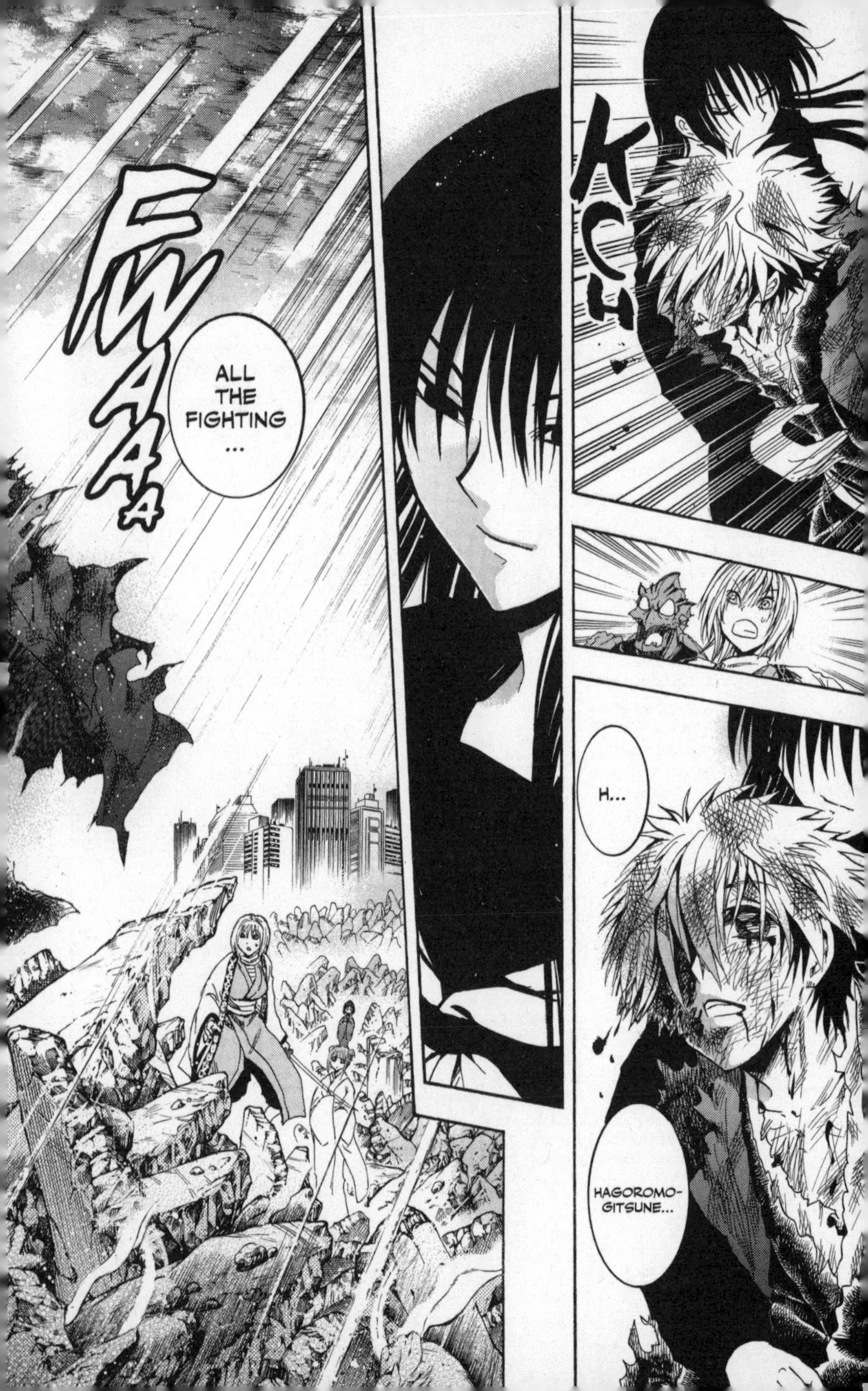
KCH
H...
HAGOROMO-GITSUNE...
FWAAAA
ALL THE FIGHTING ...

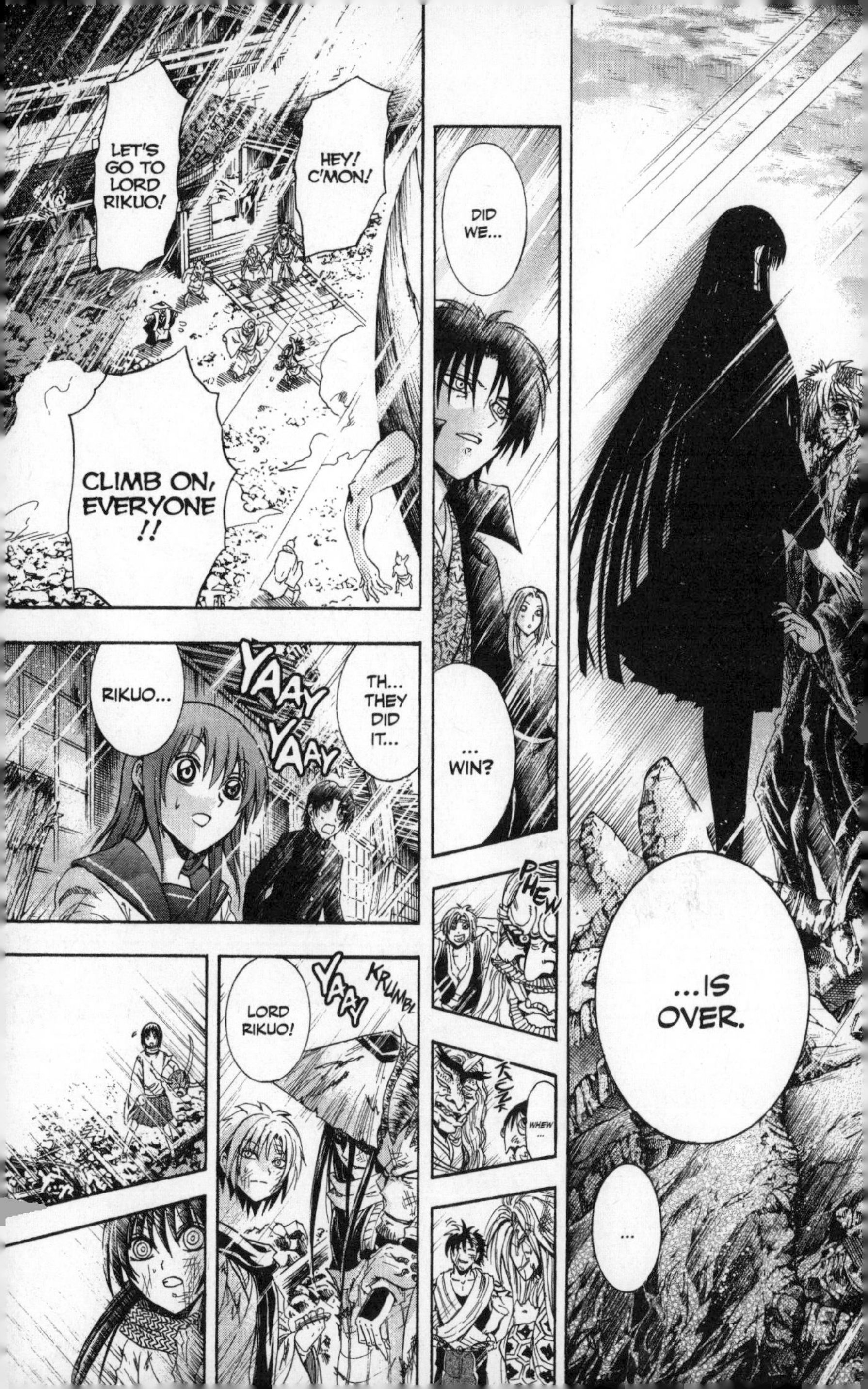
...IS OVER.
...
DID WE...
... WIN?
PHEW
KTUNK
WHEW ...
HEY! C'MON!
LET'S GO TO LORD RIKUO!
CLIMB ON, EVERYONE!!
TH... THEY DID IT...
YAAY YAAY
RIKUO...
KRUMBL
YAAY
LORD RIKUO!

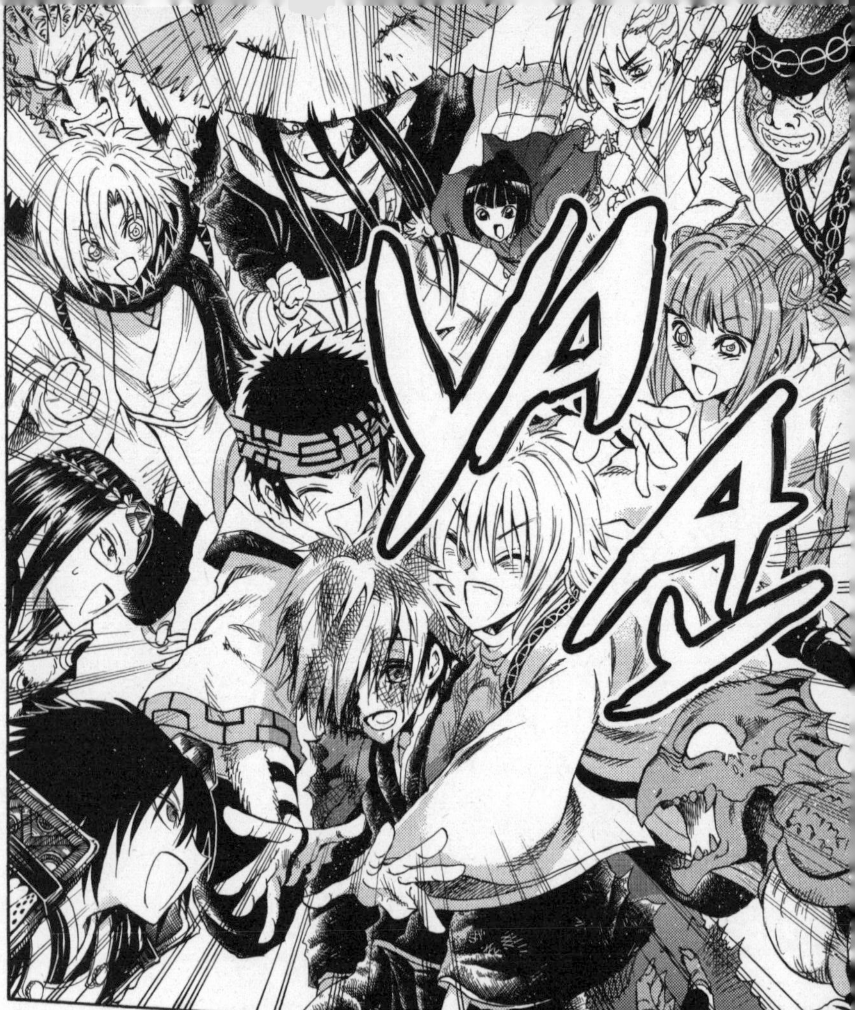
YAA

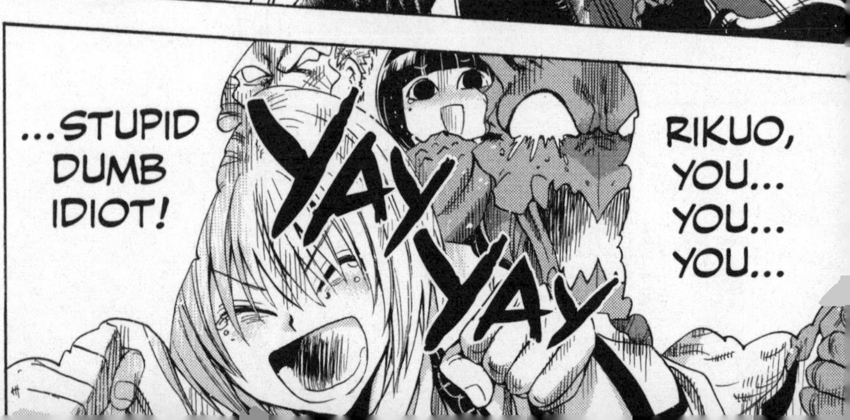
RIKUO,
YOU...
YOU...
YOU...
YAY YAY
...STUPID
DUMB
IDIOT!

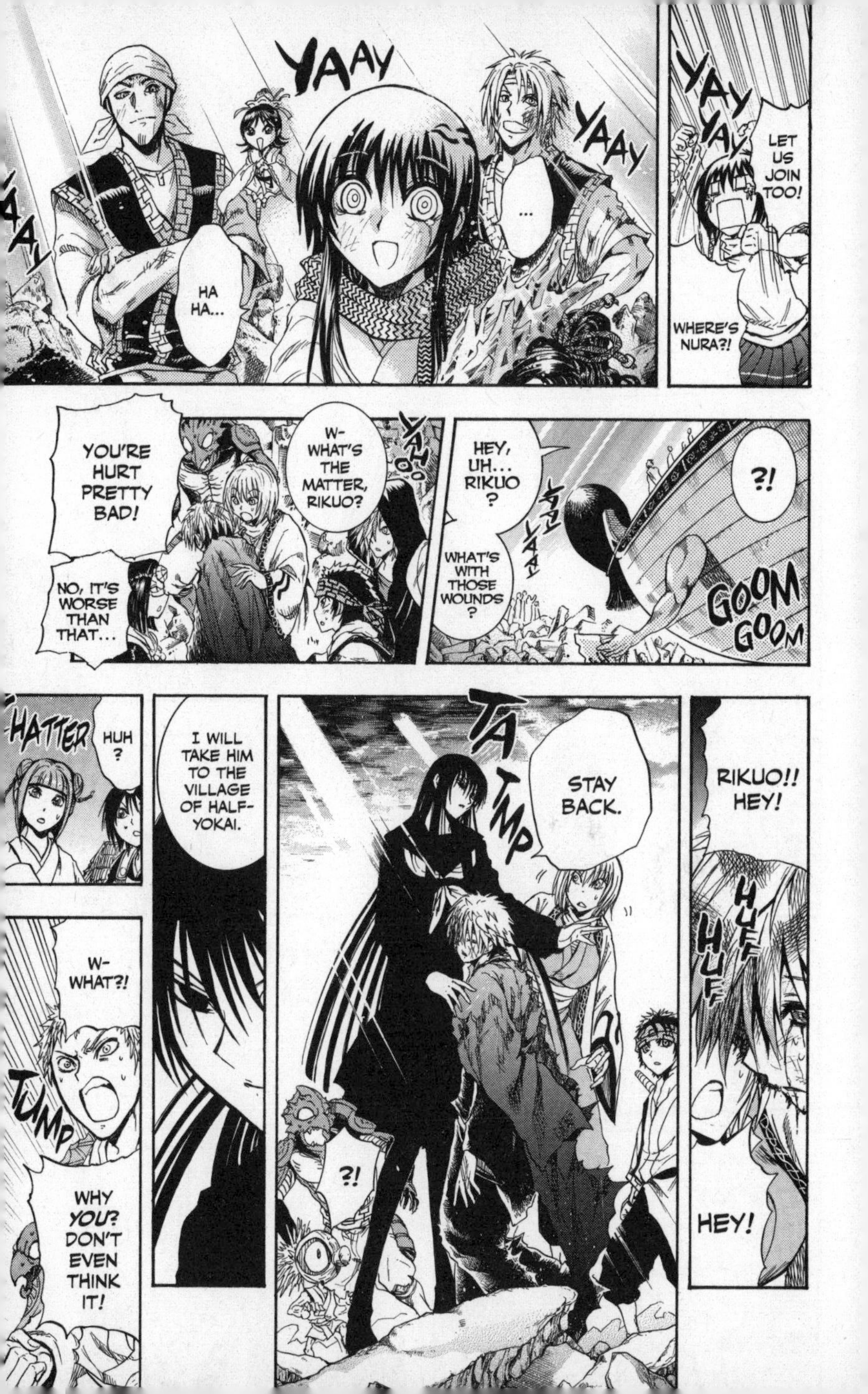
YAY YAY
LET US JOIN TOO!
WHERE'S NURA?!
YAAY
YAAY
...
HA HA...
YAAY
?!
GOOM GOOM
HEY, UH... RIKUO?
WHAT'S WITH THOSE WOUNDS?
W- WHAT'S THE MATTER, RIKUO?
YOU'RE HURT PRETTY BAD!
NO, IT'S WORSE THAN THAT...
RIKUO!! HEY!
HUFF HUFF
HEY!
TA TMP
STAY BACK.
?!
I WILL TAKE HIM TO THE VILLAGE OF HALF-YOKAI.
CHATTER
HUH?
W- WHAT?!
TUMP
WHY *YOU*? DON'T EVEN THINK IT!

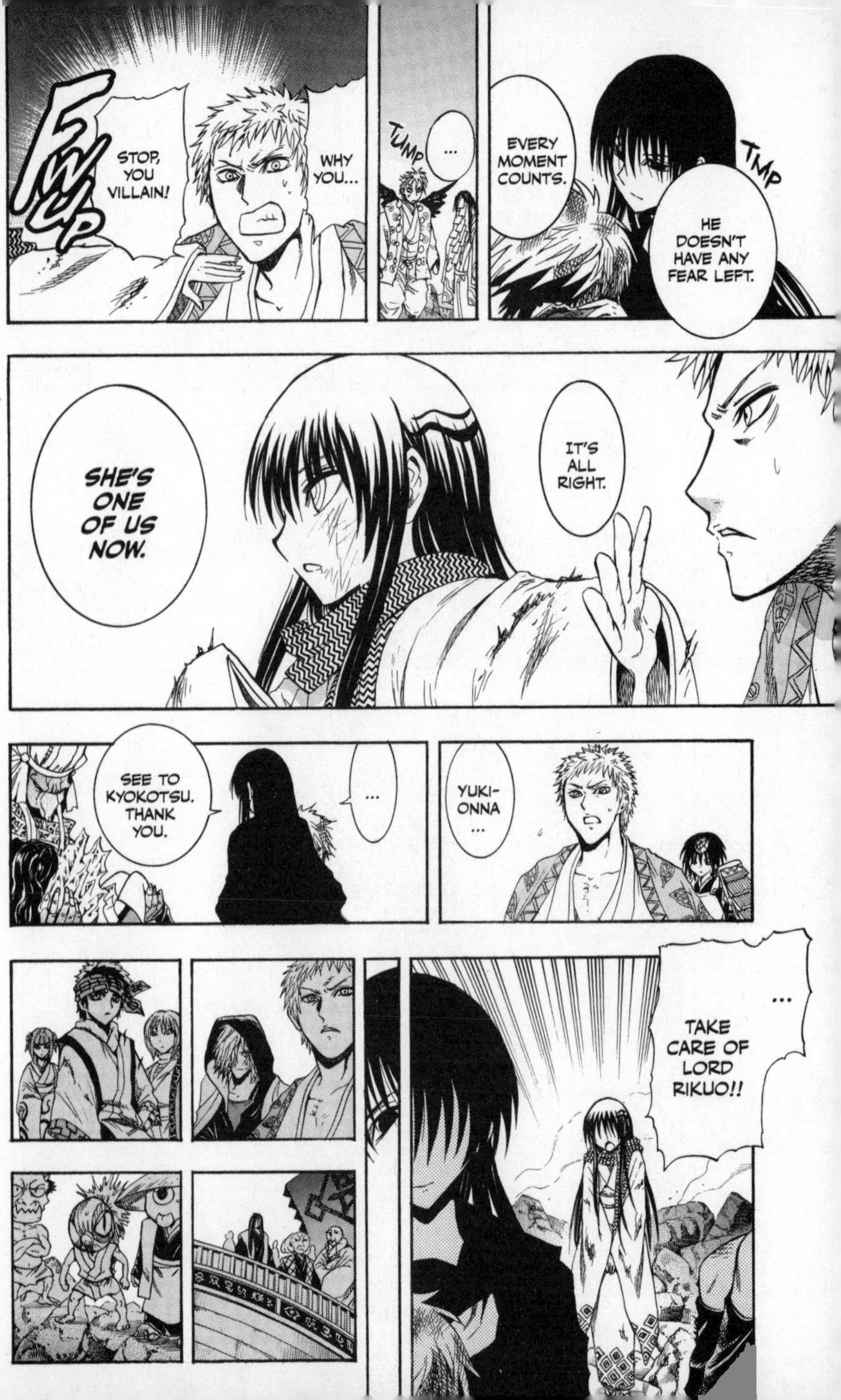
TMP
EVERY MOMENT COUNTS.
HE DOESN'T HAVE ANY FEAR LEFT.
...
TUMP
WHY YOU...
STOP, YOU VILLAIN!
FWUP
IT'S ALL RIGHT.
SHE'S ONE OF US NOW.
YUKI-ONNA ...
...
SEE TO KYOKOTSU. THANK YOU.
... TAKE CARE OF LORD RIKUO!!

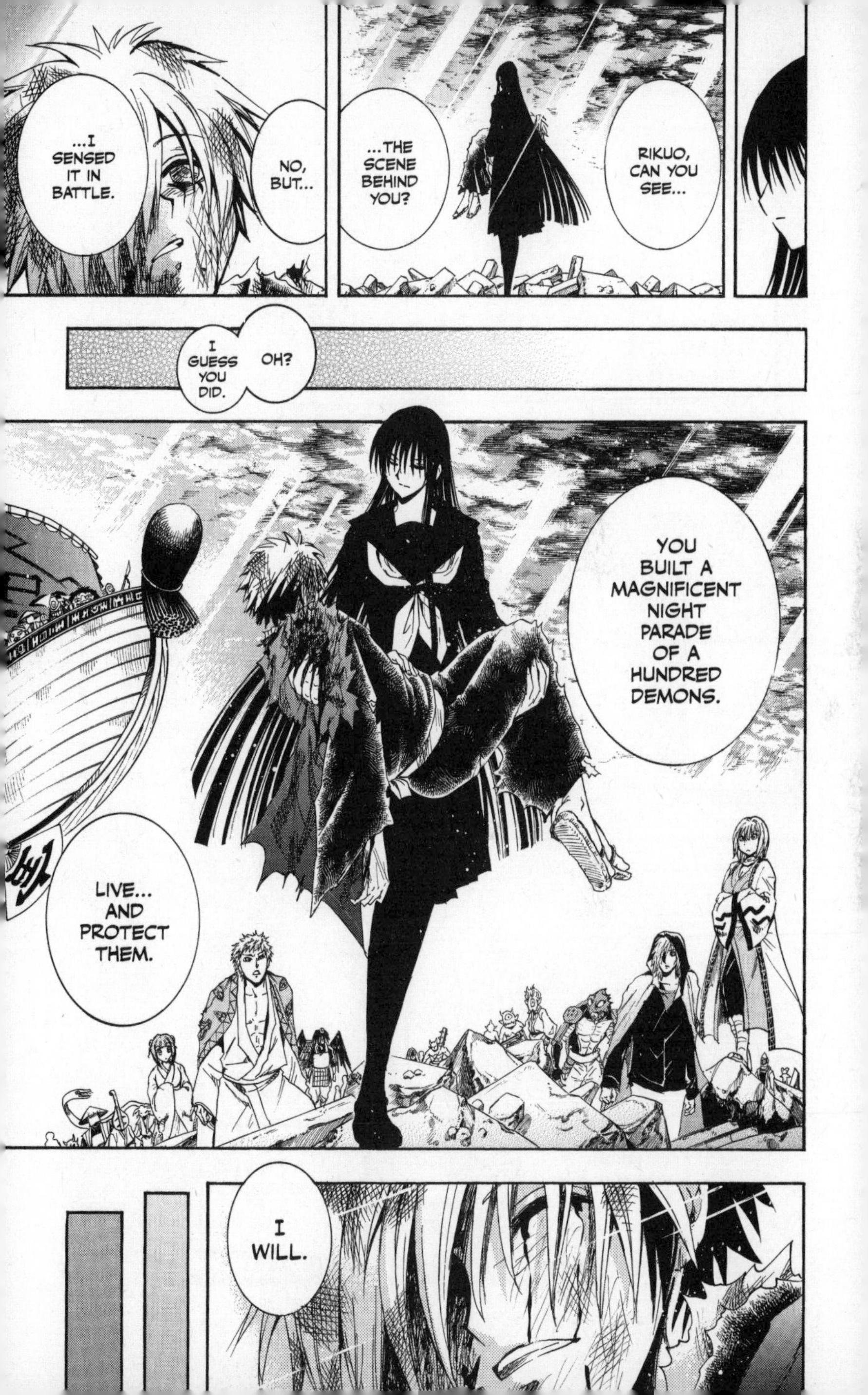
RIKUO, CAN YOU SEE...
...THE SCENE BEHIND YOU?
NO, BUT...
...I SENSED IT IN BATTLE.
OH?
I GUESS YOU DID.
YOU BUILT A MAGNIFICENT NIGHT PARADE OF A HUNDRED DEMONS.
LIVE... AND PROTECT THEM.
I WILL.

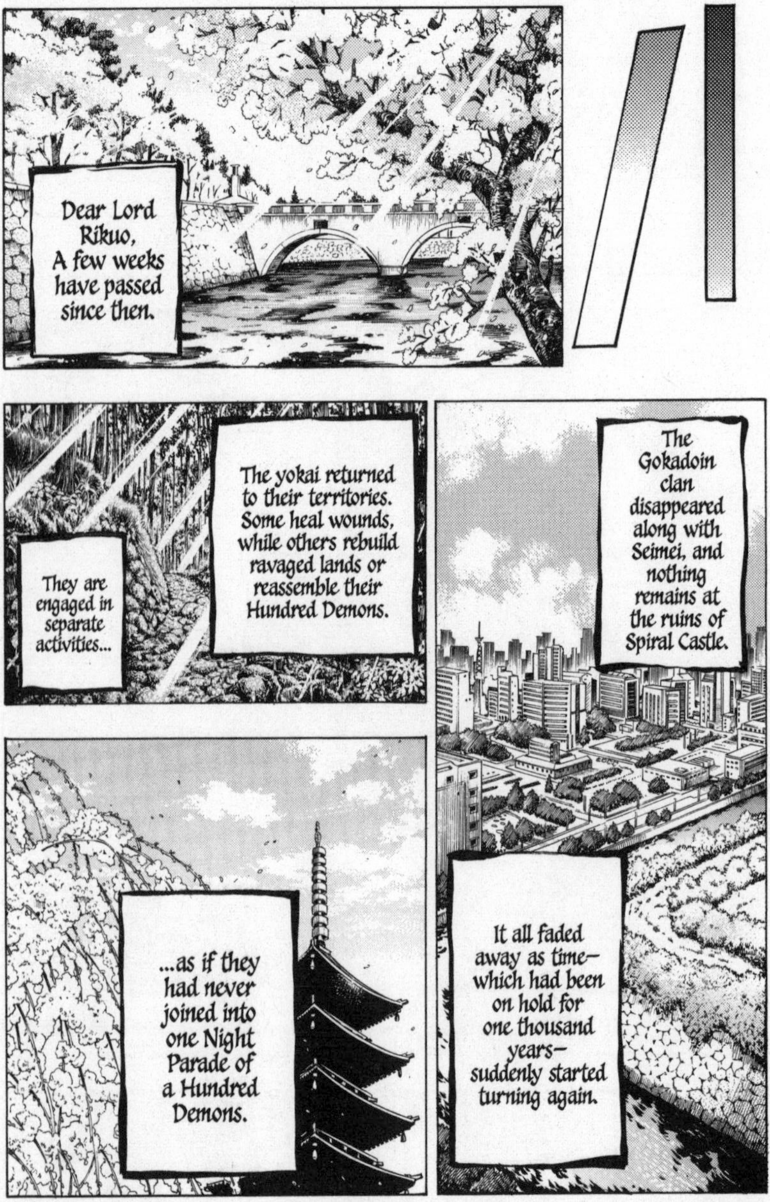
Dear Lord Rikuo, A few weeks have passed since then.
The Gokadoin clan disappeared along with Seimei, and nothing remains at the ruins of Spiral Castle.
It all faded away as time—which had been on hold for one thousand years—suddenly started turning again.
The yokai returned to their territories. Some heal wounds, while others rebuild ravaged lands or reassemble their Hundred Demons.
They are engaged in separate activities...
...as if they had never joined into one Night Parade of a Hundred Demons.

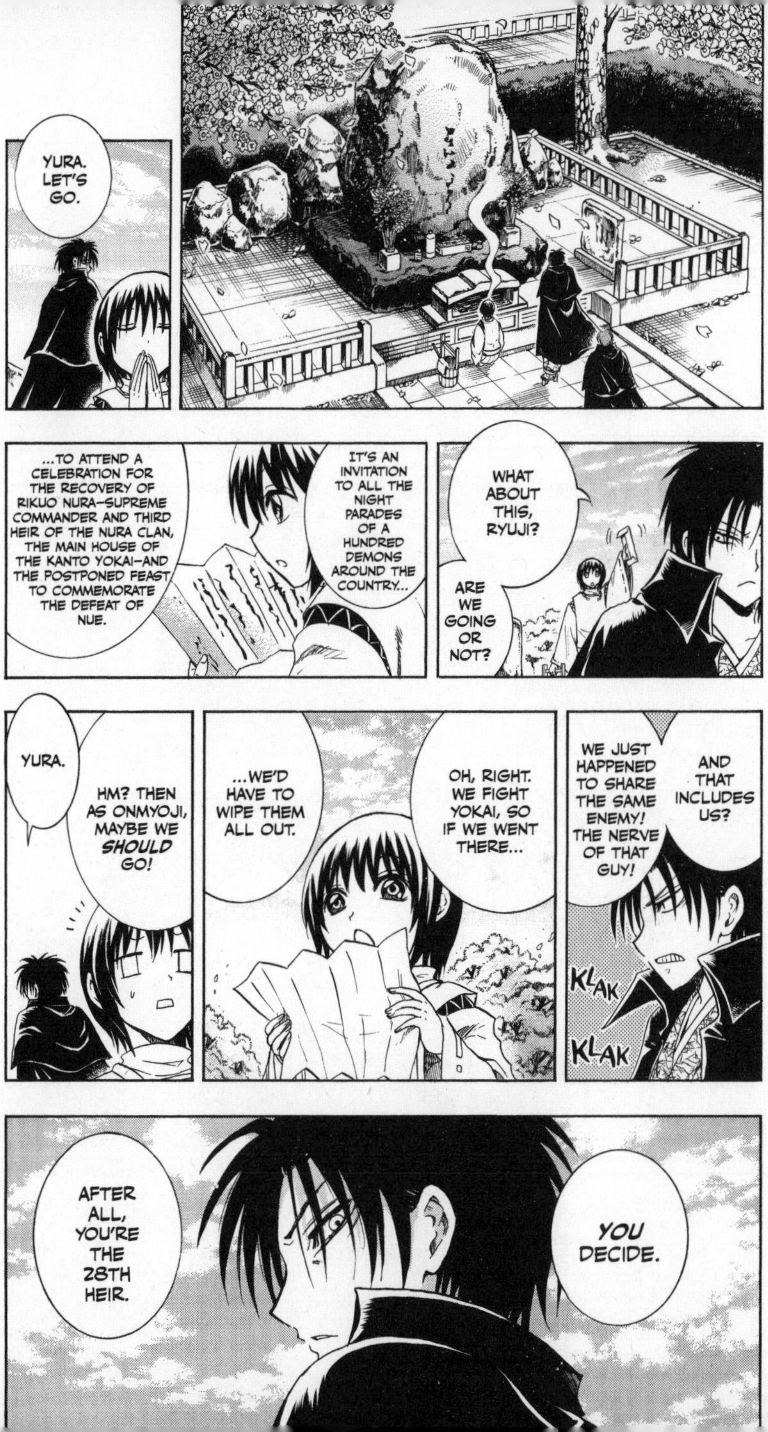
YURA. LET'S GO.
WHAT ABOUT THIS, RYUJI?
ARE WE GOING OR NOT?
IT'S AN INVITATION TO ALL THE NIGHT PARADES OF A HUNDRED DEMONS AROUND THE COUNTRY...
...TO ATTEND A CELEBRATION FOR THE RECOVERY OF RIKUO NURA—SUPREME COMMANDER AND THIRD HEIR OF THE NURA CLAN, THE MAIN HOUSE OF THE KANTO YOKAI—AND THE POSTPONED FEAST TO COMMEMORATE THE DEFEAT OF NUE.
AND THAT INCLUDES US?
WE JUST HAPPENED TO SHARE THE SAME ENEMY! THE NERVE OF THAT GUY!
KLAK
KLAK
OH, RIGHT. WE FIGHT YOKAI, SO IF WE WENT THERE...
...WE'D HAVE TO WIPE THEM ALL OUT.
HM? THEN AS ONMYOJI, MAYBE WE *SHOULD* GO!
YURA.
YOU DECIDE.
AFTER ALL, YOU'RE THE 28TH HEIR.

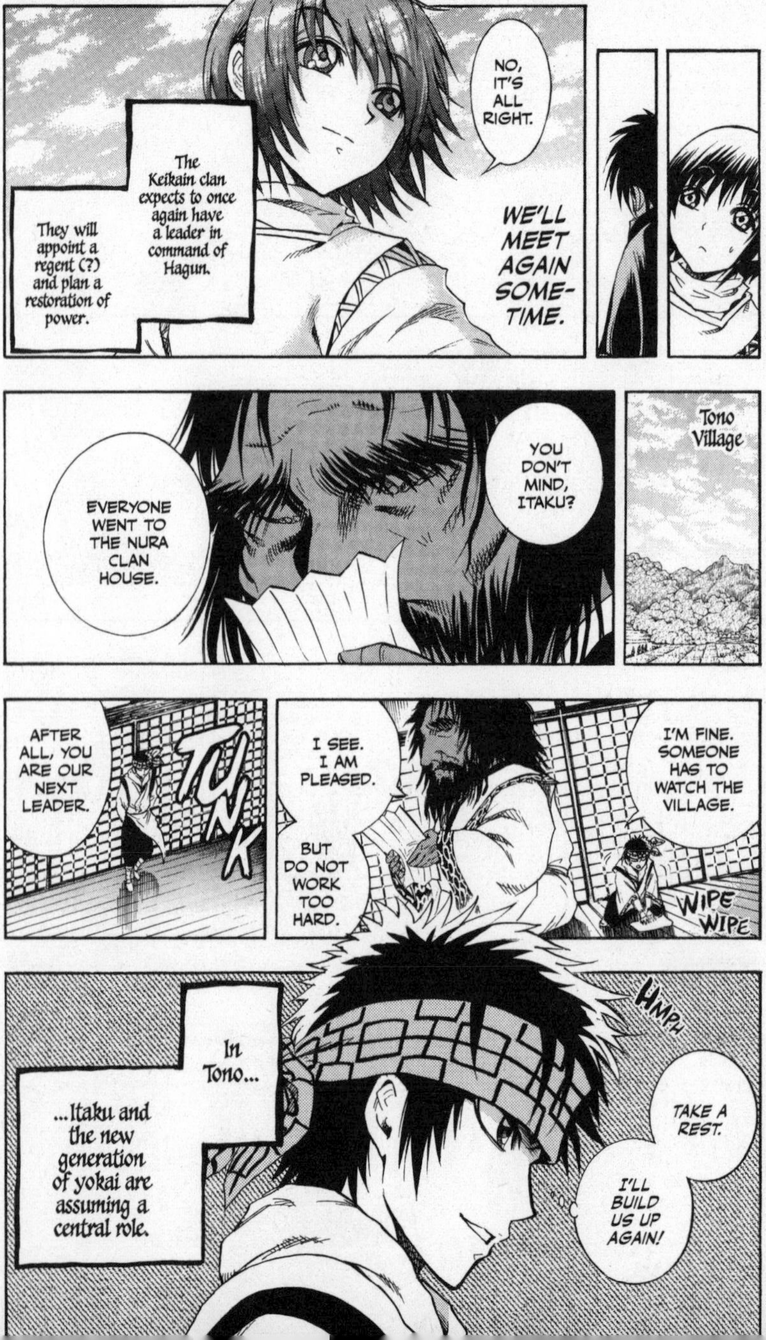
NO, IT'S ALL RIGHT.
WE'LL MEET AGAIN SOMETIME.
The Keikain clan expects to once again have a leader in command of Hagun.
They will appoint a regent (?) and plan a restoration of power.
Tono Village
YOU DON'T MIND, ITAKU?
EVERYONE WENT TO THE NURA CLAN HOUSE.
I'M FINE. SOMEONE HAS TO WATCH THE VILLAGE.
WIPE WIPE
I SEE. I AM PLEASED.
BUT DO NOT WORK TOO HARD.
AFTER ALL, YOU ARE OUR NEXT LEADER.
TUNK
HMPH
TAKE A REST.
I'LL BUILD US UP AGAIN!
In Tono...
...Itaku and the new generation of yokai are assuming a central role.

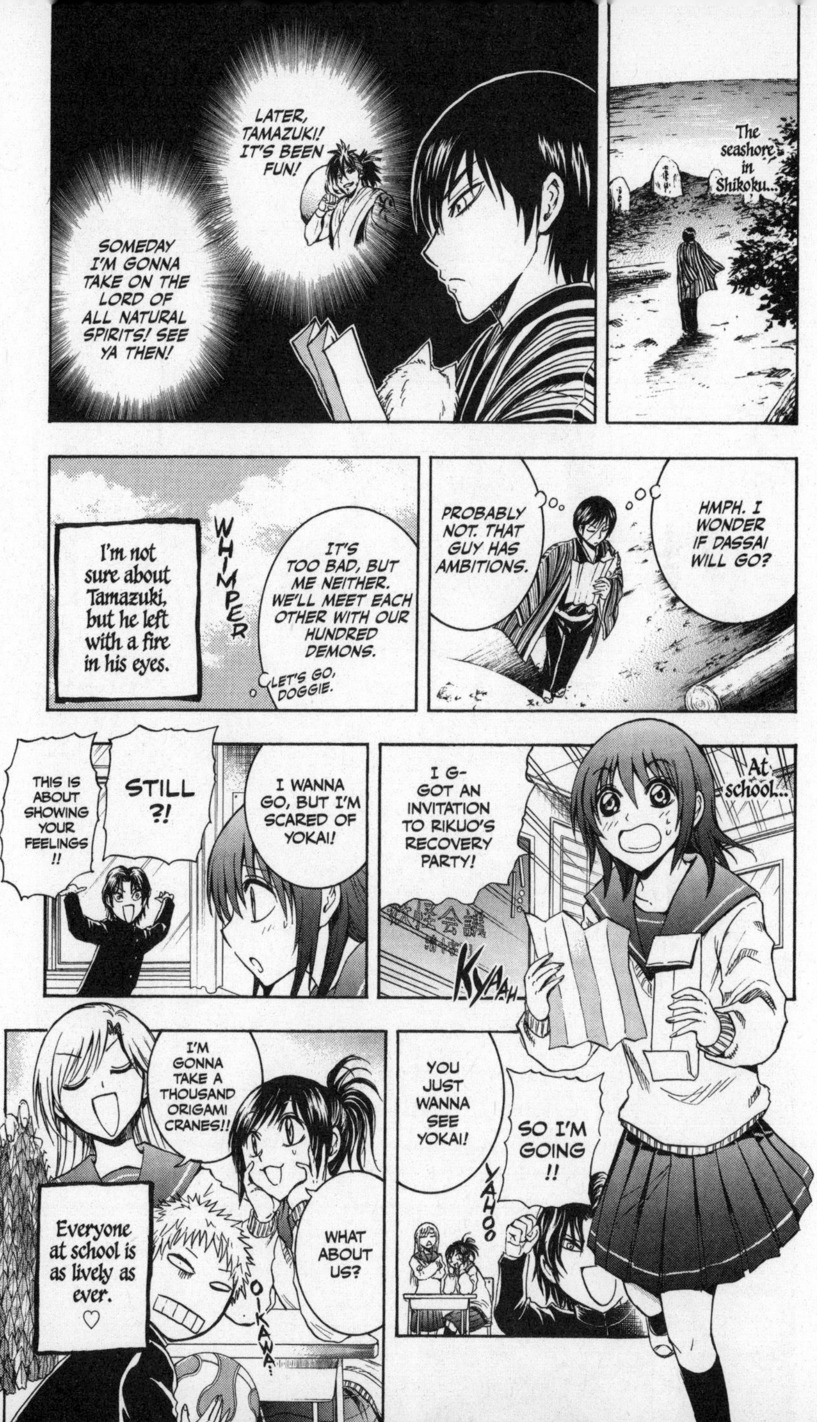
The seashore in Shikoku...
LATER, TAMAZUKI! IT'S BEEN FUN!
SOMEDAY I'M GONNA TAKE ON THE LORD OF ALL NATURAL SPIRITS! SEE YA THEN!
HMPH. I WONDER IF DASSAI WILL GO?
PROBABLY NOT. THAT GUY HAS AMBITIONS.
IT'S TOO BAD, BUT ME NEITHER. WE'LL MEET EACH OTHER WITH OUR HUNDRED DEMONS.
LET'S GO, DOGGIE.
WHIMPER
I'm not sure about Tamazuki, but he left with a fire in his eyes.
At school...
I G-GOT AN INVITATION TO RIKUO'S RECOVERY PARTY!
KYAAH
I WANNA GO, BUT I'M SCARED OF YOKAI!
STILL ?!
THIS IS ABOUT SHOWING YOUR FEELINGS !!
SO I'M GOING !!
YOU JUST WANNA SEE YOKAI!
YAHOO
I'M GONNA TAKE A THOUSAND ORIGAMI CRANES!!
WHAT ABOUT US?
OIKAWA...
Everyone at school is as lively as ever. ♡

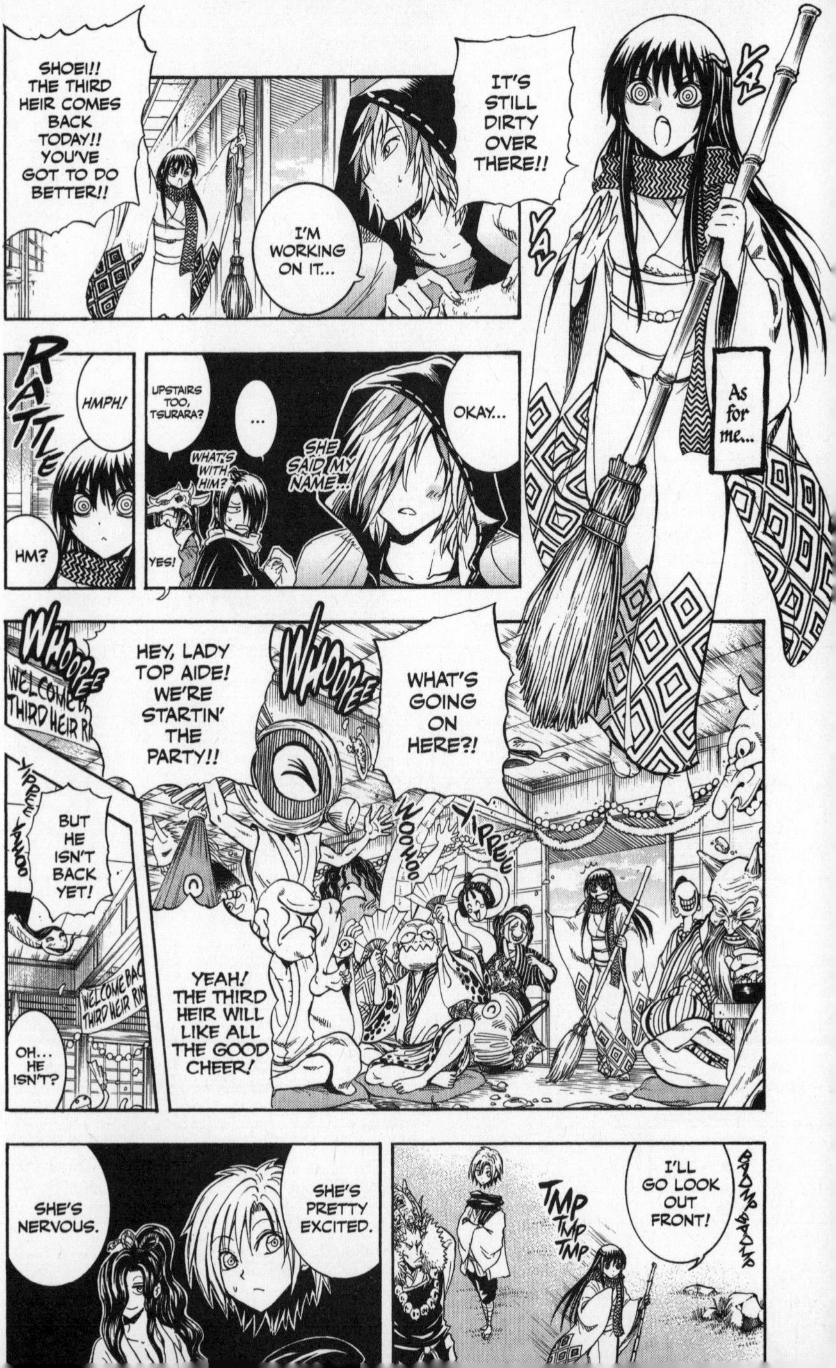
YAY
IT'S STILL DIRTY OVER THERE!!
YAY
As for me...
SHOEI!! THE THIRD HEIR COMES BACK TODAY!! YOU'VE GOT TO DO BETTER!!
I'M WORKING ON IT...
OKAY...
SHE SAID MY NAME...
...
UPSTAIRS TOO, TSURARA?
WHAT'S WITH HIM?
YES!
HMPH!
RATTLE
HM?
WHAT'S GOING ON HERE?!
WHOOPEE
HEY, LADY TOP AIDE! WE'RE STARTIN' THE PARTY!!
WHOOPEE
YIPPEE
WOOWOO
YIPPEE YAHOO
BUT HE ISN'T BACK YET!
YEAH! THE THIRD HEIR WILL LIKE ALL THE GOOD CHEER!
OH... HE ISN'T?
I'LL GO LOOK OUT FRONT!
TMP TMP TMP
SHE'S PRETTY EXCITED.
SHE'S NERVOUS.

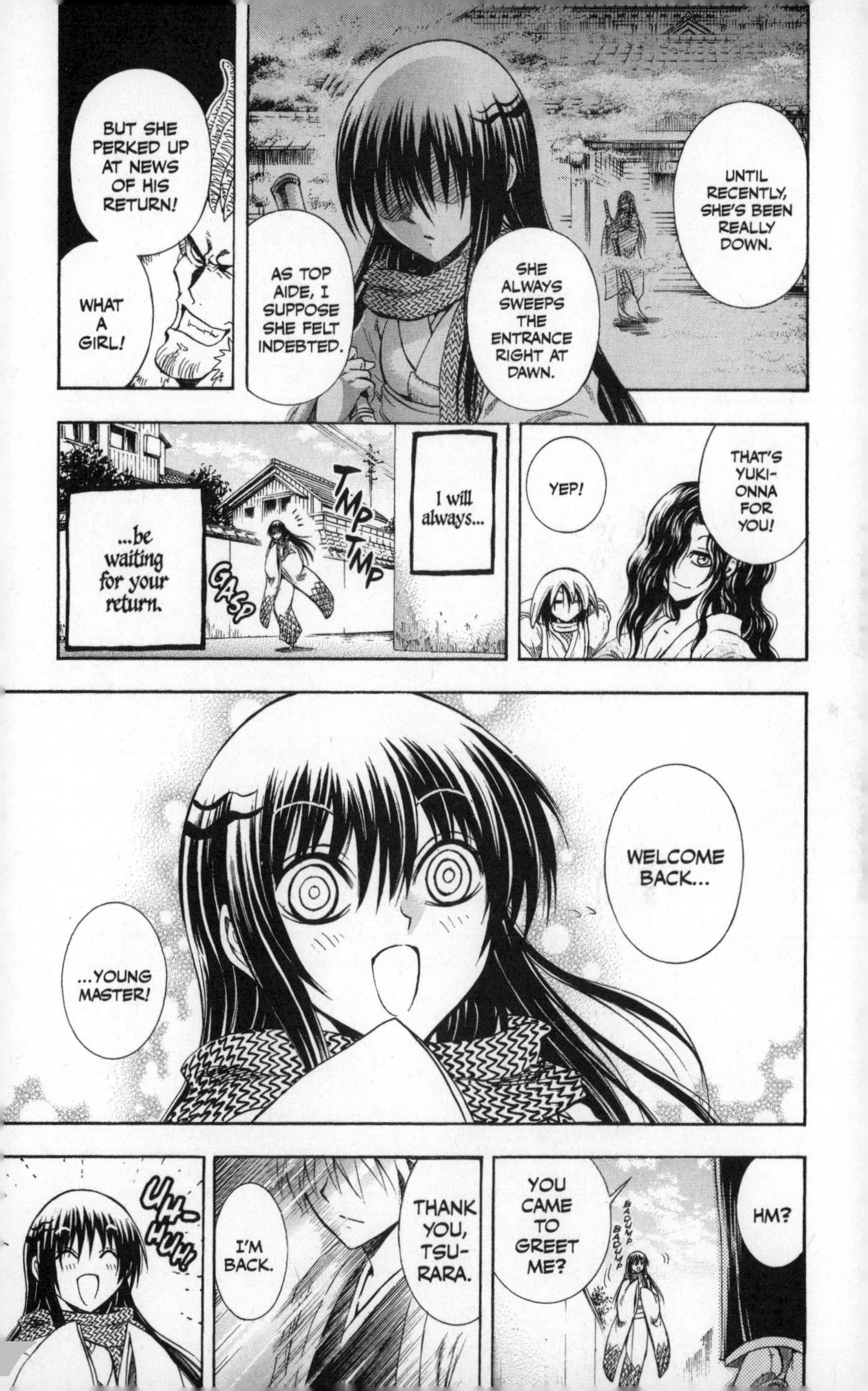
UNTIL RECENTLY, SHE'S BEEN REALLY DOWN.
SHE ALWAYS SWEEPS THE ENTRANCE RIGHT AT DAWN.
AS TOP AIDE, I SUPPOSE SHE FELT INDEBTED.
BUT SHE PERKED UP AT NEWS OF HIS RETURN!
WHAT A GIRL!
THAT'S YUKI-ONNA FOR YOU!
YEP!
I will always...
TMP TMP
...be waiting for your return.
GASP
WELCOME BACK...
...YOUNG MASTER!
HM?
YOU CAME TO GREET ME?
BADUMP BADUMP
THANK YOU, TSURARA.
I'M BACK.
UH-HUH!

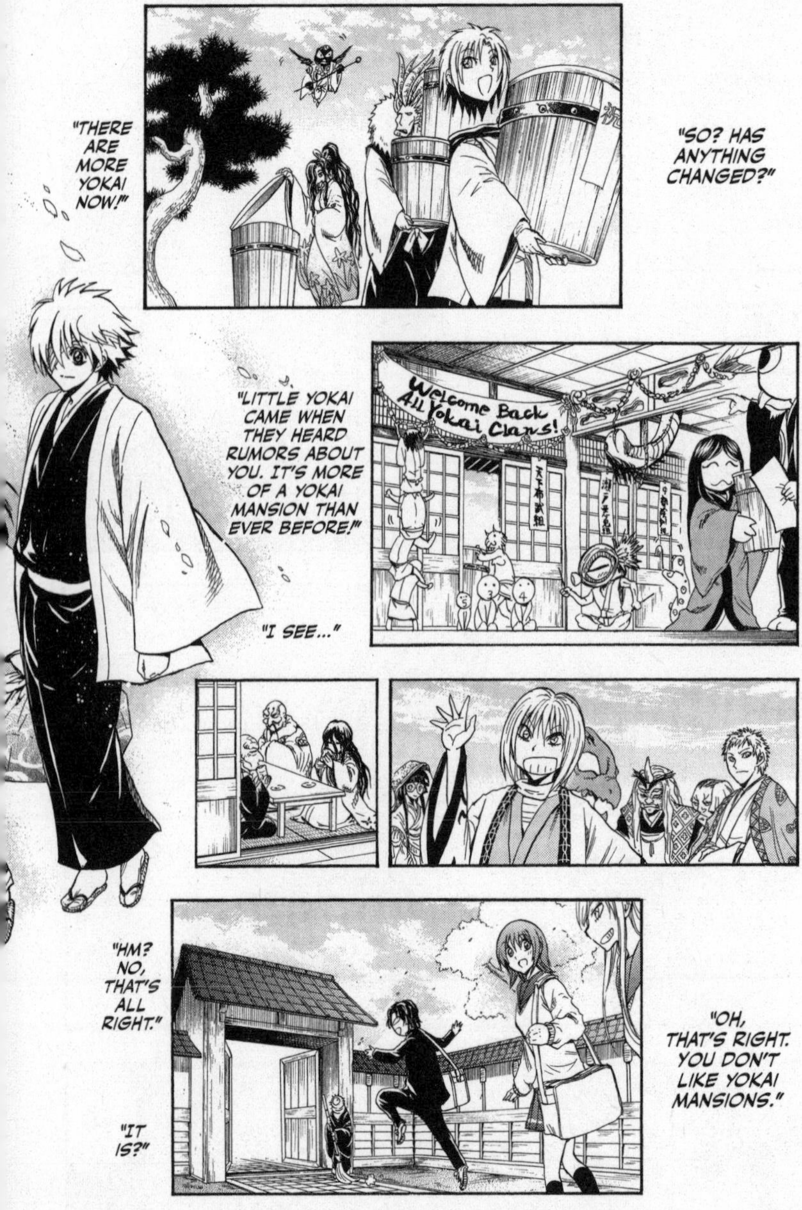
"SO? HAS ANYTHING CHANGED?"
"THERE ARE MORE YOKAI NOW!"
Welcome Back All Yokai Clans!
"LITTLE YOKAI CAME WHEN THEY HEARD RUMORS ABOUT YOU. IT'S MORE OF A YOKAI MANSION THAN EVER BEFORE!"
"I SEE..."
"OH, THAT'S RIGHT. YOU DON'T LIKE YOKAI MANSIONS."
"HM? NO, THAT'S ALL RIGHT."
"IT IS?"

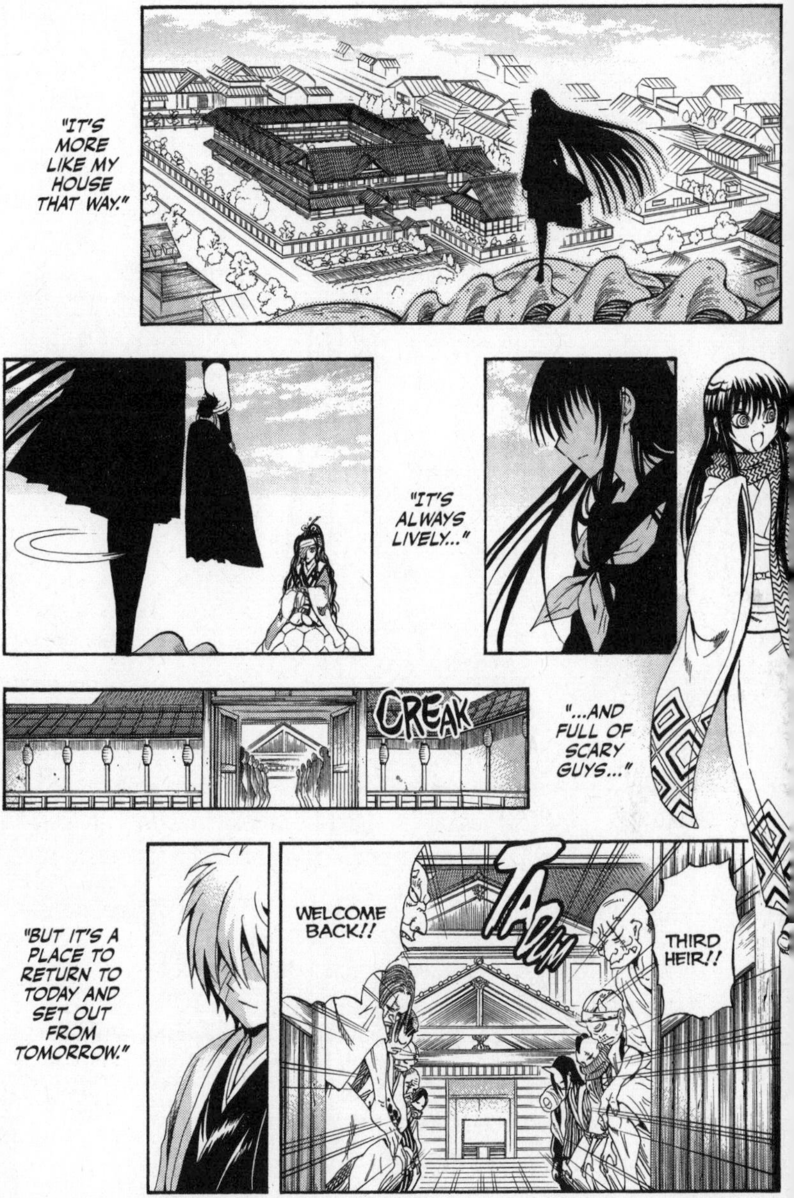
"IT'S MORE LIKE MY HOUSE THAT WAY."
"IT'S ALWAYS LIVELY..."
"...AND FULL OF SCARY GUYS..."
CREAK
THIRD HEIR!!
WELCOME BACK!!
"BUT IT'S A PLACE TO RETURN TO TODAY AND SET OUT FROM TOMORROW."

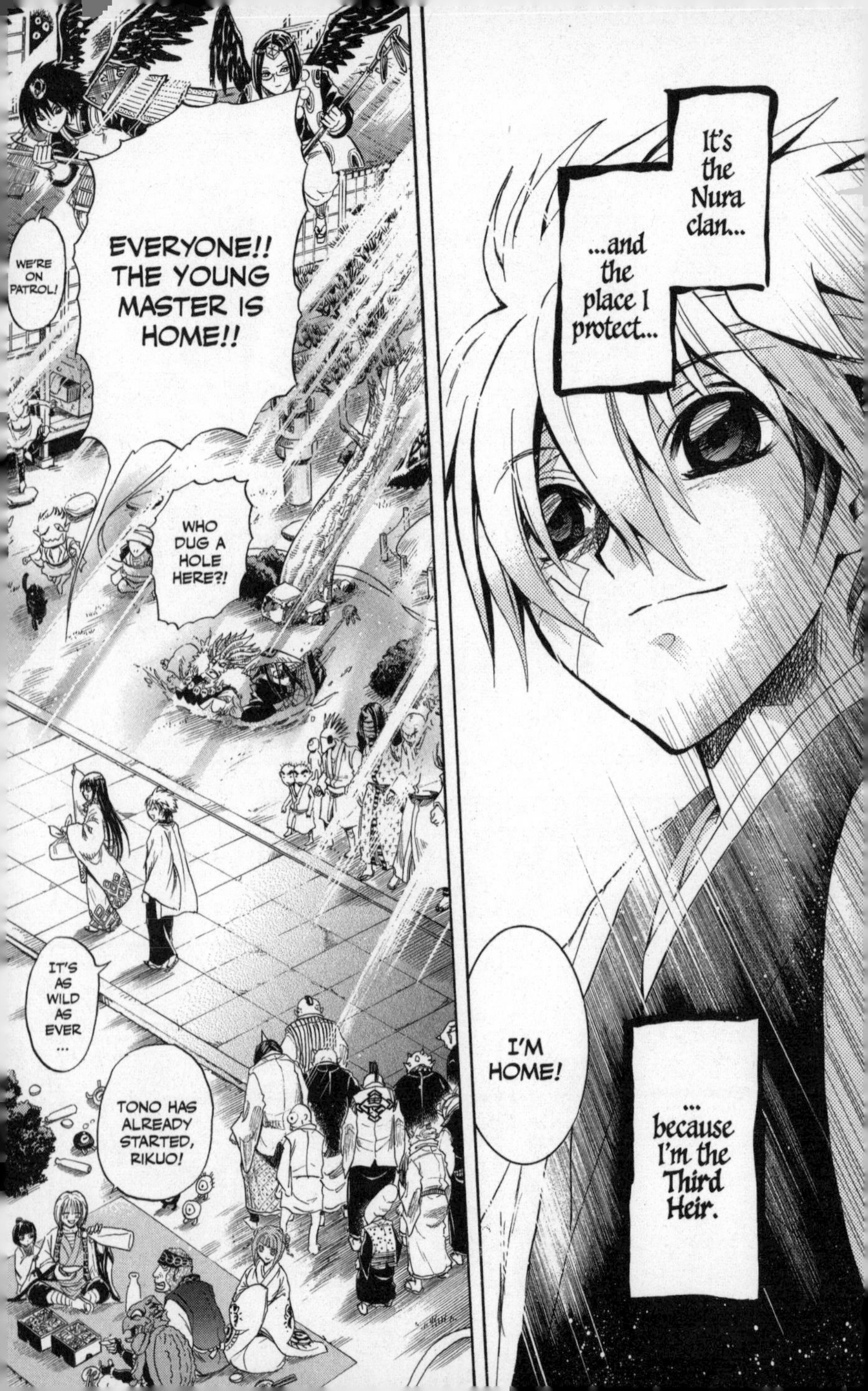
It's the Nura clan...
...and the place I protect...
I'M HOME!
...because I'm the Third Heir.
EVERYONE!! THE YOUNG MASTER IS HOME!!
WE'RE ON PATROL!
WHO DUG A HOLE HERE?!
IT'S AS WILD AS EVER...
TONO HAS ALREADY STARTED, RIKUO!

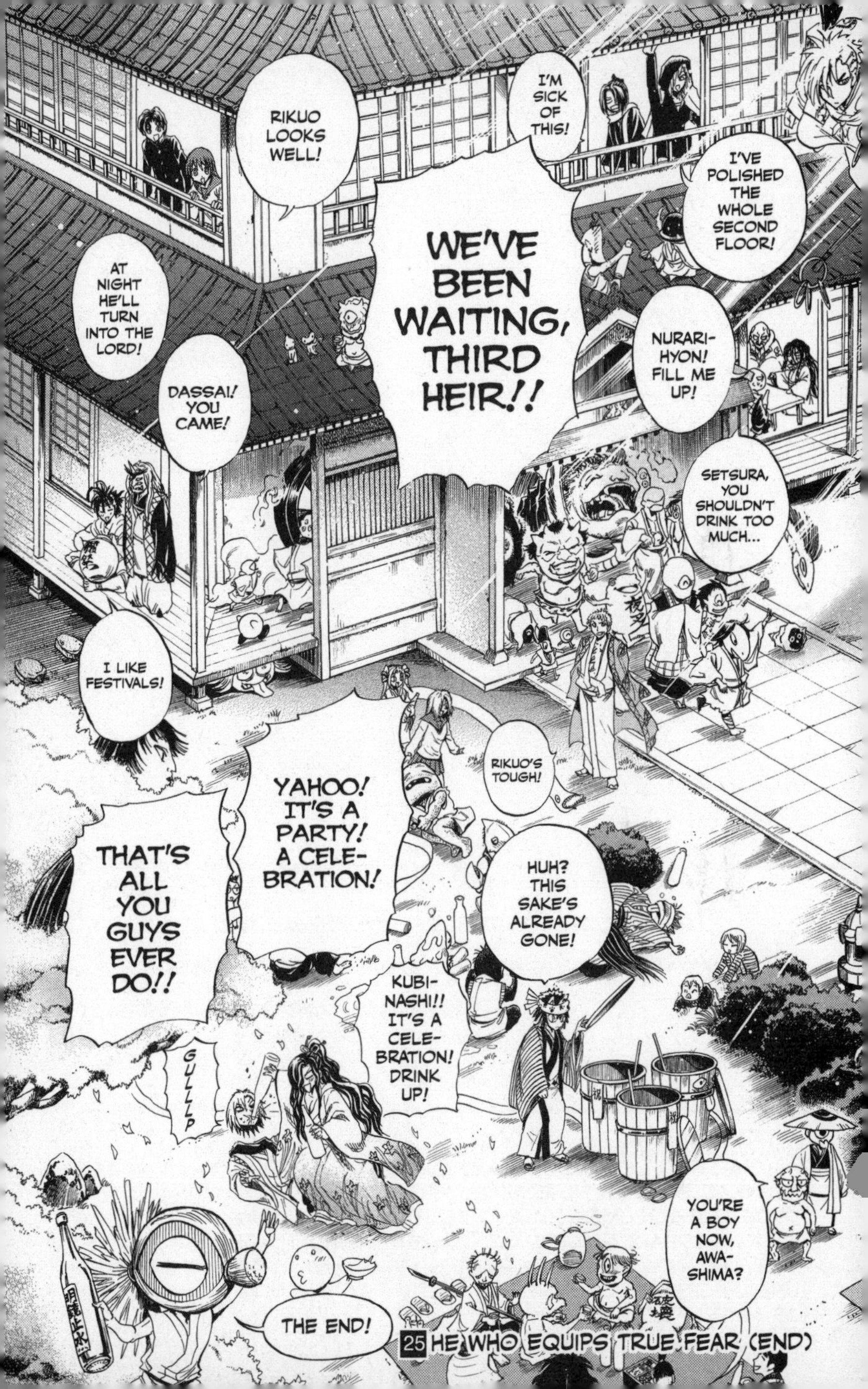
I'M SICK OF THIS!
I'VE POLISHED THE WHOLE SECOND FLOOR!
RIKUO LOOKS WELL!
WE'VE BEEN WAITING, THIRD HEIR!!
NURARIHYON! FILL ME UP!
AT NIGHT HE'LL TURN INTO THE LORD!
SETSURA, YOU SHOULDN'T DRINK TOO MUCH...
DASSAI! YOU CAME!
I LIKE FESTIVALS!
RIKUO'S TOUGH!
YAHOO! IT'S A PARTY! A CELEBRATION!
HUH? THIS SAKE'S ALREADY GONE!
THAT'S ALL YOU GUYS EVER DO!!
YOU'RE A BOY NOW, AWASHIMA?
KUBINASHI!! IT'S A CELEBRATION! DRINK UP!
GULLLP
THE END!

25 HE WHO EQUIPS TRUE FEAR (END)

Art Staff:
  Hideaki Nakajima
  Hiroyuki Senda
  Miori Nishikubo
  Kana Yoshimura
  Tadao Fukuda
  Nobuaki Yamamori
  Kentaro Hidano
  Takuma Yokota

Editors
  Seijiro Nakaji
  Amane Murakoshi

Graphic Novel Editors
  Shinya Toyama
  Hiromi Koshimura
  (planning)

THE *END*

CLOAK: FEAR

I dedicate this to all readers of Nura: Rise of the Yokai Clan and all my friends who love Japanese culture and provided encouragement.
      Hiroshi Shiibashi

⇦(ABOUT BONUS STORIES 1 AND 2)
   THESE TWO EPISODES ARE BASED ON STORIES THAT WERE PLANNED BUT NEVER REALIZED FOR THE RESERVATION-ONLY DVDS FOR VOLUMES 24 AND 25. THE CREDITS ARE AS FOLLOWS: PLOT / HIDEAKI KOYASU AND MANGA / HIROSHI SHIIBASHI. SINCE THEY INCLUDE SOMEONE ELSE'S VIEWPOINT, THERE ARE SOME UNEXPECTED RELATIONSHIPS AND SOME EPISODES THAT SERVE AS NICE EPILOGUES. ENJOY!

Bonus Story 1: Inherited Bonds

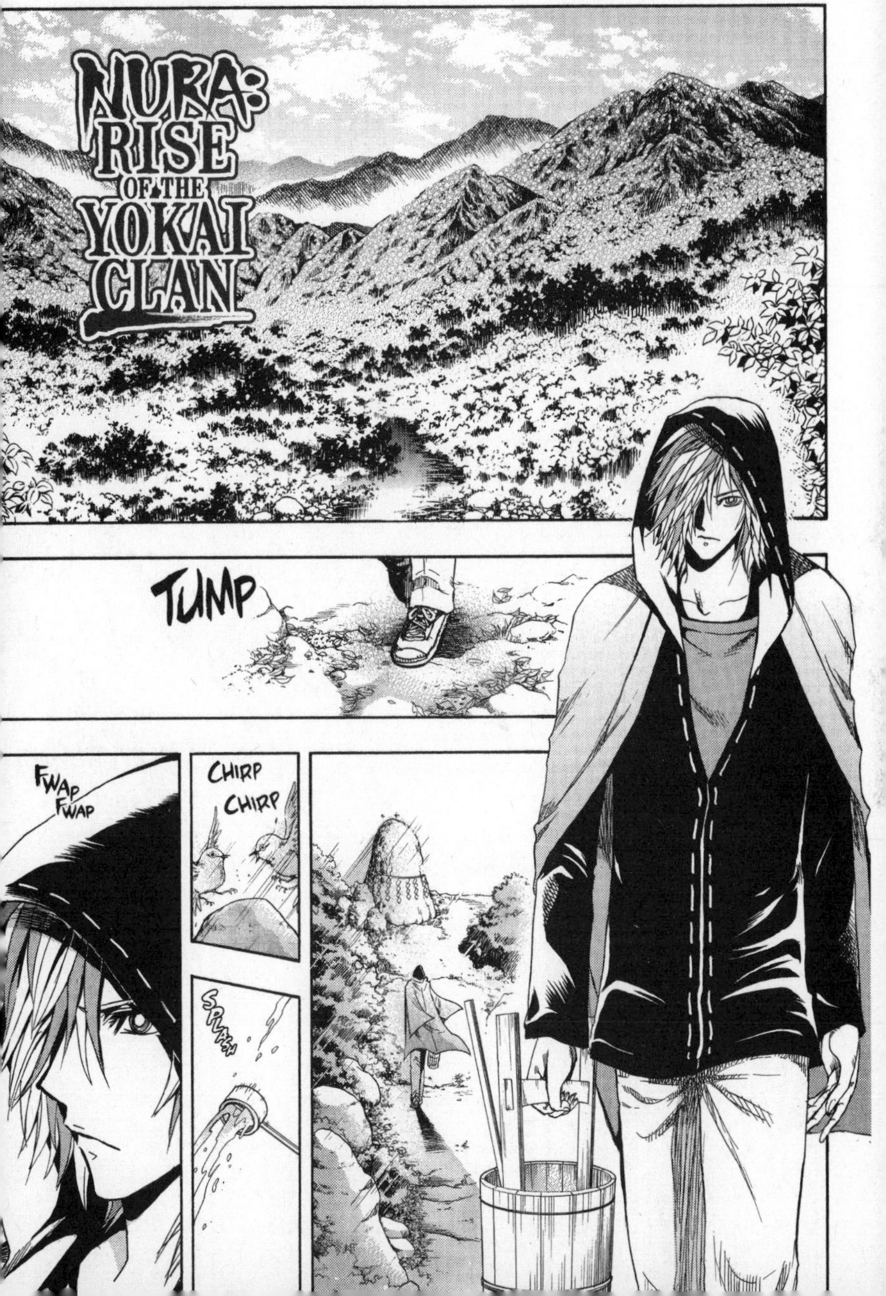
NURA: RISE OF THE YOKAI CLAN
TUMP
SPLASH
CHIRP
CHIRP
FWAP
FWAP

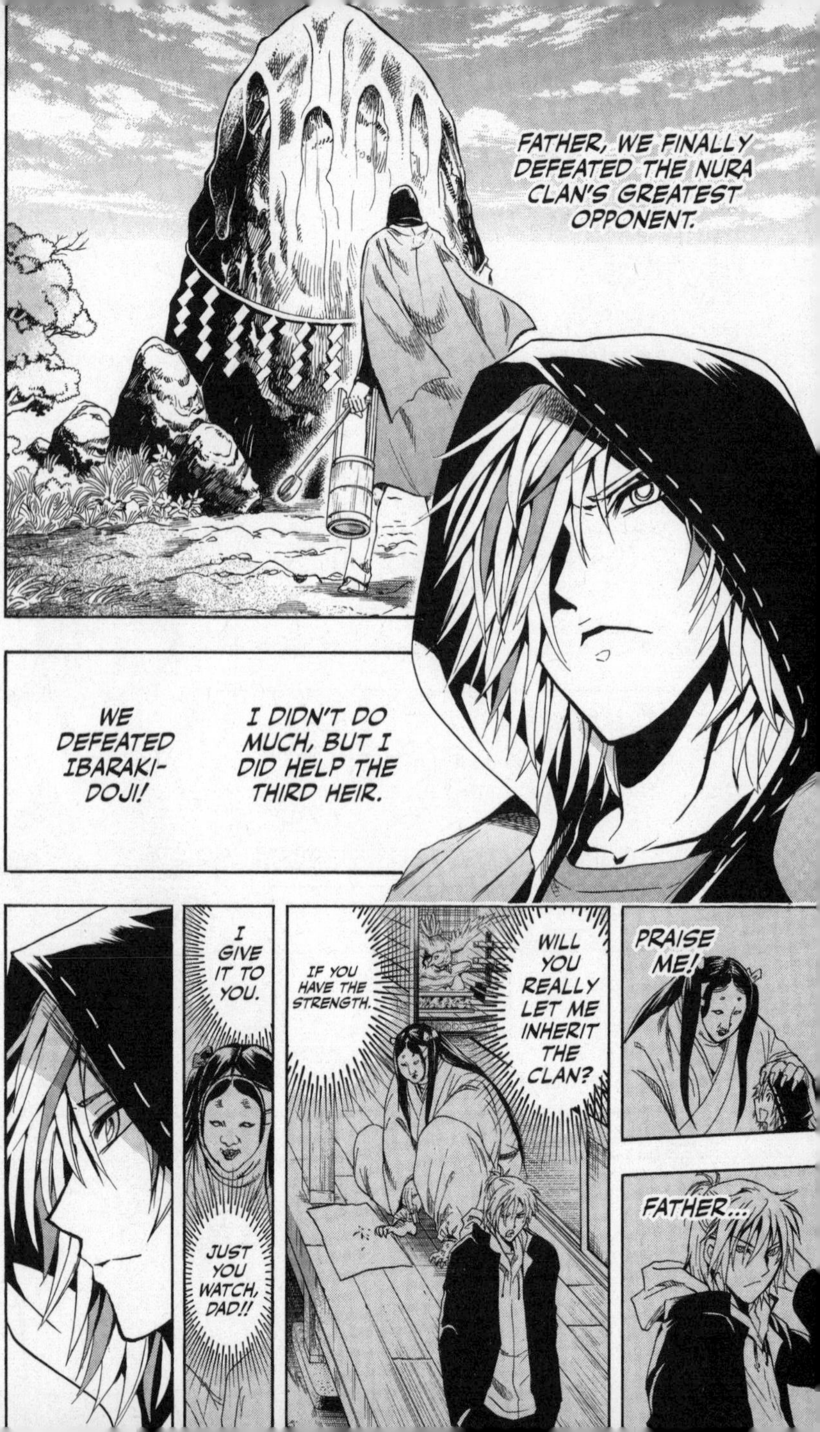
FATHER, WE FINALLY DEFEATED THE NURA CLAN'S GREATEST OPPONENT.
I DIDN'T DO MUCH, BUT I DID HELP THE THIRD HEIR.
WE DEFEATED IBARAKI-DOJI!
PRAISE ME!
FATHER...
WILL YOU REALLY LET ME INHERIT THE CLAN?
IF YOU HAVE THE STRENGTH.
I GIVE IT TO YOU.
JUST YOU WATCH, DAD!!

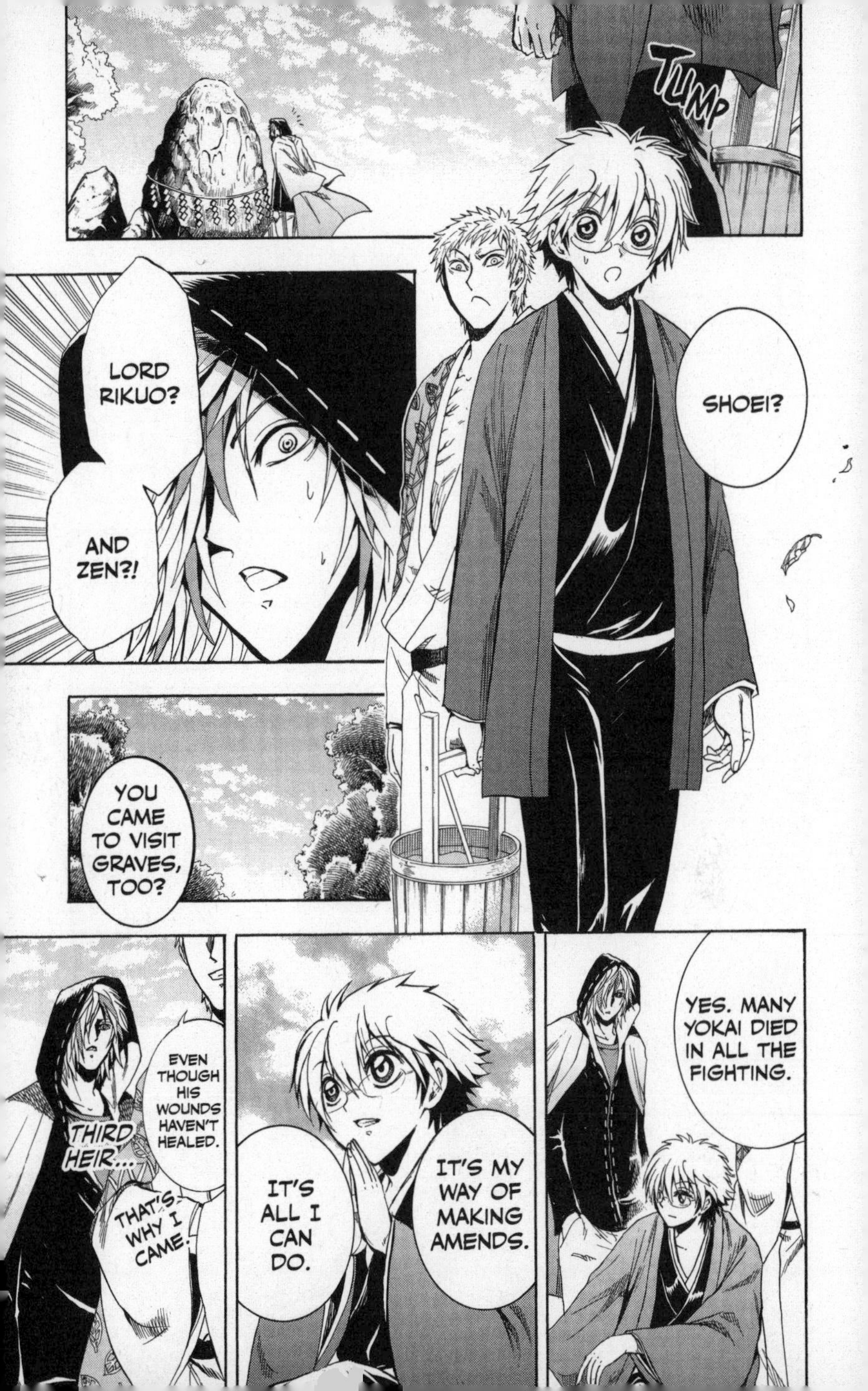
TUMP
SHOEI?
LORD RIKUO?
AND ZEN?!
YOU CAME TO VISIT GRAVES, TOO?
YES. MANY YOKAI DIED IN ALL THE FIGHTING.
IT'S MY WAY OF MAKING AMENDS.
IT'S ALL I CAN DO.
EVEN THOUGH HIS WOUNDS HAVEN'T HEALED.
THIRD HEIR...
THAT'S WHY I CAME.

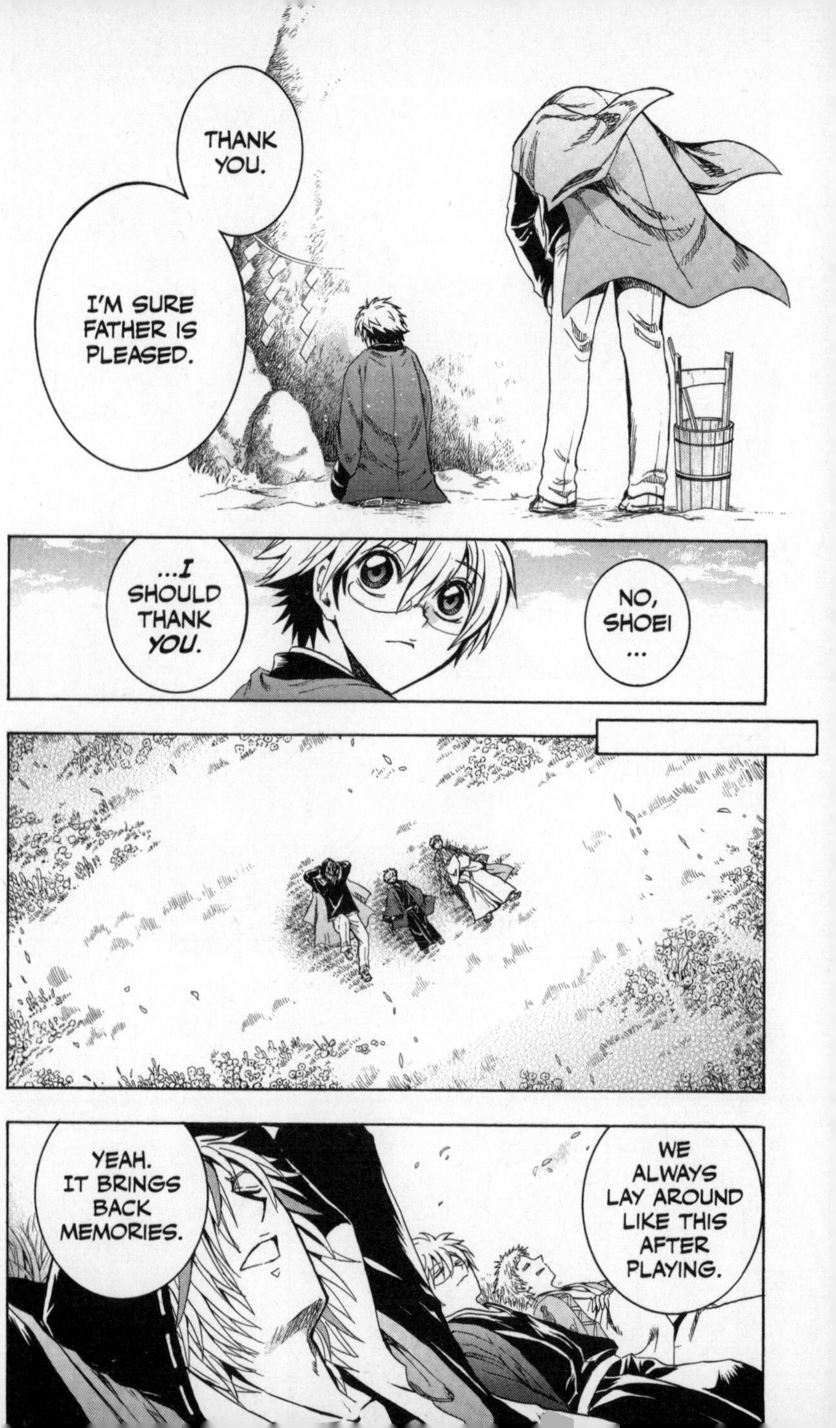
THANK YOU.
I'M SURE FATHER IS PLEASED.
NO, SHOEI ...
...I SHOULD THANK *YOU*.
WE ALWAYS LAY AROUND LIKE THIS AFTER PLAYING.
YEAH. IT BRINGS BACK MEMORIES.

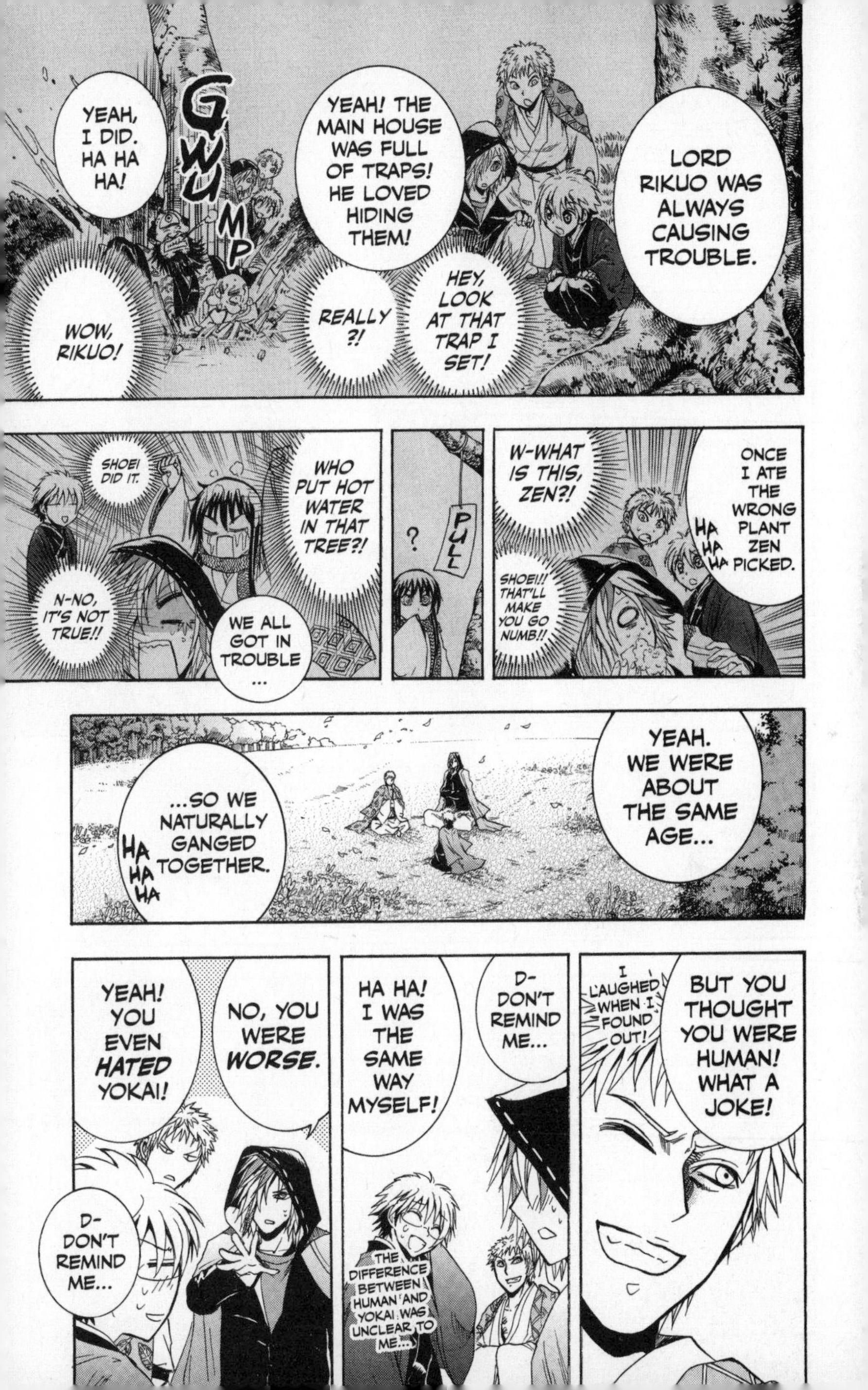
LORD RIKUO WAS ALWAYS CAUSING TROUBLE.
YEAH! THE MAIN HOUSE WAS FULL OF TRAPS! HE LOVED HIDING THEM!
HEY, LOOK AT THAT TRAP I SET!
REALLY?!
YEAH, I DID. HA HA HA!
GWUMP
WOW, RIKUO!
ONCE I ATE THE WRONG PLANT ZEN PICKED.
HA HA HA
W-WHAT IS THIS, ZEN?!
SHOEI!! THAT'LL MAKE YOU GO NUMB!!
?
PULL
WHO PUT HOT WATER IN THAT TREE?!
SHOEI DID IT.
N-NO, IT'S NOT TRUE!!
WE ALL GOT IN TROUBLE...
YEAH. WE WERE ABOUT THE SAME AGE...
...SO WE NATURALLY GANGED TOGETHER.
HA HA HA
BUT YOU THOUGHT YOU WERE HUMAN! WHAT A JOKE!
I LAUGHED WHEN I FOUND OUT!
D-DON'T REMIND ME...
HA HA! I WAS THE SAME WAY MYSELF!
THE DIFFERENCE BETWEEN HUMAN AND YOKAI WAS UNCLEAR TO ME...
NO, YOU WERE WORSE.
YEAH! YOU EVEN HATED YOKAI!
D-DON'T REMIND ME...

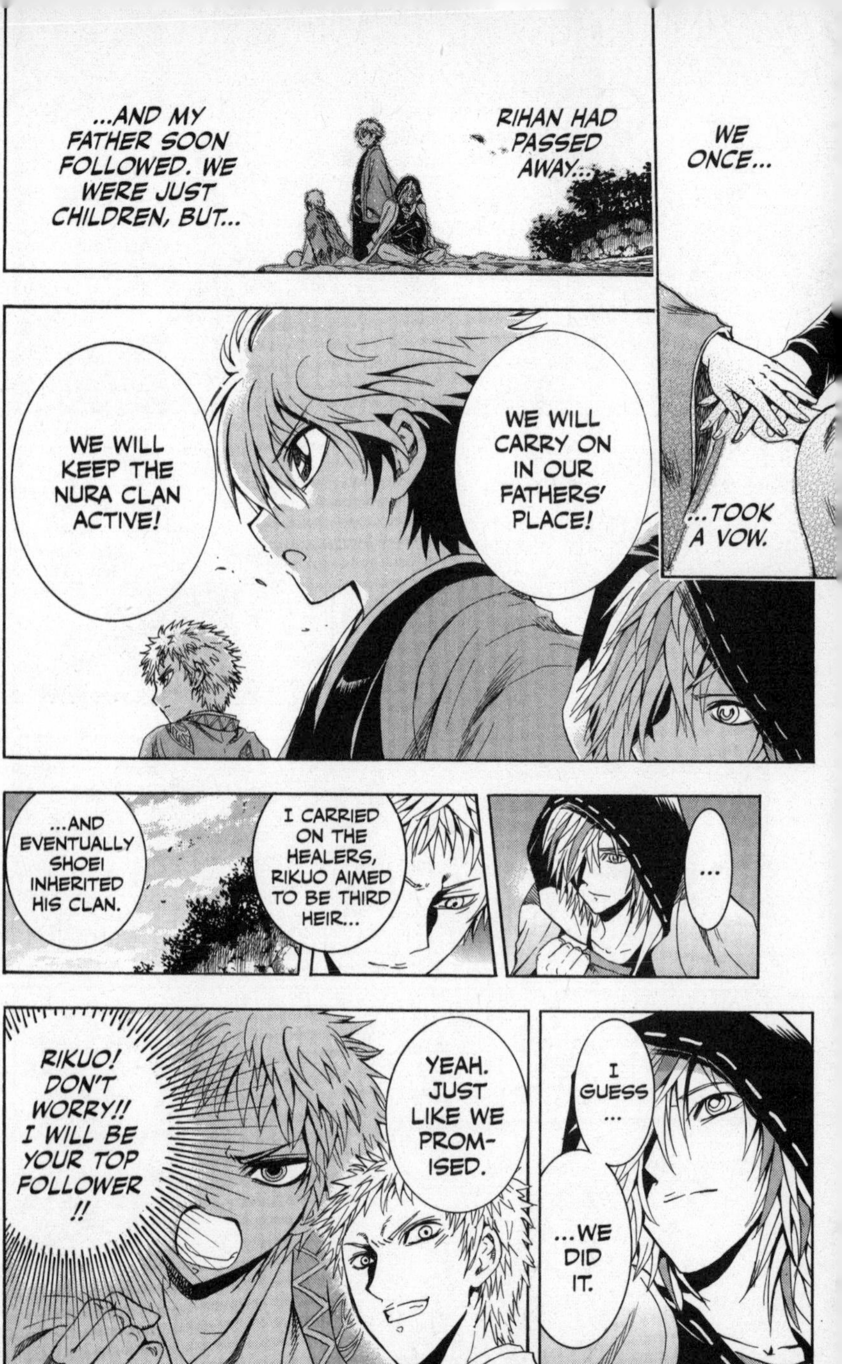
WE ONCE...
RIHAN HAD PASSED AWAY...
...AND MY FATHER SOON FOLLOWED. WE WERE JUST CHILDREN, BUT...
...TOOK A VOW.
WE WILL CARRY ON IN OUR FATHERS' PLACE!
WE WILL KEEP THE NURA CLAN ACTIVE!
...
I CARRIED ON THE HEALERS, RIKUO AIMED TO BE THIRD HEIR...
...AND EVENTUALLY SHOEI INHERITED HIS CLAN.
I GUESS...
...WE DID IT.
YEAH. JUST LIKE WE PROM-ISED.
RIKUO! DON'T WORRY!! I WILL BE YOUR TOP FOLLOWER!!

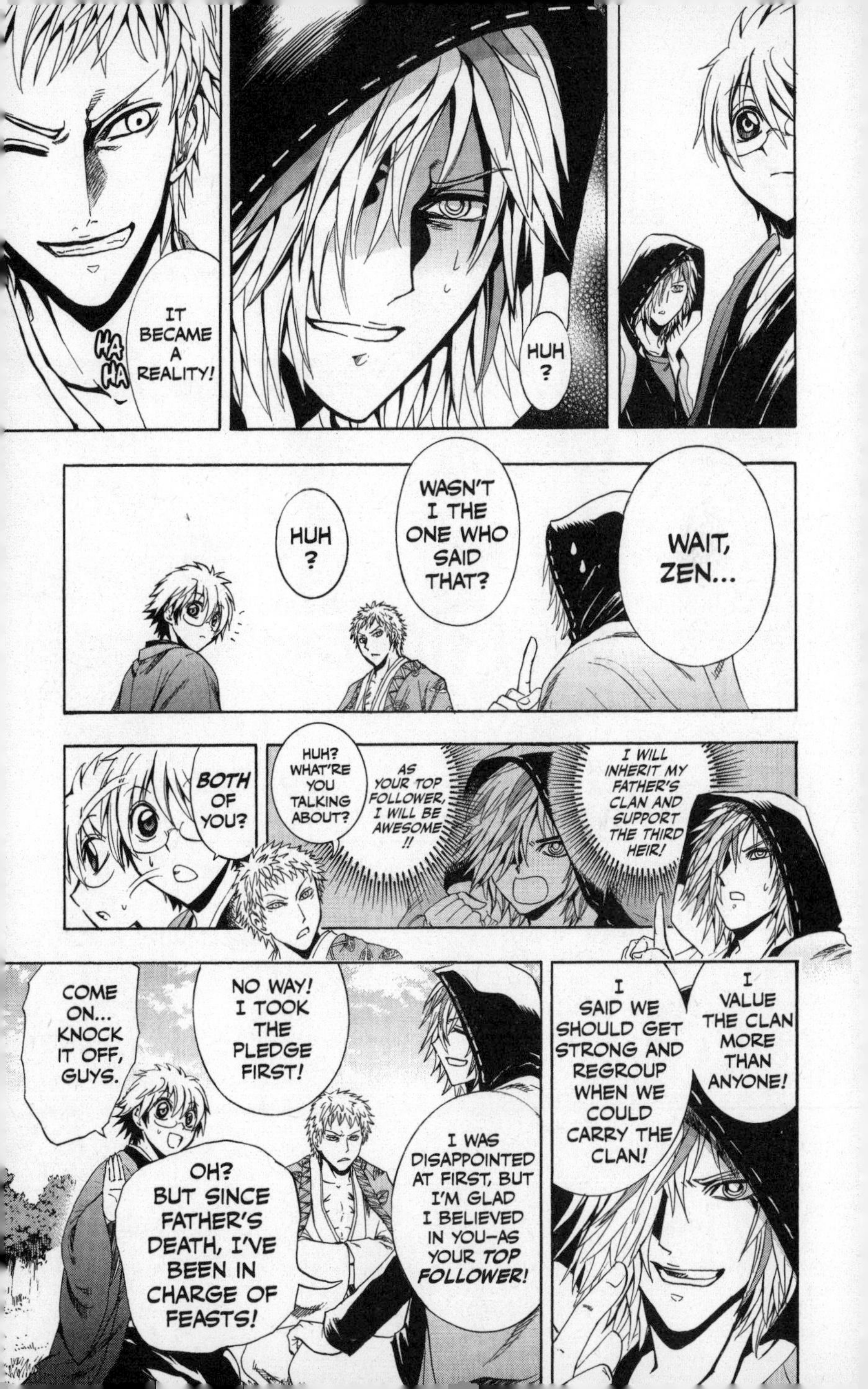
HUH ?
IT BECAME A REALITY!
HA HA
WAIT, ZEN...
WASN'T I THE ONE WHO SAID THAT?
HUH ?
I WILL INHERIT MY FATHER'S CLAN AND SUPPORT THE THIRD HEIR!
AS YOUR TOP FOLLOWER, I WILL BE AWESOME!!
HUH? WHAT'RE YOU TALKING ABOUT?
BOTH OF YOU?
I VALUE THE CLAN MORE THAN ANYONE!
I SAID WE SHOULD GET STRONG AND REGROUP WHEN WE COULD CARRY THE CLAN!
NO WAY! I TOOK THE PLEDGE FIRST!
COME ON... KNOCK IT OFF, GUYS.
I WAS DISAPPOINTED AT FIRST, BUT I'M GLAD I BELIEVED IN YOU—AS YOUR TOP FOLLOWER!
OH? BUT SINCE FATHER'S DEATH, I'VE BEEN IN CHARGE OF FEASTS!

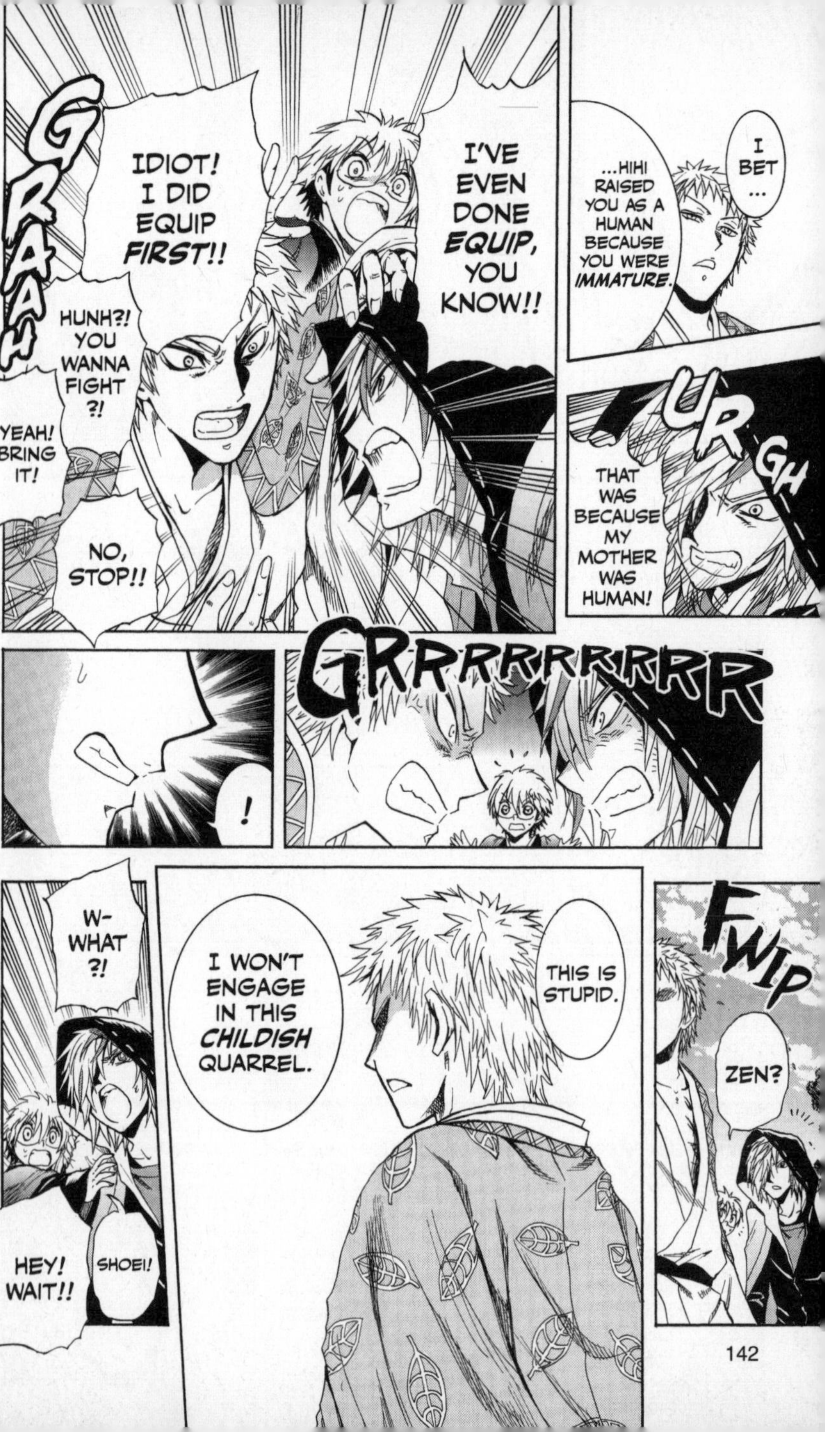
I BET ...
...HIHI RAISED YOU AS A HUMAN BECAUSE YOU WERE *IMMATURE*.
URGH
THAT WAS BECAUSE MY MOTHER WAS HUMAN!
I'VE EVEN DONE *EQUIP*, YOU KNOW!!
IDIOT! I DID EQUIP *FIRST*!!
GRAAAH
HUNH?! YOU WANNA FIGHT ?!
YEAH! BRING IT!
NO, STOP!!
GRRRRRRRRR
!
FWIP
ZEN?
THIS IS STUPID.
I WON'T ENGAGE IN THIS *CHILDISH* QUARREL.
W-WHAT ?!
SHOEI!
HEY! WAIT!!

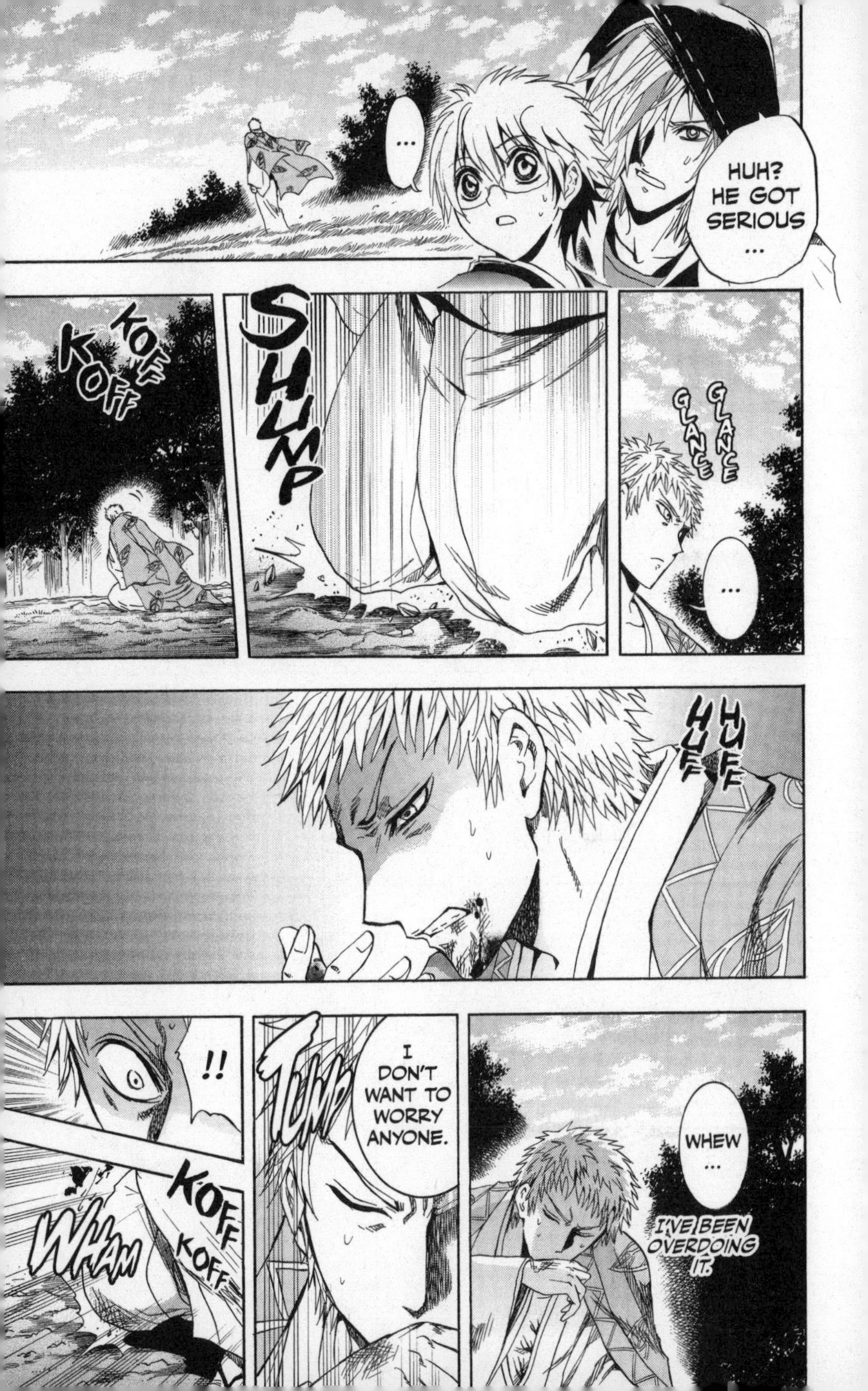
HUH? HE GOT SERIOUS ...
...
GLANCE GLANCE
...
SHUMP
KOFF KOFF
HUFF HUFF
WHEW ...
I'VE BEEN OVERDOING IT.
I DON'T WANT TO WORRY ANYONE.
TOMP
!!
KOFF KOFF
WHAM

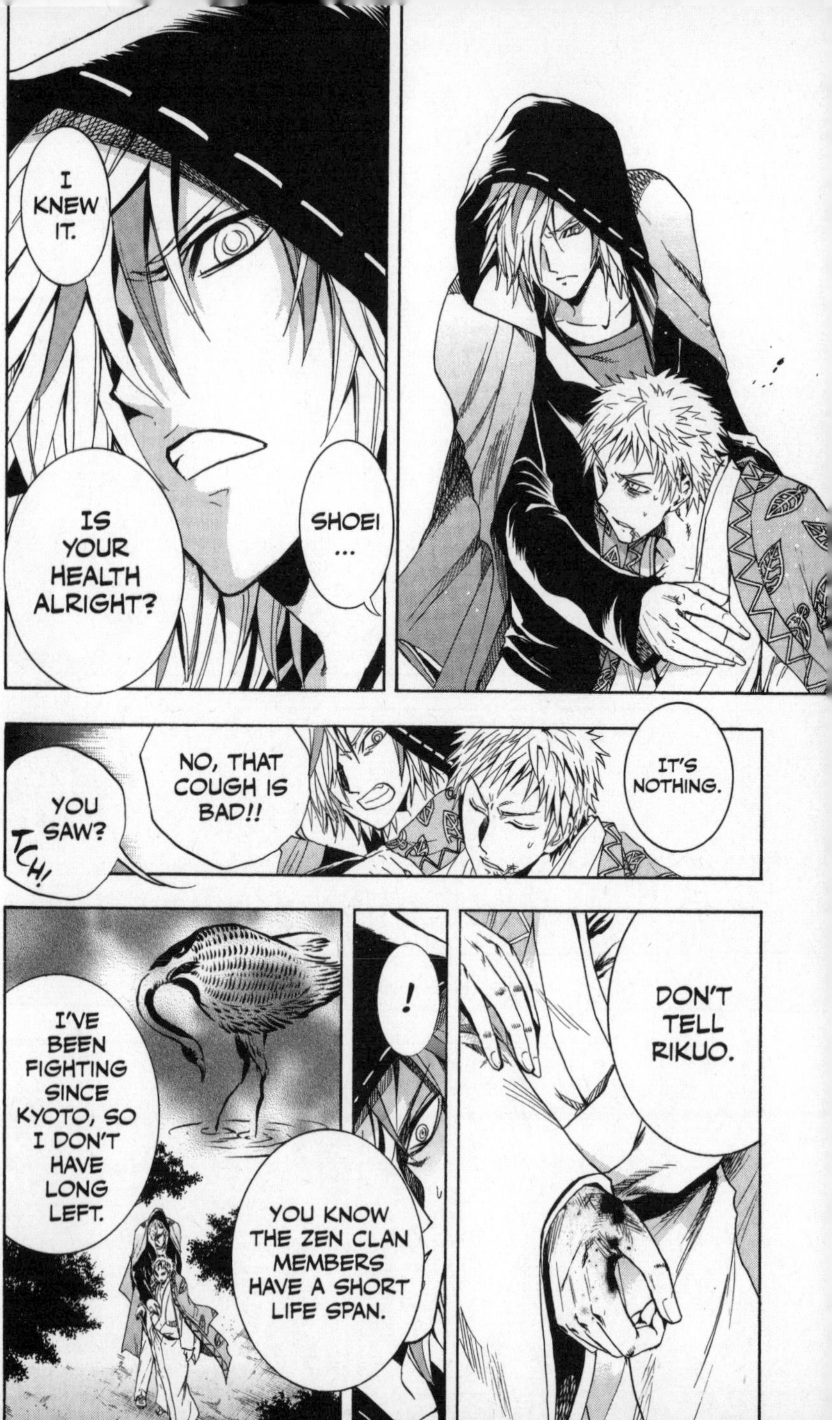
I KNEW IT.
SHOEI...
IS YOUR HEALTH ALRIGHT?
IT'S NOTHING.
NO, THAT COUGH IS BAD!!
YOU SAW?
TCH!
DON'T TELL RIKUO.
!
YOU KNOW THE ZEN CLAN MEMBERS HAVE A SHORT LIFE SPAN.
I'VE BEEN FIGHTING SINCE KYOTO, SO I DON'T HAVE LONG LEFT.

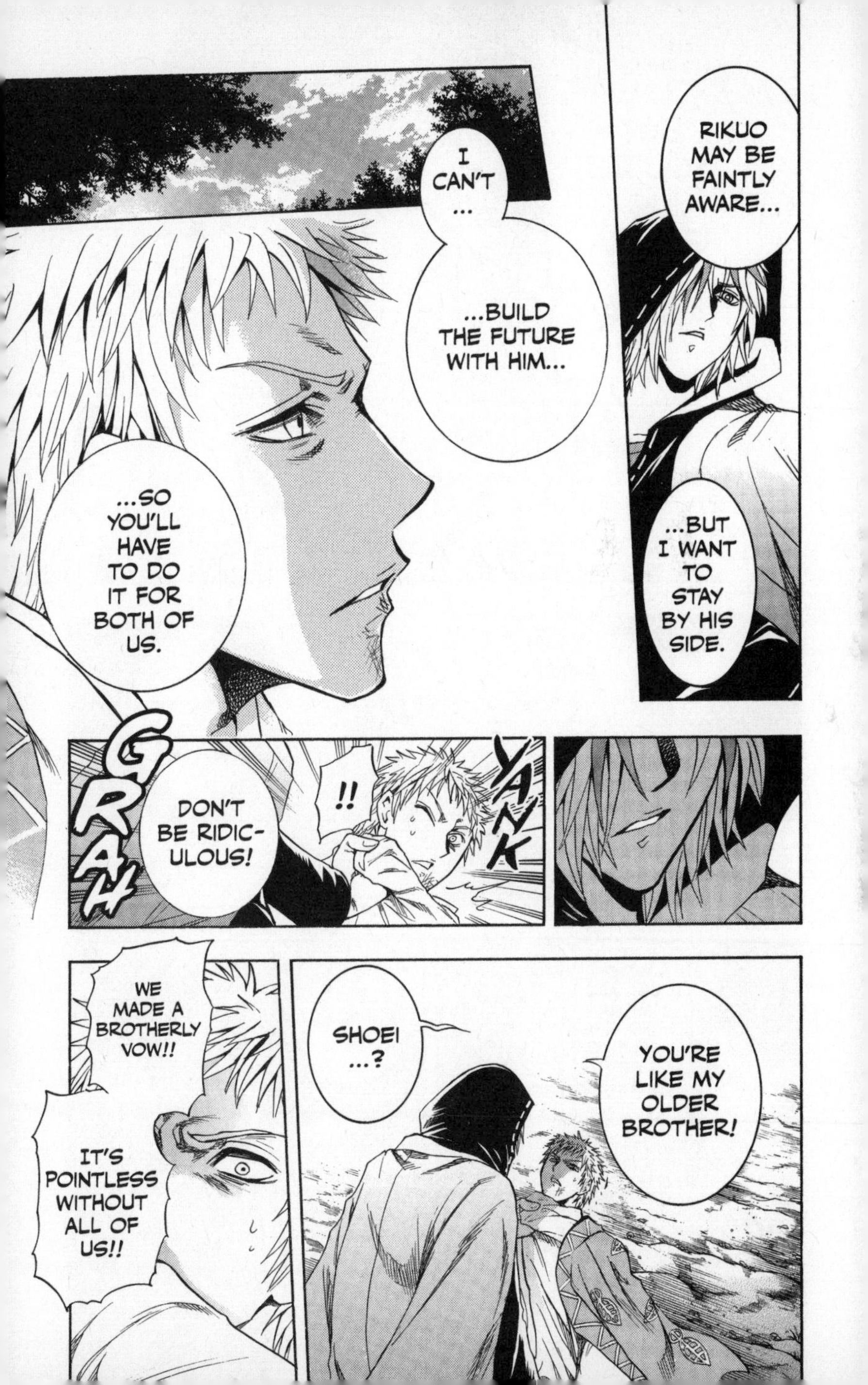
RIKUO MAY BE FAINTLY AWARE...
...BUT I WANT TO STAY BY HIS SIDE.
I CAN'T ...
...BUILD THE FUTURE WITH HIM...
...SO YOU'LL HAVE TO DO IT FOR BOTH OF US.
YANK
!!
DON'T BE RIDIC-ULOUS!
GRAH
YOU'RE LIKE MY OLDER BROTHER!
SHOEI ...?
WE MADE A BROTHERLY VOW!!
IT'S POINTLESS WITHOUT ALL OF US!!

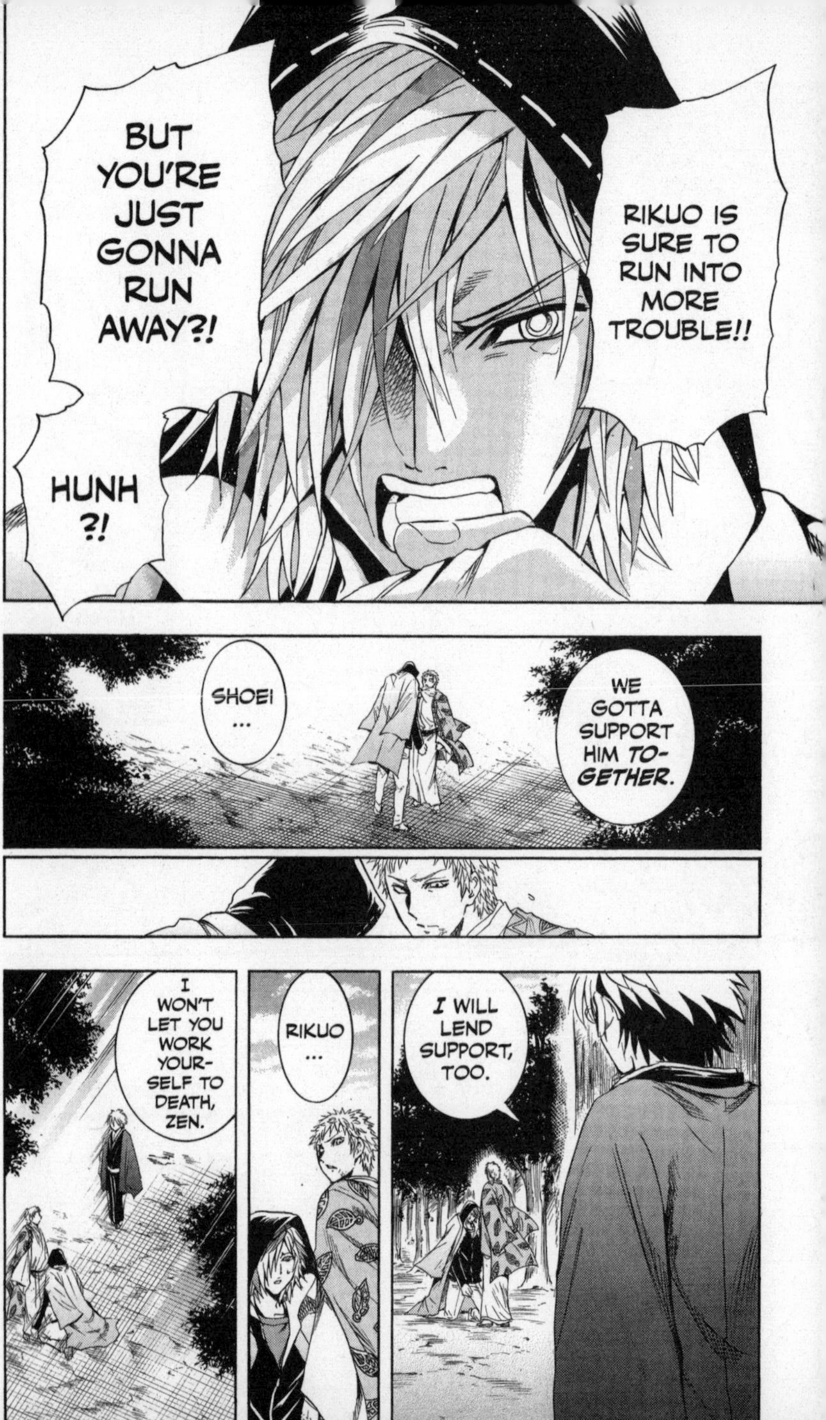
RIKUO IS SURE TO RUN INTO MORE TROUBLE!!
BUT YOU'RE JUST GONNA RUN AWAY?!
HUNH ?!
WE GOTTA SUPPORT HIM *TOGETHER*.
SHOEI ...
I WILL LEND SUPPORT, TOO.
RIKUO ...
I WON'T LET YOU WORK YOURSELF TO DEATH, ZEN.

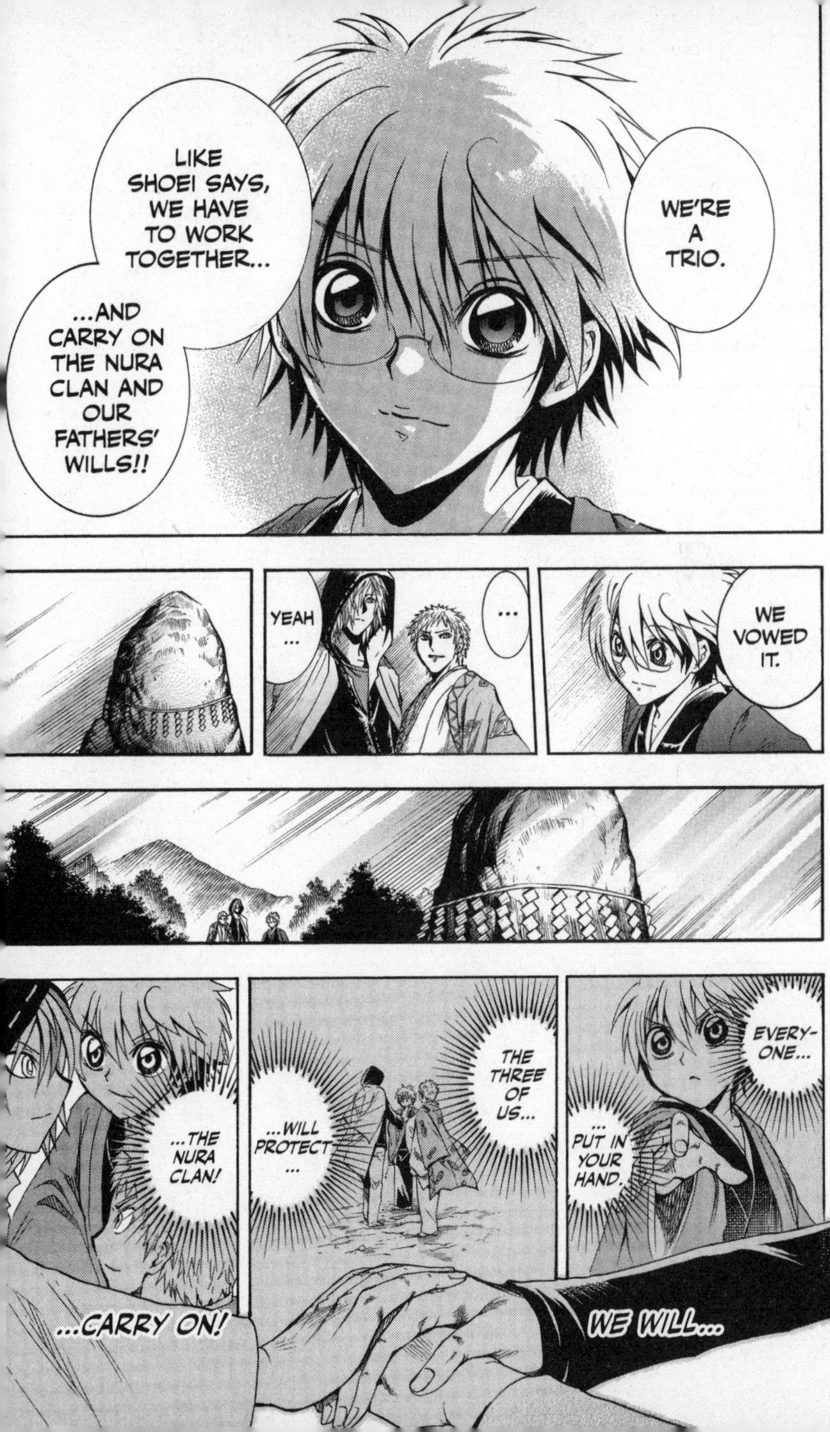
WE'RE A TRIO.
LIKE SHOEI SAYS, WE HAVE TO WORK TOGETHER...
...AND CARRY ON THE NURA CLAN AND OUR FATHERS' WILLS!!
WE VOWED IT.
...
YEAH ...
EVERY-ONE...
... PUT IN YOUR HAND.
THE THREE OF US...
...WILL PROTECT ...
...THE NURA CLAN!
WE WILL...
...CARRY ON!

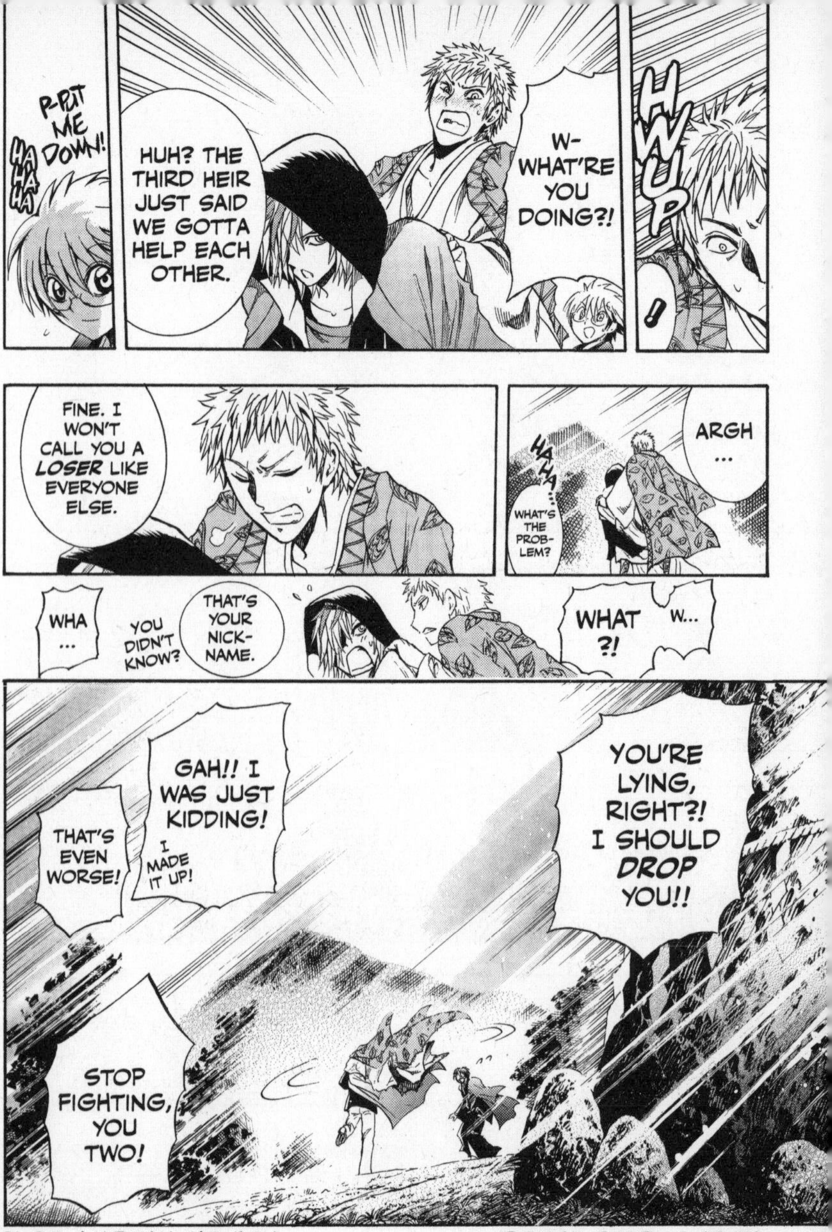
HWUP
!
W- WHAT'RE YOU DOING?!
HUH? THE THIRD HEIR JUST SAID WE GOTTA HELP EACH OTHER.
P-PUT ME DOWN!
HAHAHA
ARGH ...
HAHA...
WHAT'S THE PROB-LEM?
FINE. I WON'T CALL YOU A *LOSER* LIKE EVERYONE ELSE.
W...
WHAT ?!
THAT'S YOUR NICK-NAME.
YOU DIDN'T KNOW?
WHA ...
YOU'RE LYING, RIGHT?! I SHOULD *DROP* YOU!!
GAH!! I WAS JUST KIDDING!
I MADE IT UP!
THAT'S EVEN WORSE!
STOP FIGHTING, YOU TWO!

PLOT / HIDEAKI KOYASU

BONUS STORY 1 (END)

Bonus Story 2: The Third Heir Gone Wild?!

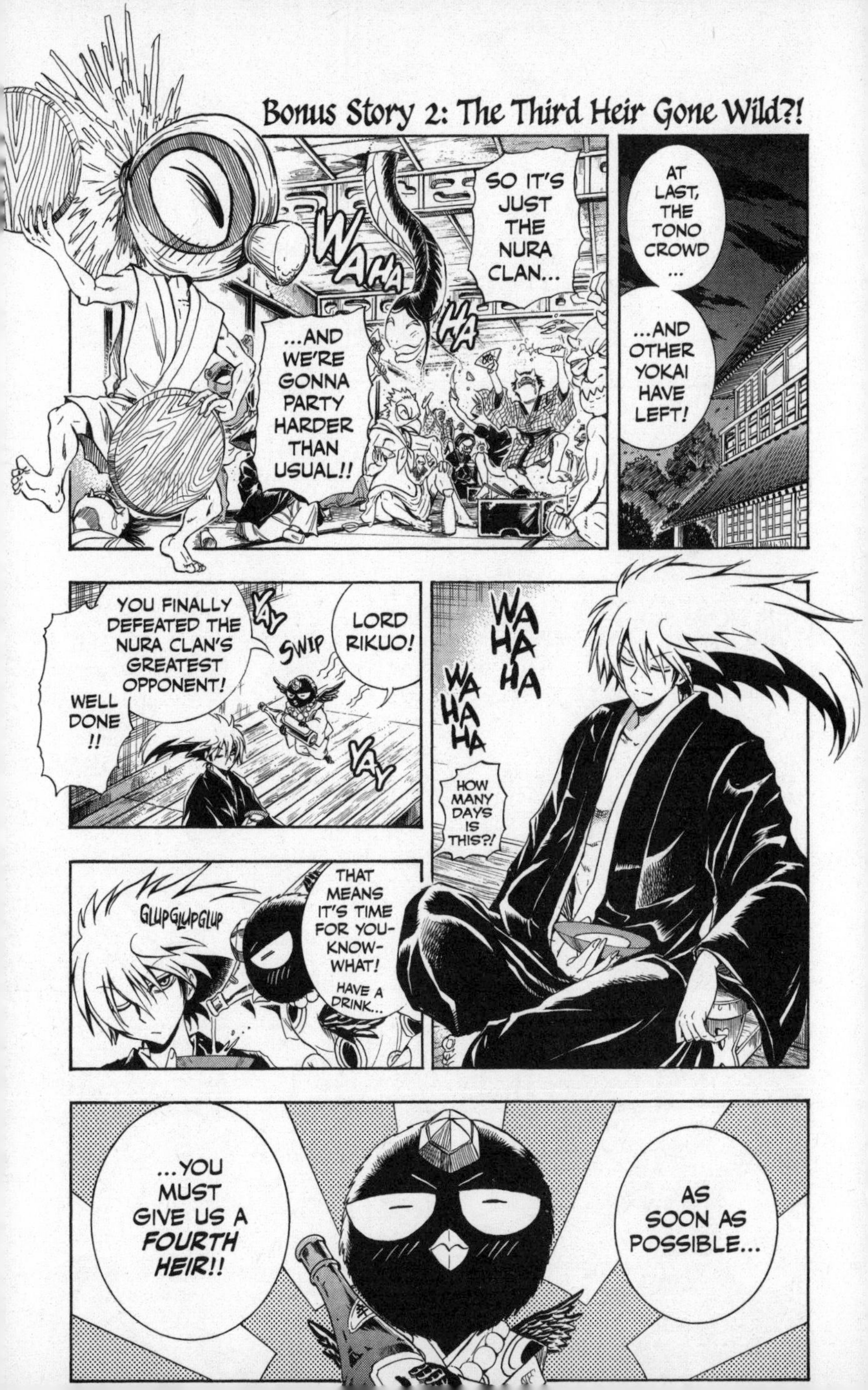
AT LAST, THE TONO CROWD ...
...AND OTHER YOKAI HAVE LEFT!
SO IT'S JUST THE NURA CLAN...
WAHAHA
HA
...AND WE'RE GONNA PARTY HARDER THAN USUAL!!
WAHAHA
WAHAHA
HOW MANY DAYS IS THIS?!
LORD RIKUO!
YAY
SWIP
YOU FINALLY DEFEATED THE NURA CLAN'S GREATEST OPPONENT!
WELL DONE !!
YAY
THAT MEANS IT'S TIME FOR YOU-KNOW-WHAT!
HAVE A DRINK...
GLUPGLUPGLUP
AS SOON AS POSSIBLE...
...YOU MUST GIVE US A *FOURTH HEIR*!!

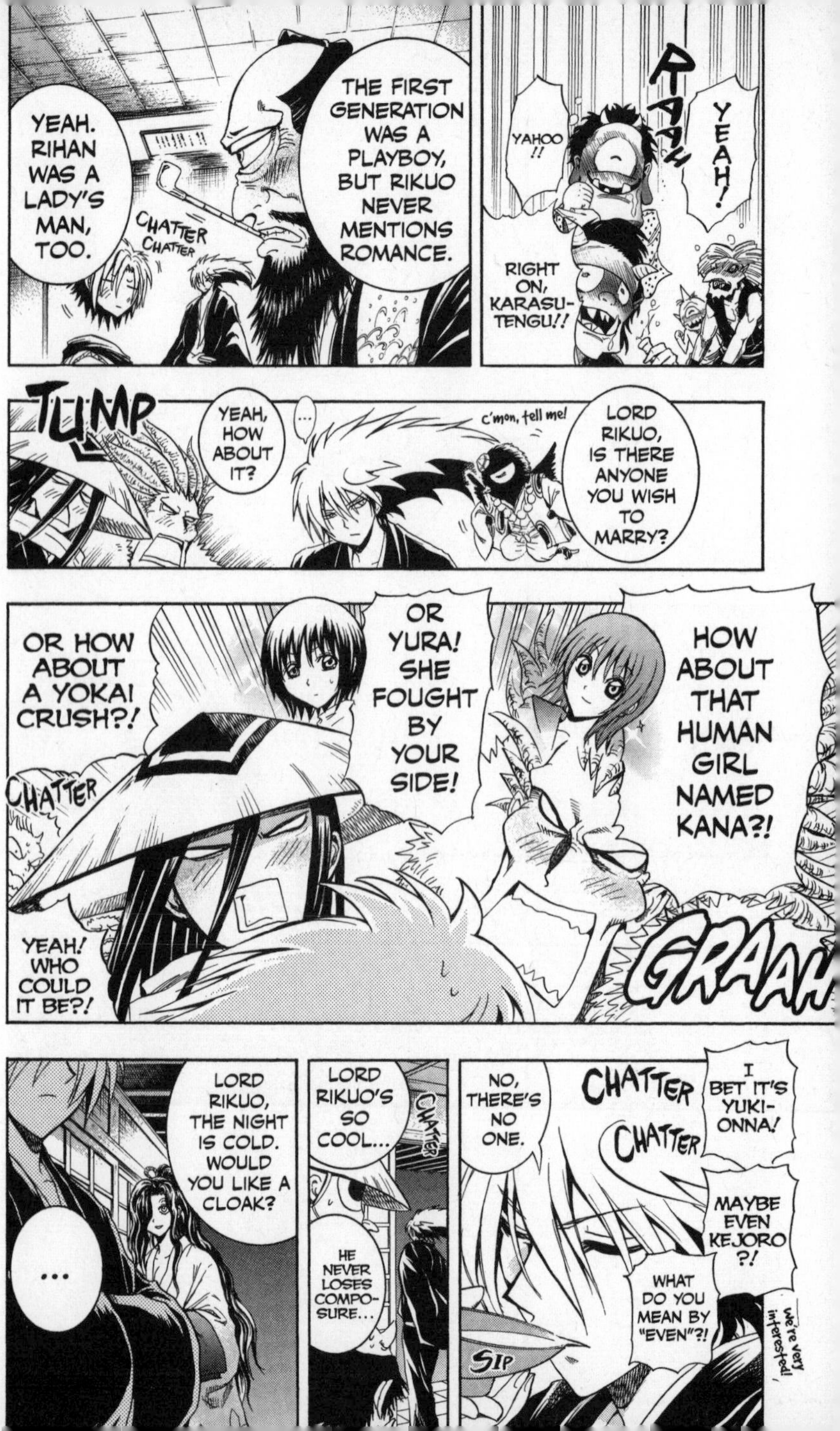
RAAAH
YEAH!
YAHOO!!
RIGHT ON, KARASU-TENGU!!
THE FIRST GENERATION WAS A PLAYBOY, BUT RIKUO NEVER MENTIONS ROMANCE.
YEAH. RIHAN WAS A LADY'S MAN, TOO.
CHATTER CHATTER
LORD RIKUO, IS THERE ANYONE YOU WISH TO MARRY?
c'mon, tell me!
...
YEAH, HOW ABOUT IT?
TUMP
HOW ABOUT THAT HUMAN GIRL NAMED KANA?!
OR YURA! SHE FOUGHT BY YOUR SIDE!
OR HOW ABOUT A YOKAI CRUSH?!
CHATTER
GRAAAH
YEAH! WHO COULD IT BE?!
I BET IT'S YUKI-ONNA!
CHATTER
CHATTER
NO, THERE'S NO ONE.
MAYBE EVEN KEJORO?!
WHAT DO YOU MEAN BY "EVEN"?!
we're very interested!
SIP
LORD RIKUO'S SO COOL...
CHATTER
HE NEVER LOSES COMPOSURE...
LORD RIKUO, THE NIGHT IS COLD. WOULD YOU LIKE A CLOAK?
...

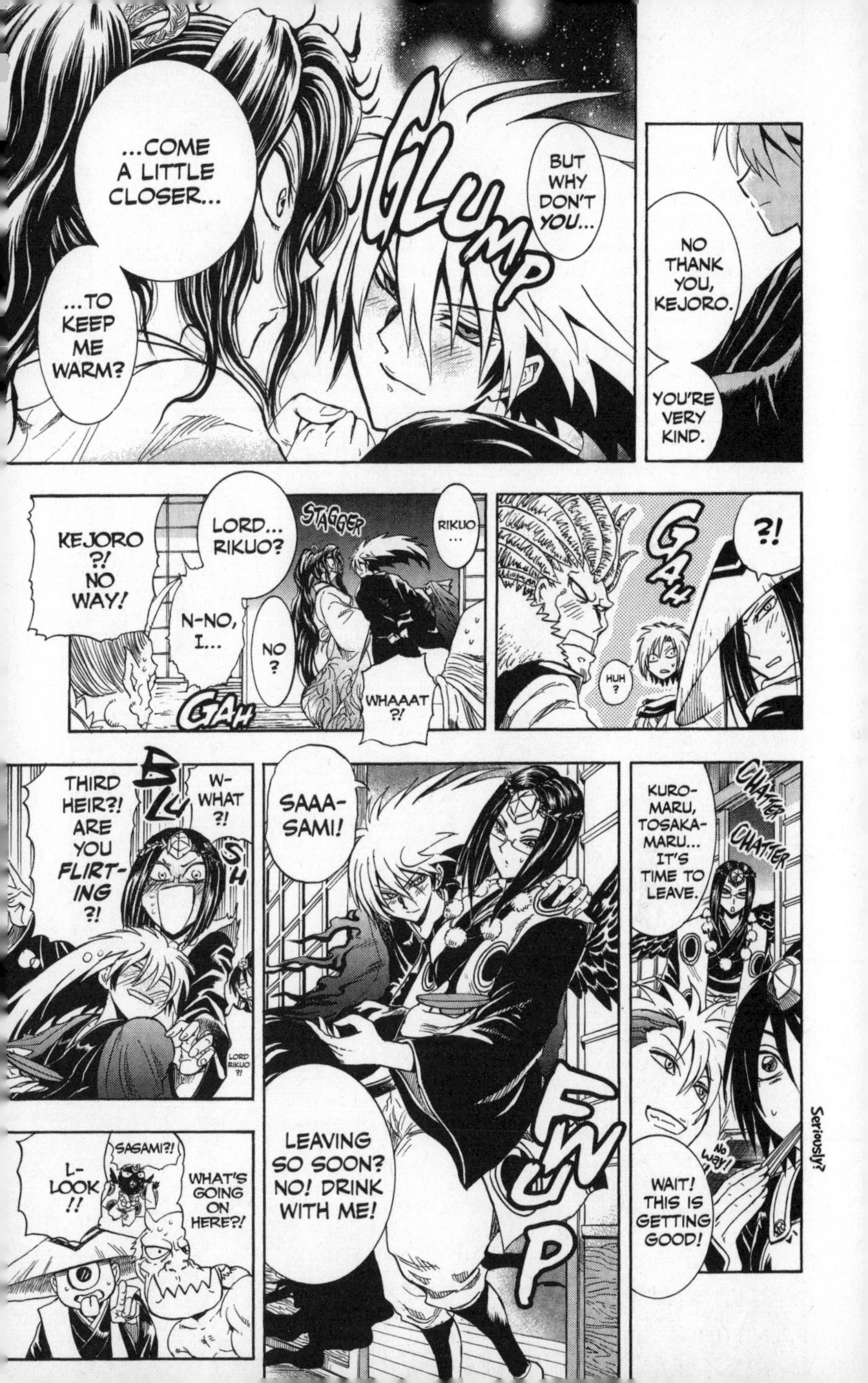
NO THANK YOU, KEJORO.
YOU'RE VERY KIND.
BUT WHY DON'T YOU...
GLUMP
...COME A LITTLE CLOSER...
...TO KEEP ME WARM?
?!
GAH
HUH?
RIKUO...
STAGGER
LORD... RIKUO?
KEJORO?! NO WAY!
N-NO, I...
NO?
WHAAAT?!
GAH
CHATTER
CHATTER
KURO-MARU, TOSAKA-MARU... IT'S TIME TO LEAVE.
No way!
WAIT! THIS IS GETTING GOOD!
Seriously?
SAAA-SAMI!
LEAVING SO SOON? NO! DRINK WITH ME!
FWUP
W-WHAT?!
BLUSH
THIRD HEIR?! ARE YOU FLIRTING?!
LORD RIKUO?!
SASAMI?!
WHAT'S GOING ON HERE?!
L-LOOK!!

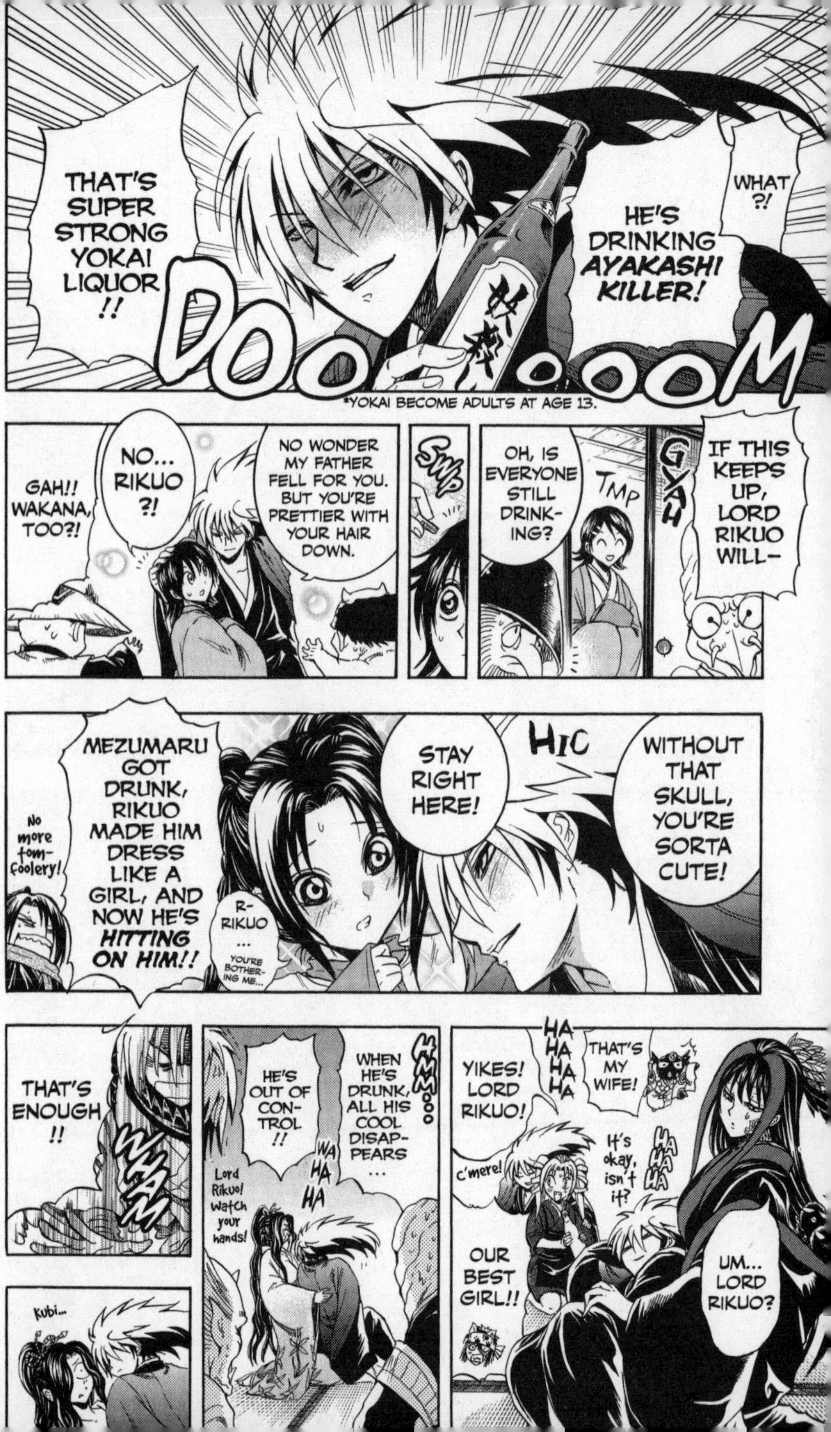
WHAT?!
HE'S DRINKING AYAKASHI KILLER!
THAT'S SUPER STRONG YOKAI LIQUOR!!
DOO...OOOM
*YOKAI BECOME ADULTS AT AGE 13.
IF THIS KEEPS UP, LORD RIKUO WILL-
GYAH
TMP
OH, IS EVERYONE STILL DRINKING?
SWP
NO WONDER MY FATHER FELL FOR YOU. BUT YOU'RE PRETTIER WITH YOUR HAIR DOWN.
NO... RIKUO?!
GAH!! WAKANA, TOO?!
WITHOUT THAT SKULL, YOU'RE SORTA CUTE!
HIC
STAY RIGHT HERE!
R-RIKUO...
YOU'RE BOTHERING ME...
MEZUMARU GOT DRUNK, RIKUO MADE HIM DRESS LIKE A GIRL, AND NOW HE'S HITTING ON HIM!!
No more tom-foolery!
THAT'S MY WIFE!
HA HA HA HA HA
YIKES! LORD RIKUO!
c'mere!
It's okay, isn't it?
HA HA HA
OUR BEST GIRL!!
UM... LORD RIKUO?
HMMOOO
WHEN HE'S DRUNK, ALL HIS COOL DISAPPEARS...
HE'S OUT OF CONTROL!!
WA HA HA
Lord Rikuo! Watch your hands!
THAT'S ENOUGH!!
WHAM
Kubi...

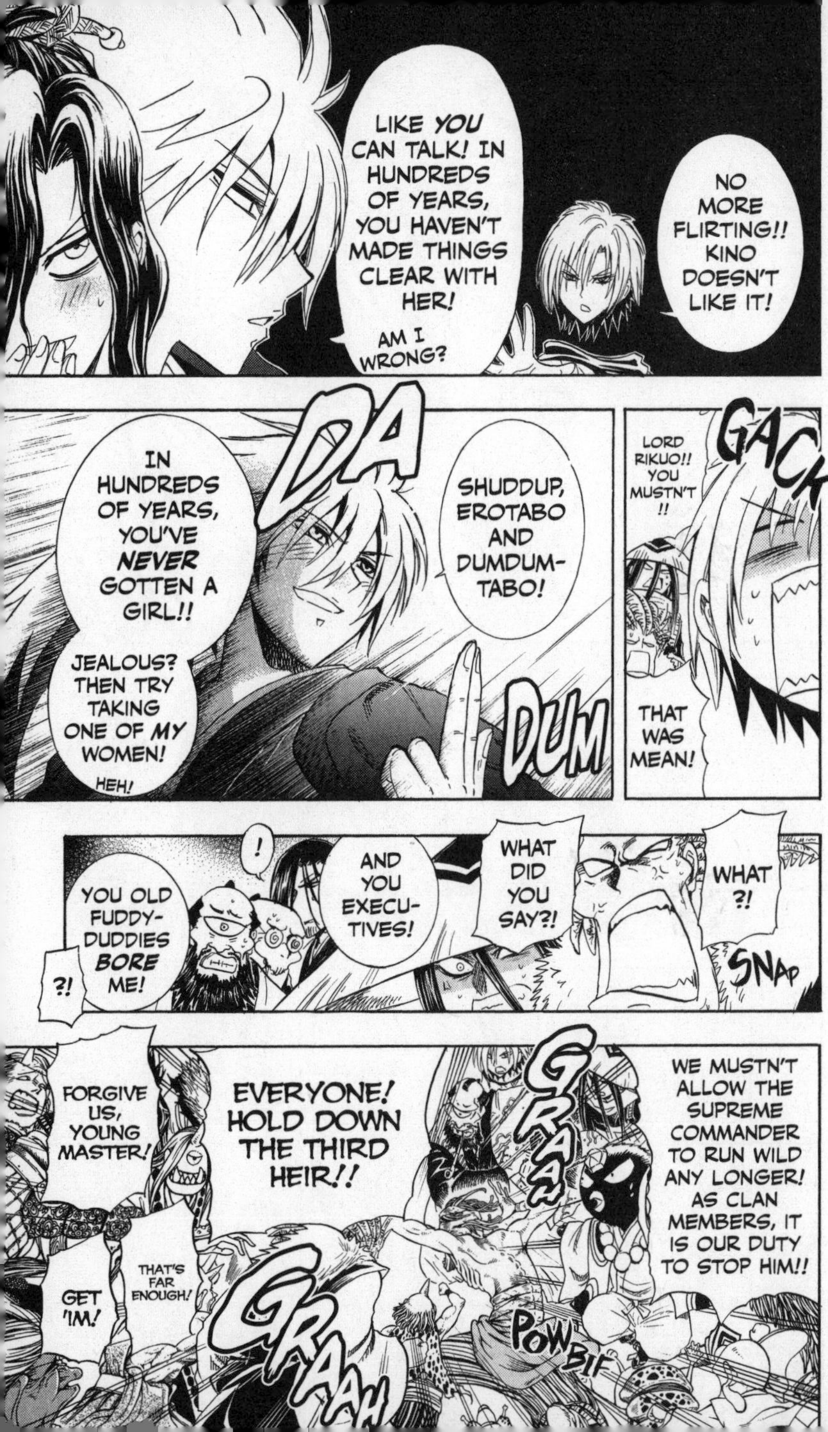

NO MORE FLIRTING!! KINO DOESN'T LIKE IT!
LIKE YOU CAN TALK! IN HUNDREDS OF YEARS, YOU HAVEN'T MADE THINGS CLEAR WITH HER!
AM I WRONG?
GACK
LORD RIKUO!! YOU MUSTN'T!!
THAT WAS MEAN!
DA
SHUDDUP, EROTABO AND DUMDUM-TABO!
IN HUNDREDS OF YEARS, YOU'VE NEVER GOTTEN A GIRL!!
DUM
JEALOUS? THEN TRY TAKING ONE OF MY WOMEN!
HEH!
WHAT?!
SNAP
WHAT DID YOU SAY?!
AND YOU EXECUTIVES!
!
YOU OLD FUDDY-DUDDIES BORE ME!
?!
WE MUSTN'T ALLOW THE SUPREME COMMANDER TO RUN WILD ANY LONGER! AS CLAN MEMBERS, IT IS OUR DUTY TO STOP HIM!!
GRAAH
EVERYONE! HOLD DOWN THE THIRD HEIR!!
FORGIVE US, YOUNG MASTER!
THAT'S FAR ENOUGH!
GET 'IM!
GRAAH
POW
BIF

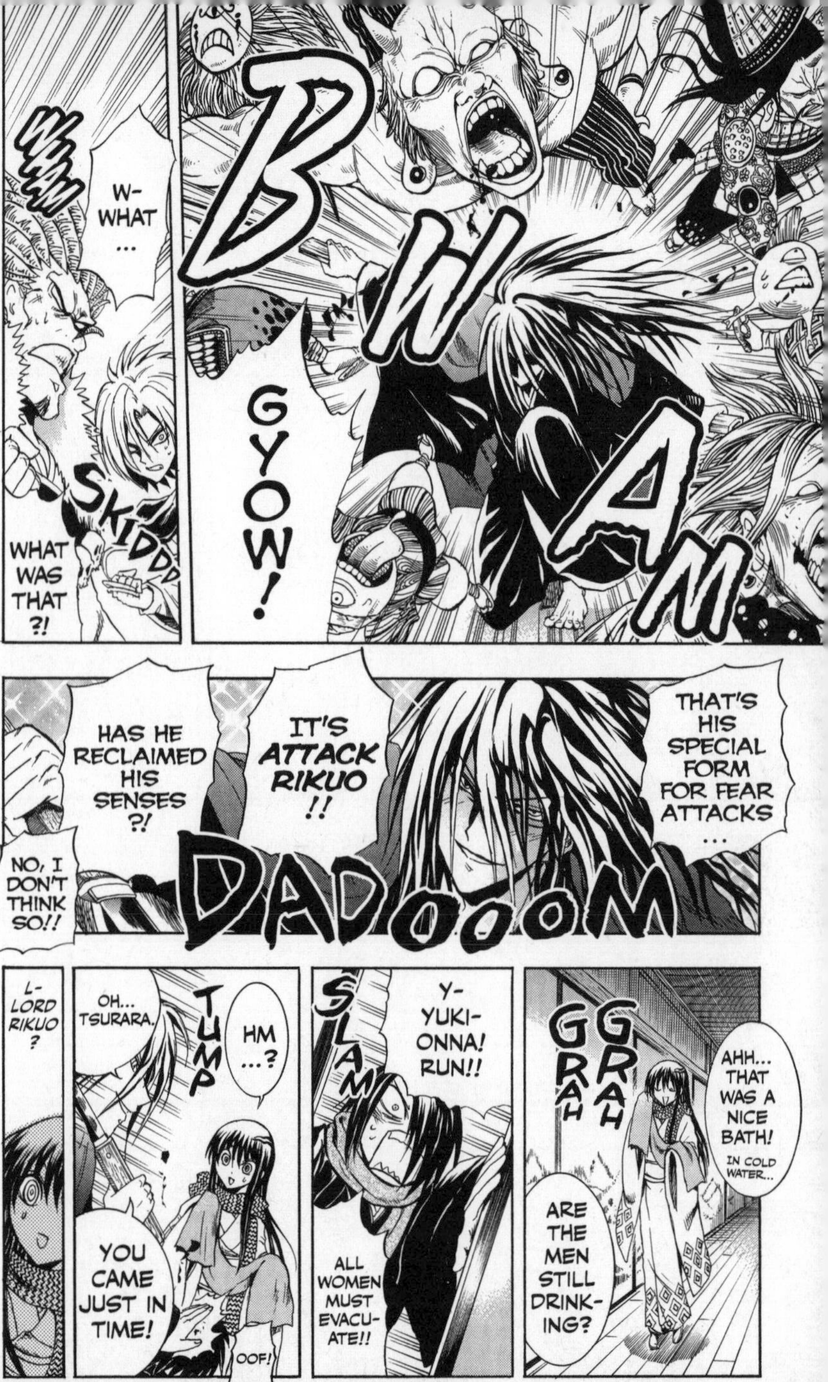
BWAM
GYOW!
W-WHAT ...
SKIDDD
WHAT WAS THAT ?!
THAT'S HIS SPECIAL FORM FOR FEAR ATTACKS ...
DADOOOM
IT'S ATTACK RIKUO !!
HAS HE RECLAIMED HIS SENSES ?!
NO, I DON'T THINK SO!!
GGRAH GRAH
AHH... THAT WAS A NICE BATH!
IN COLD WATER...
ARE THE MEN STILL DRINK-ING?
SLAM
Y-YUKI-ONNA! RUN!!
ALL WOMEN MUST EVACU-ATE!!
TUMP
HM ...?
OH... TSURARA.
YOU CAME JUST IN TIME!
OOF!
L-LORD RIKUO ?

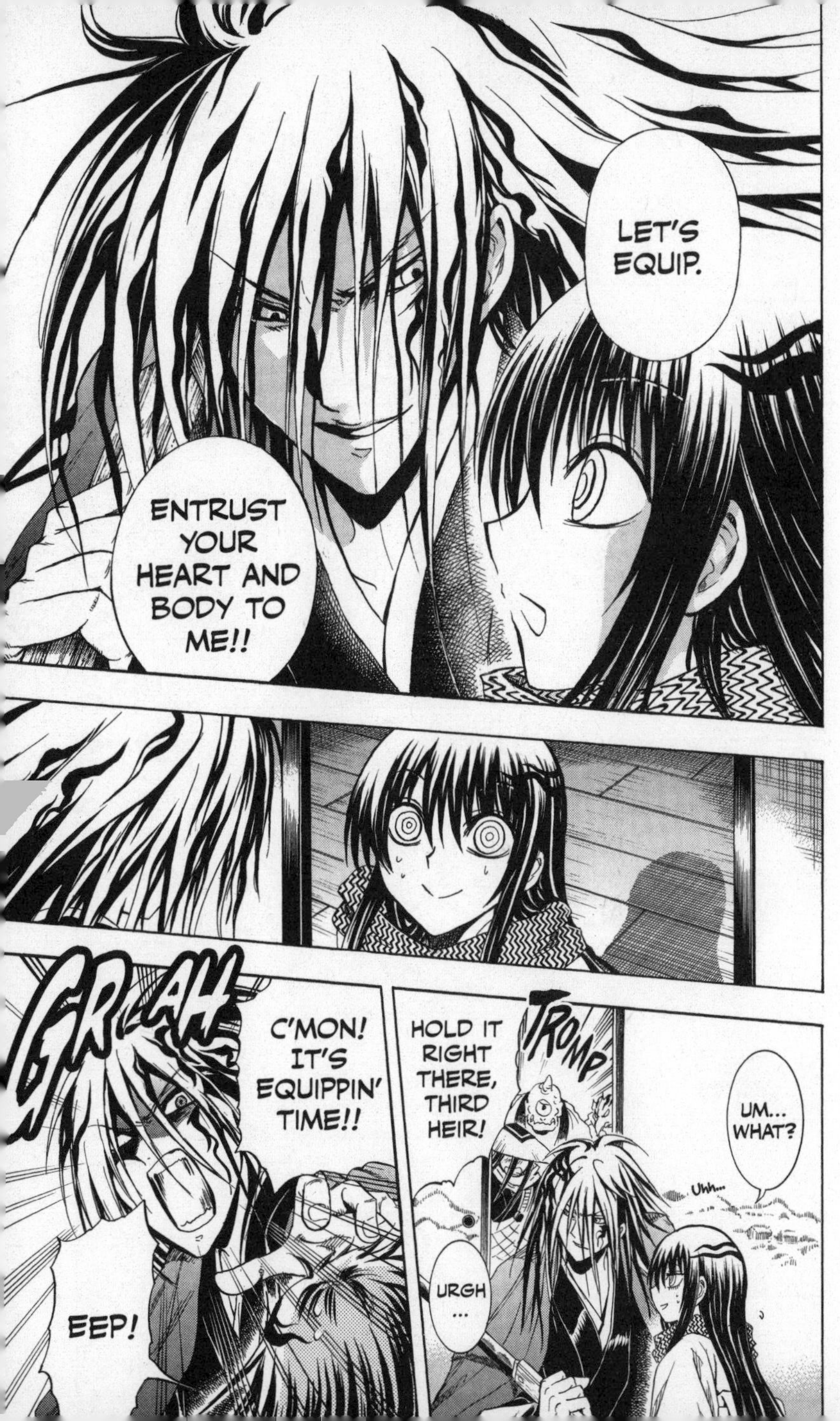
LET'S EQUIP.
ENTRUST YOUR HEART AND BODY TO ME!!
UM... WHAT?
TROMP
HOLD IT RIGHT THERE, THIRD HEIR!
Uhh...
URGH ...
C'MON! IT'S EQUIPPIN' TIME!!
GRAH
EEP!

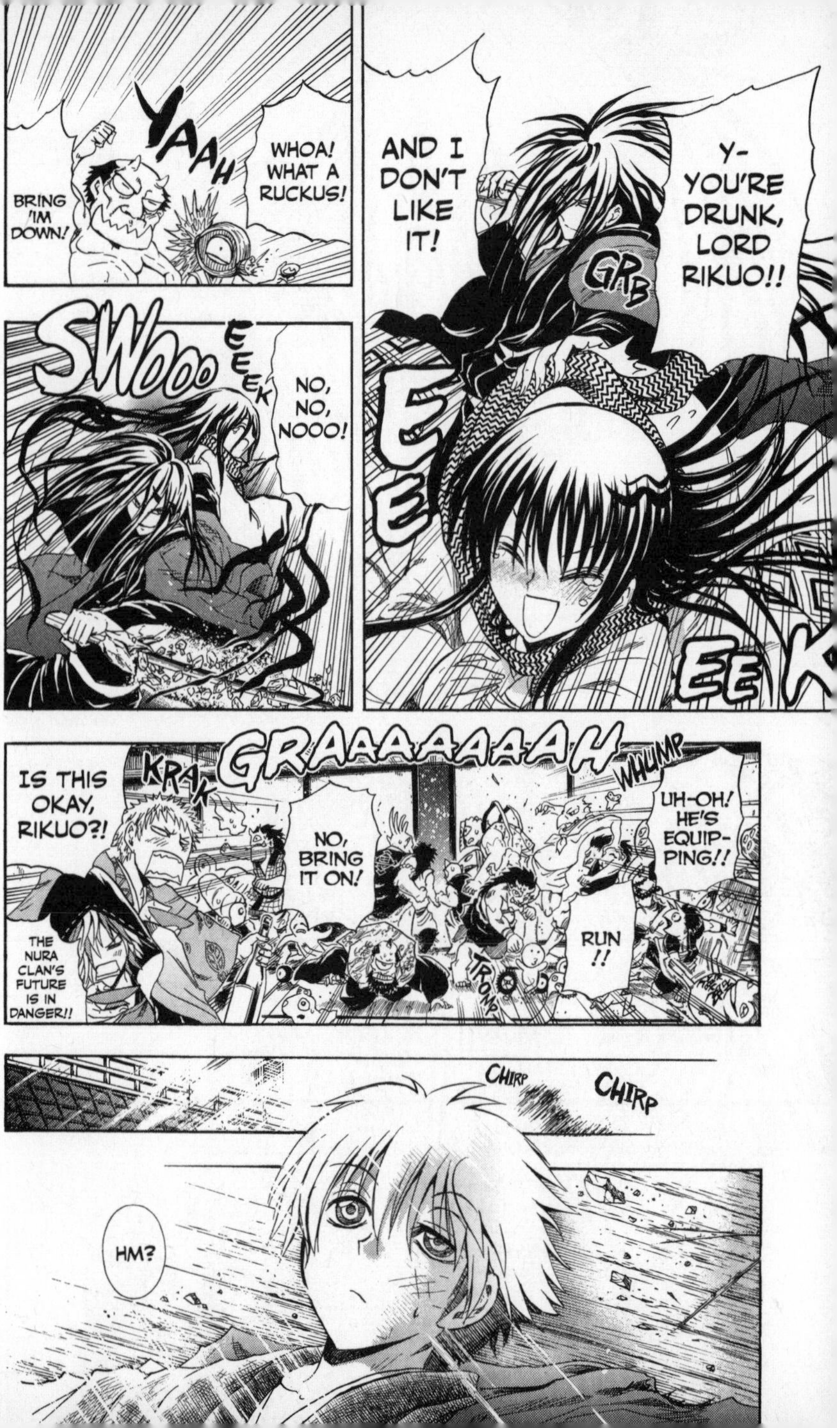
Y- YOU'RE DRUNK, LORD RIKUO!!
AND I DON'T LIKE IT!
GRB
EEEEK
WHOA! WHAT A RUCKUS!
YAAAH
BRING 'IM DOWN!
SWOOO
EEEEK
NO, NO, NOOO!
GRAAAAAAAAH
WHUMP
UH-OH! HE'S EQUIP-PING!!
RUN!!
NO, BRING IT ON!
KRAK
IS THIS OKAY, RIKUO?!
TROMP
THE NURA CLAN'S FUTURE IS IN DANGER!!
CHIRP
CHIRP
HM?

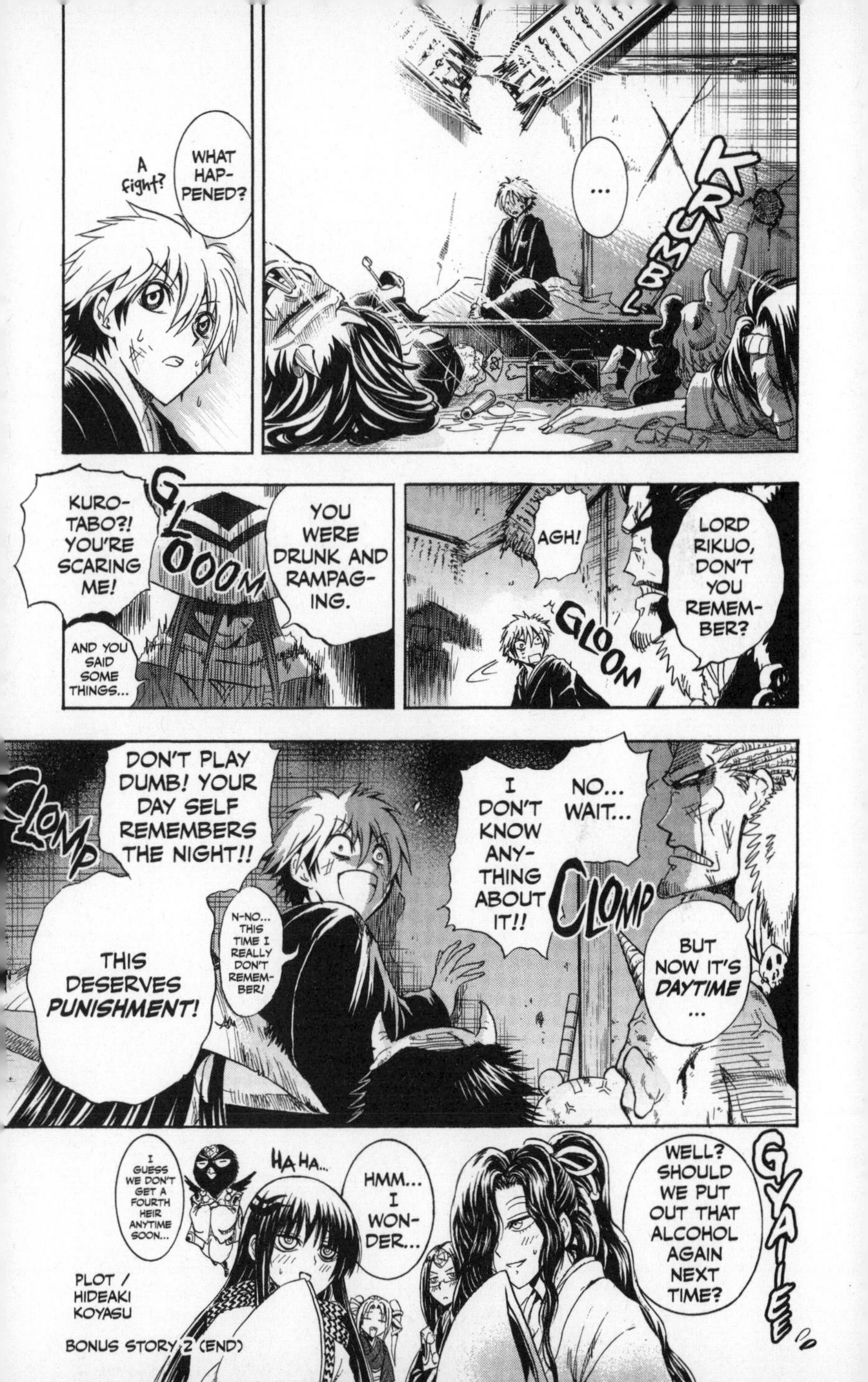
...
KRUMBL
WHAT HAP-PENED?
A fight?
LORD RIKUO, DON'T YOU REMEMBER?
AGH!
GLOOM
YOU WERE DRUNK AND RAMPAG-ING.
GLOOOM
KURO-TABO?! YOU'RE SCARING ME!
AND YOU SAID SOME THINGS...
NO... WAIT...
BUT NOW IT'S *DAYTIME* ...
CLOMP
I DON'T KNOW ANY-THING ABOUT IT!!
DON'T PLAY DUMB! YOUR DAY SELF REMEMBERS THE NIGHT!!
N-NO... THIS TIME I REALLY DON'T REMEM-BER!
CLOMP
THIS DESERVES *PUNISHMENT*!
GYAIEE
WELL? SHOULD WE PUT OUT THAT ALCOHOL AGAIN NEXT TIME?
HMM... I WON-DER...
HA HA...
I GUESS WE DON'T GET A FOURTH HEIR ANYTIME SOON...
PLOT / HIDEAKI KOYASU
BONUS STORY 2 (END)

At Spiral castle

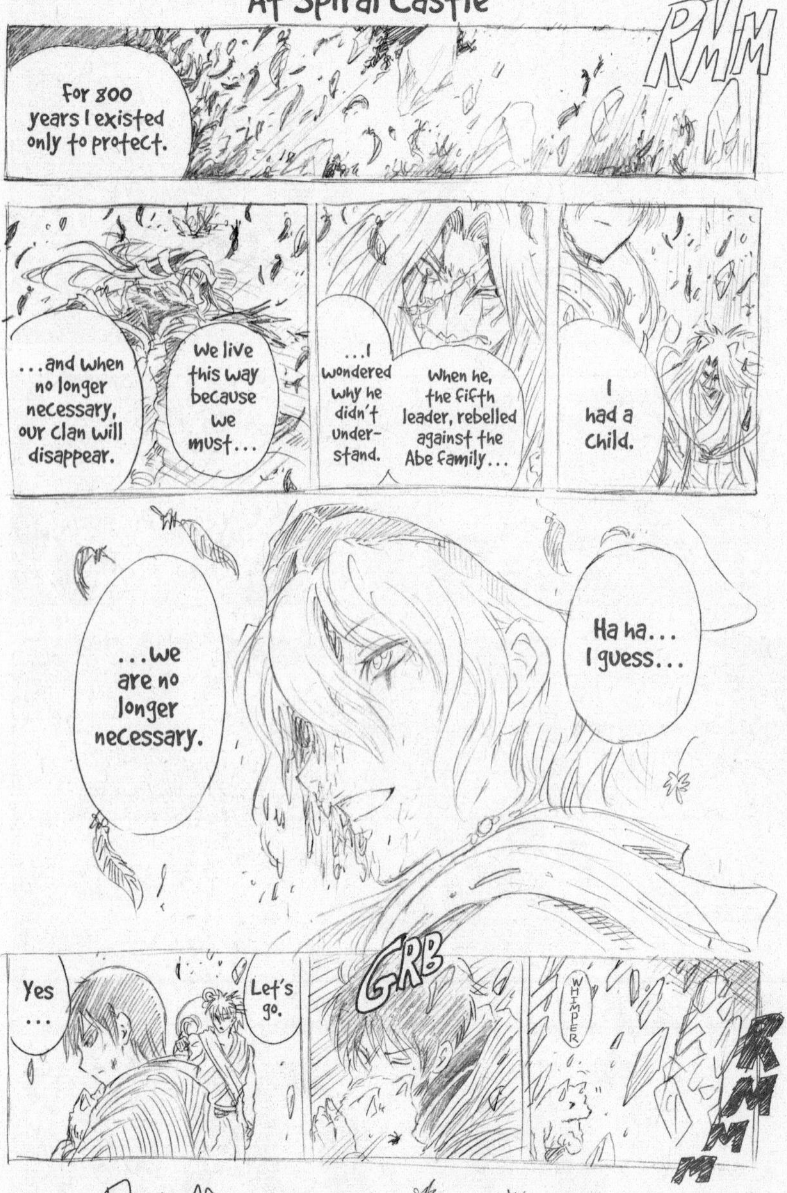
RMM
For 800 years I existed only to protect.
I had a child.
When he, the fifth leader, rebelled against the Abe family...
...I wondered why he didn't under-stand.
We live this way because we must...
...and when no longer necessary, our clan will disappear.
Ha ha... I guess...
...we are no longer necessary.
WHIMPER
RMMM
GRB
Let's go.
Yes ...
RMM

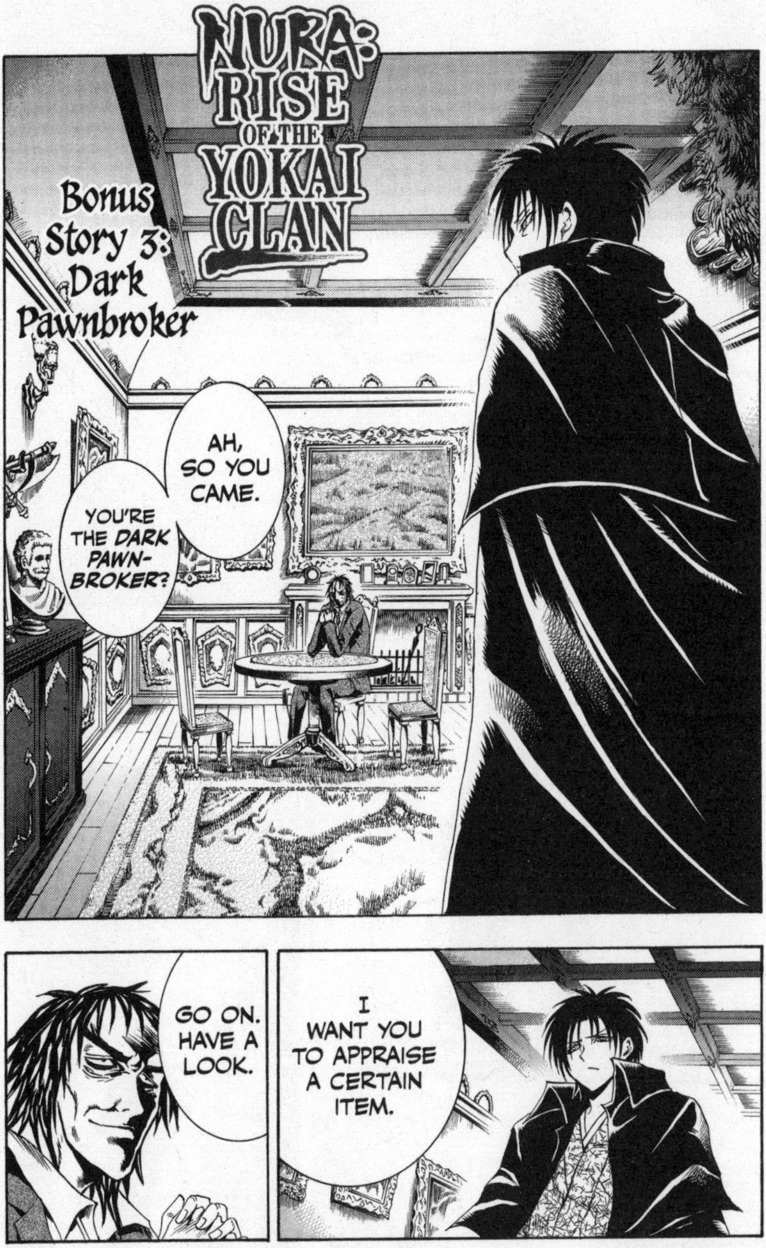
NURA: RISE OF THE YOKAI CLAN
Bonus Story 3: Dark Pawnbroker
AH, SO YOU CAME.
YOU'RE THE DARK PAWN-BROKER?
I WANT YOU TO APPRAISE A CERTAIN ITEM.
GO ON. HAVE A LOOK.

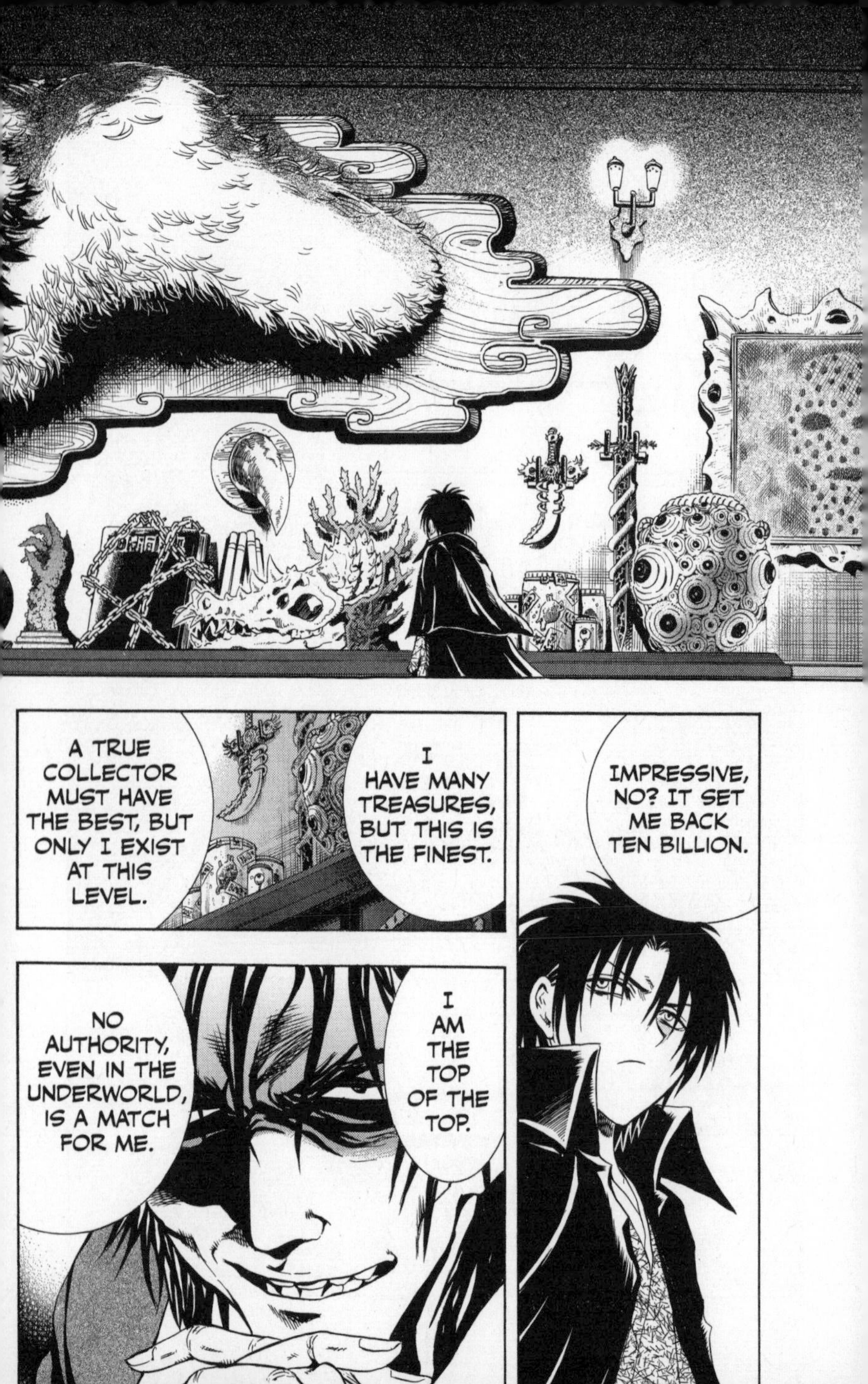
IMPRESSIVE, NO? IT SET ME BACK TEN BILLION.
I HAVE MANY TREASURES, BUT THIS IS THE FINEST.
A TRUE COLLECTOR MUST HAVE THE BEST, BUT ONLY I EXIST AT THIS LEVEL.
I AM THE TOP OF THE TOP.
NO AUTHORITY, EVEN IN THE UNDERWORLD, IS A MATCH FOR ME.

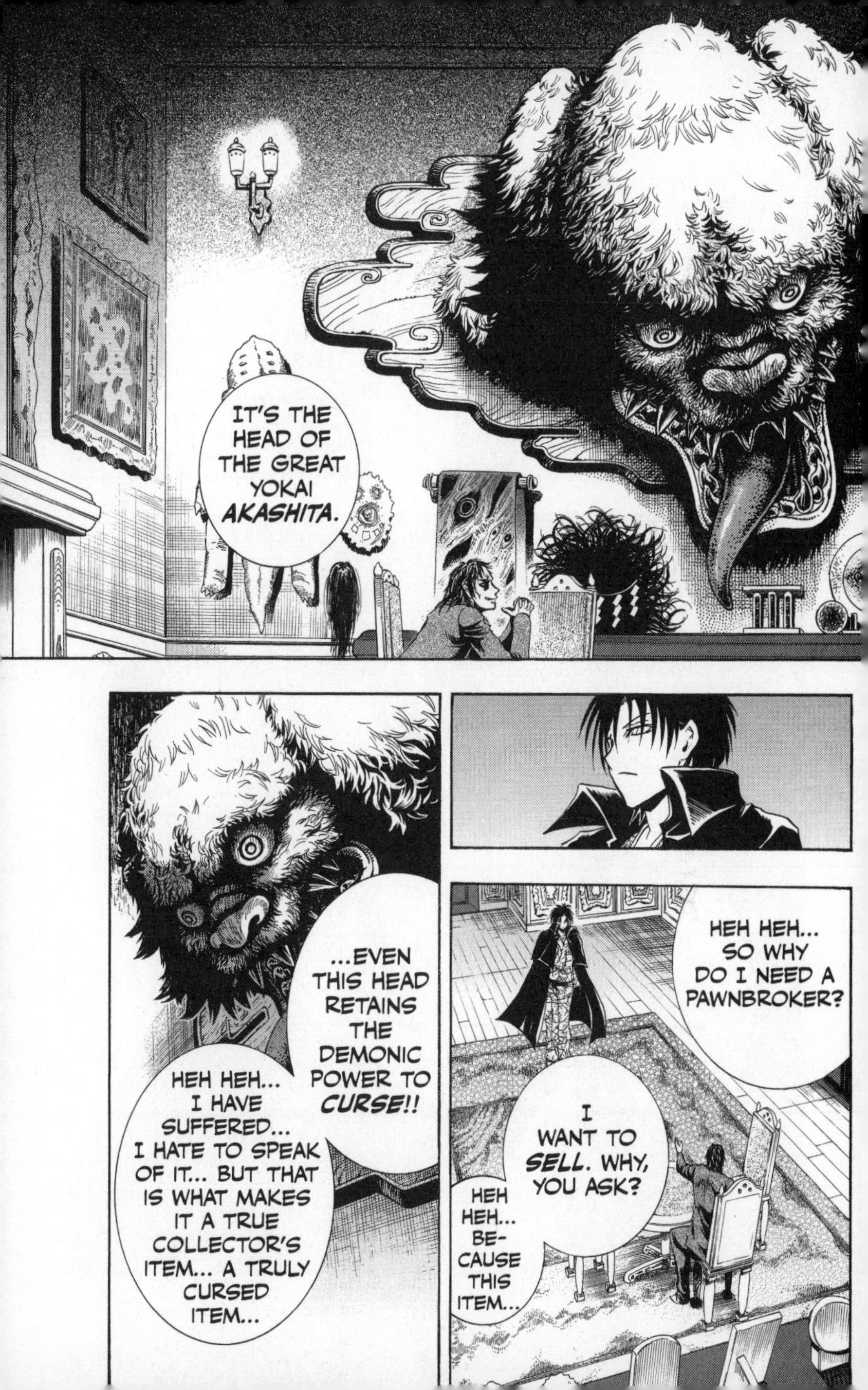
IT'S THE HEAD OF THE GREAT YOKAI AKASHITA.
HEH HEH... SO WHY DO I NEED A PAWNBROKER?
I WANT TO SELL. WHY, YOU ASK?
HEH HEH... BE-CAUSE THIS ITEM...
...EVEN THIS HEAD RETAINS THE DEMONIC POWER TO CURSE!!
HEH HEH... I HAVE SUFFERED... I HATE TO SPEAK OF IT... BUT THAT IS WHAT MAKES IT A TRUE COLLECTOR'S ITEM... A TRULY CURSED ITEM...

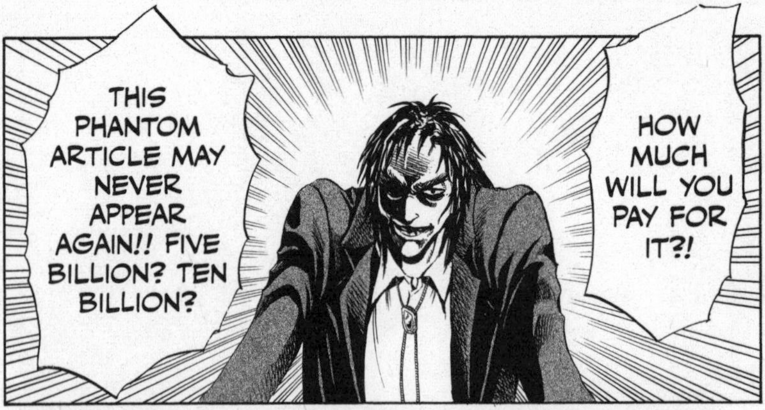
HOW MUCH WILL YOU PAY FOR IT?!
THIS PHANTOM ARTICLE MAY NEVER APPEAR AGAIN!! FIVE BILLION? TEN BILLION?
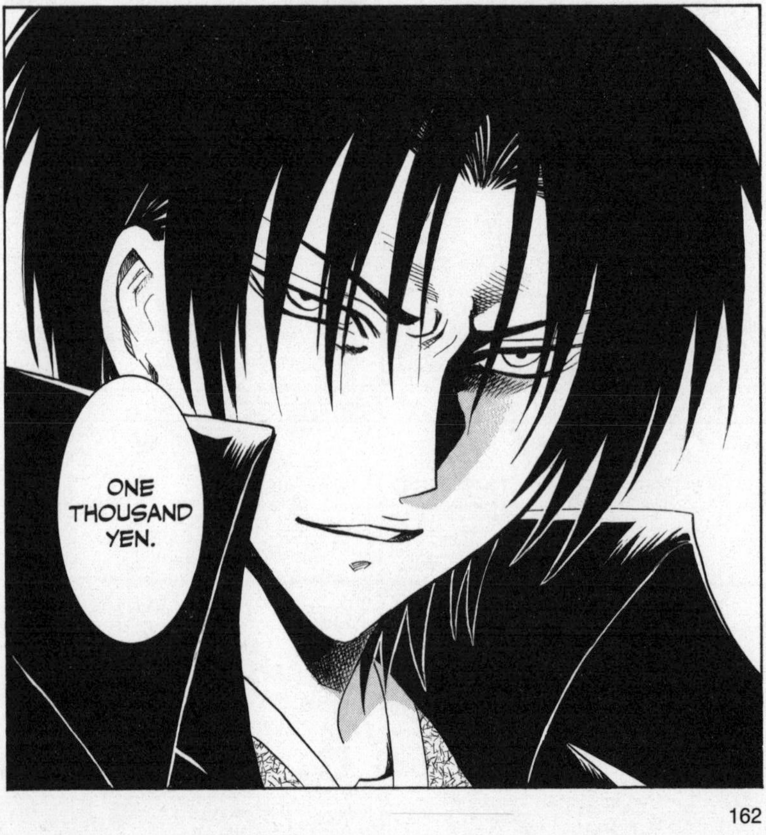
ONE THOUSAND YEN.

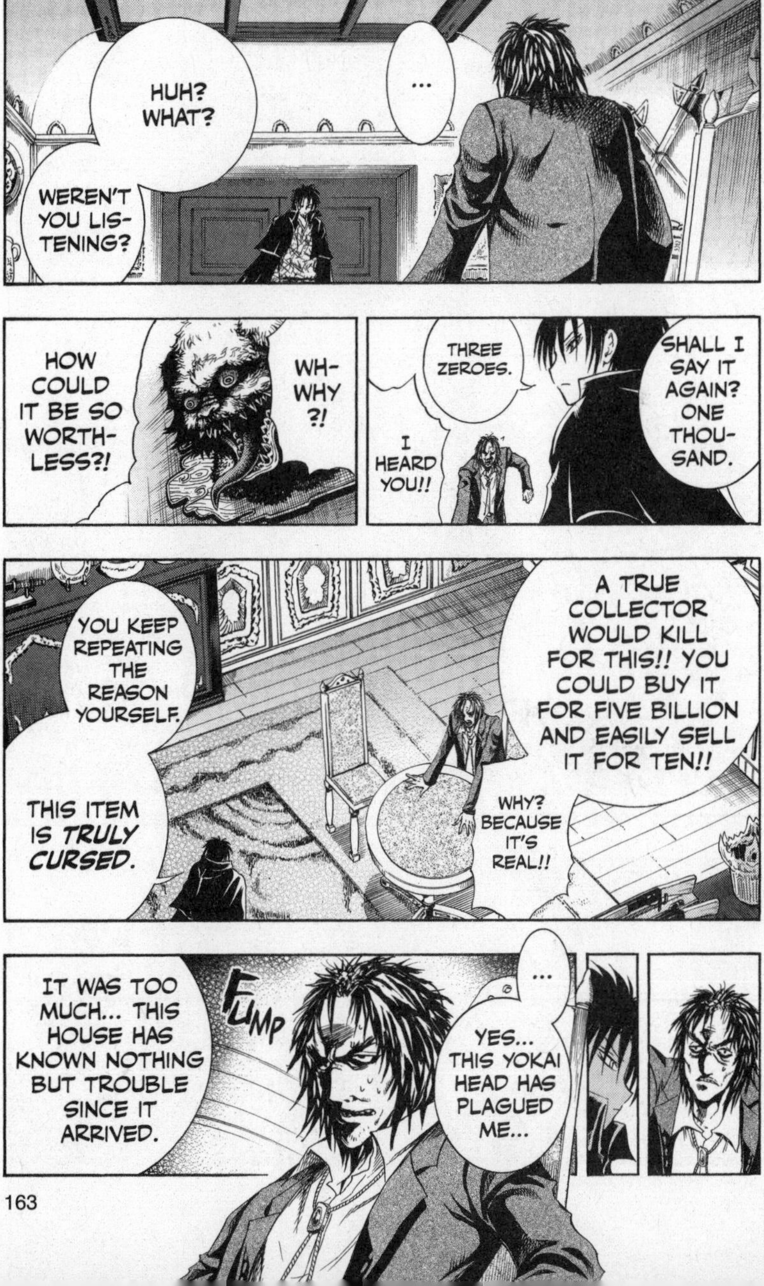
...
HUH? WHAT?
WEREN'T YOU LIS-TENING?
SHALL I SAY IT AGAIN? ONE THOU-SAND.
THREE ZEROES.
I HEARD YOU!!
WH-WHY?!
HOW COULD IT BE SO WORTH-LESS?!
A TRUE COLLECTOR WOULD KILL FOR THIS!! YOU COULD BUY IT FOR FIVE BILLION AND EASILY SELL IT FOR TEN!!
WHY? BECAUSE IT'S REAL!!
YOU KEEP REPEATING THE REASON YOURSELF.
THIS ITEM IS *TRULY CURSED*.
...
YES... THIS YOKAI HEAD HAS PLAGUED ME...
FUMP
IT WAS TOO MUCH... THIS HOUSE HAS KNOWN NOTHING BUT TROUBLE SINCE IT ARRIVED.

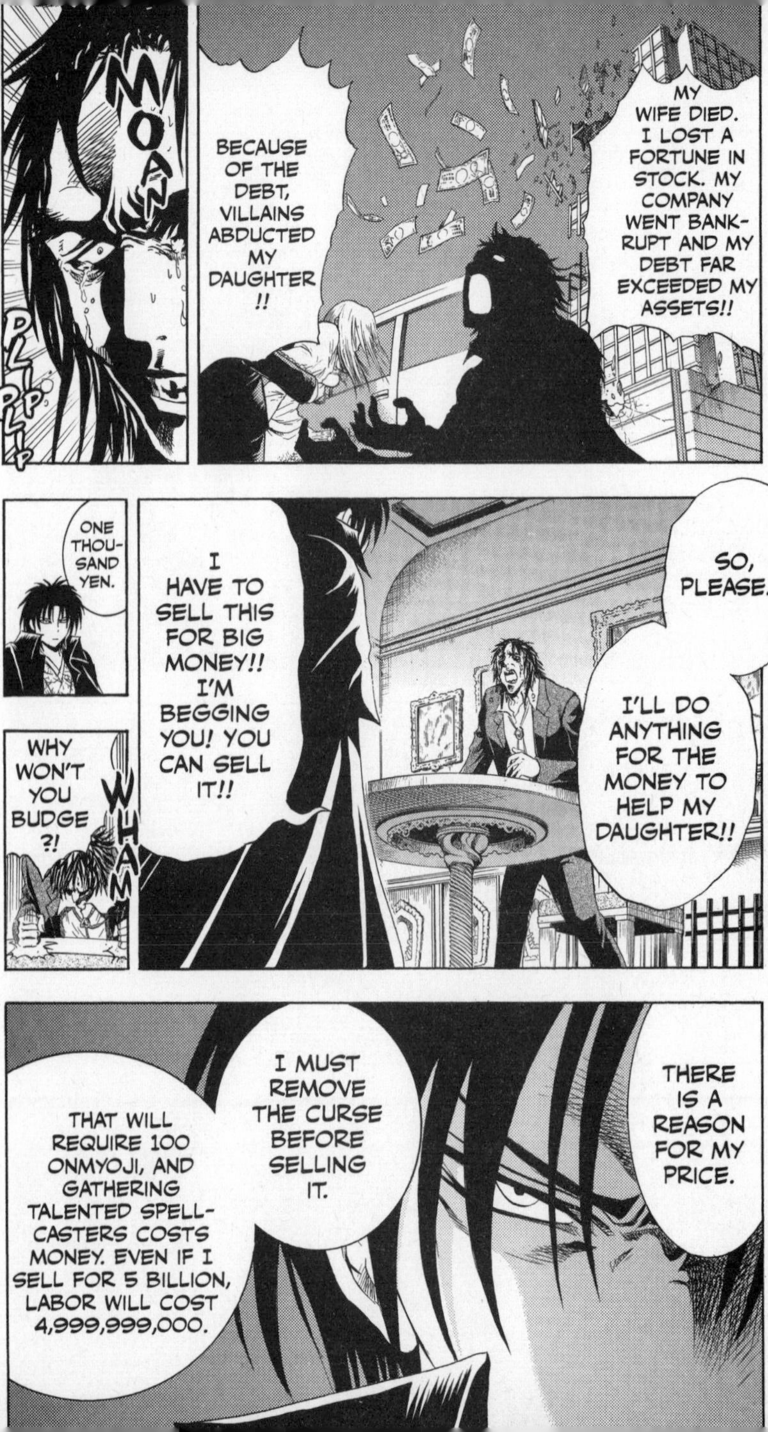
MY WIFE DIED. I LOST A FORTUNE IN STOCK. MY COMPANY WENT BANK-RUPT AND MY DEBT FAR EXCEEDED MY ASSETS!!
BECAUSE OF THE DEBT, VILLAINS ABDUCTED MY DAUGHTER!!
MOAN
PLIP PLIP
SO, PLEASE...
I'LL DO ANYTHING FOR THE MONEY TO HELP MY DAUGHTER!!
I HAVE TO SELL THIS FOR BIG MONEY!! I'M BEGGING YOU! YOU CAN SELL IT!!
ONE THOU-SAND YEN.
WHY WON'T YOU BUDGE?!
WHAM
THERE IS A REASON FOR MY PRICE.
I MUST REMOVE THE CURSE BEFORE SELLING IT.
THAT WILL REQUIRE 100 ONMYOJI, AND GATHERING TALENTED SPELL-CASTERS COSTS MONEY. EVEN IF I SELL FOR 5 BILLION, LABOR WILL COST 4,999,999,000.

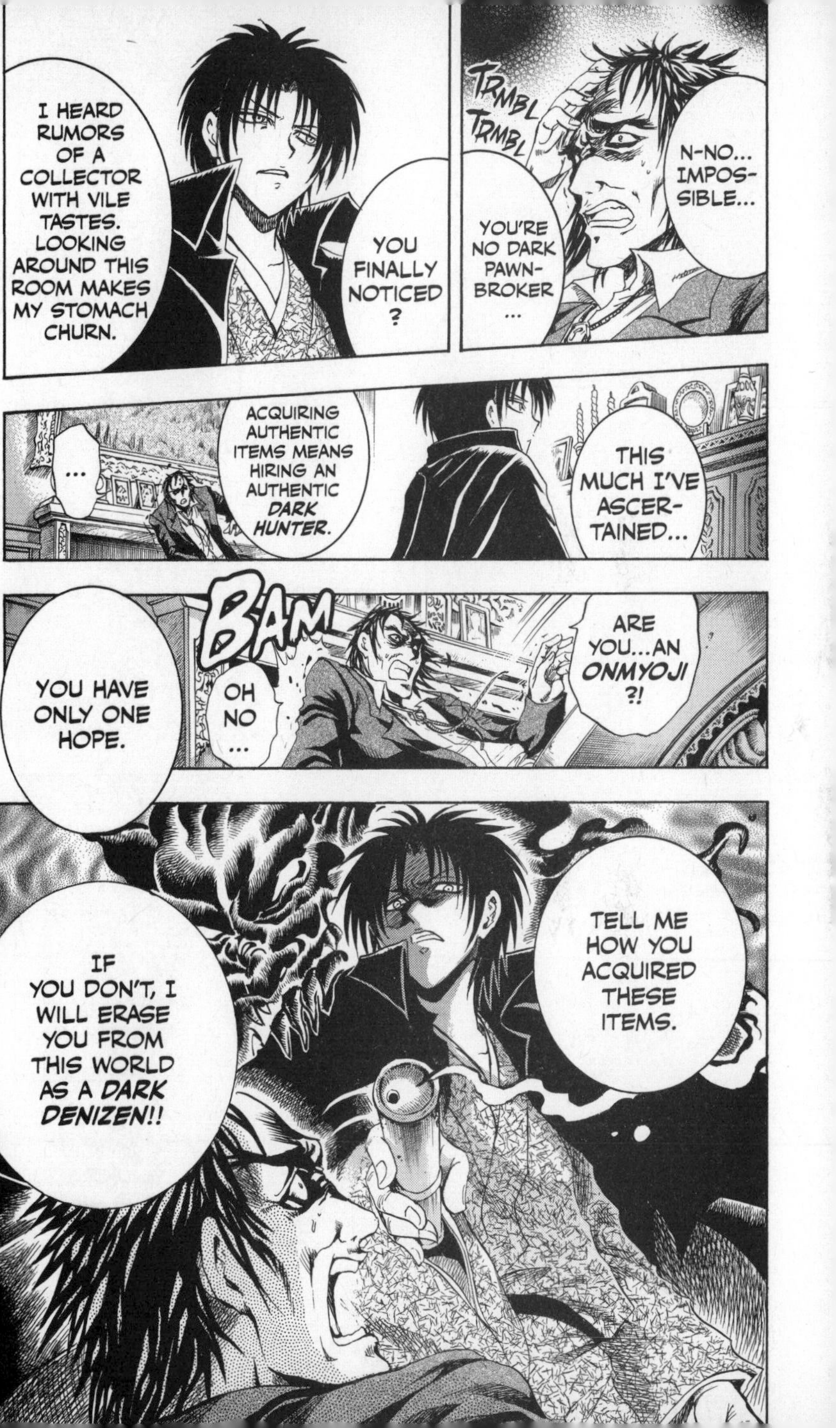
N-NO... IMPOSSIBLE...
TRMBL TRMBL
YOU'RE NO DARK PAWNBROKER...
YOU FINALLY NOTICED?
I HEARD RUMORS OF A COLLECTOR WITH VILE TASTES. LOOKING AROUND THIS ROOM MAKES MY STOMACH CHURN.
THIS MUCH I'VE ASCERTAINED...
ACQUIRING AUTHENTIC ITEMS MEANS HIRING AN AUTHENTIC *DARK HUNTER*.
...
ARE YOU...AN *ONMYOJI*?!
BAM
OH NO...
YOU HAVE ONLY ONE HOPE.
TELL ME HOW YOU ACQUIRED THESE ITEMS.
IF YOU DON'T, I WILL ERASE YOU FROM THIS WORLD AS A *DARK DENIZEN*!!

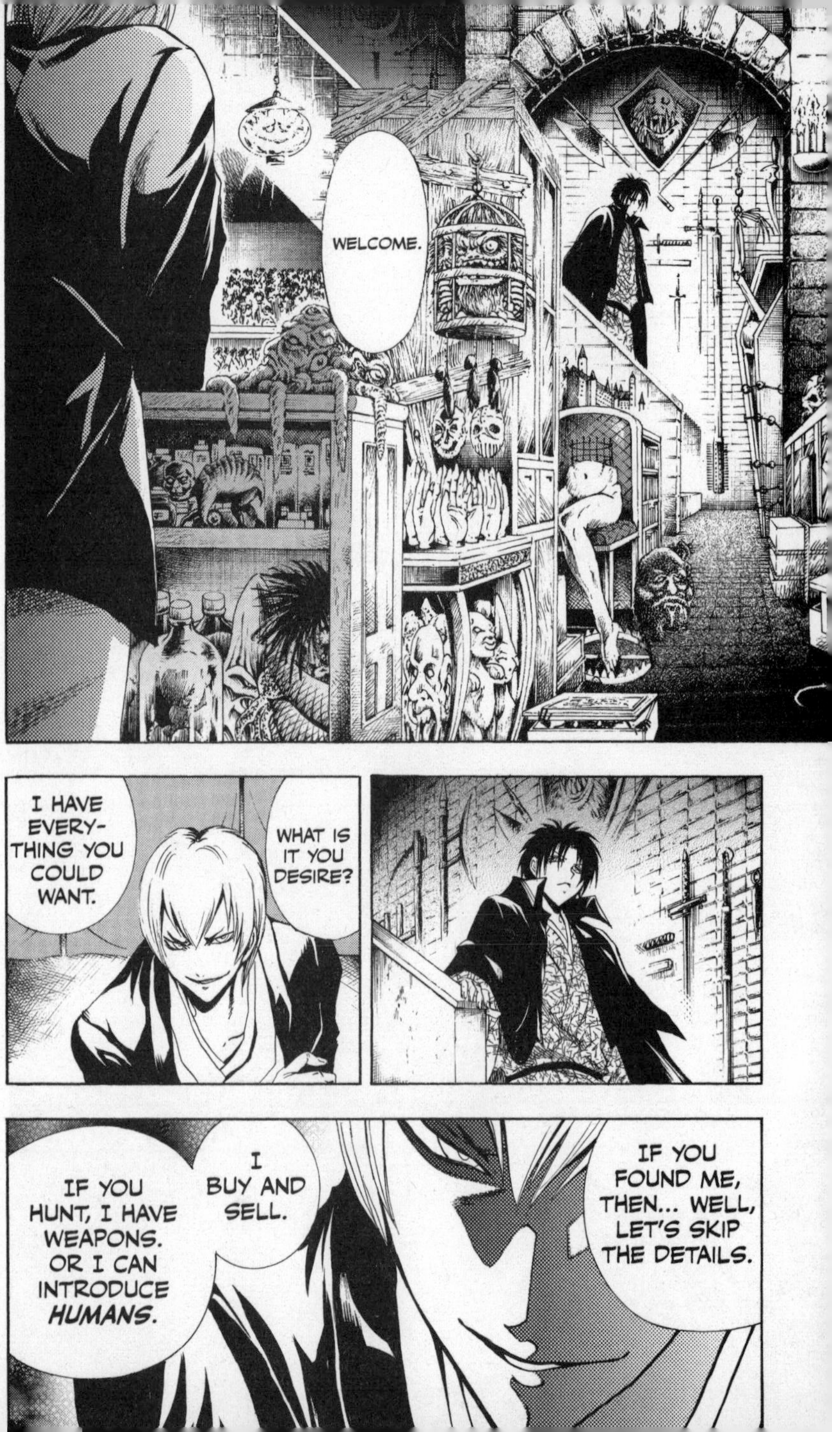
WELCOME.
WHAT IS IT YOU DESIRE?
I HAVE EVERYTHING YOU COULD WANT.
IF YOU FOUND ME, THEN... WELL, LET'S SKIP THE DETAILS.
I BUY AND SELL.
IF YOU HUNT, I HAVE WEAPONS. OR I CAN INTRODUCE *HUMANS*.

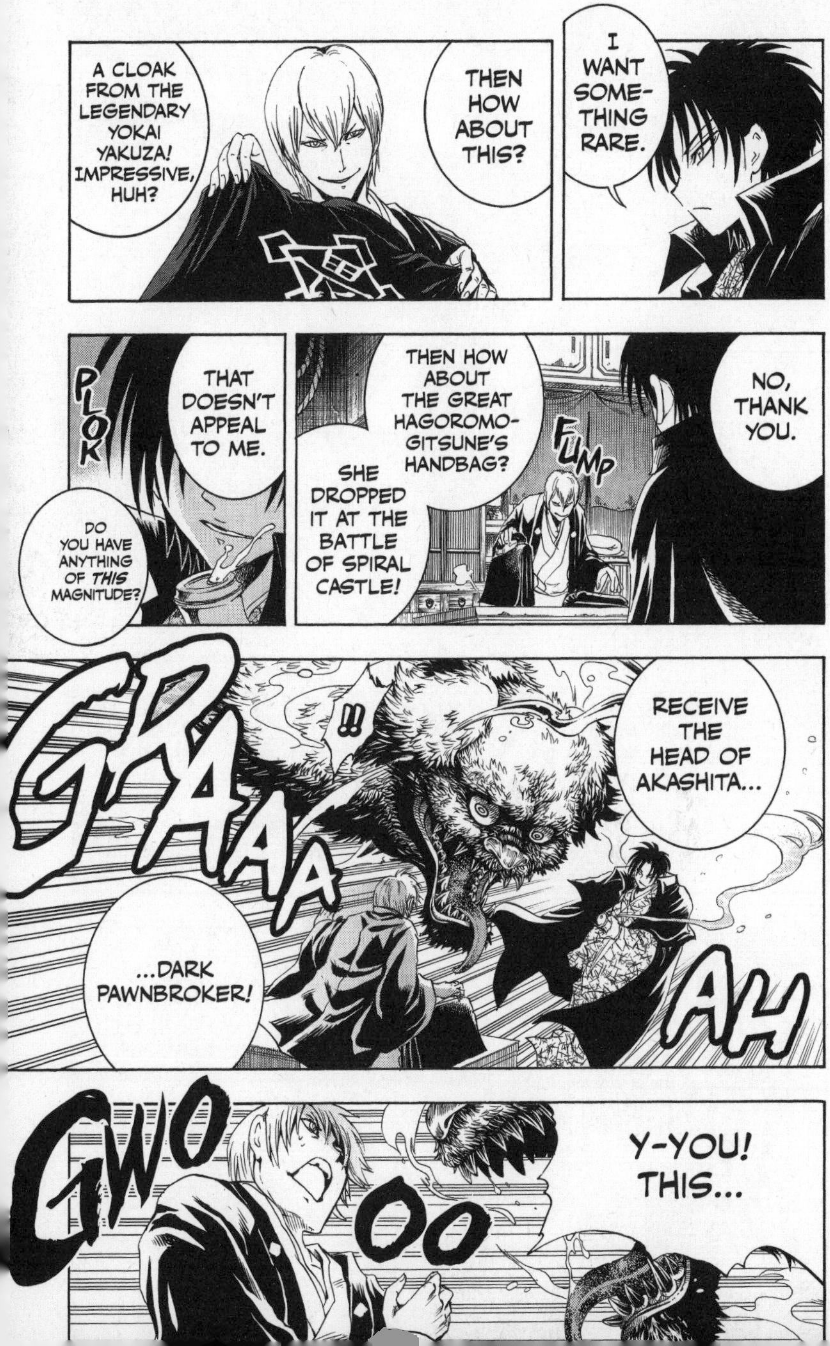
I WANT SOMETHING RARE.
THEN HOW ABOUT THIS?
A CLOAK FROM THE LEGENDARY YOKAI YAKUZA! IMPRESSIVE, HUH?
NO, THANK YOU.
FUMP
THEN HOW ABOUT THE GREAT HAGOROMO-GITSUNE'S HANDBAG?
SHE DROPPED IT AT THE BATTLE OF SPIRAL CASTLE!
THAT DOESN'T APPEAL TO ME.
PLOK
DO YOU HAVE ANYTHING OF *THIS* MAGNITUDE?
RECEIVE THE HEAD OF AKASHITA...
!!
GPAAAA
AH
...DARK PAWNBROKER!
Y-YOU! THIS...
GWOOO

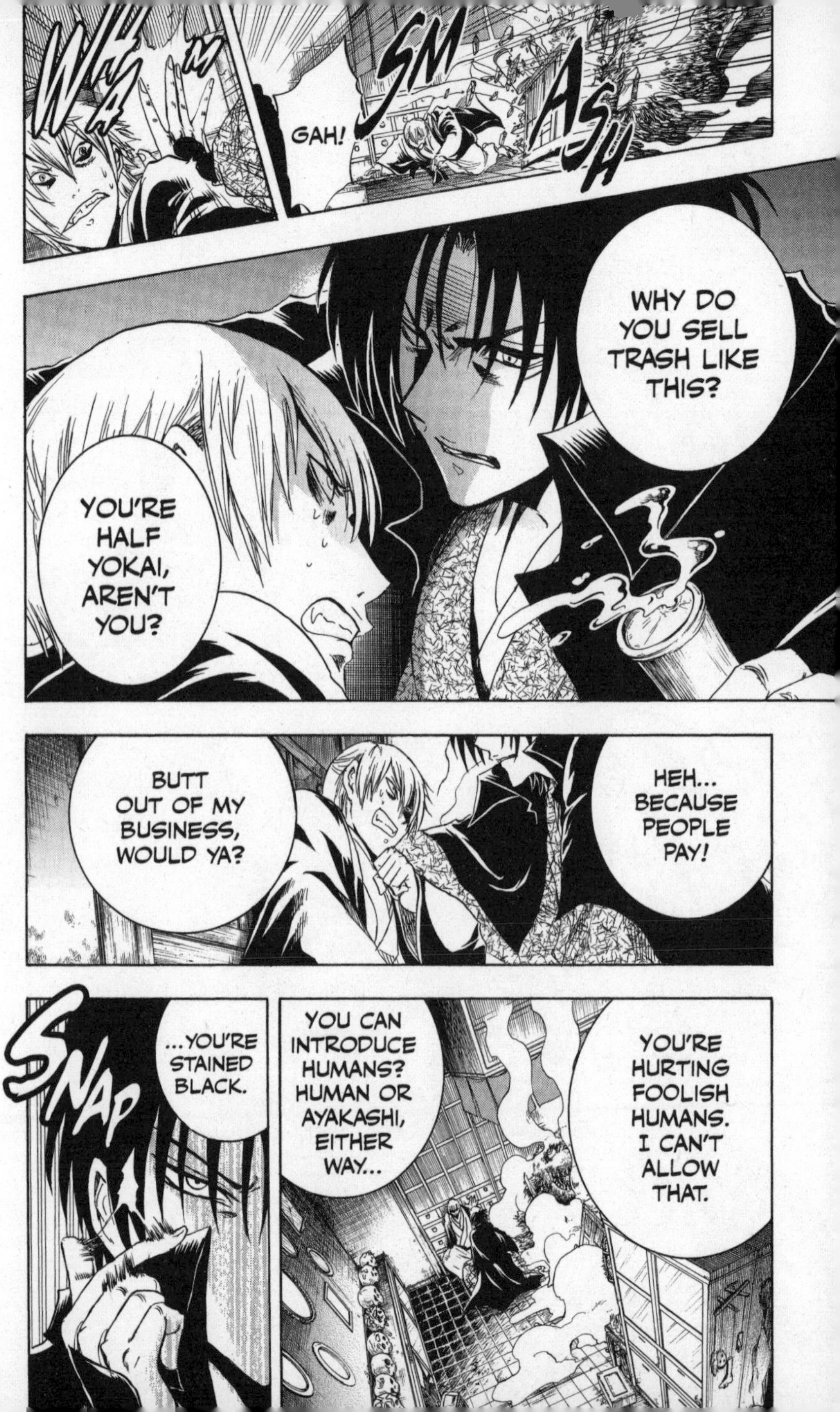
SMASH
GAH!
WHAM
WHY DO YOU SELL TRASH LIKE THIS?
YOU'RE HALF YOKAI, AREN'T YOU?
HEH... BECAUSE PEOPLE PAY!
BUTT OUT OF MY BUSINESS, WOULD YA?
YOU'RE HURTING FOOLISH HUMANS. I CAN'T ALLOW THAT.
YOU CAN INTRODUCE HUMANS? HUMAN OR AYAKASHI, EITHER WAY...
...YOU'RE STAINED BLACK.
SNAP

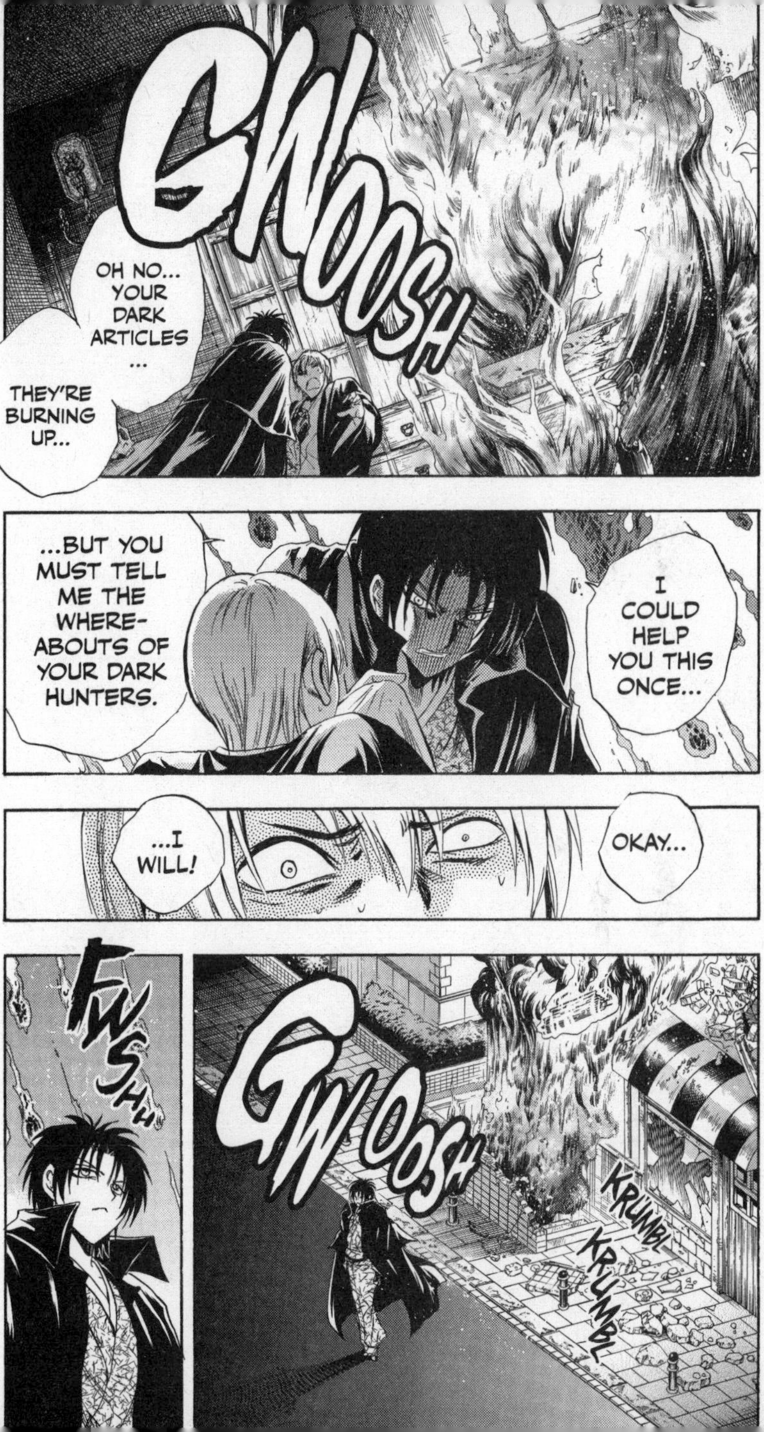
GWOOSH
OH NO... YOUR DARK ARTICLES...
THEY'RE BURNING UP...
I COULD HELP YOU THIS ONCE...
...BUT YOU MUST TELL ME THE WHERE-ABOUTS OF YOUR DARK HUNTERS.
OKAY...
...I WILL!
GWOOSH
KRUMBL
KRUMBL
FWSHH

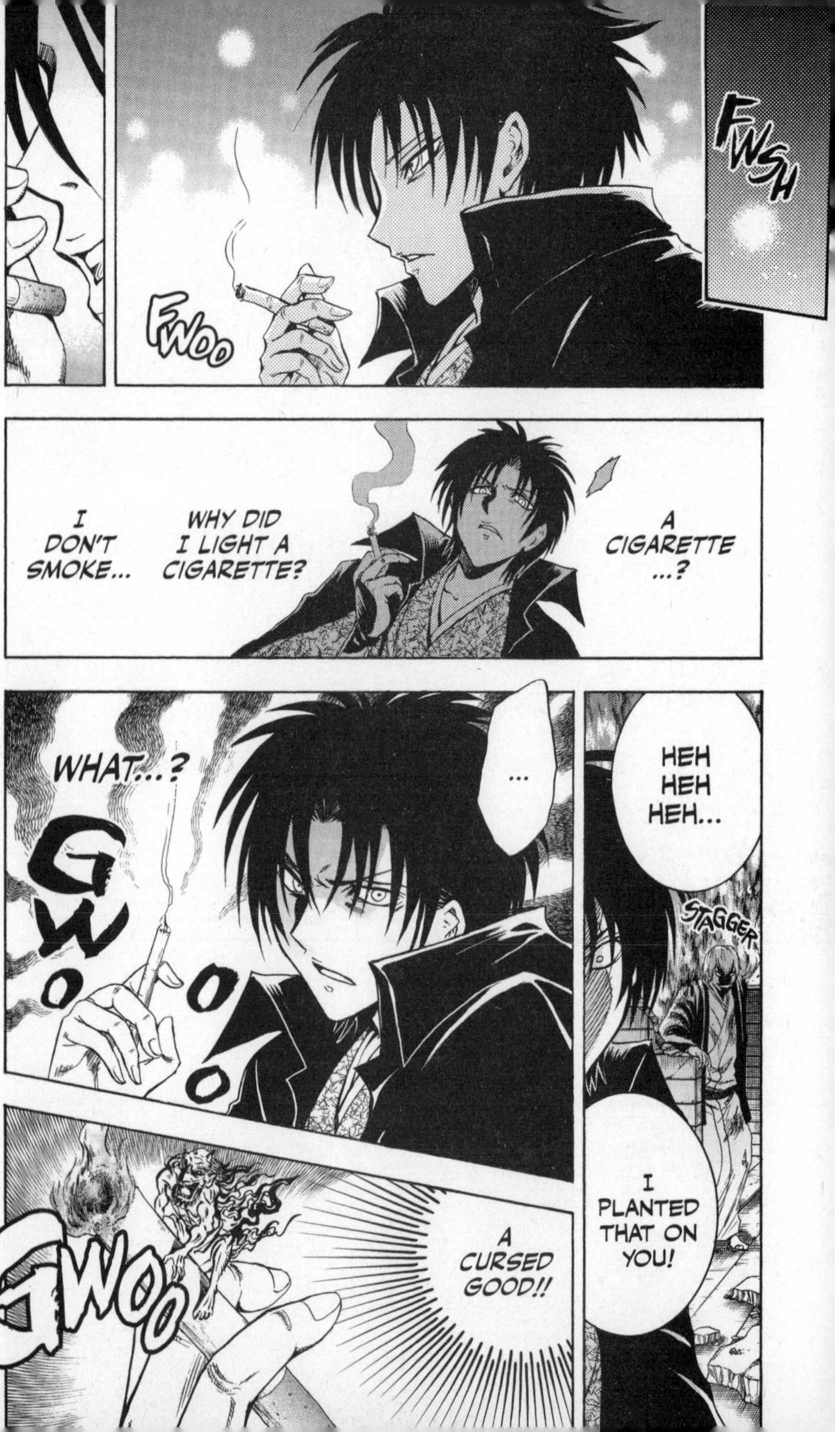
FWSH
FWOO
A CIGARETTE ...?
WHY DID I LIGHT A CIGARETTE?
I DON'T SMOKE...
HEH HEH HEH...
STAGGER
I PLANTED THAT ON YOU!
...
WHAT...?
GWOOOO
A CURSED GOOD!!
GWOO

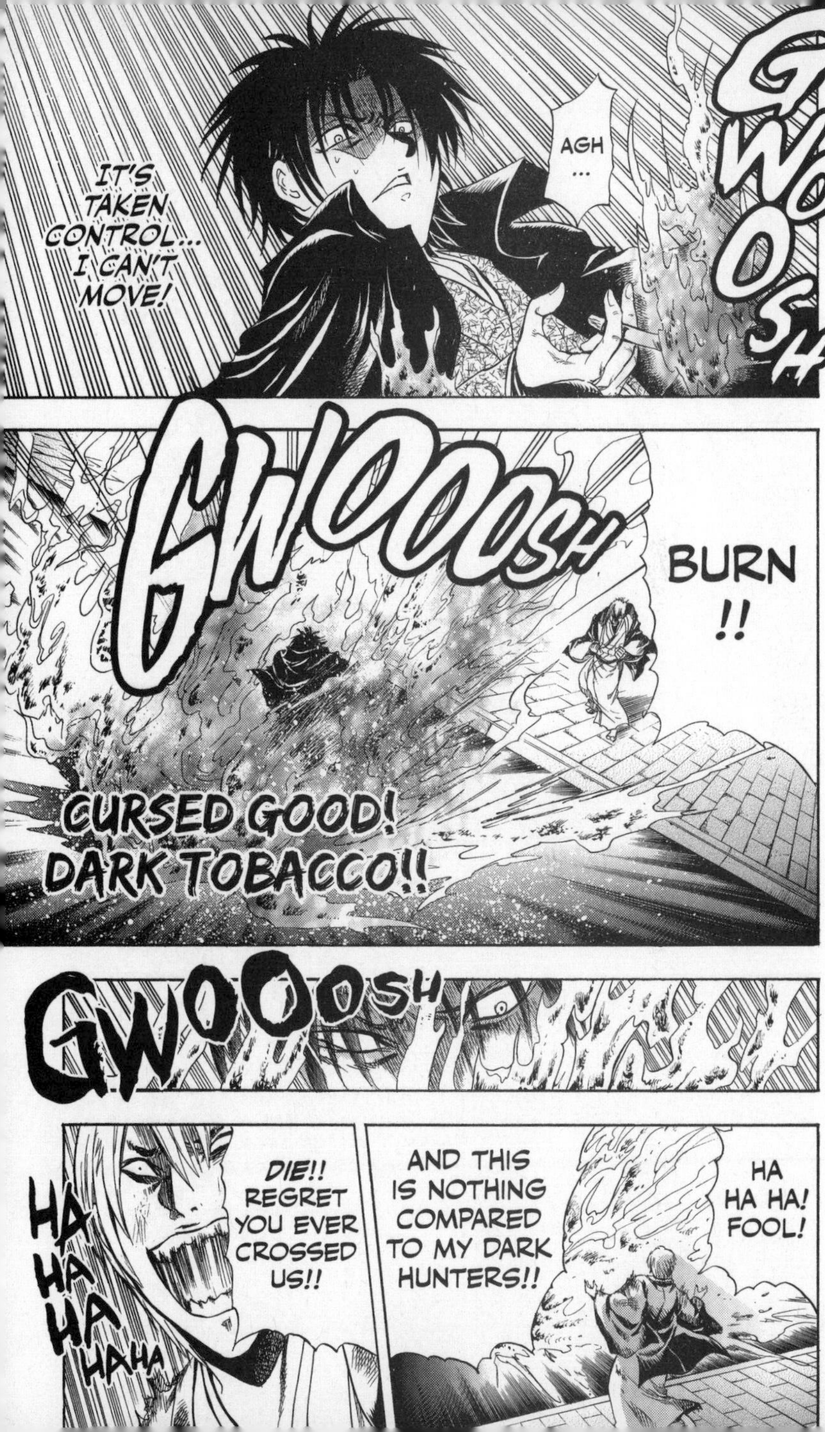
GWOOOSH
AGH ...
IT'S TAKEN CONTROL... I CAN'T MOVE!
BURN !!
GWOOOSH
CURSED GOOD! DARK TOBACCO!!
GWOOOSH
HA HA HA! FOOL!
AND THIS IS NOTHING COMPARED TO MY DARK HUNTERS!!
DIE!! REGRET YOU EVER CROSSED US!!
HA HA HA HA HAHA

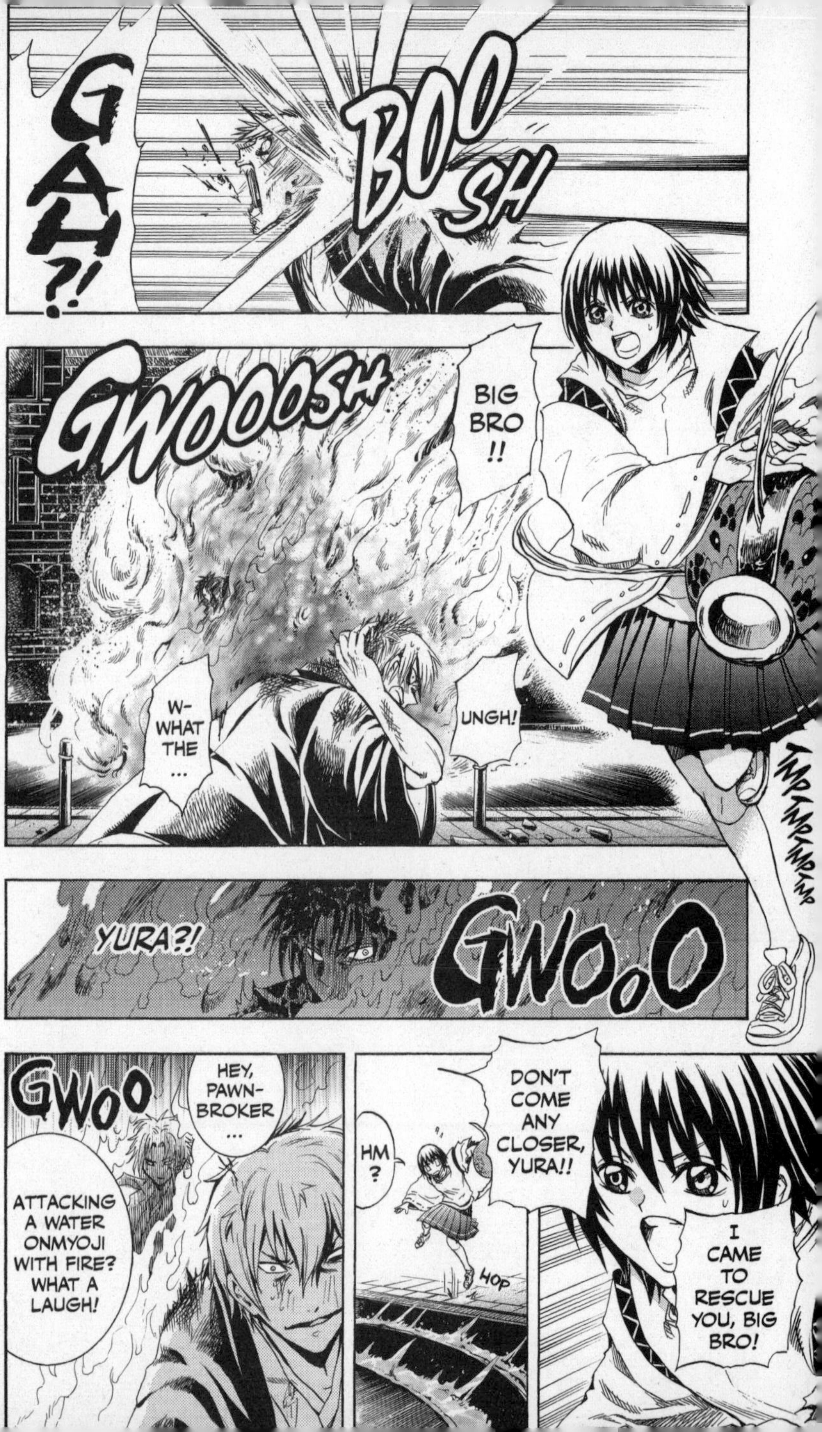
BOOSH
GAH?!
BIG BRO!!
GWOOOSH
UNGH!
W-WHAT THE...
TMPTMPTMP
GWO.O
YURA?!
DON'T COME ANY CLOSER, YURA!!
HM?
I CAME TO RESCUE YOU, BIG BRO!
HOP
HEY, PAWN-BROKER...
GWOO
ATTACKING A WATER ONMYOJI WITH FIRE? WHAT A LAUGH!

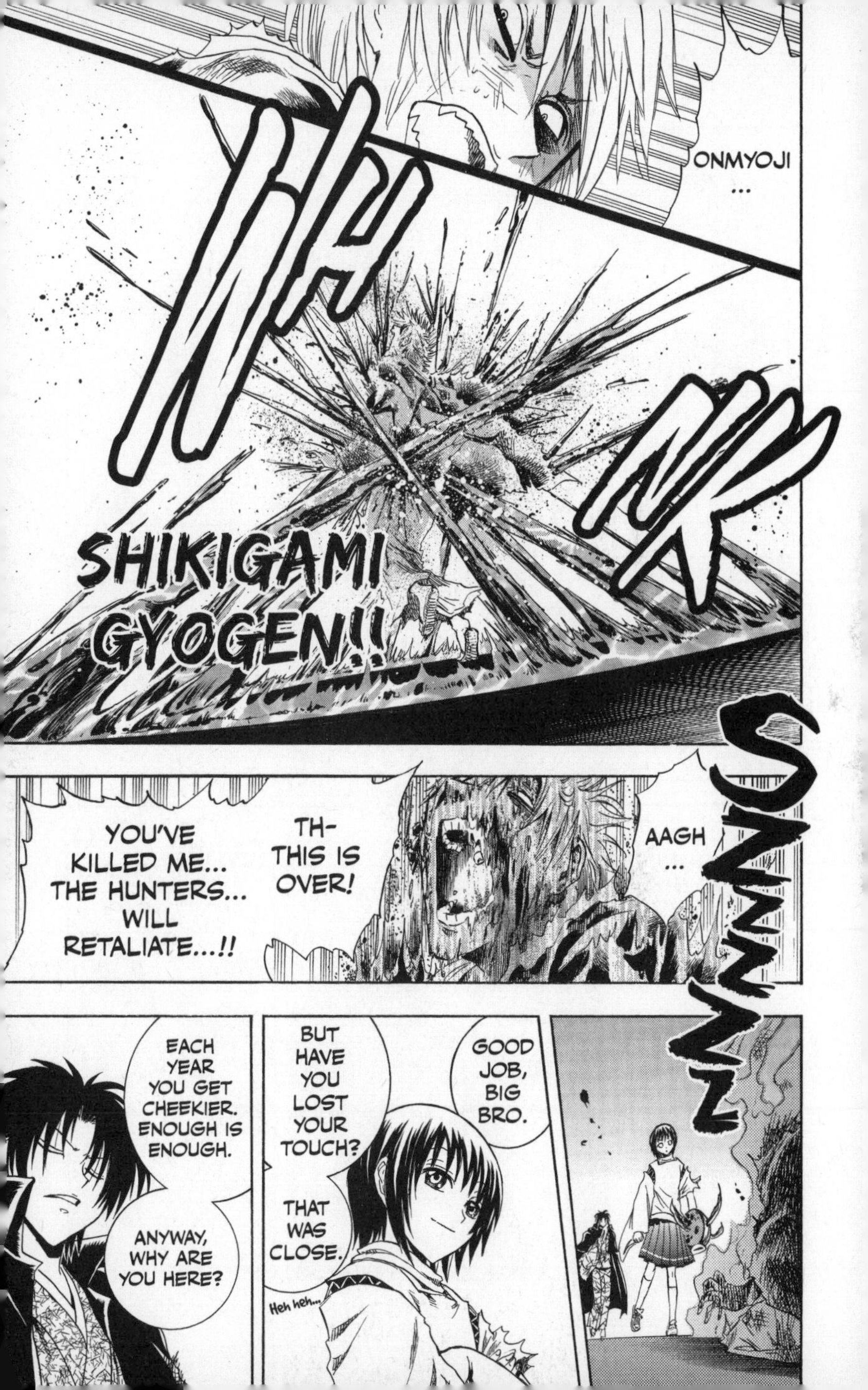
ONMYOJI ...
SHIKIGAMI GYOGEN!!
AAGH ...
TH- THIS IS OVER!
YOU'VE KILLED ME... THE HUNTERS... WILL RETALIATE...!!
GOOD JOB, BIG BRO.
BUT HAVE YOU LOST YOUR TOUCH?
THAT WAS CLOSE.
Heh heh...
EACH YEAR YOU GET CHEEKIER. ENOUGH IS ENOUGH.
ANYWAY, WHY ARE YOU HERE?

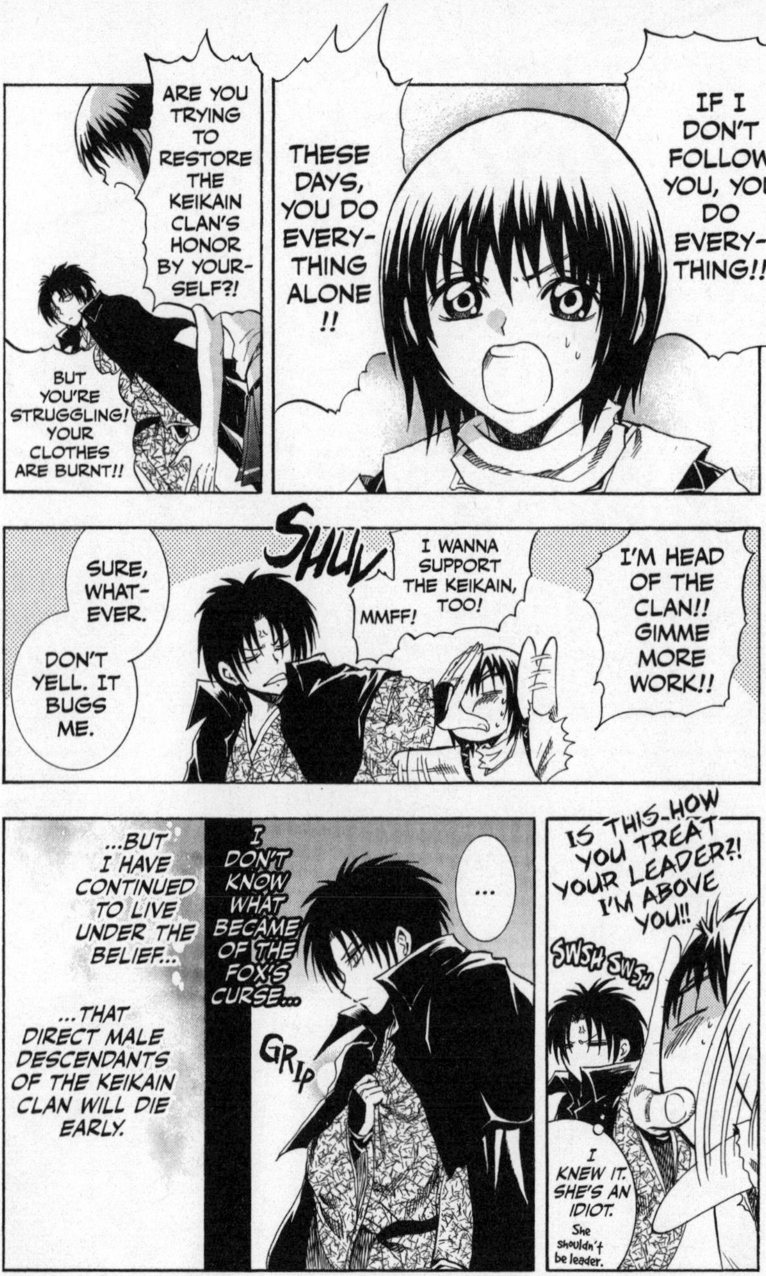
IF I DON'T FOLLOW YOU, YOU DO EVERYTHING!!
THESE DAYS, YOU DO EVERYTHING ALONE!!
ARE YOU TRYING TO RESTORE THE KEIKAIN CLAN'S HONOR BY YOURSELF?!
BUT YOU'RE STRUGGLING! YOUR CLOTHES ARE BURNT!!
I'M HEAD OF THE CLAN!! GIMME MORE WORK!!
I WANNA SUPPORT THE KEIKAIN, TOO!
SHUV
MMFF!
SURE, WHATEVER.
DON'T YELL. IT BUGS ME.
IS THIS HOW YOU TREAT YOUR LEADER?! I'M ABOVE YOU!!
SWSH SWSH
I KNEW IT. SHE'S AN IDIOT.
She shouldn't be leader.
...
I DON'T KNOW WHAT BECAME OF THE FOX'S CURSE...
GRIP
...BUT I HAVE CONTINUED TO LIVE UNDER THE BELIEF...
...THAT DIRECT MALE DESCENDANTS OF THE KEIKAIN CLAN WILL DIE EARLY.

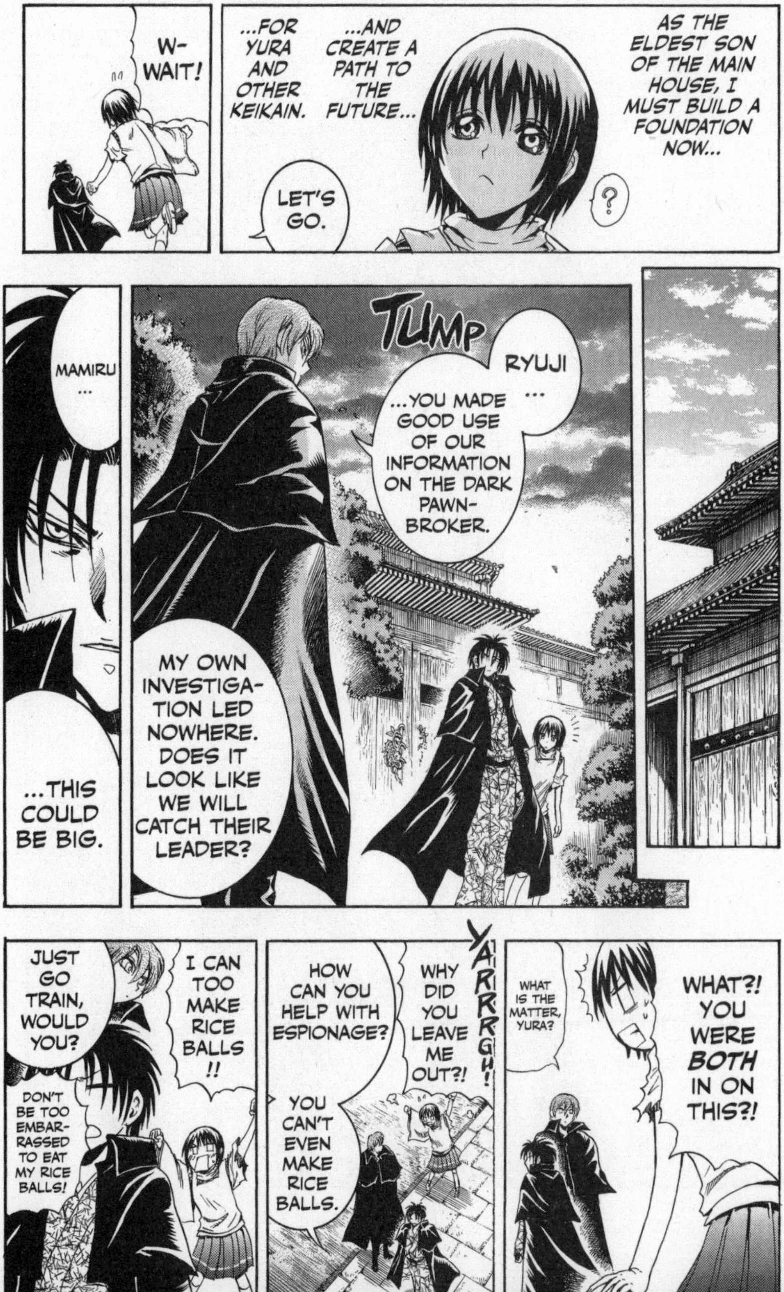
AS THE ELDEST SON OF THE MAIN HOUSE, I MUST BUILD A FOUNDATION NOW...
...AND CREATE A PATH TO THE FUTURE...
...FOR YURA AND OTHER KEIKAIN.
?
LET'S GO.
W-WAIT!
TUMP
RYUJI ...
...YOU MADE GOOD USE OF OUR INFORMATION ON THE DARK PAWN-BROKER.
MY OWN INVESTIGATION LED NOWHERE. DOES IT LOOK LIKE WE WILL CATCH THEIR LEADER?
MAMIRU ...
...THIS COULD BE BIG.
WHAT?! YOU WERE *BOTH* IN ON THIS?!
WHAT IS THE MATTER, YURA?
YARRRGH!
WHY DID YOU LEAVE ME OUT?!
HOW CAN YOU HELP WITH ESPIONAGE?
YOU CAN'T EVEN MAKE RICE BALLS.
I CAN TOO MAKE RICE BALLS!!
JUST GO TRAIN, WOULD YOU?
DON'T BE TOO EMBARRASSED TO EAT MY RICE BALLS!

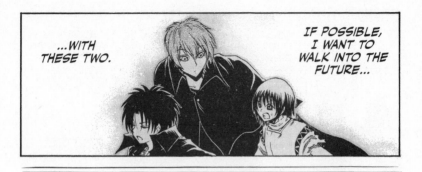

IF POSSIBLE, I WANT TO WALK INTO THE FUTURE...
...WITH THESE TWO.

THE FOX'S CURSE DISAPPEARED. NOW I WILL BELIEVE THAT.

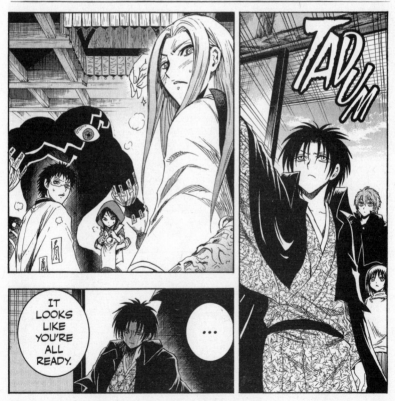

TADUM
...
IT LOOKS LIKE YOU'RE ALL READY.

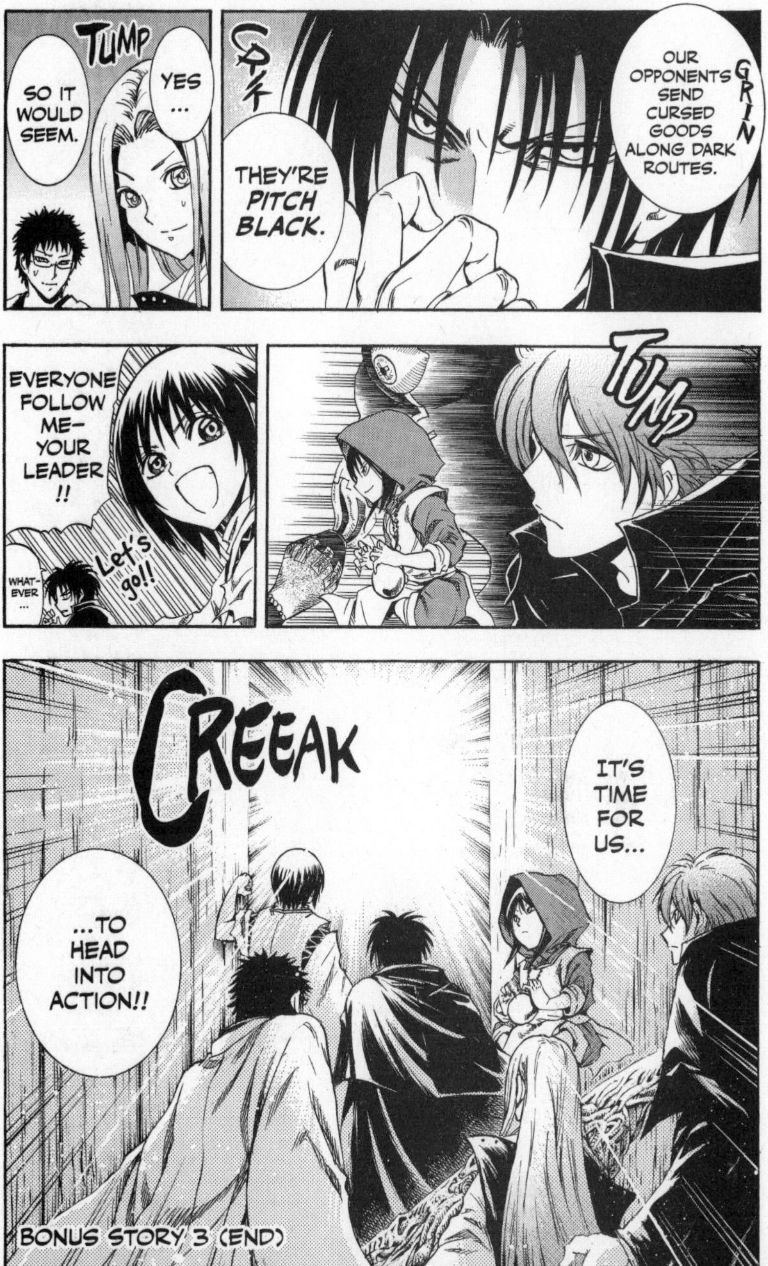
GRIN
OUR OPPONENTS SEND CURSED GOODS ALONG DARK ROUTES.
THEY'RE PITCH BLACK.
YES ...
TUMP
SO IT WOULD SEEM.
TUMP
EVERYONE FOLLOW ME— YOUR LEADER !!
Let's go!!
WHAT-EVER ...
CREEAK
IT'S TIME FOR US...
...TO HEAD INTO ACTION!!
BONUS STORY 3 (END)

In the Underground Passage

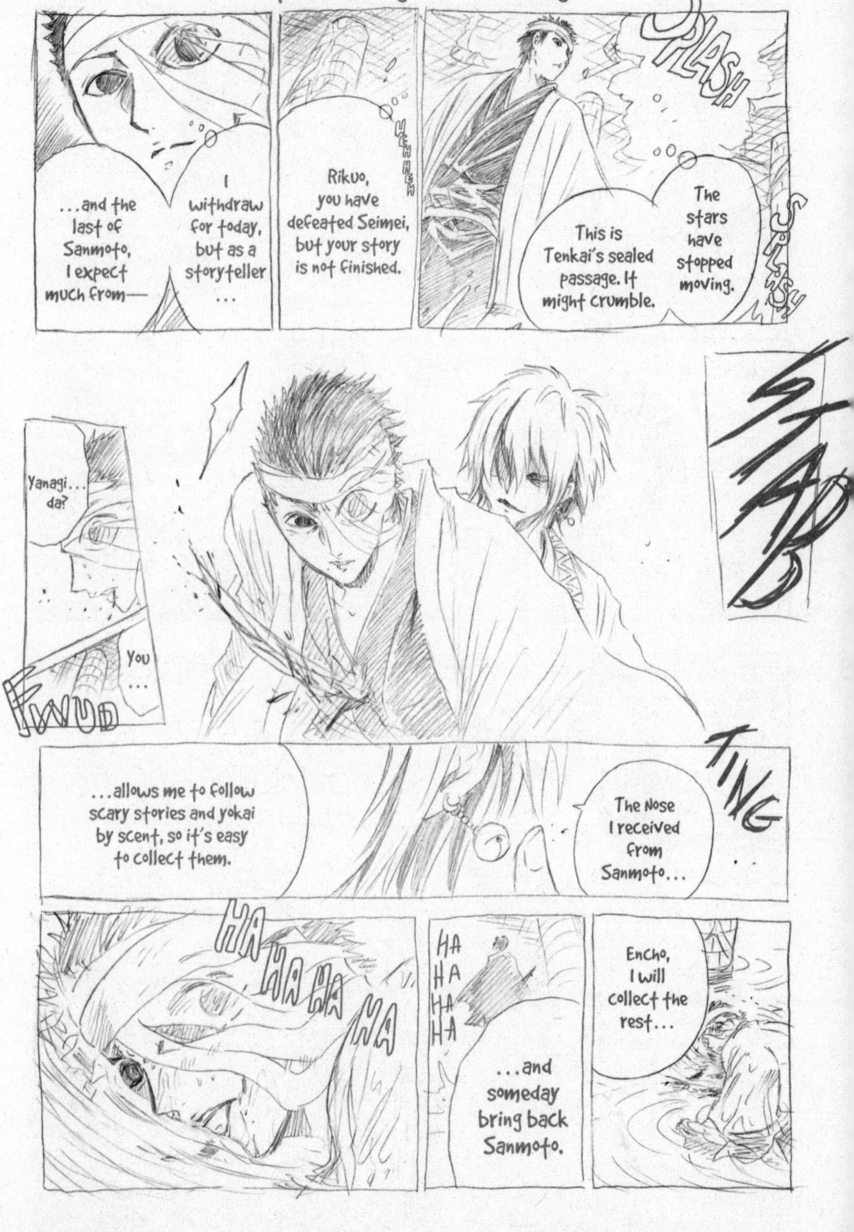
SPLASH
The stars have stopped moving.
This is Tenkai's sealed passage. It might crumble.
SPLASH
HEH HEH
Rikuo, you have defeated Seimei, but your story is not finished.
I withdraw for today, but as a storyteller...
...and the last of Sanmoto, I expect much from—
STAB
Yanagi... da?
You...
FWUD
TING
The Nose I received from Sanmoto...
...allows me to follow scary stories and yokai by scent, so it's easy to collect them.
Encho, I will collect the rest...
HA HA HA HA HA
...and someday bring back Sanmoto.
HA HA HA HA HA

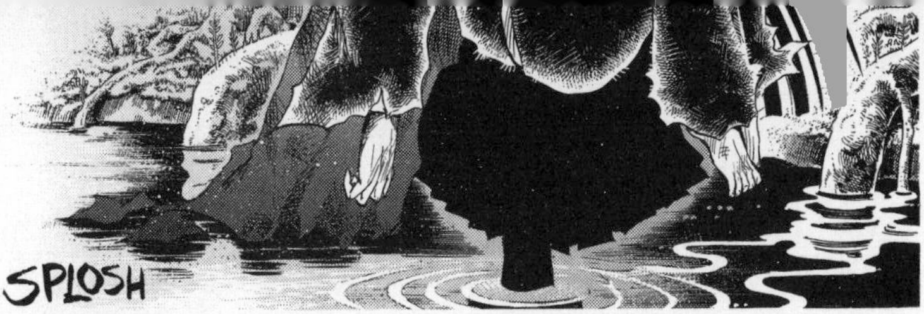
SPLOSH

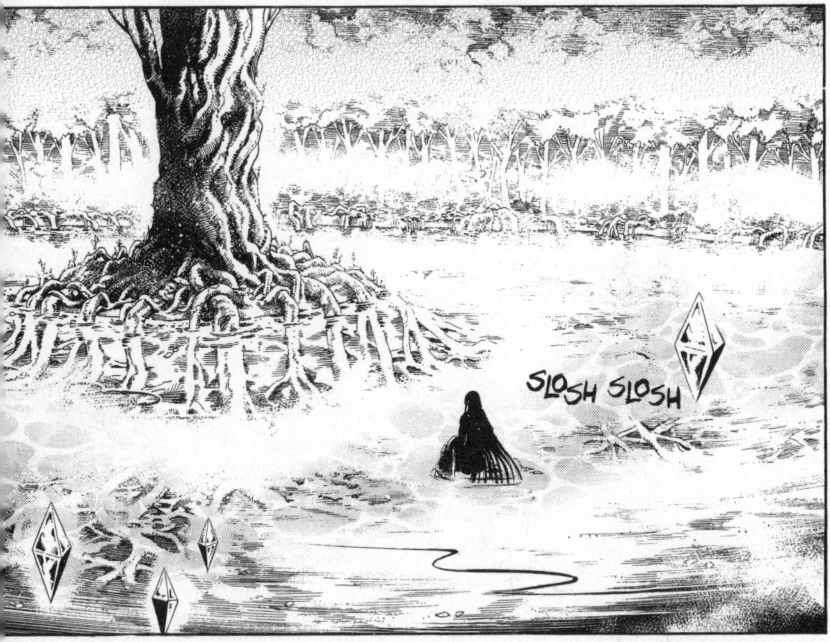
SLOSH SLOSH

Bonus Story 4: In the Village of Half-Yokai

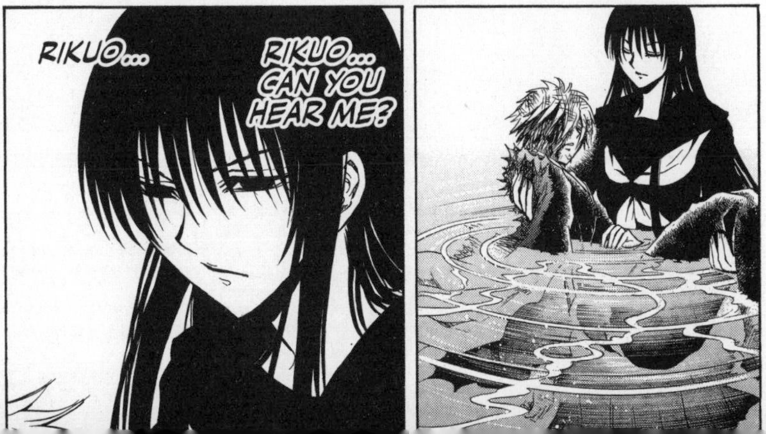
RIKUO...
RIKUO... CAN YOU HEAR ME?

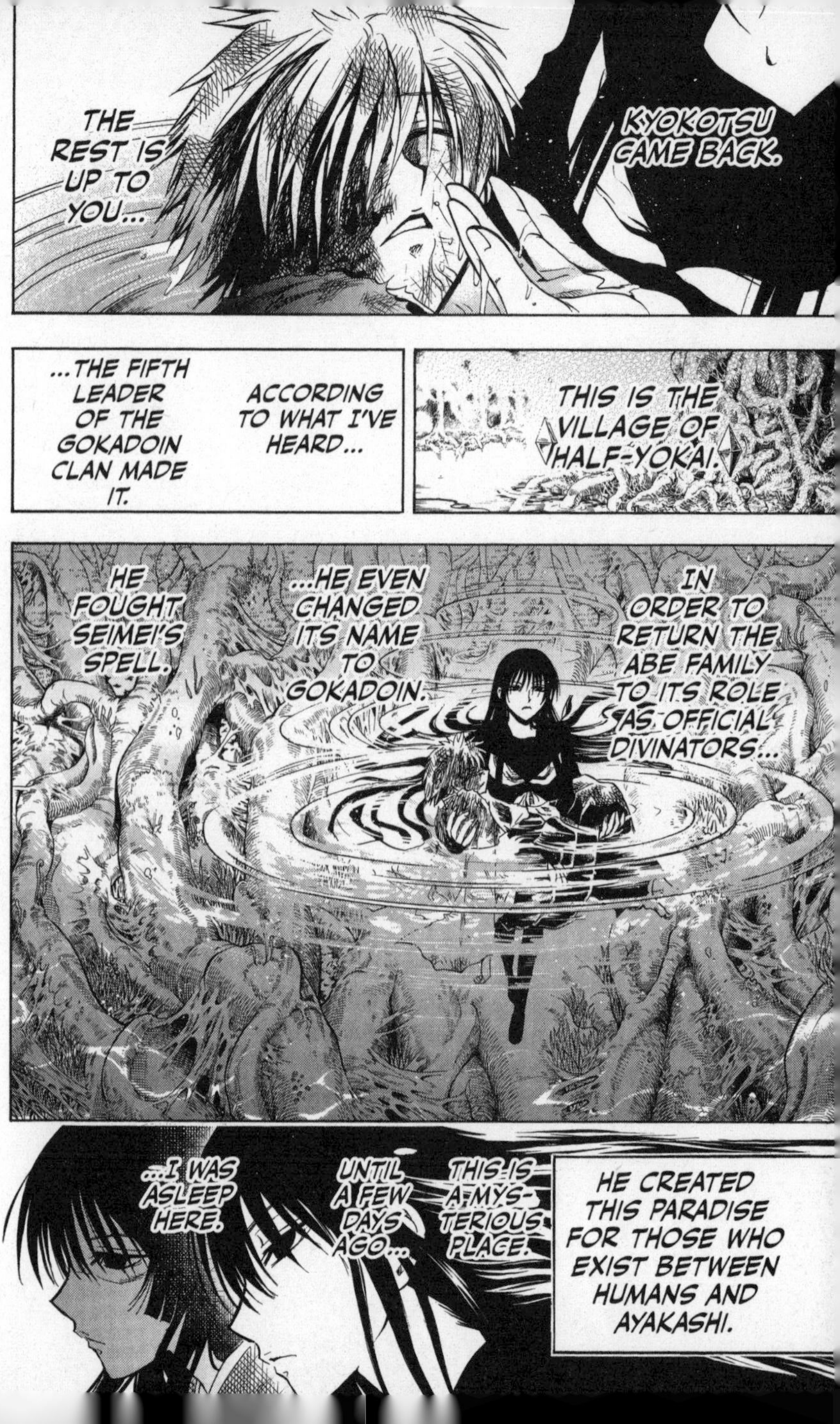
KYOKOTSU CAME BACK.
THE REST IS UP TO YOU...
THIS IS THE VILLAGE OF HALF-YOKAI.
ACCORDING TO WHAT I'VE HEARD...
...THE FIFTH LEADER OF THE GOKADOIN CLAN MADE IT.
IN ORDER TO RETURN THE ABE FAMILY TO ITS ROLE AS OFFICIAL DIVINATORS...
...HE EVEN CHANGED ITS NAME TO GOKADOIN.
HE FOUGHT SEIMEI'S SPELL.
HE CREATED THIS PARADISE FOR THOSE WHO EXIST BETWEEN HUMANS AND AYAKASHI.
THIS IS A MYS-TERIOUS PLACE.
UNTIL A FEW DAYS AGO...
...I WAS ASLEEP HERE.

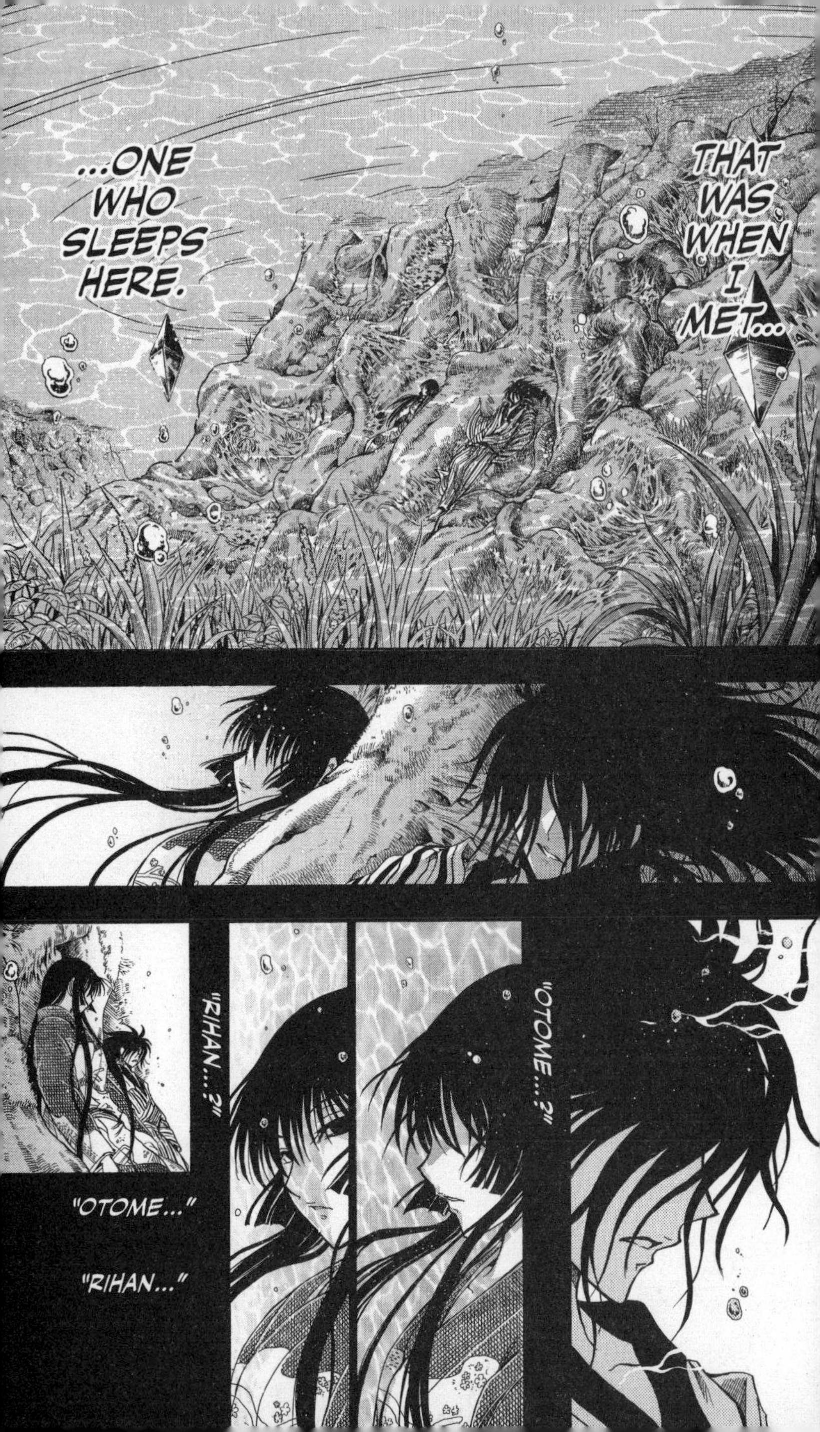
THAT WAS WHEN I MET...
...ONE WHO SLEEPS HERE.
"OTOME...?"
"RIHAN...?"
"OTOME..."
"RIHAN..."

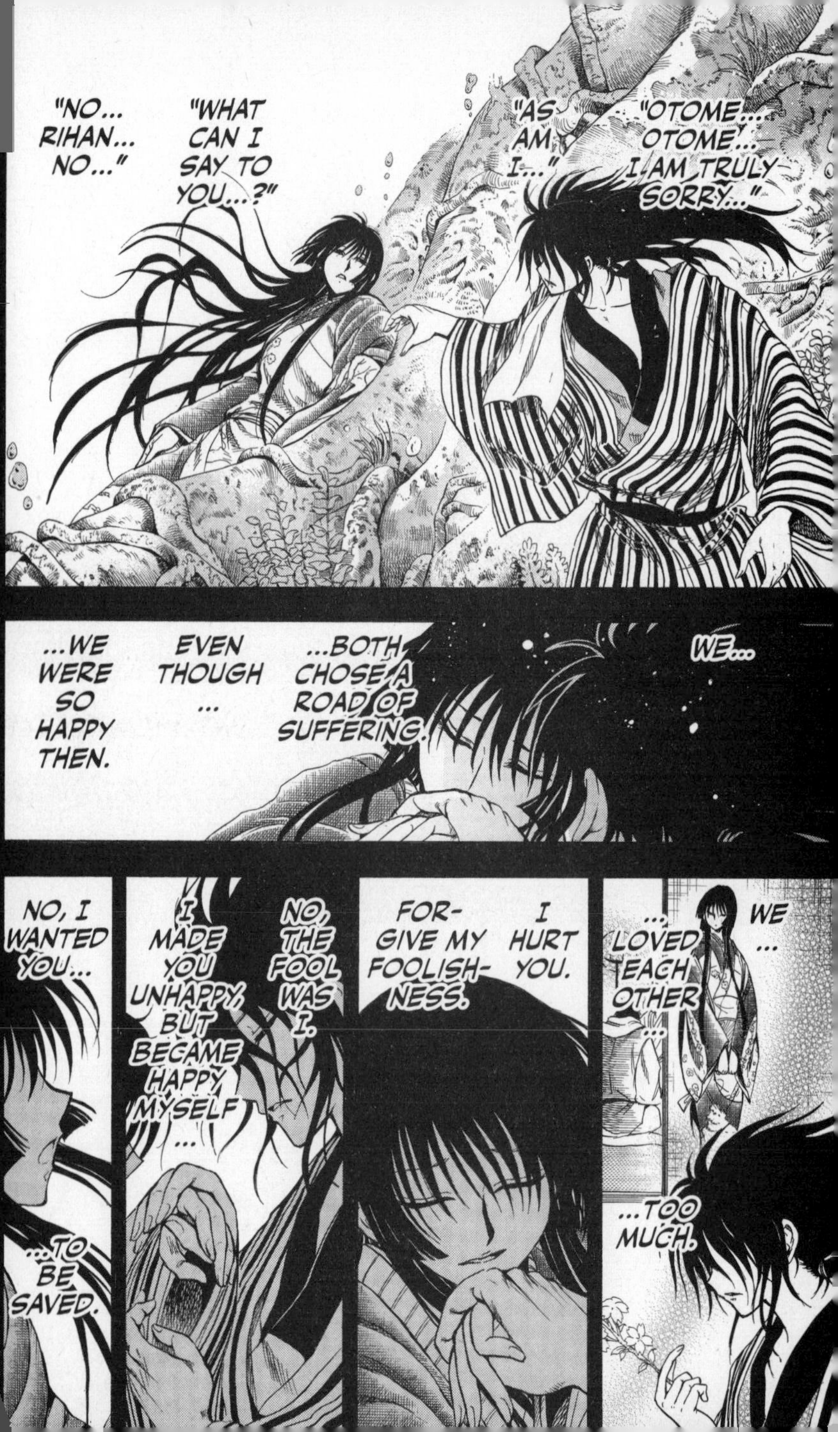
"OTOME... OTOME... I AM TRULY SORRY..."
"AS AM I..."
"WHAT CAN I SAY TO YOU...?"
"NO... RIHAN... NO..."
WE...
...BOTH CHOSE A ROAD OF SUFFERING.
EVEN THOUGH...
...WE WERE SO HAPPY THEN.
WE...
...LOVED EACH OTHER...
...TOO MUCH.
I HURT YOU.
FOR-GIVE MY FOOLISH-NESS.
NO, THE FOOL WAS I.
I MADE YOU UNHAPPY, BUT BECAME HAPPY MYSELF...
NO, I WANTED YOU...
...TO BE SAVED.

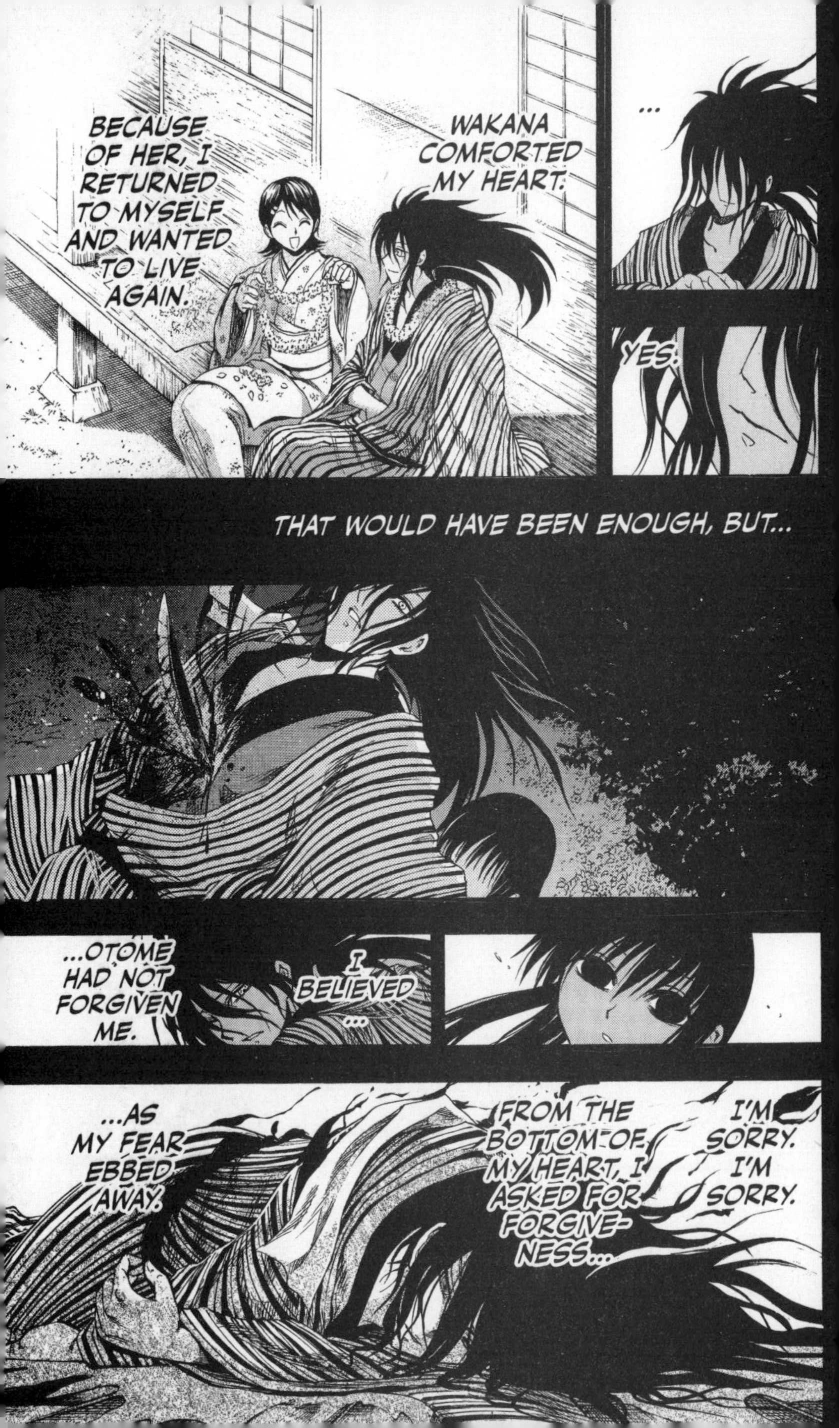
...
YES.
WAKANA COMFORTED MY HEART.
BECAUSE OF HER, I RETURNED TO MYSELF AND WANTED TO LIVE AGAIN.
THAT WOULD HAVE BEEN ENOUGH, BUT...
I BELIEVED...
...OTOME HAD NOT FORGIVEN ME.
I'M SORRY. I'M SORRY.
FROM THE BOTTOM OF MY HEART, I ASKED FOR FORGIVE-NESS...
...AS MY FEAR EBBED AWAY.

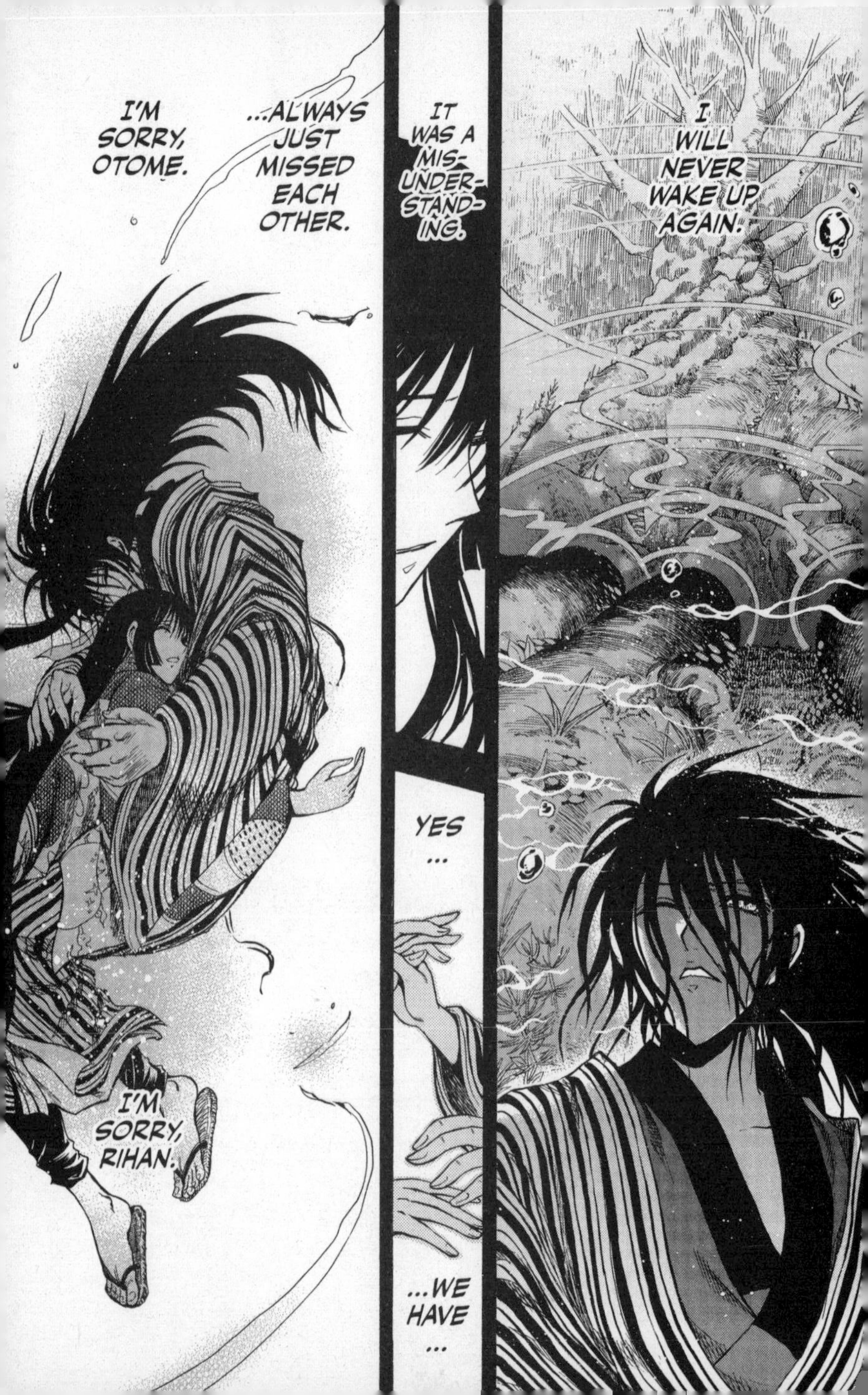
I WILL NEVER WAKE UP AGAIN.
IT WAS A MIS-UNDER-STAND-ING.
YES ...
...WE HAVE ...
...ALWAYS JUST MISSED EACH OTHER.
I'M SORRY, OTOME.
I'M SORRY, RIHAN.

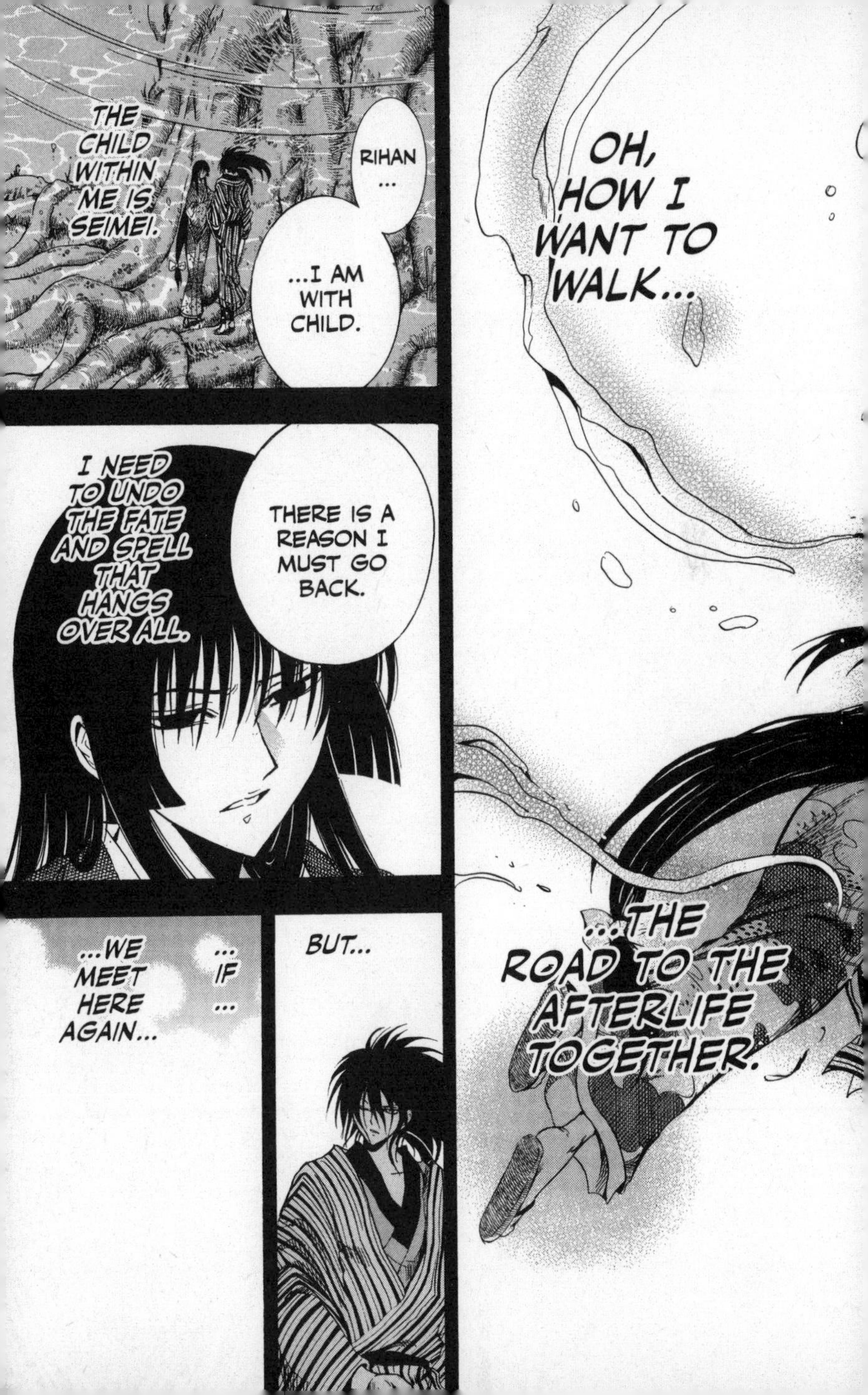
RIHAN ...
...I AM WITH CHILD.
THE CHILD WITHIN ME IS SEIMEI.
THERE IS A REASON I MUST GO BACK.
I NEED TO UNDO THE FATE AND SPELL THAT HANGS OVER ALL.
BUT...
... IF ...
...WE MEET HERE AGAIN...
OH, HOW I WANT TO WALK...
...THE ROAD TO THE AFTERLIFE TOGETHER.

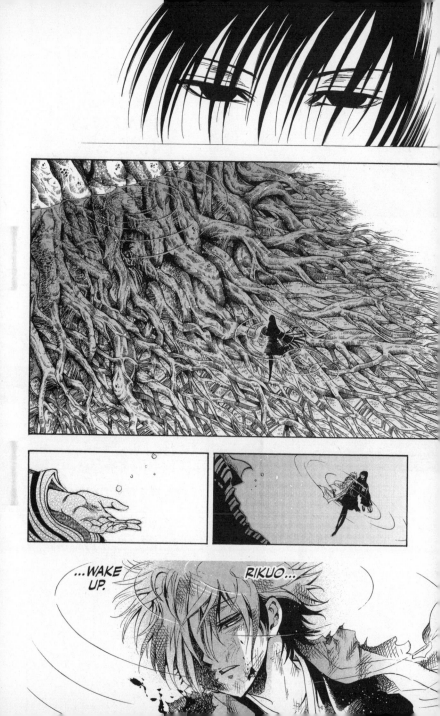

...WAKE UP.

RIKUO...

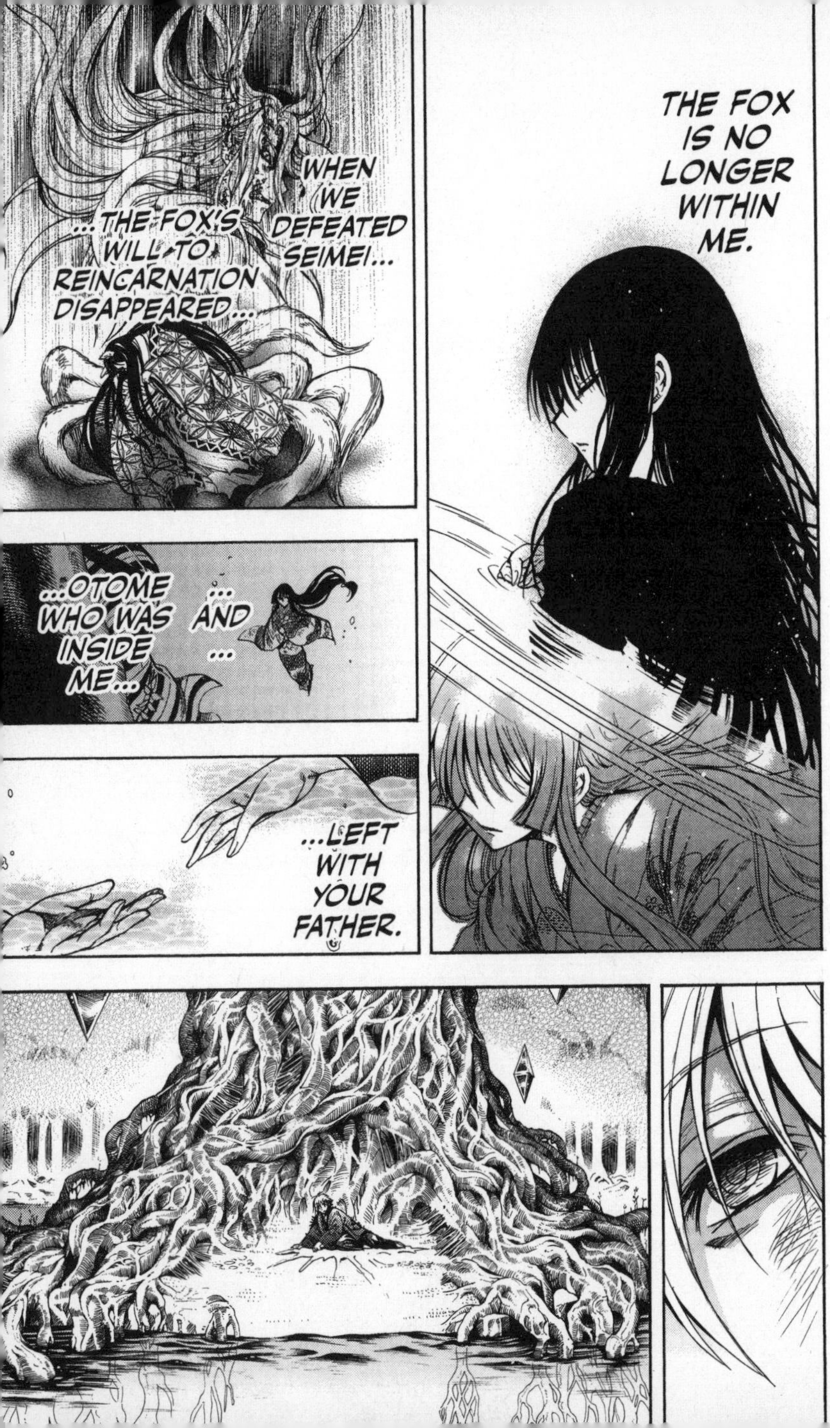
THE FOX IS NO LONGER WITHIN ME.
WHEN WE DEFEATED SEIMEI...
...THE FOX'S WILL TO REINCARNATION DISAPPEARED...
... AND ...
...OTOME WHO WAS INSIDE ME...
...LEFT WITH YOUR FATHER.

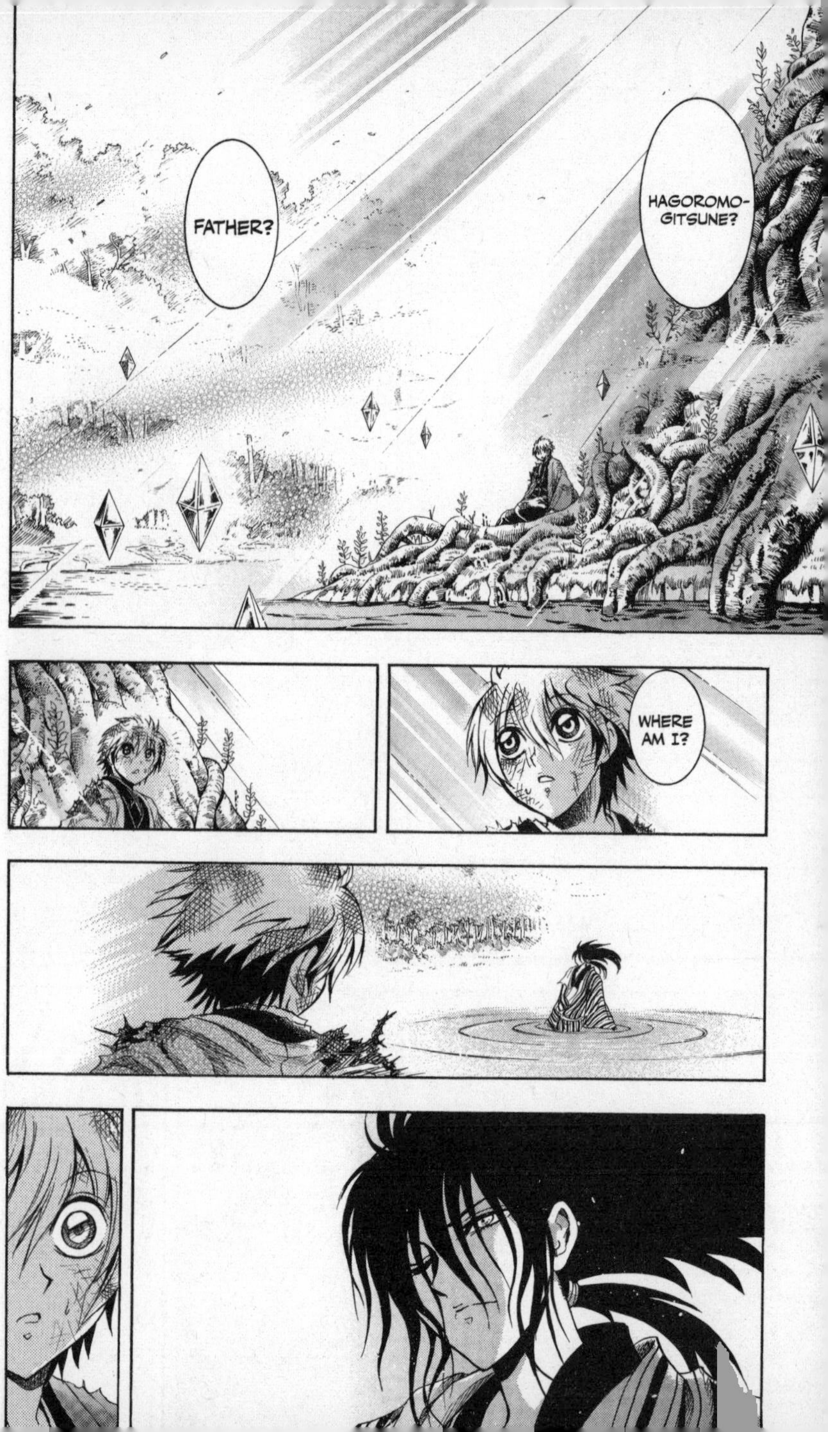
HAGOROMO-GITSUNE?
FATHER?
WHERE AM I?

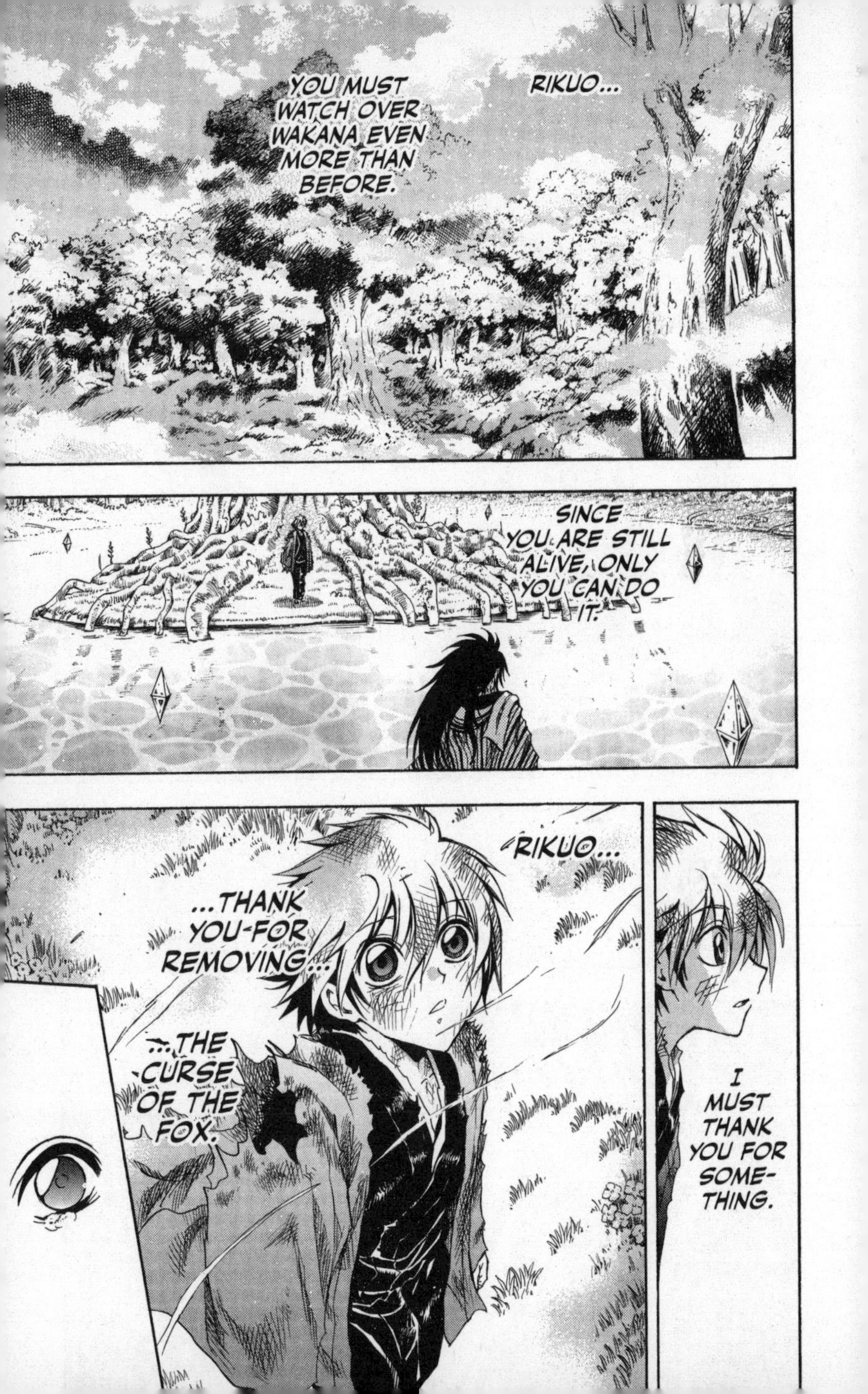
RIKUO...
YOU MUST WATCH OVER WAKANA EVEN MORE THAN BEFORE.
SINCE YOU ARE STILL ALIVE, ONLY YOU CAN DO IT.
I MUST THANK YOU FOR SOME-THING.
RIKUO...
...THANK YOU FOR REMOVING...
...THE CURSE OF THE FOX.

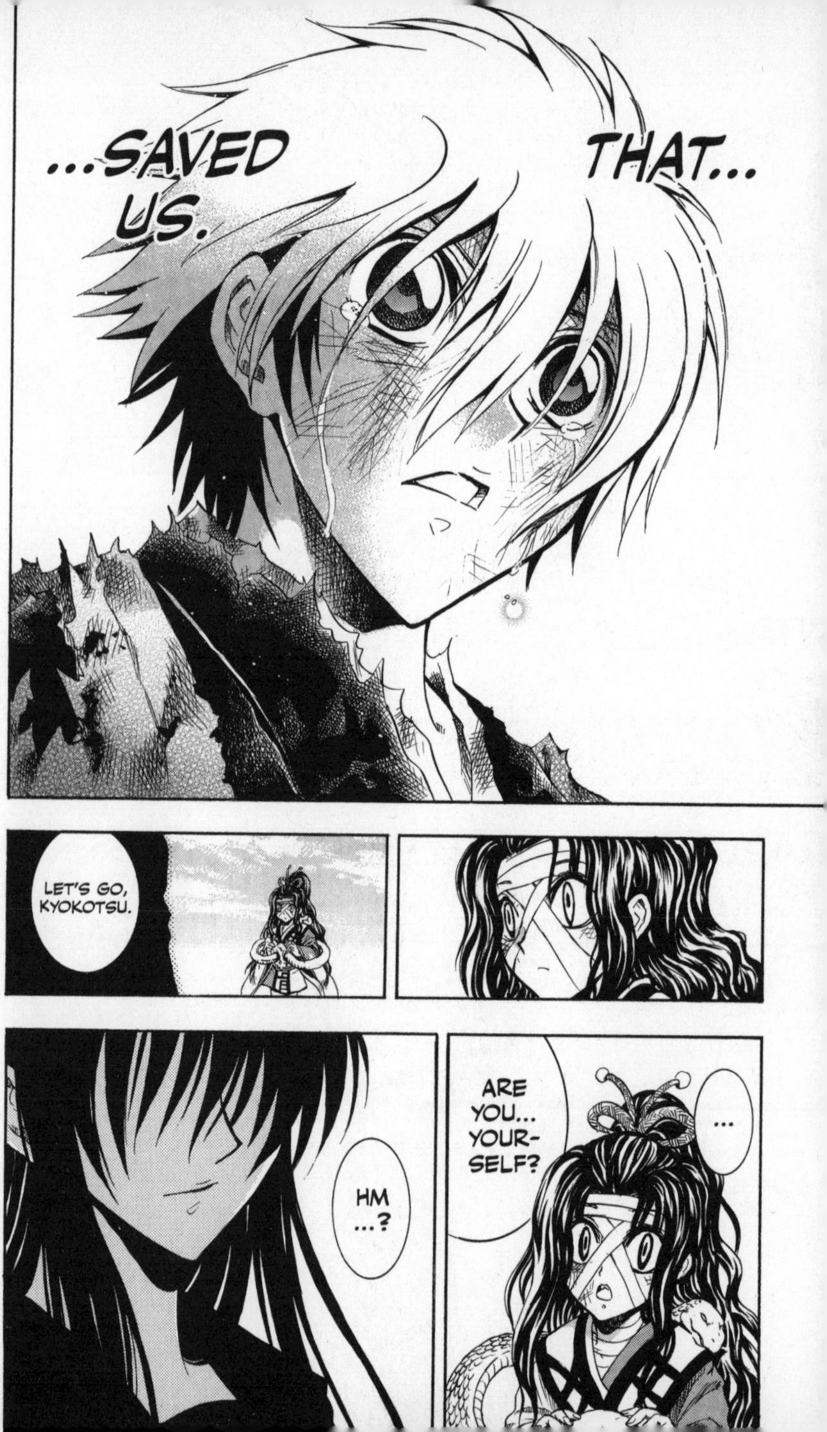
THAT...
...SAVED US.
LET'S GO, KYOKOTSU.
...
ARE YOU... YOURSELF?
HM ...?

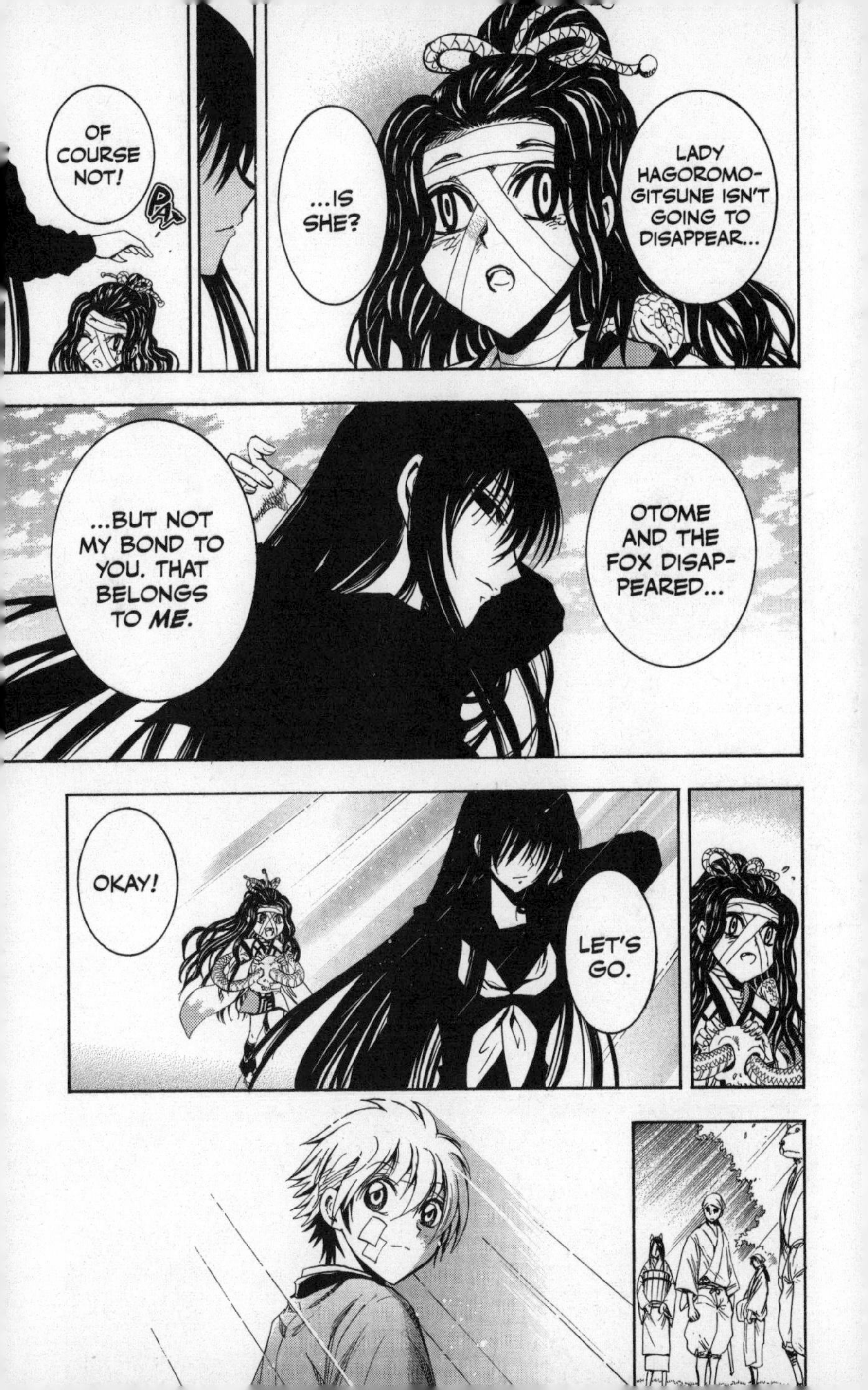
LADY HAGOROMO-GITSUNE ISN'T GOING TO DISAPPEAR...
...IS SHE?
OF COURSE NOT!
PAT
OTOME AND THE FOX DISAPPEARED...
...BUT NOT MY BOND TO YOU. THAT BELONGS TO *ME*.
LET'S GO.
OKAY!

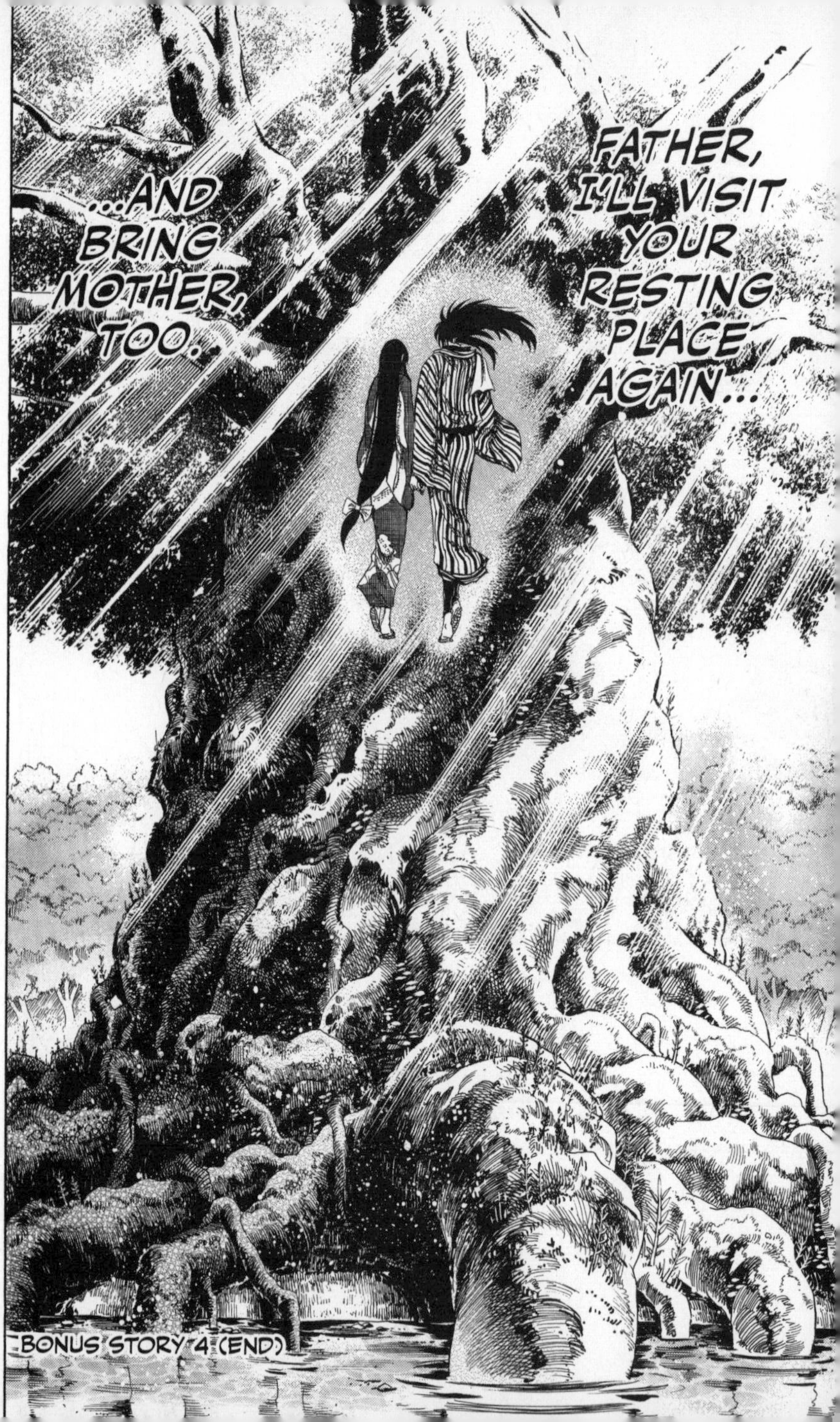
FATHER, I'LL VISIT YOUR RESTING PLACE AGAIN...
...AND BRING MOTHER, TOO.
BONUS STORY 4 (END)

Extra Bonus

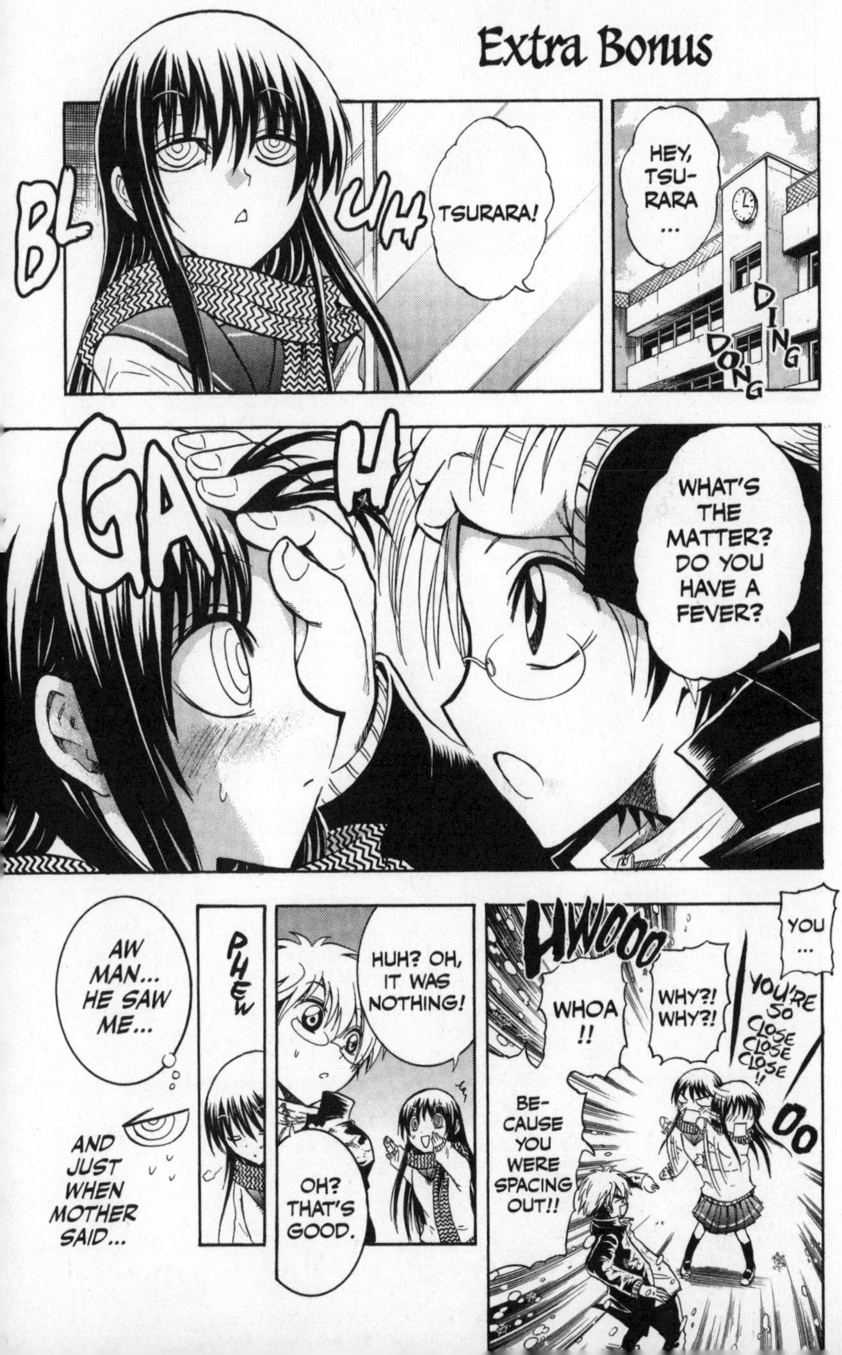
HEY, TSURARA ...
DING DONG
TSURARA!
BLUH
WHAT'S THE MATTER? DO YOU HAVE A FEVER?
GAH
YOU ...
YOU'RE SO CLOSE CLOSE CLOSE!!
WHY?! WHY?!
WHOA !!
HWOOOOO
BECAUSE YOU WERE SPACING OUT!!
HUH? OH, IT WAS NOTHING!
PHEW
OH? THAT'S GOOD.
AW MAN... HE SAW ME...
AND JUST WHEN MOTHER SAID...

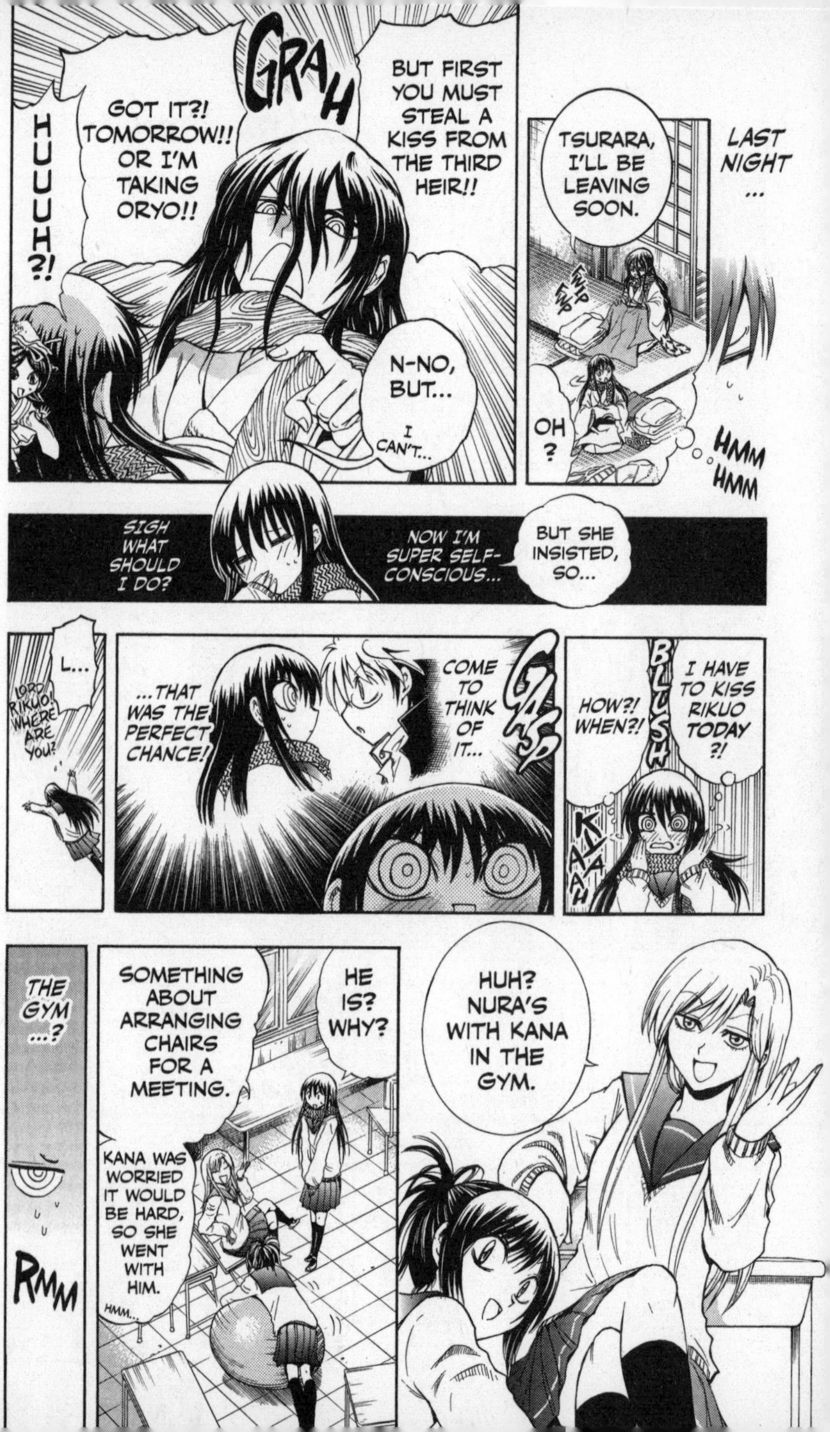
LAST NIGHT ...
TSURARA, I'LL BE LEAVING SOON.
FWIP FWIP
HMM HMM
OH?
BUT FIRST YOU MUST STEAL A KISS FROM THE THIRD HEIR!!
GRAH
GOT IT?! TOMORROW!! OR I'M TAKING ORYO!!
HUUUUH?!
N-NO, BUT...
I CAN'T...
BUT SHE INSISTED, SO...
NOW I'M SUPER SELF-CONSCIOUS...
SIGH WHAT SHOULD I DO?
I HAVE TO KISS RIKUO TODAY?!
BLUSH
HOW?! WHEN?!
KYAAH
GASP
COME TO THINK OF IT...
...THAT WAS THE PERFECT CHANCE!
L...
LORD RIKUO! WHERE ARE YOU?
HUH? NURA'S WITH KANA IN THE GYM.
HE IS? WHY?
SOMETHING ABOUT ARRANGING CHAIRS FOR A MEETING.
KANA WAS WORRIED IT WOULD BE HARD, SO SHE WENT WITH HIM.
HMM...
THE GYM...?
RMM

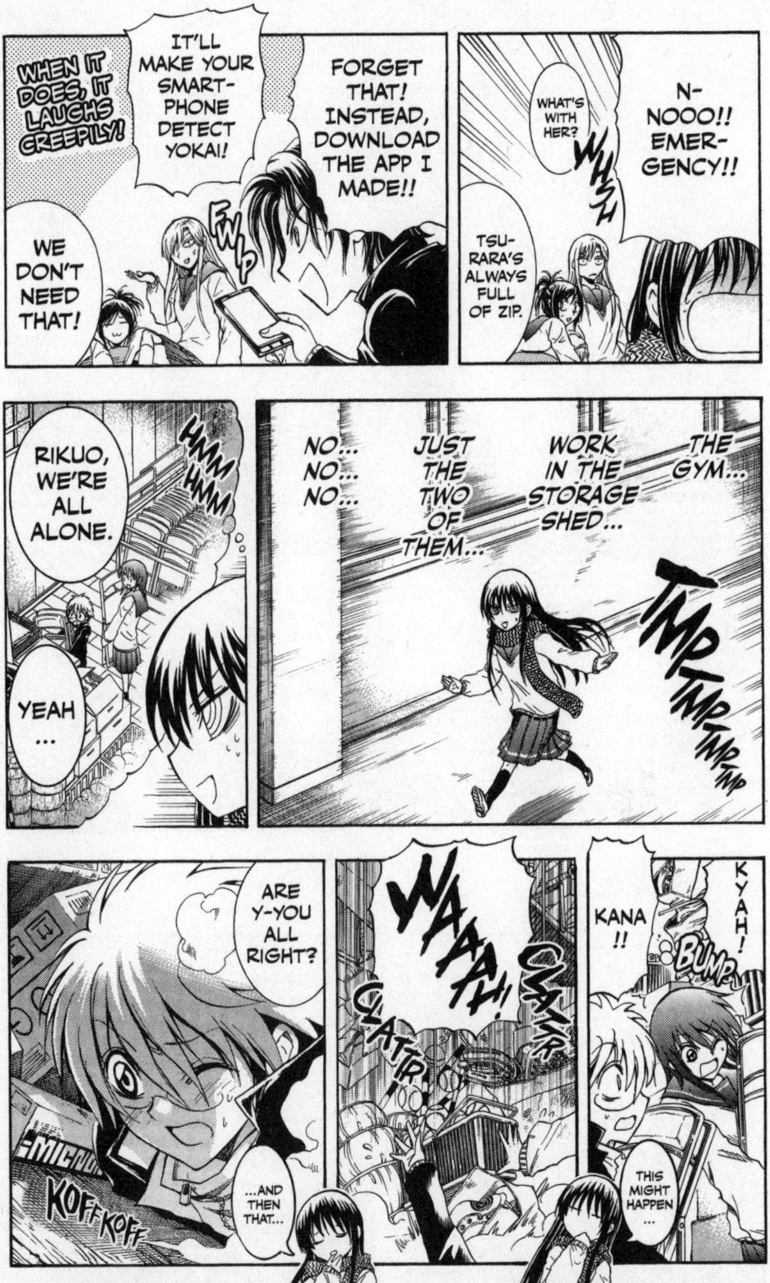
N-
NOOO!!
EMER-
GENCY!!
WHAT'S WITH HER?
WHSH
TSU-RARA'S ALWAYS FULL OF ZIP.
FORGET THAT! INSTEAD, DOWNLOAD THE APP I MADE!!
IT'LL MAKE YOUR SMART-PHONE DETECT YOKAI!
WHEN IT DOES, IT LAUGHS CREEPILY!
FWIP
WE DON'T NEED THAT!
THE GYM...
WORK IN THE STORAGE SHED...
JUST THE TWO OF THEM...
NO... NO... NO...
TMP-TMP-TMP-TMP
HMM HMM
RIKUO, WE'RE ALL ALONE.
YEAH ...
KYAH!
KANA !!
BUMP
THIS MIGHT HAPPEN ...
WAAAH!
CLATR
CLATTR
...AND THEN THAT...
ARE Y-YOU ALL RIGHT?
KOFF KOFF

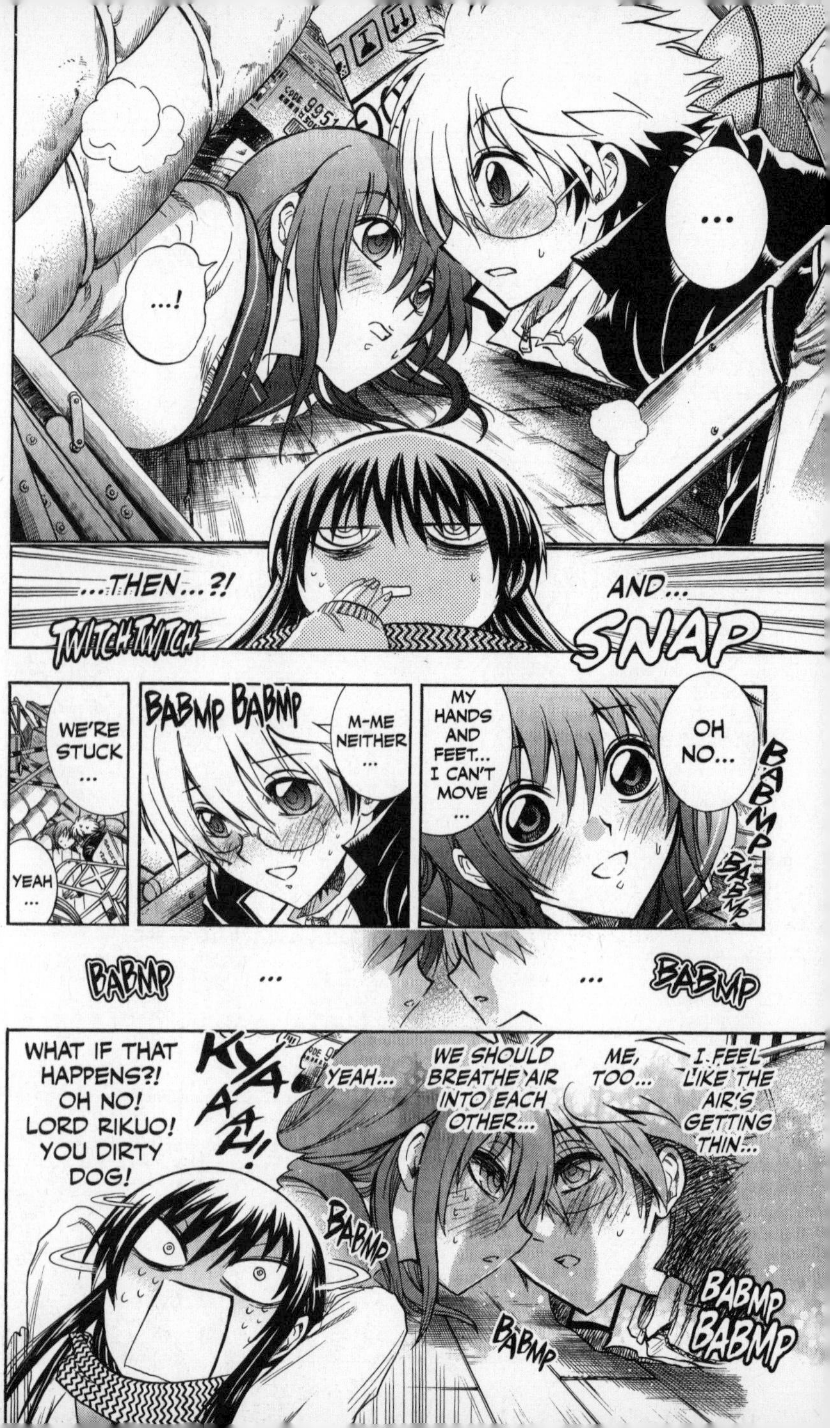
...
...!
AND...
SNAP
...THEN...?!
TWITCH TWITCH
OH NO...
BABMP
BABMP
BABMP
MY HANDS AND FEET... I CAN'T MOVE ...
M-ME NEITHER ...
BABMP BABMP
WE'RE STUCK ...
YEAH ...
BABMP
...
...
BABMP
I FEEL LIKE THE AIR'S GETTING THIN...
ME, TOO...
WE SHOULD BREATHE AIR INTO EACH OTHER...
YEAH...
BABMP BABMP
BABMP
BABMP
KYAAAH!
WHAT IF THAT HAPPENS?! OH NO! LORD RIKUO! YOU DIRTY DOG!

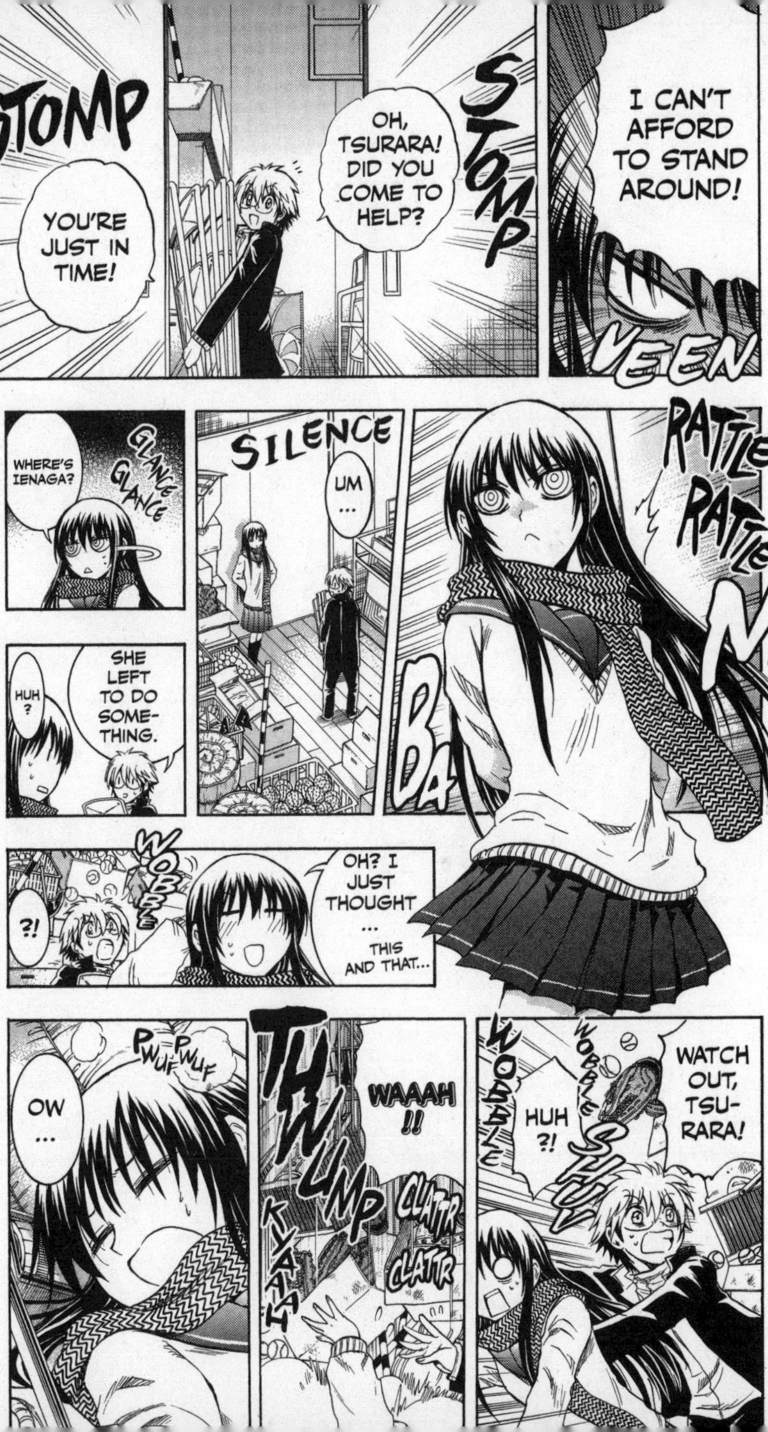
I CAN'T AFFORD TO STAND AROUND!
VEEN
STOMP
OH, TSURARA! DID YOU COME TO HELP?
STOMP
YOU'RE JUST IN TIME!
RATTLE RATTLE
M
BADA
SILENCE
UM ...
GLANCE GLANCE
WHERE'S IENAGA?
SHE LEFT TO DO SOME-THING.
HUH ?
OH? I JUST THOUGHT ...
THIS AND THAT...
WOBBLE
?!
WATCH OUT, TSU-RARA!
WOBBLE
HUH ?!
WOBBLE
SHUU
THWUMP
WAAAH !!
CLATR
CLATR
KYAAAH
PWUF PWUF
OW ...

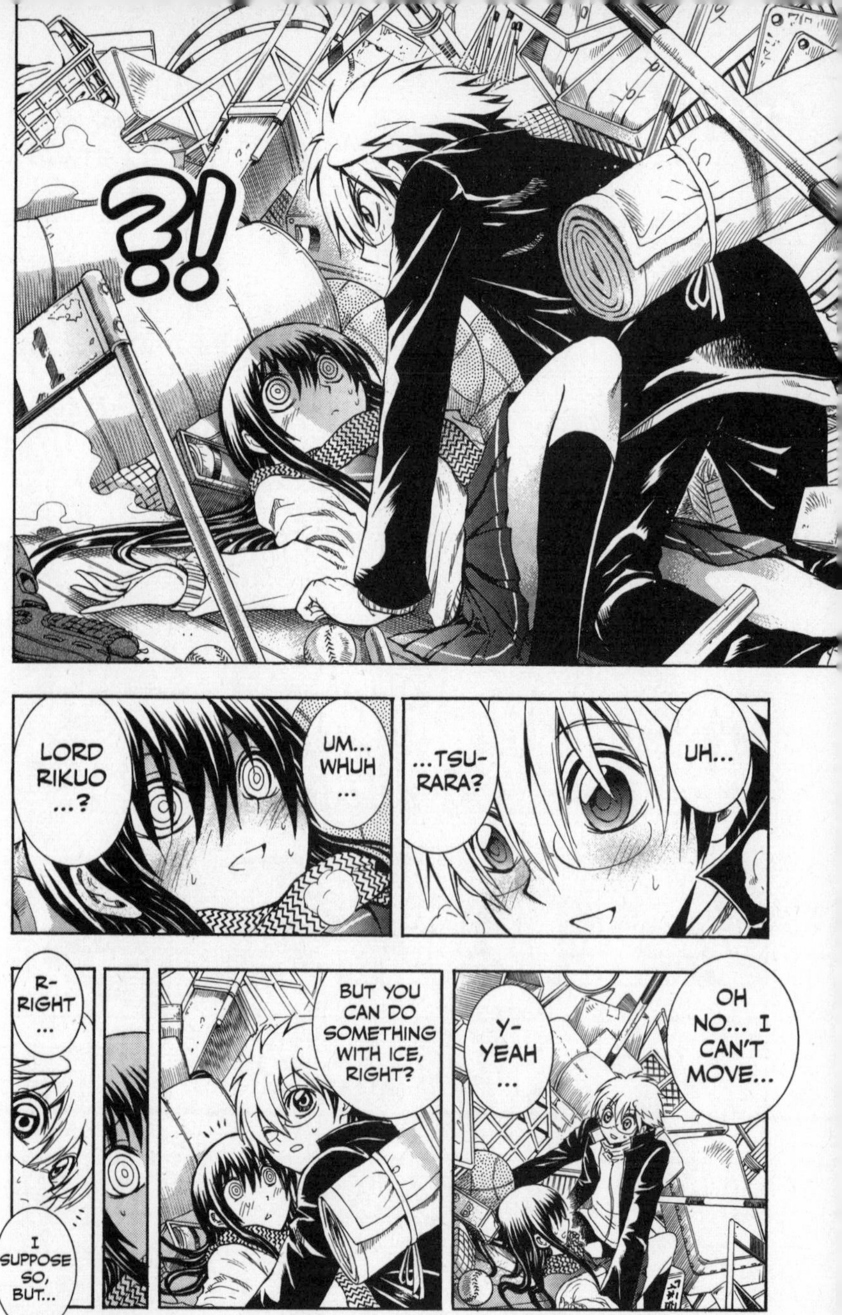
?!
UH...
...TSU-RARA?
UM... WHUH ...
LORD RIKUO ...?
OH NO... I CAN'T MOVE...
Y-YEAH ...
BUT YOU CAN DO SOMETHING WITH ICE, RIGHT?
R-RIGHT ...
I SUPPOSE SO, BUT...

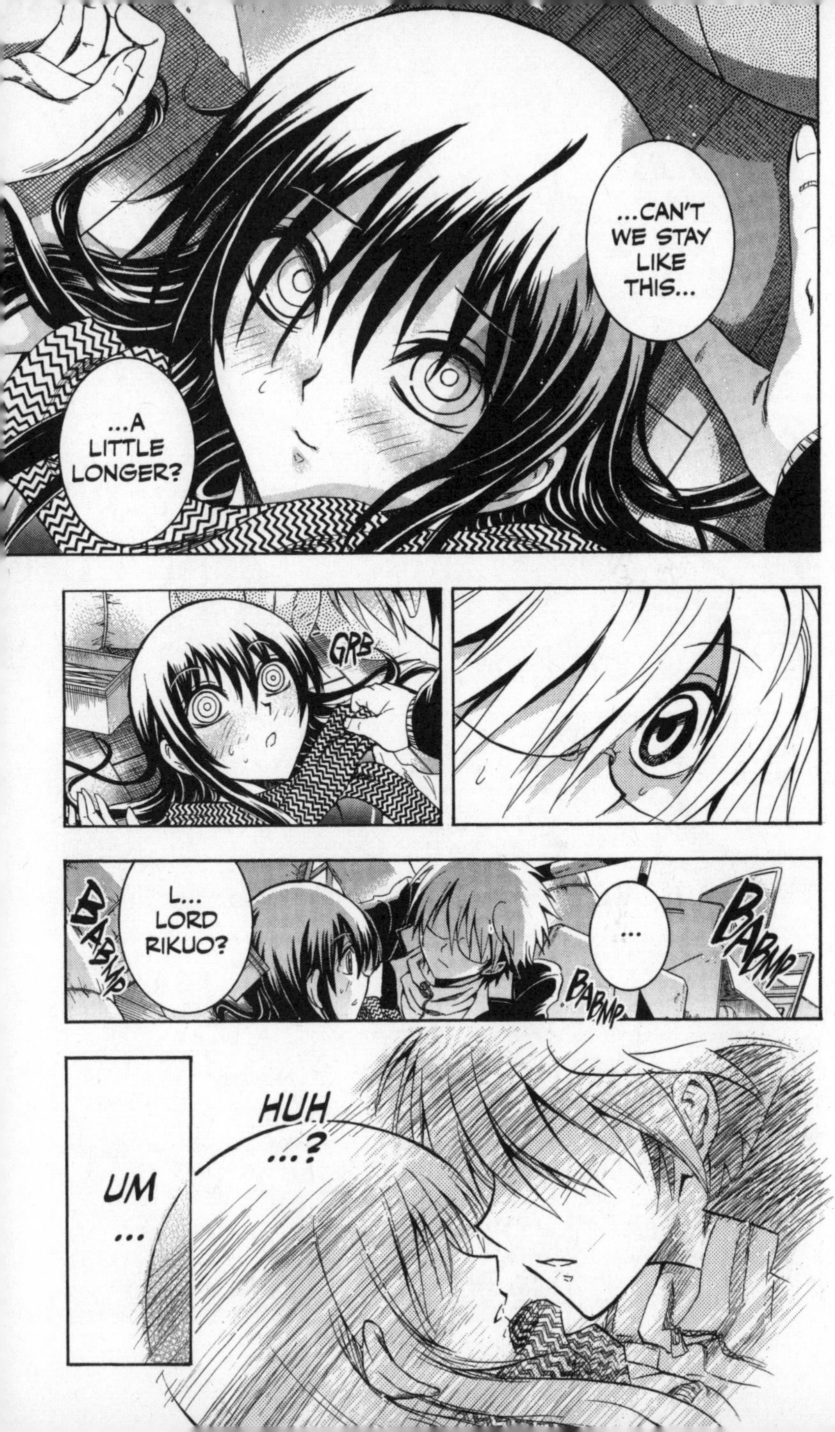
...CAN'T WE STAY LIKE THIS...
...A LITTLE LONGER?
GRB
BABMP
...
BABMP
L... LORD RIKUO?
BABMP
HUH ...?
UM ...

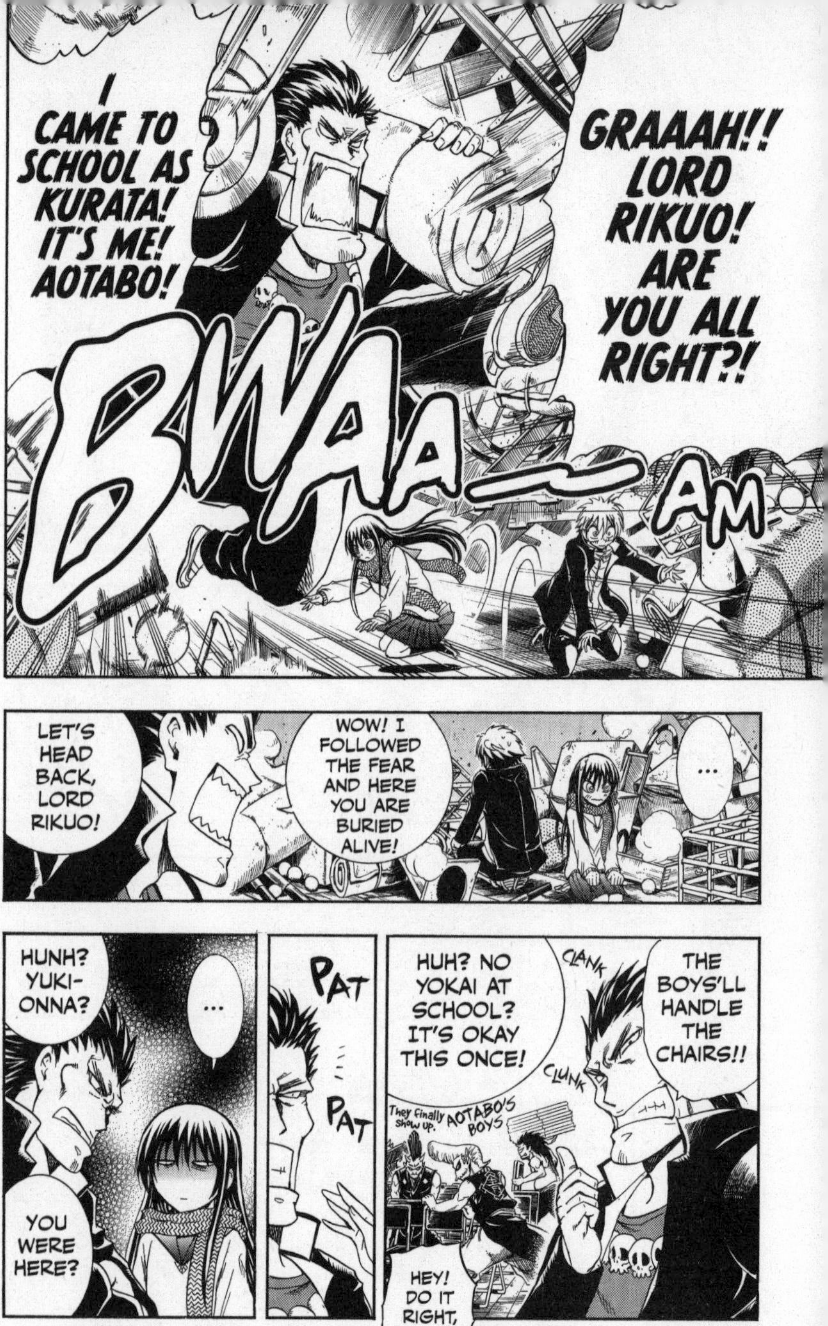
GRAAAH!! LORD RIKUO! ARE YOU ALL RIGHT?!
I CAME TO SCHOOL AS KURATA! IT'S ME! AOTABO!
BWAA—AM
...
WOW! I FOLLOWED THE FEAR AND HERE YOU ARE BURIED ALIVE!
LET'S HEAD BACK, LORD RIKUO!
THE BOYS'LL HANDLE THE CHAIRS!!
CLANK
CLUNK
HUH? NO YOKAI AT SCHOOL? IT'S OKAY THIS ONCE!
AOTABO'S BOYS
They finally show up.
HEY! DO IT RIGHT, FELLAS!
PAT
PAT
...
HUNH? YUKI-ONNA?
YOU WERE HERE?

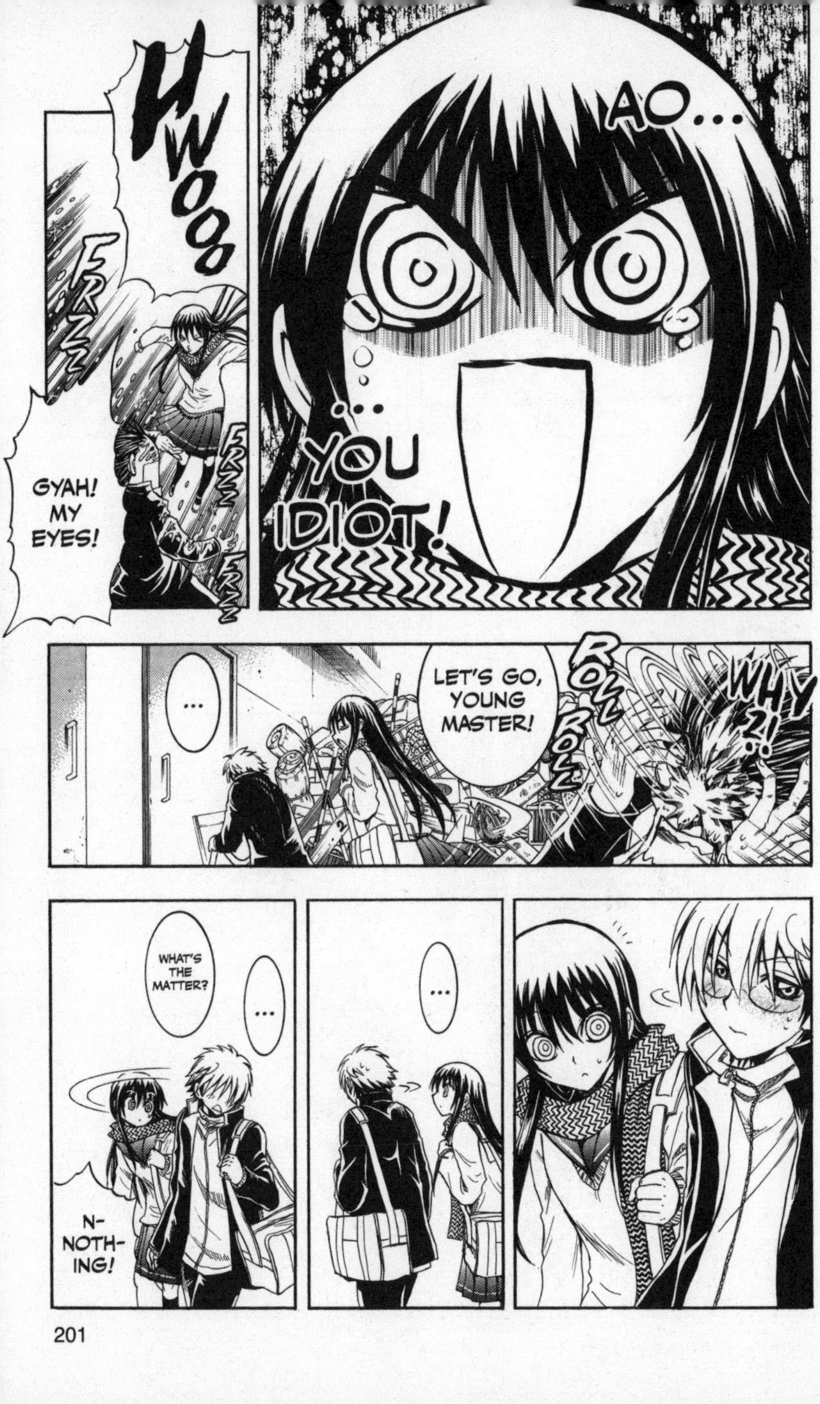
AO...
...YOU IDIOT!
HWOOO
FRZZ
FRZZ
FRZZ
GYAH! MY EYES!
WHY?!
ROLL ROLL
LET'S GO, YOUNG MASTER!
...
...
WHAT'S THE MATTER?
...
N-NOTHING!

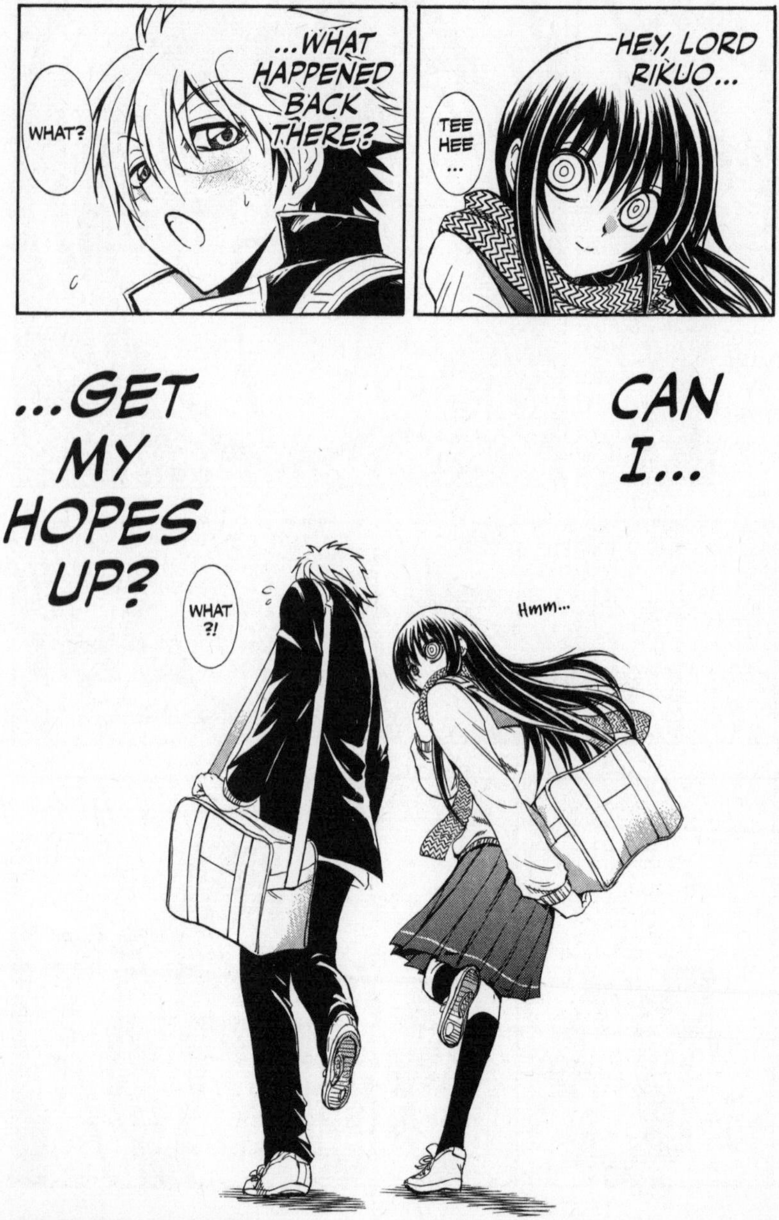
HEY, LORD RIKUO...
TEE HEE ...
...WHAT HAPPENED BACK THERE?
WHAT?
CAN I...
...GET MY HOPES UP?
Hmm...
WHAT ?!

EXTRA BONUS (END)

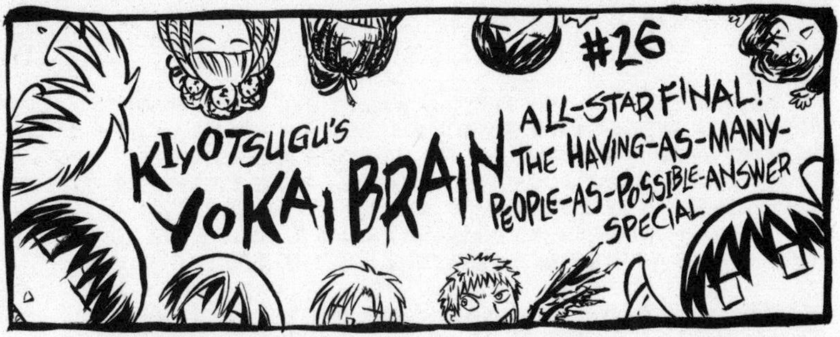
#26
KIYOTSUGU'S YOKAI BRAIN
ALL-STAR FINAL! THE HAVING-AS-MANY-PEOPLE-AS-POSSIBLE-ANSWER SPECIAL

Q: THIS QUESTION'S FOR RIKUO! HOW DO YOU REALLY FEEL ABOUT TSURARA? PLEASE HAVE TSURARA HERSELF ASK RIKUO. *-FURATTOMO, AICHI PREFECTURE*

TSURARA: WELL, HOW ABOUT IT, LORD RIKUO?

RIKUO: W-WHAT DO YOU MEAN HOW ABOUT IT?! DON'T ASK ME THAT HERE!

TSURARA: HMF! AT LEAST LOOK AT ME!!

Q: THIS IS A QUESTION FOR THE COOL AND LAID-BACK KAPPA!♪ HE OFTEN REFERS TO ROMANCE AS "REPRODUCTIVE BEHAVIOR." DOESN'T HE EVER FALL IN LOVE? I SUPPOSE HE LIKES WOMEN KAPPA? *-KARYU, KANAGAWA PREFECTURE*

KAPPA: HMM. I'VE NEVER REALLY THOUGHT ABOUT IT. BUT I GUESS I DO LIKE THEM. WOMEN AND REPRODUCTIVE BEHAVIOR, THAT IS.

KUBINASHI: H-HEY... THE WAY YOU PUT THAT SOUNDS DIRTY...

Q: I HAVE A QUESTION FOR YUIYUI. HOW LONG HAVE YOU BEEN WEARING GOTHIC LOLITA CLOTHES? THEY REALLY SUIT YOU! *-EIGETSU, AICHI PREFECTURE*

YUIYUI: THANK YOU. SINCE WESTERN CULTURE BEGAN TO ENTER JAPAN. I'VE LIKED THIS STYLE OF CLOTHING SINCE THE MEIJI PERIOD! ♡

Q: I HAVE AN IDEA FOR ZEN. WOULD CUTTING OFF YOUR WINGS IMPROVE YOUR HEALTH? AND PLEASE, TAKE CARE OF YOURSELF! *-NASHUA, AOMORI PREFECTURE*

ZEN: YOU'VE GOT SOME NERVE! CUT MY WINGS? IMPOSSIBLE. THEY'RE MY FEAR ITSELF! BUT THANKS FOR YOUR CONCERN.

Q: TAMAZUKI, WHEN YOU FOUGHT RIKUO TOWARD THE BEGINNING, I THINK YOU COULD HAVE BEATEN HIM WITH AUTUMN LEAF PELLETS. WHY DIDN'T YOU USE IT? *-IBARAKI'S BROTHER, HYOGO PREFECTURE*

TAMAZUKI: WHAT'S IT TO YOU? I WASN'T IN MY RIGHT MIND AT THE TIME. THE MAGIC OF THE SWORD HAD AHOLD OF ME.

Q: I LOVE HIRUKO! IF HIS HANDS ARE WATER AND FIRE, HOW DOES HE EAT? OR TAKE A BATH? WERE HIS HANDS AND FEET NORMAL WHEN HE WAS BORN? *-NIOIDAMA, TOKYO PREFECTURE*

HIRUKO: BECOMING CLAN LEADER WAS HARD. I GAINED RECOGNITION AS A LEADER BY DEVOTING MY BODY TO THE FIVE ELEMENTS!! SO I DON'T REGRET THE WAY MY BODY IS. BATHS AND MEALS ARE HARD!!

Q: THIS QUESTION IS ABOUT THE KEIKAIN CLAN. WHY DO YOU HAVE SO FEW FEMALE ONMYOJI? *-SHIRACHIKO, NAGASAKI PREFECTURE*

YURA: WE HAVE QUITE A FEW, BUT NOT MANY STRONG ENOUGH FOR BATTLE. THERE WERE ONLY MEN UNTIL THE MEIJI PERIOD, BUT THERE WILL BE MORE FROM NOW ON!!

Q: WHAT WAS IT LIKE RIDING TSUCHIGUMO? HIS HAIR LOOKS ITCHY... *-UKOKKEI, NAGASAKI PREFECTURE*

YURA: HIS HAIR WAS SURPRISINGLY SILKY!

Q: A QUESTION FOR TSURARA!! WHO DO YOU LIKE BETTER, KUBINASHI OR RIKUO? *-WHAT?! RIDICULOUS!, CHIBA PREFECTURE*

TSURARA: KUBINASHI? THE ANSWER IS LORD RIKUO, OF COURSE! WAIT...WHAT DID YOU JUST MAKE ME SAY?!

Q: RIKUO! WHAT DO YOU THINK OF YURA, KANA AND TSURARA?! I WANT BOTH DAY AND NIGHT RIKUOS TO ANSWER!! *-KUREHATSUBUTE, IWATE PREFECTURE*

Q: THIS QUESTION IS FOR THE DAY AND NIGHT RIKUOS! DO YOU LIKE TSURARA? DO YOU WANT TO MARRY HER? -SAKURAYO DANCING GIRL, YAMAGATA PREFECTURE

RIKUO: W-W-WHAH!!

TSURARA: EVERYONE W-WANTS TO KNOW!

RIKUO: I CAN'T ANSWER THAT!!

TSURARA: HEH HEH... I THINK I KNOW!!

RIKUO: W-WHAT? WHAT?!

TSURARA: KEEP CHEERING US ON, EVERYONE!♡

TO BE HONEST, I HAD THIS FEELING WHEN I BEGAN THE SERIES: "THIS WORK WILL GIVE ME SOMETHING BIG THAT MOVES MY LIFE IN DRASTIC WAYS." AND I THINK MY PREMONITION WAS ACCURATE. IT DIDN'T JUST GIVE ME SOMETHING BIG, IT GAVE ME EVERYTHING. IT TRULY WAS A HAPPY OCCURRENCE. A LONG SERIALIZATION, ANIME AND A FULL MEDIA MIX... AS A MANGA CREATOR, MY DREAMS CAME TRUE. I HAVE NOTHING BUT GRATITUDE FOR THE READERS.

HOWEVER, THAT'S WHY MY UNEASE GREW PARTWAY THROUGH. THE CHARACTERS GAVE ME EVERYTHING, BUT I WORRIED I WOULDN'T BE ABLE TO GIVE THEM A HAPPY ENDING. MOST OF THE CHARACTERS, LIKE TSURARA AND RIKUO, ARE STRONG ENOUGH TO OVERCOME WHATEVER HAPPENS IN THE FUTURE. BUT WHEN IT CAME TO YAMABUKI-OTOME, I DIDN'T THINK I COULD END IT WITHOUT DRAWING AN ENDING FOR HER. IT WAS ALL MY FAULT, THOUGH. BUT NOW I'M RELIEVED. I HOPE YOU READERS FEEL THE SAME WAY—THAT SHE WAS ABLE TO BE HAPPY. BECAUSE OF CERTAIN CIRCUMSTANCES, I DREW TWO FINAL EPISODES FOR THIS MANGA, AND WHEN I DREW THAT SCENE, I FELT LIKE I HAD FINALLY FINISHED IT.

AND THAT SCENE WITH TSURARA AND RIKUO, TOO! (LOL)

AS A CLUMSY FIRST EFFORT FOR ME, I IMAGINE THERE WERE A LOT OF DIFFICULT PLACES TO READ, SPOTS WITH POOR COMPOSITION, AND THINGS THAT STUCK OUT. AND I'M AWARE THAT THERE MUST BE A TON OF STUFF THAT MAKES YOU WONDER "WHATEVER HAPPENED TO SO-AND-SO?" AND OTHER THINGS I COULDN'T QUITE DRAW TO THE END. I'M SORRY ABOUT THAT. ALONG THE WAY, ALL I COULD SEE WERE MY OWN FAULTS, AND PERHAPS THAT HAD A POOR EFFECT.

HMM... BUT ENOUGH NEGATIVITY. HERE AT THE END, I SHOULD MENTION WHAT I LIKED ABOUT *NURA: RISE OF THE YOKAI CLAN!* I LIKED THE UNGAIKYO STORY! STORIES THE LENGTH OF THE ONE ABOUT LORD SODEMOGI ARE EASY TO DO! TSURARA VERSUS YOSUZUME WAS THE BEST PART OF THE SHIKOKU ARC! RIKUO VERSUS RYUJI OPENED MY EYES ABOUT A LOT!

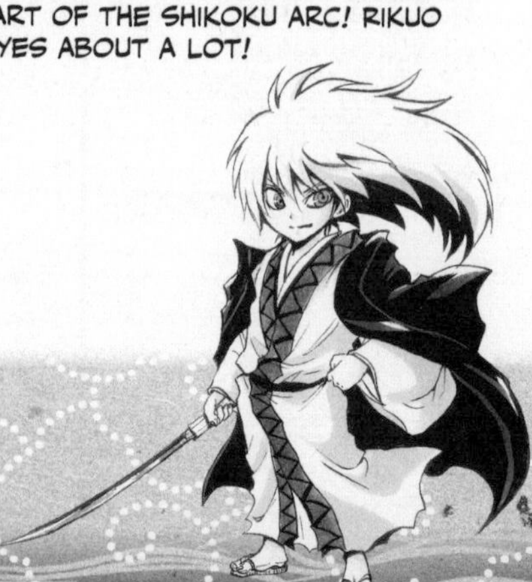

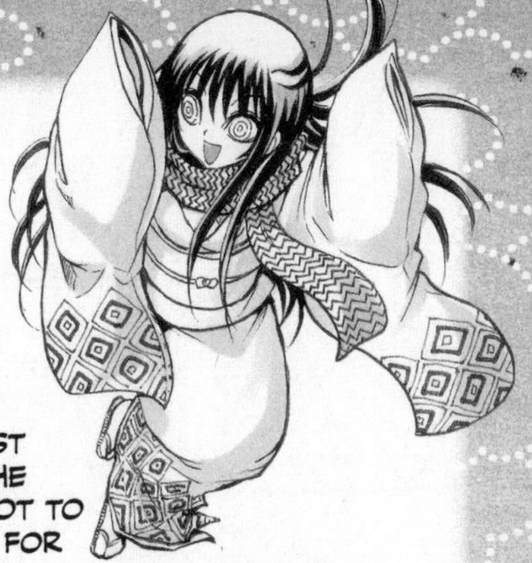

THE PART ABOUT NURARIHYON'S PAST ALWAYS MADE THE TOP THREE IN SURVEYS! "LEAVING TONO!!" MADE NUMBER TWO! YAY! I ALSO THOUGHT RYUJI VERSUS AKIFUSA WAS PRETTY GOOD! AWASHIMA IN THE FOREST OF *TORII* WAS SORT OF LIKE *JOJO*. (LOL) I LIKED THE ART IN RIKUO VERSUS KIDOMARU. I WEPT AS I DREW THE LAST TWO CHAPTERS OF THE KYOTO ARC. THE SURVEY ALSO TURNED OUT WELL. I GOT TO DRAW TSURARA AS MUCH AS I WANTED FOR THE BIRTH OF TEAM TSURARA. AND THE PART FOCUSING ON TORYANSE PUT MY INTERESTS ON FULL DISPLAY! AKIMOTO SENSEI COMPLIMENTED ME ON "SUBWAY GIRL." FUJIMAKI SENSEI COMPLIMENTED ME ON "HOW EROTIC ARE YOU?!" (LOL) RIHAN VERSUS KUROTABO WAS A GOOD FIGHT. AND I THINK THE STUFF ABOUT THE HUNDRED STORIES CLAN FROM "NUMBER 100" UP TO KUDAN'S APPEARANCE WASN'T BAD AT ALL. RIKUO VERSUS KYOSAI WAS SO GROSS THAT THE STAFF FELT SICK... AND DURING RIKUO VERSUS ABE NO YOSHIHIRA, I REALIZED THAT OF ALL THE CHARACTERS IN *NURA: RISE OF THE YOKAI CLAN*, I MOST CLOSELY RESEMBLE YOSHIHIRA. I DIDN'T HAVE MANY PAGES TO WORK WITH, SO I REALLY POURED MY SOUL INTO THEM.

AND SO ON. THERE'S NO END TO THE EXAMPLES I COULD LIST. OH, AND I LIKE ALL THE EXTRA CHAPTERS. INCLUDING THE FIVE IN THIS VOLUME! (LOL) WHAT'S MORE, I LOVE THE BONUS PAGES IN THE GRAPHIC NOVELS! (LOL) LISTEN TO ALL THIS SELF-PRAISE! OH, AND I LIKE OITEKEBORI, TOO! (LOL) IF YOU GET THE URGE, TELL ME YOUR FAVORITE EPISODES!

THIS MEANS AT LEAST A TEMPORARY PARTING WITH *NURA: RISE OF THE YOKAI CLAN*, BUT THE WORLD IT CREATED WON'T DISAPPEAR. MY NEXT WORK MAY HAVE LINKS TO IT AND THE CHARACTERS MIGHT SHOW UP SOMEWHERE ELSE. I LOVE THEM SO MUCH THEY WON'T JUST DISAPPEAR. SORT OF LIKE A LAND GOD. IF YOU REMEMBER THEM, YOU'LL SEE THEM AGAIN SOMETIME. I HAVE A FEELING ABOUT THAT.

UNTIL THEN, THANKS FOR READING!

HIROSHI SHIIBASHI
JANUARY 2013

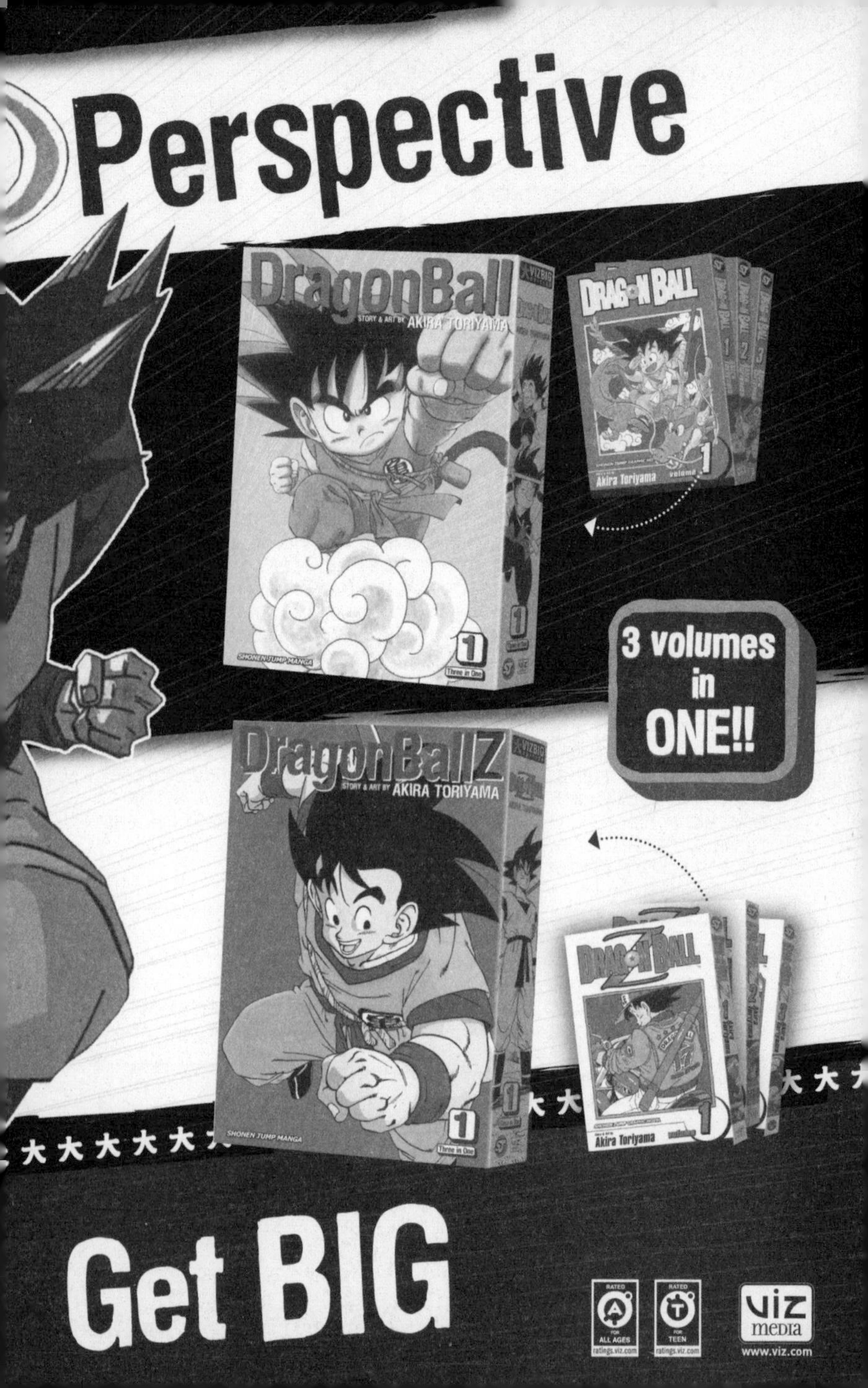
Perspective
DragonBall
STORY & ART BY AKIRA TORIYAMA
SHONEN JUMP MANGA
Three in One
Akira Toriyama
3 volumes in ONE!!
DragonBallZ
STORY & ART BY AKIRA TORIYAMA
Get BIG
RATED A FOR ALL AGES ratings.viz.com
RATED T FOR TEEN ratings.viz.com
VIZ media
www.viz.com